A·N·N·U·A·L E·D·I·T·I·O·N·S

Adolescent Psychology
04/05

Fourth Edition

EDITOR

Karen G. Duffy

State University of New York, Geneseo

Karen G. Duffy obtained her Ph.D. in psychology from Michigan State University. She is a Distinguished Service Professor, emeritus, at the State University of New York, Geneseo. Dr. Duffy has practiced as a family mediator and Employee Assistance Program specialist as well as serves on several community boards for human and social services. She is an editor for other Annual Editions as well as author of books in other areas of psychology.

McGraw-Hill/Dushkin

2460 Kerper Blvd., Dubuque, Iowa 52001

Visit us on the Internet
http://www.dushkin.com

Credits

1. **Perspectives on Adolescence**
   Unit photo—Ryan McVay/Getty Images
2. **Puberty and Biology**
   Unit photo—Vicky Kasala/Getty Images
3. **Cognitive Growth and Education**
   Unit photo—PhotoLink/Getty Images
4. **Identity and Socioemotional Development**
   Unit photo—Keith Brofsky/Getty Images
5. **Family Relationships**
   Unit photo—Amos Morgan/Getty Images
6. **Peers and Youth Culture**
   Unit photo—Ryan McVay/Getty Images
7. **Teen Sexuality**
   Unit photo—Kirk Weddle/Getty Images
8. **Problem Behaviors and Interventions**
   Unit photo—Barbara Penoyar/Getty Images

Copyright

Cataloging in Publication Data
Main entry under title: Annual Editions: Adolescent Psychology. 2004/2005.
1.Adolescent Psychology—Periodicals. I. Duffy, Karen G.,Title: Adolescent psychology.
ISBN 0–07–294949-X   658'.05   ISSN 1094–2610

Fourth Edition

Cover image © Photos.com
Printed in the United States of America   1234567890QPDQPD0987654   Printed on Recycled Paper

Editors/Advisory Board

Members of the Advisory Board are instrumental in the final selection of articles for each edition of ANNUAL EDITIONS. Their review of articles for content, level, currentness, and appropriateness provides critical direction to the editor and staff. We think that you will find their careful consideration well reflected in this volume.

Staff

To the Reader

In publishing ANNUAL EDITIONS we recognize the enormous role played by the magazines, newspapers, and journals of the public press in providing current, first-rate educational information in a broad spectrum of interest areas. Many of these articles are appropriate for students, researchers, and professionals seeking accurate, current material to help bridge the gap between principles and theories and the real world. These articles, however, become more useful for study when those of lasting value are carefully collected, organized, indexed, and reproduced in a low-cost format, which provides easy and permanent access when the material is needed. That is the role played by ANNUAL EDITIONS.

No longer a child and not yet an adult, adolescents find themselves caught in the middle. Popular culture often depicts adolescence as a period of raging hormones, emotional upheaval, rejection of parents, and blind conformity to peers. One goal of this anthology is to present a more balanced picture of adolescence, including both positive and negative aspects of this developmental period. I chose articles that address time-less adolescent issues such as puberty, the identity crisis, and the establishment of independence from parents. I also chose articles that discuss contemporary issues affecting adolescents, their parents, and the professionals who interact with them. For example, articles examine violence in schools, use of the Internet, academic dishonesty, and global culture. I also made an effort to include readings that focus on effective strategies and interventions for helping adolescents—particularly at-risk adolescents—through this transition period.

This anthology is arranged into eight units. The units cover issues related to the fundamental biological, cognitive, and socioemotional changes of adolescence as well as the contexts of adolescent development (e.g. family, school, peer groups, and work). In keeping with the perspective that the ecological context or "environment" of adolescent development is crucial to understanding it, I also incorporated articles that examine the impact of socioeconomic, gender, culture, and other contexts on adolescent development. Unit 1 explores adolescence in historical and contemporary perspectives. Unit 2 examines the biological and psychological impact of puberty. Unit 3 discusses issues related to cognitive growth and education, while unit 4 addresses identity and socioemotional development. Unit 5 covers family relationships during adolescence, and unit 6 focuses on peers and youth culture. Teen sexuality issues are examined in unit 7. Finally, problem behaviors, like teen suicide, are included in unit 8.

Many of the readings present issues I hope will spur classroom debate. Are standardized tests ensuring that high schools have met educational standards? Are today's teens too image-conscious? Is the internet a safe place for meeting people? Should sex education stress abstinence or safe sex?

I hope that the articles of *Annual Editions: Adolescent Psychology* are thought-provoking, interesting, and foster understanding of adolescent development. I also would like to know what you think of this edition. Please take a few minutes to complete the article rating form at the back of this volume. Anything can be improved, so I need your feedback to improve future editions of *Annual Editions: Adolescent Psychology*.

Karen G. Duffy
Editor

Contents

UNIT 1
Perspectives and Adolescence

Three articles in this section examine what defines adolescence.

UNIT 2
Puberty and Biology

Five selections in this section consider what impact puberty has on the maturing adolescent.

The concepts in bold italics are developed in the article. For further expansion, please refer to the Topic Guide and the Index.

UNIT 3
Cognitive Growth and Education

The dynamics encountered by adolescents as they learn to cope with society and educational experiences are discussed in the nine articles in this section.

The concepts in bold italics are developed in the article. For further expansion, please refer to the Topic Guide and the Index.

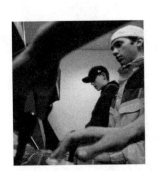

UNIT 4
Identity and Socioemotional Development

Five articles in this section look at how an adolescent copes with self-esteem, establishing a sense of identity, emotional development, and emotional intelligence.

The concepts in bold italics are developed in the article. For further expansion, please refer to the Topic Guide and the Index.

UNIT 5
Family Relationships

In this section, four articles examine how much influence family life has on adolescent development.

Unit Overview

The concepts in bold italics are developed in the article. For further expansion, please refer to the Topic Guide and the Index.

UNIT 6
Peers and Youth Culture

Three articles in this section consider the extent that gender roles, peer group pressure, drugs, and mass media influence the socialization of an adolescent.

UNIT 7
Teenage Sexuality

Five articles in this section discuss how adolescents view sexual behavior and the importance of sex education.

The concepts in bold italics are developed in the article. For further expansion, please refer to the Topic Guide and the Index.

UNIT 8
Problem Behaviors and Interventions

In this section, six articles address some of the problems faced by today's adolescents. These include drug abuse, violence, steroid use, suicide, and alienation.

The concepts in bold italics are developed in the article. For further expansion, please refer to the Topic Guide and the Index.

Topic Guide

This topic guide suggests how the selections in this book relate to the subjects covered in your course. You may want to use the topics listed on these pages to search the Web more easily.

On the following pages a number of Web sites have been gathered specifically for this book. They are arranged to reflect the units of this *Annual Edition.* You can link to these sites by going to the DUSHKIN ONLINE support site at *http://www.dushkin.com/online/.*

ALL THE ARTICLES THAT RELATE TO EACH TOPIC ARE LISTED BELOW THE BOLD-FACED TERM.

World Wide Web Sites

The following World Wide Web sites have been carefully researched and selected to support the articles found in this reader. The easiest way to access these selected sites is to go to our DUSHKIN ONLINE support site at *http://www.dushkin.com/online/*.

AE: Adolescent Psychology 04/05

The following sites were available at the time of publication. Visit our Web site—we update DUSHKIN ONLINE regularly to reflect any changes.

General Sources

Health Information Resources

http://www.health.gov/nhic/

Here is a long list of toll-free numbers that provide health-related information.

Knowledge Exchange Network (KEN)

http://www.mentalhealth.org/aboutken/index.htm

The CMHS National Mental Health Services Exchange Network (KEN) provides information about mental health via toll-free telephone services.

Mental Health Net

http://mentalhelp.net/

A comprehensive guide to mental health online, featuring 6,300 individual resources, can be found at this site.

Psychnet

http://www.apa.org/topics/homepage.html

Access *APA Monitor,* the American Psychological Association newspaper, APA Books on a wide range of topics, PsychINFO (an electronic database of abstracts on over 1,350 scholarly journals), and HelpCenter here.

UNIT 1: Perspectives and Adolescence

Facts for Families

http://www.aacap.org/info_families/index.htm

The American Academy of Child and Adolescent Psychiatry provides concise, up-to-date information on issues that affect teenagers and their families. Fifty-six fact sheets include teenagers' issues, such as coping with life, sad feelings, inability to sleep, or not getting along with family and friends.

The Opportunity of Adolescence

http://www.winternet.com/~webpage/adolescencepaper.html

This paper considers adolescence as the turning point in life—after which the future is redirected and confirmed. Discussion on the opportunities and problems of this period to the individual and society, using quotations from Erik Erikson, Jean Piaget, and others, is presented.

UNIT 2: Puberty and Biology

Biological Changes in Adolescence

http://inside.bard.edu/academic/specialproj/darling/adolesce.htm

This site offers a discussion of puberty, sexuality, biological changes, cross-cultural differences, and nutrition for adolescents.

UNIT 3: Cognitive Growth and Education

At-Risk Children and Youth

http://www.ncrel.org/sdrs/areas/at0cont.htm

North Central Regional Educational Laboratory (NCREL) offers this list of resources. Critical issues include rethinking learning for students at risk, linking at-risk students to integrated services, providing effective schooling for students at risk, and using technology to enhance engaged learning.

UNIT 4: Identity and Socioemotional Development

ADOL: Adolescence Directory On-Line

http://education.indiana.edu/cas/adol/adol.html

This is an electronic guide to information on adolescent issues. Some of the issues concern conflict and violence, peer mediation, mental health problems, and health issues.

UNIT 5: Family Relationships

CYFERNET: Cooperative Extension System's Children, Youth, and Family Information Service

http://www.cyfernet.org/

CYFERNET provides hundreds of complete online publications featuring practical, research-based information in six major areas.

Help for Parents of Teenagers

http://www.bygpub.com/parents/

In addition to discussing the book, *The Teenager's Guide to the Real World,* and how it can help parents, this site lists other book sources and Web sites for parents and teens.

Stepfamily Association of America

http://www.stepfam.org

The problems that surround step-parenting and stepchildren are discussed at this site. Just click on Facts and Figures and then on FAQs to reach many aspects of adolescent adjustments based on the type of family in which they live.

UNIT 6: Peers and Youth Culture

Higher Education Center for Alcohol and Other Drug Prevention

http://www.edc.org/hec/

This U.S. Department of Education site has interactive discussion forums and a Just for Students section.

Justice Information Center (NCJRS): Drug Policy Information

http://www.ncjrs.org/drgswww.html

National and international World Wide Web sites on drug policy information are provided on this NCJRS site.

National Clearinghouse for Alcohol and Drug Information

http://www.health.org/

This is an excellent general site for information on drug and alcohol facts that relates to adolescence and the issues of peer pressure and youth culture.

www.dushkin.com/online/

UNIT 7: Teenage Sexuality

American Sexual Behavior
http://www.norc.uchicago.edu/online/sex.pdf

This article, "American Sexual Behavior," discusses trends, sociodemographics, and risky behavior.

CDC National AIDS Clearinghouse
http://www.cdcnpin.org/

This complete source on AIDS includes "Respect Yourself, Protect Yourself," which are public service announcements that target youth.

Welcome to AboutHealth
http://www.abouthealth.com/

This health site includes information about sexuality, HIV and AIDS, peer pressure, and other information to help adolescents. Sites include In Our Own Words: Teens & AIDS, Risky Times, and links to other sites.

UNIT 8: Problem Behaviors and Interventions

Mental Health Net: Eating Disorder Resources
http://eatingdisorders.mentalhelp.net/

This is a very complete list of Web references on eating disorders, including anorexia, bulimia, and obesity.

Mental Health Risk Factors for Adolescents
http://education.indiana.edu/cas/adol/mental.html

This collection of Web resources is useful for parents, educators, researchers, health practitioners, and teens. It covers abuse, conduct disorders, stress, and support.

Questions & Answers about Child & Adolescent Psychiatry
http://www.aacap.org/about/q&a.htm

The American Academy of Child & Adolescent Psychiatry attempts to answer questions related to feelings and behaviors that cause disruption in the lives of children and young adults and the people around them.

Suicide Awareness: Voices of Education
http://www.save.org/

This is one of the Internet's most popular sites that address the issue of suicide. It provides detailed information on suicide along with material from the organization's many education sessions.

Youth Suicide League
http://www.unicef.org/pon96/insuicid.htm

This UNESCO Web site provides international suicide rates of young adults in selected countries.

We highly recommend that you review our Web site for expanded information and our other product lines. We are continually updating and adding links to our Web site in order to offer you the most usable and useful information that will support and expand the value of your Annual Editions. You can reach us at: *http://www.dushkin.com/annualeditions/*.

UNIT 1
Perspectives and Adolescence

Unit Selections

1. **Harnessing the Energies of Youth**, Isaac C. Lamba
2. **On (not) "Coloring in the Outline" (Transformations from Youth Through Relationships)**, Linda C. Powell
3. **The Future of Adolescence: Lengthening Ladders to Adulthood**, Reed Larson

Key Points to Consider

- Do you think various generations of adolescents (e.g. from the 1940s, 1960s, 1990s) are more alike than they are different? How so?

- What recent cultural and social changes have altered the way today's teens think and act?

- When in a person's development does the individual emerge as an adult rather than an adolescent?

- What do you think is the driving force behind today's adolescents: family, schools, pop culture, world events, or something else?

- How has technology altered the way teens interact with each other and the rest of the world?

 **Links: www.dushkin.com/online/**
These sites are annotated in the World Wide Web pages.

Facts for Families
http://www.aacap.org/info_families/index.htm
The Opportunity of Adolescence
http://www.winternet.com/~webpage/adolescencepaper.html

Serita applies her lipstick expertly without a mirror, wears the most popular fashions to school, and clutches her new CD player as she worries that a friend might give her a Barbie doll for her birthday when she clearly has outgrown them. This 13-year old is not a young child, but neither is she an adult. She is in that stage between childhood and adulthood known today as adolescence.

Exactly what characterizes adolescence is not clearly established. G. Stanley Hall, who is credited with founding the scientific study of adolescence in the early part of the 1900s, saw adolescence as corresponding roughly to the teen years. He believed individuals of this age had great potential but also experienced extreme mood swings. He labeled adolescence a period of "storm and stress." Because of their labile emotions, Hall believed that adolescents were typically maladjusted. But what did he believe was the cause of this storm and stress? He essentially believed that the cause was biological. Hall's views had a profound effect on the subsequent study of adolescence. Biological factors that underlie adolescence and direct the transition from childhood to adulthood have repeatedly been studied and refined.

Historically, other researchers hold very different views on the causes and characteristics of adolescence. For example, Erik Erikson, a psychologist interested in how people formed normal or abnormal personalities, believed that adolescence was a key period in development. He theorized that during adolescence, individuals did develop their identity. Just as Hall did, Erikson believed that there was some biological basis underlying development. Unlike Hall, however, Erikson emphasized the role society played in the formation of the individual. Erikson proposed that adolescents must confront a number of conflicts (for example, understanding gender roles and understanding oneself as male or female) in order to develop an identity. The form of these conflicts and the problems the adolescent faced coping with them were influenced by the individual's culture. If adolescents were successful in meeting the conflicts, they would develop a healthy identity; if unsuccessful, they would suffer role diffusion or a negative identity. Similar to Hall, Erikson saw adolescence as a period where the individual's sense of self is disrupted, so it was typical for adolescents to be disturbed. Today, Erikson's ideas on identity formation are still influential. However, his stereotype of adolescents as all suffering because of psychological problems has been called into question.

Margaret Mead, an anthropologist who started studying adolescents in the 1920s, presented a perspective on adolescence that differs from both Hall's and Erikson's. She concluded that culture, rather than biology, was the underlying cause of the transitional stage between childhood and adulthood. In cultures that held the same expectations for children as for adults, the transition from childhood to adulthood was smooth; there was no need for a clearly demarcated period where one was neither child nor adult. In addition, adolescence did not have to be a period of storm and stress or of psychological problems. Although some of Mead's work has since been criticized, many of her ideas remain influential. Today's psychologists concur with Mead that adolescence need not be a time of psychological maladjustment. Modern anthropologists agree that biology alone does not define adolescence. Rather, the sociocultural environment in which an individual is raised affects how adolescence is manifested and what characterizes it.

A cogent question is, what social and cultural factors lead to the development of adolescence in our society? And why in the world was Serita, the teen in the introduction to this unit, so worried about what her peers would think. Modern scholars believe that adolescence as we know it today, did not even exist until the end of the 1800s. During the end of the nineteenth century and the beginning of the twentieth century, societal changes caused the stage of adolescence to be "invented". In this period, job opportunities for young people doing either farm labor or apprenticeships in factories were decreasing. For middle-class children, the value of staying in school in order to get a good job was stressed. Since there were fewer job opportunities, young people were less likely to be financially independent and had to rely on their families. By the beginning of the twentieth century, legislation ensuring that adolescents could not assume adult status was passed, child labor laws restricted how much time young people could work, and compulsory education laws required adolescents to stay in school. In the 1930s, for the first time in this country's history, the majority of high school age individuals were enrolled in school. These teenagers were physically mature people who were dependent on their parents—they were neither children nor adults.

Ryan McVay/Getty Images

The articles in this unit focus on the images of adolescence in our culture as well as around the world. The first article by Isaac C. Lamba, provides a global perspective on adolescence. American adolescents indeed are different from others who are experiencing wars, epidemics, and other serious social upheavals. In the second article by Linda C. Powell, we hear from the adolescents themselves. Through their voices, Powell introduces us to themes in adolescent development such as the centrality of schools, the role of justice in their lives, and other issues that transform youth. In the final article, Reed Larson guides us through a look at the future of adolescence. He addresses a seminal question, "Are today's youth prepared to become adults?" His answer is "yes", despite the many challenges that face our teenagers such as terrorism and the AIDS epidemic.

Harnessing the Energies of Youth

Isaac C. Lamba

Any discussion of children and youth now must inevitably relate to the United Nations Millennium Development Goals, which provide the road map for human development. The recent United Nations Special Session on Children exposed failures of Governments in creating an enabling environment for youth within the Millennium Goals. Heads of State and Government reaffirmed the crucial importance of recognizing the rights of youth for any development agenda to work. As they conceded, children's greatest needs and aspirations point to a world that facilitates a rich human development based on "principles and democracy, equality, non-discrimination, peace, social justice and the universality, indivisibility, interdependence and interrelatedness of all human rights, including the right to development. Children and adolescents are resourceful citizens capable of building a better future for all" [A World Fit for Children]. The Special Session sounded a wake-up call to address the continuing neglect of children and youth in an uncaring world.

For a long time, the general public has viewed youth as a category wasteful of opportunity through frustration and lawlessness. The negative images of youth, who now form close to a half of the world's population, exclude and ignore the great potential in them which needs only to be given opportunity, cultivation and guidance.

The goal of a productive world of peace is often marred by selfish individuals in positions of influence, who have no tangible commitment or concern for the enrichment of the human condition of youth in order to launch them into meaningful adulthood. The quality of our young will depend on the bequest they receive; this forms a basic challenge of the twenty-first century. The identified and recognized needs of youth will constitute the agenda of the United Nations to be translated into action through its various agencies. Children need to be listened to for their proper participation in charting out their future as important partners in the custodianship of the world. Productivity in every nation originates from children and youth properly grounded in the cultural, social and economic virtues and aspirations of the nation,

which must exclude the dehumanizing and traumatic abduction into training as child soldiers in conflict situations or into forced child labour and prostitution.

In preparation for the Special Session, held from 8 to 10 May 2002, the youth in Malawi convened a "Children's Parliament" on 16 and 17 August, with the theme "A Malawi Fit for Children".

Areas of great concern defined by the children, whose recommendations the main Parliament adopted in toto, included education, HIV/AIDS, child participation in decision-making, poverty and the problem of orphans. The enormous challenge for lawmakers in Malawi was the realization of the children's desire and ability to eloquently articulate concerns affecting them, which called for relevance in policy formulation. Malawian children's concerns are repeated everywhere in the world, with the problem of violence against children on the list.

According to the Malawi National Youth Policy, factors contributing to the vulnerability of youth include inadequate educational and training facilities, exacerbated by social and cultural practices, early pregnancies and marriages, sexual harassment, violence and exploitation, HIV/AIDS and sexually transmitted diseases, drug and alcohol abuse, marginalization and non-involvement in decision-making, homelessness, unemployment and lack of sporting and proper entertainment facilities. These areas of preoccupation dovetail with the interests related to the UN mission.

However, for the UN to help harness the energies and potential of youth, Member States need to demonstrate the political and general will to assist them. Malawi President Bakili Muluzi, in a "State of the Nation" address on 31 May, called upon "all people in the country to work on giving our boys and girls equal opportunities to participate in the development of this country. They are our future. This is the time to prepare them for meaningful contribution".

In Africa, the situation of children and youth has been quite troubling: one in three children suffers from malnutrition; the AIDS pandemic has created huge numbers of orphans; and child labour, sex exploitation and child soldiers in war crises, with their terrible humanitarian tragedies, have impacted negatively the prospects of a humane, educated and enlightened society. Efforts by national governments to address these problems have failed to register much notable success because of the lack of financial resources and capacity. The United Nations has an important role to play here, but we must also recognize its successful performance often depends on the level of investment by the international community in societies riddled by poverty.

If education represents the backbone of socioeconomic empowerment and development, UN agencies, such as the UN Educational, Scientific and Cultural Organization (UNESCO), the International Bureau of Education and, to some extent the International Labour Organization (ILO) in the area of vocational training, can make a significant contribution by way of different programmes and projects. The Education for All concept was launched in Jomtien, Cambodia in the early 1990s with great expectations. The United Nations Children's Fund (UNICEF) and the United Nations Population Fund (UNFPA) continue to play important supporting roles in addressing the problem of physical infrastructure in education to promote some of the goals of Jomtien. The task for Government is extremely challenging in a poverty stricken country. In Malawi, universal primary education, introduced in 1994 by the United Democratic Front (UDF), has increased enrollment from 1.9 million to about 3.4 million today. This has brought enormous logistical and infrastructural problems which, however, should be seen as a stepping stone. Attempts to reduce the gap of educational opportunity to equally empower both girls and boys have formed an important agenda in countries such as Malawi, which has attained sex parity, although as yet only in the first five years of primary school. Out of the 100 million children out of school worldwide, 60 per cent are girls. The United Nations can continue to support the development of physical facilities and appropriate school curriculum, accompanied by incentives for girls. UNICEF has demonstrated conspicuous practical interest in funding curriculum revision, which must now include cross-cutting areas, such as gender and HIV/AIDS.

HIV/AIDS today constitutes the greatest threat to human development. The negative impact comes not just from the loss of millions of lives and the reversal of economic development efforts and insecurity, but also from the plight inflicted on children and youth, most of them in the poverty-ridden developing world. Of the close to 11 million children and youth living with AIDS, 70 per cent are in sub-Saharan Africa, while 12.1 million struggle as AIDS orphans in need of institutionalized care, about 90 per cent of them in sub-Saharan Africa (1.2 million in Zambia and 1 million in Malawi). Youth, for their part, need education, information and services that will emphasize self-respect, rights and informed choices to reduce their vulnerability to HIV infection, in order to assist

the pledges by Governments to visibly cut HIV prevalence among 15- to 24-year-olds by 25 per cent by 2005. HIV/AIDS is a shared concern in the work of UNICEF, UNESCO and UNFPA. UN partnerships with Governments in financial support and technical assistance aim at arresting the scourge through training, public education and other interventions, which most Governments, given their poverty, are unable to mount on their own.

The fundamental issue of addressing alternatives that can engage youth profitably to supplement verbal messages through the curriculum and traditional forums must be addressed.

Every child or youth has a right to a dignified life free from exploitation and discrimination in a world that needs to be protected for them. Education without gainful occupation fails to appeal to the youth who see schooling as a gateway to a better economic life.

Governments may have the will to improve the welfare of youth, but lack of resources cripples the optimism. As the UN Secretary-General has noted, goals for youth improvement have been hampered by inadequate government funding—a most critical factor in developing youth capabilities and capacities, and a serious challenge for the UN global agenda in the creation of a world fit for children.

Lack of employment has frequently created a negative incentive to education and has given rise to pursuits, such as substance (drugs) abuse, premarital sex, violence and even crimes of theft. Training youth for self-employment would reduce deviance and promote balanced socio-economic development and dignified ambitions. A UN agency such as the ILO could contribute to this training through support to a college or even setting up a vocational training centre. Skills for building self-reliance would help to reduce youth indiscipline on the streets and in cities.

Youth have enormous mental and physical energy that seek expression. Quite often, official attention to the physical requirement has been minimal. Government investment in community youth recreational centres constitutes positive action as a potent strategy to build self-esteem among them, particularly in the absence of sufficient youth employment.

Support for small business enterprise has sometimes been dubbed risky for funding agencies. Malawi's experience in giving loans to youths has revealed promise through training. President Muluzi has declared his government's support for youth employment and entrepreneurship projects and programmes that will assist youth in developing not only skills for sustainable livelihood but also the leadership potential and confidence which the youth of Malawi exhibited during the children's parliament. As concerns projects and vocational training, the supportive role of the ILO and other UN agencies cannot be overemphasized.

In Bolivia, a moral leadership training programme, with a coverage that includes youth, has shown great promise in the development of character and leadership among young. (One Country, Bahai Magazine, Jan-March 2002). Small youth groups have been organized to undertake community projects, drawing the youth away from unworthy engagements. UNESCO could assist in leadership training.

If youth represent the custodians of the future of the world, they are the determinants of the quality of the world today, which must reflect our contribution to them. Our role is to enrich the process of developing youth into useful, productive and responsible architects of a world of peace. The United Nations in this process must take on and execute a partnership with Governments to ensure the raising of youth well grounded in the commendable socio-economic and cultural virtues for the sustainability of humankind.

Ambassador Isaac C. Lamba is Permanent Representative of the Republic of Malawi to the United Nations. In addition to a distinguished diplomatic career, he has an extensive background in academia.

From *UN Chronicle*, September/November 2002, pp. 60-61. © 2002 by United Nations. Reprinted with permission.

On (not) "coloring in the outline"

(Transformations From Youth Through Relationships)

Linda C. Powell

This article provides an overview and analysis of 10 studies on violence and injustice from the perspective of youth. These articles are contained in the issue of Journal of Social Issues entitled Youth Perspectives on Violence and Injustice and, in the articles, the authors offer a unique opportunity to go far beyond the current discursive terrains of youth and violence. Through a reinterpretation of what is conceptualized as normative, an expansion of the conceptualization of "youth" and an exploration of a broad range of topics, contexts and methods, the issue explores five provocative and significant critical themes. These themes are: methodology is critical; youth as subject, not object; girl and danger of a clinical approach; centrality of schools? and at the intersection of social justice and development. The impact of popular culture on youth and violence and the importance of examining what adults value as "entertainment" are discussed also.

Adding a new voice to a conversation, a new point of view, does more than just increase the content in a linear way (Walkerdine, 2002). Including a voice that has previously been excluded contains the potential for changing the entire discussion. "Facts" and other notions once taken for granted are opened to scrutiny. "Natural" connections and causalities yield to new ways of organizing ideas and relationships. Notions assumed "settled" lead to new questions and implicate new players. In scientific terms (Kuhn, 1962), science moves forward not by careful and gradual research programs, but by huge new ideas that replace old ones. The action of moving youth voices toward the center of the study of violence is such a paradigm shift.

Daiute and Fine (this issue), the editors of this issue, report 10 studies that go beyond what Mahiri and Conner (this issue) describe as the public discourse about Black youth violence or "the outline" which sets boundaries of a somewhat proscribed conversation that adults have about young people and violence. Daiute and Fine (this issue) echo Mahiri and Conner's desire to go beyond this kind of "coloring in the outline" (Mahiri and Conner). This issue offers an opportunity to color far beyond the lines of the currently overlapping terrains of youth and violence. The 10 studies featured reinterpret what counts as normative, expand the conceptualization of "youth," and explore a broad range of topics, contexts and methods. The editors and contributors to this issue assume that there are ongoing, multiple systems that influence the lives of young people, that these systems can interact in paradoxical and counterintuitive ways and that when we listen, young people can describe their experiences in ways that are multi-layered and complex. As the studies report, listening to these stories can dramatically enlarge our sense of and the nature of the "problem" of violence and the "meaning" of youth. In taking an important theoretical turn that young people have something to say about their own lives, and these young people do not disappoint—this issue creates the possibility of shifting the conversation and public discourse about youth and violence.

Lewin (1951) and Fallis and Opotow (this issue) remind us that social behavior is a function of both persons and their environments. From a youth-based perspective, this issue's ambitious task is to begin to make the function of both individual and contextual elements of youth and violence clearer and more precise. Youth narratives and experiences map in detail and in color the connections between their internal lives and their environmental context—looking at interactions, relationships, causality, and influences between the multiple ways they describe their experiences, and their life contexts and behaviors and the impact of social institutions. In many of these studies, the authors have, as Phoenix, Frosh, and Pattman (this issue) describe it, "gotten out of our way," giving us the actual words of young people. They let us decide whether or not we agree with the researchers' interpretation. In others, the authors (e.g., Cross, this issue) have carefully interwoven history with present day realities so we may re-view youth and violence.

Coloring outside of the line is not simply about the shape of the boundaries, but also about the hues and textures around the boundaries. The authors offer not just studies of "kids of color" but they enter the more dangerous area of seeing the experiences of kids of all colors through the prisms of race, gender and class. We begin to see the ways in which social identity matters in the social construction and attributions of behavior and the development of identities. In particular, young people have different experiences of similar stimuli and different consequences of their behavior depending on race, ethnicity, gender, or class (Bailey, 1992-93; Giles, 2001; Style & Powell, 1995; Wellesley College, 1992). These "embodied" studies give us additional insights into the experiences of youth that are always influenced by status, history, and position. For instance, we learn that violence is not something that "Black young men do," but violence becomes a phenomenon affecting all young people, but with potentially differential impact and consequence based on race and class. In this issue, we hear the voices of girls and of boys; of young people from elementary school through adolescence and early adulthood; of young people living in and migrating to the United States, Israel, and Britain. We meet these youth in their classrooms, in community organizations, on the streets, and in history. We see them through the lenses of psychology and sociology, through feminism, and through antiracist analyses. Some of these young people live in circumstances of war, racism, or tremendous social dislocation. Some studies dare to ask youth about "violence," itself. And they respond by telling us about their relationships, their homes, and their schools. More frightening, when they are asked about their relationships or about school, we learn how violence and the antecedents to violence weave into the everyday fabric of friendships, romance, and learning. Conducting research that surfaces youth perspectives in an authentic way requires a cognitive shift, a move away from the idea of "youth as problem" to an empathic entering into and with the experience of young people themselves. Making this cognitive shift leads to a set of theoretical and methodological "taken for granteds" that are provocative, significant, and subtly understated. In the following section, I discuss these shifts as critical themes that run across these papers.

Critical Themes

Methodology Is Critical

The studies are explicit in generating methods that allow researchers to "hear," theorize, interpret, and analyze critically what youth say about violence and how they say it. This may require some departures from more typical research methods. These methodological investments and innovations come in many forms and at every stage of research. Writers such as Phoenix et al. (this issue) and Tolman, Spencer, Rosen-Reynoso, and Porche (this issue) create research situations in which adults must listen deeply to youth, following their lead in inquiry and interpretation. Daiute, Stem, and Lelutiu-Weinberger (this issue) designed their project so that youth talk to adults could be contrasted to youth talk with peers, while studying the values of adults and students. Fine et al. (this issue) build research and survey questions with young people, turning over unexpected rocks in the differences between adult and youth experience. Using historical and sociological methods, Cross (this issue) excavates and examines the myths that generate and potentially pervert approaches to youth problems today. Spencer,

Dupree, Cunningham, Harpalani, and Munoz-Miller (this issue) use a specific theoretical framework that "integrate[s] salient issues of context and development". In exploring young people's experience with victimization via their thoughts, fears, and physical symptoms they attempt to "[capture] the meaning-making processes underlying foundational identity development and outcomes" (Spencer et al.). Hertz-Lazarowitz (this issue) applies concepts from a model of Social Drama (Harre, 1979) that seems uniquely useful in understanding the action and intergroup dynamics on a university campus.

These approaches are a far cry from the traditional approaches to studying youth violence. First, these studies investigate the experiences of "normal" kids, those not officially identified as violent or "at risk" for violence. In this way, these are truly studies "of" violence from the perspective "of" youth. Secondly, these studies care about development as a dynamic. Violence is not conceived as a one time event. Rather, it is viewed as an experience that will influence what occurs next in their lives, coming at a vulnerable time in the lifespan and having impact on learning, relational development, feelings of engagement/alienation, etc. Finally, each of these studies comments in some way on the "essentialist versus systemic perspective" (Cross). For instance, Cross (this issue) states that observers essentialize problems when Blacks (or youth) are involved and those same problems are perceived as more systemic when Whites and other social groups (like adults) are studied. Most of these studies are interdisciplinary, including the methods of social, developmental and clinical psychology, sociology, history, public health, and education. Fine et al. (this issue) worked with young people at the outset of the research to generate questions, discovering a vein of experience that the adults could not access. Most of the studies used multiple methods, including clinical interviewing. Phoenix et al. (this issue) remind us that since "we 'make' our identities through our autobiographical narratives", we can learn from young people by having them tell rich, complex potentially contradictory stories about their experience. Tolman et al. (this issue) describe this process as creating a "... dialogue between theory and youth perspectives...". Solis's (this issue) theoretical framework holds that violence is "a dialectical process that is constantly unfolding between social structures and individuals". Therefore, for her, violence has social, rather than natural or individual, origins. Fallis and Opotow (this issue) included dissemination as a critical part of their data analysis; this phase challenged student researchers to become conceptually clear about their work and allowed each stage of the project to generate new questions.

Youth as Subject, Not Object

What each of these studies indicates is the potential for empowerment and, hence, new results when young people are involved as subject and even researcher, rather than simply objects of someone else's inquiry. As Hertz-Lazarowitz (this issue) sums up, "... we sought to document young people in conflict and confrontation using events of injustice and surveillance to develop critical and political thinking". The phenomenology of meaning making rather than remaining object in someone else's study requires new kinds of supportive and interpretive research environments. The results of these studies suggest (not counter-intuitively) that young people tell different stories when they trust that their authentic experiences are genuinely valued and respected. This may be an inadvertent "metafinding" of these studies. Wells (1985) has usefully given us the "radio" metaphor for thinking about multiple levels of analysis, and how to think usefully about group-level variables. Daiute and Fine (this issue) state that youth today are growing up with a sense of adult betrayal and alienation. If we imagine that many stations are playing all the time, it becomes possible to "tune in" to a single station and listen. This is not to say that no young people have good relationships with adults, but that when we tune in on the "youth station" we hear the absence of sufficient holding environments constructed and honored by adults for youth.

Group relations theory (Rioch, 1975; Shapiro and Carr, 1991; Wells, 1985) uses psychoanalysis and social psychology to build complex understandings of individuals, groups, and social systems. It can help with the interactions between institutional and personal factors and how these influences conspire to create identities and connecting individual lives, personal narrations and institutional effects. Fallis and Opotow (this issue) introduce the notion of multiple levels of analysis (individual, interpersonal, and institutional) when identifying what gets addressed and what remains latent within a system. They offer a sophisticated interpretation of school cutting, an activity they conceive of as challenging the authority of the school to avoid conflict or direct challenges of systems and processes they see as alienating. A purely behavioral and individual focus protects the system from investigating its own contributions, dynamics, and interests. Systemic failure (disengagement, alienation due to the nature of school) is handled by individual interventions. As long as we see only individuals, the systemic or group level problem will persist, unfettered and unaddressed.

Fallis and Opotow's (this issue) complex definition of "boring" as a reason to cut class is instructive as we think about young people and violence. When students describe something as boring, they are not just describing the absence of something or being disinterested. Upon investigation, they mean something very specific: a one way, top down, unengaged relationship with a teacher whose pedagogy feels disrespectful because it is not designed to "tempt, engage or include" them. From a youth perspective, boring is not a naturally occurring phenomenon. It is the predictable outcome of specific decisions and actions of the teacher and school.

The third major assumption of these writings, again refreshing and understated, is that the social world is not necessarily neutral for young people. Researchers must be willing to suspect that some young person isn't personally troubled or some issue isn't just "pesty...." We have to be willing to look at institutional structures that contribute to youth behavior. Fallis and Opotow (this issue) note that "moral exclusion is the alchemy that transforms intransigent, unaddressed conflict into structural violence [and] ... situates responsibility for negative outcomes in victims rather than those with institutional resources and power". This notion indicts our adult, researcher at-tention, spotlighting what it emphasizes or what it doesn't seem to notice.

Institutions cannot be taken as helpful or supportive simply because adults intend for them to be. Young people develop a variety of ways of navigating their complex social world. These studies document how much can be learned by listening to the experiences of young people as they challenge public institutions. From the perspective of young people, history, schools, and communities can oppress and create inequity. As an example, many policing programs are allegedly designed to protect citizens. However, Fine et al. (this issue) discovered that young people experience themselves as a population at risk of police targeting. That is a youth perspective on adult surveillance.

What is the impact on identity development when receiving a constant message that you are untrustworthy, suspicious and potential criminals and it "shows" on you—your look determines your criminality, not your behavior? As Fine et al. (this issue) note, even good behavior does not protect Black youth from police surveillance. Similarly, the voices of young people have rarely been heard in discussions of police violence, despite being a target of more aggressive policing initiatives.

Finally, these essays recognize that adult definitions of social problems can be social defenses (Jaques, 1955; Menzies, 1975; Powell, 1994) against the anxiety stirred by youth perspectives on social problems. Why is it still an unusual idea to take students' concerns seriously when planning school reform efforts or to work with them collaboratively in creating youth policy? This avoidance of authentic engagement serves as a psychological defense for adults. For example, what happens when we look beyond cutting class as an individual issue to the systemic issues giving rise to cutting? What happens when we consider youth behavior as data and even a critique, not just as individual errant behavior (Fine, 1991)? When teachers see cutting class as a disciplinary matter, it protects them from the hypothesis that it is a comment on their teaching.

Girl and Danger of a Clinical Approach

The authors of these studies honor young people's experiences with and explanations about the risks of violence to their physical and psychological well-being. For the purpose of this issue, youth violence is not a "disease" and violence against and by young people must be addressed as a social and political problem. This moves beyond individual behavior, into the realm of phenomenology, or the meaning making systems that young people employ to understand and organize their experiences. These studies require stepping back from individually framed behavior and looking at the big picture of affective experiences of young people. This issue assumes that youth do have internal worlds that are products, reflections, and defenses against their experiences.

Across these essays we hear a psychoanalytic or clinical language through which researchers stretch to recognize the relation of adult fetishes and youth behavior; adult anxieties and our projections onto youth. Further, the researchers seek to move into the internal world which inevitably brings us into the world of clinical dynamics. For example, Daiute and Fine (this issue) note that "Research in the field of youth violence … rarely reports from the standpoints of youths themselves who may look at the world around them as problematic … Adults project onto youth our growing concerns about violence [emphasis added]". Mahiri and Conner (this issue) use the notions of displacement and scapegoats (Banet and Hayden, 1977; Wells, 1985). In addition to the practical mechanism they quote from Chomsky (1995), in psychoanalysis this is the most extreme form of projective identification. Parallel process (Smith and Berg, 1987; Smith, Simmon, and Thames, 1989) is intimated by Hertz-Lazarowitz when she considers the possibility that lessons learned from the conflict on campus can be considered data about the university as a whole, as well as in Israel. Fallis and Opotow (this issue) remind us of Apples' (1996) poignant insight about students' "almost unconscious realization that … schooling will not enable them to go much farther than they already are", which provides a powerful glimpse into a student's internal world. Tolman et al. (this issue) organize their inquiry around Rich's (1983) definition of heterosexuality as a universally pervasive institution, with mechanisms that "insure that it functions unconsciously and imperceptibly for most individuals" (Tolman et al.).

Using clinical language about the unconscious gives us incredible firepower to more authentically construct the complexity within and between individuals and groups. It allows us to account for that which is apparent, and that which operates below the surface. Organizations, too, have an unconscious (Obholzer and Roberts, 1994), with manifest and latent content, conflict and defensive strategies. Daiute et al. (this issue) note this: "When violence prevention programs are placed in contexts where children are presumed to have experienced discrimination conflicts, it should not be surprising that they may need or want to express life experiences that the curriculum actually represses [emphasis added]". Fallis and Opotow (this issue) also comment on this, noting that "intransigent conflicts that resist standard solutions are often characterized by misdiagnoses that miss deeper issues such as the basic need for consistency, security, respect, justice, and a sense of personal control". And, above all, it lets us enter the terrain of the imagination, of dreams and images, which are developmentally and politically critical in the identities of youth.

There remains the difficulties of capturing and measuring the inner world in any respectful way: One major danger is that we have all been boys and girls. Transference—clinical, research, and theoretical—appears as a likely problem. First, we have to attempt to make some meaning out of the experiences youth share and the stories they tell. We must wonder about the questions that adults have not asked. While this is always true of the research adventure, our absences make an interesting pattern. Like Tolman's wondering why (all) the research on dating violence hasn't inquired into why there is so much violence? There is significant research on gender differences in dating behavior but a marked absence of gendered analysis (for counterexamples see Leadbeater and Way, 1996). This is similar to Fine et al. (this issue) not conceding the possibility of sexual harassment of young women by the police. Or in Phoenix et al. (this issue) wondering about repressed material in adults

leading to Black boys being seen as super-masculine. Perhaps these are the kinds of arenas we may not have conscious access to and are not eager (or encouraged) to excavate.

Hertz-Lazarowitz (this issue) looks specifically at meaning making in her study of Palestine and Israeli dynamics at Haifa University. First, she shifts the question away from personal behavior to personal experiences. One of her central interview questions clearly seeks internal meaning: Has someone in authority controlled or acted toward you in an unjust way? In this question, the research puts the question of justice right at the forefront. Her study focuses also on the social meaning, potentially offering a new understanding of the interplay between personal and collective factors.

Solis (this issue) hypothesizes a "dialectical relationship [as] a cycle between the societal abuse faced by Mexican immigrants, and the personal acts of violence and abuse enacted by Mexican immigrants". From this perspective, violence is a tool youth use to make sense of themselves, other people and institutions. She uses the term "violenced" (Solis, this issue) to describe those who have had violence perpetrated upon them as a result of their "illegal" status.

Centrality of Schools?

Schools are the only social institution that can compel young people to be present. For that reason alone, schools are important in any discussion of youth perspectives on violence. In this issue, all of the studies mention schools; six are specifically situated within them. Tragically, schools are increasingly a place where some young people enact violence. We believe, also, that schools are a key site where young people negotiate their understanding in the world and develop their capacity for social engagement and meaning making. Schools have been considered important as an agency of indoctrination, reproduction of social relations, and sites of social violence (Block, 1997). It is an important social institution where the emotional aspects of the youth social system and adult social system interact on a daily basis.

Cross (this issue) provides a complete rereading of Frazier's 1939 work about delinquency in Chicago with a systemic rather than essentialist perspective. While Frazier sought explanations for the behavior in family and community dynamics, Homel (1984) found a more persuasive systemic argument in the schools and their maladaptive attempts to deal with racism and overcrowding. These (systemic) facts undercut the myth that African Americans were crippled in some way by slavery, and yet the (essentialist) myth continues to influence our thinking about Black youth and violence today. Do we still think, as Cross (this issue) asks, that schools are designed "… to prevent delinquency through educational engagement"? Or have we given up on that?

School can be a site of violence, and the task of schools is influenced by young people's experiences of violence. Phoenix et al. (this issue) remind us that experiences of school influence how young people see their worlds. Tolman et al. (this issue) note that school is the context in which much of teen dating takes place, between people who are known to one another, and in a context where adults fail to interrupt and may even encourage harassing behaviors. Spencer et al. (this issue) note an important finding in their study: each of the post-traumatic stress disorder (PTSD) symptoms that were predicted by experience with violence was related to focus of attention. They rightly note that feelings of fear, distraction and self-consciousness in response to experiences with violence can interfere with normative learning processes.

This concern about violence in schools is not simply about social interactions, but also occurs in the pedagogy of the school. For example, in explicating the ways that teachers and students struggled together to produce a set of values, Daiute et al. (this issue) remind us that an emphasis on mastery discourages critique or transformation; from this perspective, all questions and challenges emerge as individual failures. Tolman et al. (this issue) discover that school policies that provoke individual discussion about sexual harassment and dating violence, without a critique of the larger systems which produce and perpetuate violence in intimate relationships, leave girls feeling scared and boys feeling unfairly accused.

Mahiri and Conner's (this issue) study findings reflected three broad, highly related themes that clearly contrasted with public discourse on Black youth. In particular, the lives of the youth closely correspond to the circumstances of many of the Black youth that U.S. society has characterized as violent "others" (Fordham, 1996; Payne, 2001; Ward, 2001), with one key difference. Those youth that attended small schools with teachers that were interested in and capable of teaching a unique curriculum unit engaged young people in ways that match their experiences about violence. The impact of school size (Wasley et al., 2000; Fine and Soimerville, 1998) was noted also by Fine et al. (this issue). Small schools give the opportunity for innovative curriculum. In the Mahiri and Connor article (this issue) students research and document aspects of their own lives; they interview members of their community and assess positive and negative aspects of their community. Academic work is used to mirror and explore their experience, developing their intellectual ability to think about what actually happens in their world. This schooling experience starts with the lived experience of young people, and does not demand that students create a separate school self. This integrating, unitive approach could be for young people the opposite of Fallis and Opotow's (this issue) "boring" aspects of school. Why is it still news to us that young people bring complex and competing worlds into their classrooms, worlds which require respect and negotiation for the learning task to proceed?

At the Intersection of Social Justice and Development

Unlike the linear and unidimensional "outline" that is much of the public conversation about youth and violence, the young people in these studies emerge in colorful, vivid, and complex terms. They inhabit a world which they must accept as routinely unpredictable and violent by necessity, a world where public policy may make you unsafe, and a world where huge forces like history and war will determine daily interactions with others. And as several researchers discovered, young people describe this simply as "the way things are." A world where boys must struggle to act like "real men," and romance requires violence, where girls must balance being desirable, vulnerable, and acceptable. A world where language has no meaning and homophobia is "just" a joke (although boys will go to great lengths to avoid being called "gay"). Not surprisingly, many young people, in several of the studies, "just decide not to care about it" or "to simply ignore it." The numbing burdens of this world become monotonous and debilitating. And too often the responses of adults imply that it is up to the individual young person to take action. Despite our intent, our educational and social policies often operate as if young people are our enemy rather than our future.

As a whole, these studies expand our definitions of "violence." Myth making robs and lies and distorts—and is a form of violence against the history and culture of African Americans. Being termed "illegal" is violence against the self and the identity of Mexican immigrant children and families. Microaggressions of disrespect and suspicion (Toussaint, Boyd-Franklin, & Franklin, 2000) are experienced as forms of interpersonal violence. Organizational structures and practices that diminish the sense of self and deny resources are a form of violence. The cumulative impact of these processes on identity development can be devastating. A person or a group can suffer real damage if the world mirrors back to them a confining or demeaning or contemptible picture of themselves. As Solis (this issue) notes, "… as long as violence continues to be lived privately and ignored publicly, and as long as the means to respond to violence other than with violence remains unfamiliar to [them]", young people will find themselves in a bind. The 10 studies in this issue suggest that interventions with the power to solve the intransigent problems youth face will require youth perspectives leveled "at the intersection of social justice and development" (Daiute and Fine, this issue) situated front and center. What does this issue have to say to the school reform, youth development, and violence prevention literatures? It calls into question new interpretations of seemingly straightforward data; it offers methodologies and syntheses. It makes us wonder whether perhaps we should we be interrogating "adulthood" the way we eventually had to interrogate Whiteness? If sampling the internal world of young people is important, then like psychotherapy, it is labor intensive work. It requires relationship and clinical skill, respect and courage.

An Afterthought

In a recent address to the Public Education Network national convention, Nobel laureate Toni Morrison (2002) used her own narrative as a student to inspire and provoke her audience to think about education in a post-9/11 world. Her earliest desire for academic achievement was fueled, she said, by a "terror" or desire that she wouldn't be competent in an adult world. This is the world that no longer exists for young people. In the absence of adult engagement with youth voices and experiences, popular culture (Lash, 2000; Wolff, 1999) sells a version of adult life that always feels in reach. There is less and less that schools or real adults have to teach that TV and movies don't provide a more powerful and immediate "curriculum." That terror she felt has now been assuaged by a plastic sense of order and certainty; no problem exists that is not solved by the end of the episode (with suitable commercial breaks) or turned into a meme of stimulation.

Cross (this issue) notes that it is unclear how Frazier (1939/1948) missed the role of schools overcrowding and double-shift schools in understanding youth problems in Chicago. Are researchers also overlooking the impact of popular culture now? Will we look back and wonder about the unrestrained impact of violence as entertainment on issues of identity and violence; depictions of this violence are easily found on television, in video games, and in films. Interesting that it may elude us too if we do not recognize it as a force (Daspit and Weaver, 1999; Minow and LeMay, 1995). If we fail to consider it as a potential variable-the way Frazier may never have thought about the structure of the day—then we will miss the potential impact of this multibillion-dollar, saturating industry (Daspit, 1999). The challenge is that popular culture lives in our imaginations, in our unconscious, away from our immediate awareness and public selves. The major power of advertising is its ability to convince us that we are not influenced by it (Kilbourne, 1999).

Cross (this issue) imagines the comments from the 1940s: "yes, now that you point it out to me, double-shifting probably does not help matters, but there must be some cultural or genetic reasons why so many Black teens keep getting into trouble". We ruminate in the same way about the steady diet of stimulating images fed to all of us, with young people perhaps more vulnerable than others; we know that it affects brain chemistry; we sense that it is changing the ways that we relate to ourselves and each other, we know that our consuming behaviors are sustainable only at the costs of lives around the globe, and then we look away. Like the adults that Cross describes, we assume that it must be about something else: bad genes, the education system, the mental health system, racism, etc. And while all of these contribute to our understanding of youth violence, there is a strange silence in this issue and in general about what de Zengotita (2002) calls "The Numbing of The American Mind" and the particular impact that has on children and youth. We, too, struggle with the addictive properties of popular culture; however, we would rather project all of our concern on young people. Hertz-Lazarowitz reminds us of McLaren and Giroux's (1994) reflection: "education has to be viewed as a political matter related to the power structure of the society". Maybe schools are less potent as critical sites for identity development, and popular culture reigns. Mahiri and Connor (this issue) allude to this when they suggest that "elements of hip-hop culture and rap music constituted a kind of 'pop culture pedagogy' that extended, offered alternatives to, or challenged the pedagogy of schools".

However, I would go further. The images and values of popular culture have colonized the imagination, subtly defining what is important, the ways in which we interact and the meanings we construct. Certain images, especially those that link sexuality and violence (the critical link of the last two articles in this issue) take up a place in our imaginations, whether we consciously "know" or acknowledge it. The preponderance of violence as entertainment does at least three things: First, the very medium of television, movies, video games, and the Internet pulls us into an external focus and risks making us passive and "receptive" in the most intimate areas of our own lives. This contributes to the sense reported by many young people that "this is just the way things are," and "you get used to it..." This passivity develops separate from the "content" of specific films or music. This is a meta-effect, provoked by intensity and saturation. Secondly, popular culture teaches an amazingly consistent and "standardized" curriculum of consumerist and materialist values. In a world of harsh policy battles about what young people should be taught in schools, there is a seemingly clear consensus in the curriculum of popular culture that individualism, efficiency, and materialism are the keys to a happy life. And that violence is a common, legitimate, and sometimes glamorous way of handling conflict and difference. And finally, popular culture holds identity development processes hostage to a false reality, away from the human, interactive, social field. This may be why the focus in so many of these studies on actual experience—shared between adults and young people—proved to be so riveting. Several studies note that relationships over time with youth participants led to deeper levels of comfort with process and reflection on their involvement in the study. This proves especially important in Solis's (this issue) case study of her work with one student over time.

While there is much additional research to chart this new terrain, it seems likely that popular culture has some impact on issues of youth and violence and it has some impact on how adults view and engage with issues of youth and violence. For instance, in my most recent work with educators, it has become clear that adults are often quite clear about the implications of consumerist values on the young people with whom they work. They are usually quite enthusiastic about the need for critical media training and coursework about advertising and marketing. Although they say that young people are rarely initially engaged by these ideas, believing themselves to be about this kind of influence—while they wear the clothes, buy the music, and incorporate the values of the culture that surrounds them. However, these educators are routinely less interested in exploring their own reaction to popular culture and the ways in which issues of consumption, externalization, and ambition affect them on a daily basis.

Studying this new terrain will be fraught with methodological, psychological and political difficulties. One of the greatest challenges may be the requirement that adults, researchers, and educators examine our own values about popular culture, examine our own values about "entertainment," and not simply lump it into some larger vague category called "the media." The simple fact that a multi-billion dollar industry exists and thrives on images of violence seemingly unfettered may communicate to young people what we really believe.

References

Apple, M. (1996). Cultural politics and education. New York: Teachers College Press.

Bailey, S. (1992-93). Gender equity: The unexamined basic of school reform. Stanford Law & Policy Review, 4, Winter.

Banet, A. G., Jr., & Hayden, C. (1977). The Tavistock primer. In J. E. Jones, & J. W. Pfeiffer (Eds.), The 1977 handbook for group facilitators (pp. 155-167). La Jolla, CA: University Associates.

Block, A. (1997). I'm only bleeding: Education as the practice of social violence against children. New York: Peter Lang.

Chomsky, N. (1995). A dialogue with Noam Chomsky. Harvard Educational Review, 65(2).

Daspit, T. (1999). Rap pedagogies: "Bring(ing) the noise of knowledge born on the microphone" to radical education. In T. Daspit & J. A. Weaver (Eds.), Popular culture and critical pedagogy. Reading, constructing, connecting (pp. 163-181). New York: Garland Publishing.

Daspit, T., & Weaver, J. A. (Eds.) (1999). Popular culture and critical pedagogy. Reading, constructing, connecting. New York: Garland Publishing.

de Zengotita, T. (2002). Numbing of the American mind. Harper's Magazine, 304 (1823), 33-41.

Fine, M. (1991). Framing dropouts: Notes on the politics of an urban public high school. Albany, NY: State University of New York Press.

Fine, M., & Somerville, J. I. (Eds.). (1998). Small schools, big imaginations: Creative look at urban public schools. Chicago: Cross City Campaign for Urban School Reform.

Fordham, S. (1996). Blacked out. Dilemmas of race, identity, and success at Capital High. Chicago: University of Chicago Press.

Frazier, E. F. (1939). The Negro family in the United States. Chicago: University of Chicago Press; revised edition 1948. New York: Dryden Press.

Giles, H. C. (2001). Transforming the deficit narrative: Race, class and social capital in parent-school relations. In C. Korn & A. Bursztyn (Eds.), Case studies in cultural transition: Re-thinking multi-cultural education. Wesport, CT: Greenwood Press.

Harre, R. (1979). Social being. London: Blackwell.

Homel, M. W. (1984). Down from equality: Black Chicagoans and the public schools, 1920-1940. Champaign-Urbana, IL: University of Illinois Press.

Jaques, E. (1955). Social systems as a defense against persecutory and depression anxiety. In M. Klein, P. Heimann, & R. E. Money-Kyrle (Eds.), New directions in psychoanalysis (pp. 277-299). London: Tavistock.

Kilbourne, J. (1999). Can't buy my love: How advertising changes the way we think and feel. New York: Simon & Schuster.

Kuhn, T. (1962). Structure of scientific revolutions. Chicago: University of Chicago Press.

Lasn, K. (2000). Culture jam: How to reverse America's suicidal consumer binge—And why we must. New York: Quill.

Leadbeater, B. J. R., & Way, N. (Eds.). (1996). Urban girls: Resisting stereotypes, creating identities. New York: New York University Press.

Lewin, K. (1951). Field theory in social science: Selected papers (D. Cartwright, Ed.). New York: Harper.

McLaren, P., & Giroux, H. A. (1994). Between borders: Pedagogy and the politics of cultural studies. New York: Routledge.

Menzies, I. E. P. (1975). A case-study in the functioning of social systems as a defense against anxiety. In A. D. Colman & W. H. Bexton (Eds.), Group relations reader I. Washington, DC: A.K. Rice Institute.

Minow, N. N., & LeMay, C. L. (1995). Abandoned in the wasteland: Children, television, and the first amendment. New York: Hill & Wang.

Morrison, T. (2002). Freeing the imagination of America. Keynote address, PEN Annual Conference. Assessment and Accountability: The Great Equity Debate 11/11/02-11/13/02.

Obholzer, A., & Roberts, V. Z. (Eds.). (1994). The unconscious at work: Individual and organizational stress in the human services. London, New York: Routledge.

Payne, Y. A. (2001). Black men and street life as a site of resiliency: A counter story for Black scholars. International Journal of Critical Psychology (4), 109-122.

Powell, L. C. (1994). Interpreting social defenses: Family groups in an urban setting. In M. Fine (Ed.), Chartering urban school reform: Reflections on public high schools in the midst of change. New York: Teachers College Press.

Rich, A. (1983). Compulsory heterosexuality & lesbian existence. In A. Snitow, C. Stansell, & S. Thompson (Eds.), Power of desire: The politics of sexuality (pp. 177-205). New York: Monthly Review Press.

Rioch, M. J. (1975). "All we like sheep—" [Isaiah 53:6]: Followers and leaders. In A. D. Colman & W. H. Bexton (Eds.), Group relations reader I. Washington, DC: A. K. Rice Institute.

Shapiro, E. R., & Carr, A. W. (1991). Lost in familiar places: Creating new connections between the individual and society. New Haven, CT: Yale University Press.

Senge, P. M. (1990). The fifth discipline: The art and practice of the learning organization. New York: Doubleday.

Smith, K. K., & Berg, D. N. (1987). Paradoxes of group life: Understanding conflict, paralysis, and movement in group dynamics. San Francisco: Jossey Bass.

Smith, K. K., Simmons, V. M., & Thames, T. B. (1989). "Fix the women": An intervention into an organizational conflict based on parallel process thinking. The Journal of Applied Behavioral Science, 25(1), 11-29.

Style, E., & Powell, L. C. (1995). In our own hands: A diversity primer. Transformations (2), 65-84.

Toussaint, P., Boyd-Franklin, N., & Franklin, A. J. (2000). Boys into men: Raising our African American teenage sons. New York: Dutton/Penguin Books.

Walkerdine, V. (2002). Challenging subjects. London: Palgrave Publishers.

Ward, J. (2001). Raising resisters. In M. Fine & L. Weis (Eds.), Constructions sites. New York: Teachers College Press.

Wasley, P., et al. (2000). Executive summary: Small schools: Great strides: A study of new small schools in Chicago. New York: Bank Street College.

Wellesley College, C. f. R. o. W. (1992). How schools shortchange girls: A study of major findings on girls in education. AAUW Educational Foundation.

Wells, L. (1985). The group-as-a-whole perspective and its theoretical roots. In A. D. Colman & M. H. Geller (Eds.), Group relations reader 2. Sausalito, CA: GREX.

Wolff, M. J. (1999). The entertainment economy: How media forces are transforming our lives. New York: Crown Publishing Group.

LINDA C. POWELL is a Clinical Psychologist and an internationally-known group relations consultant, in the tradition of the Tavistock Institute of Human Relations in London, England. Currently, she is Visiting Professor at the Graduate Center of the City University of New York as well as Affiliated Faculty at the Leadership Institute, University of San Diego. Using an interdisciplinary set of skills as Educator, Organizational Consultant, and Psychotherapist, Dr. Powell has been working with groups and individuals on issues of power and change for almost thirty years. In addition to her corporate consultation and coaching efforts, she works in education reforms, most recently with the nationally-noted research report on the impact of Chicago small-schools movement, "Small Schools, Great Strides." Dr. Powell has authored several articles and book chapters on leadership and urban school reform, most recently, "Savage inequalities indeed: Irrationality and urban school reform" with Maggie Barber and "From charity to justice: Toward a theology of urban school reform." She is the co-editor of Off-

White: Reading on race, power and society (Routledge Press). She is currently working on a book-length exploration of the dilemmas of social identity, leadership, and organizational change and is the President of Resources for Change, Inc., a consulting firm specializing in organizational transformation.

From *Journal of Social Issues*, Spring 2003, pp. 197-211. © 2003 by Blackwell Publishers, Ltd. Reprinted with permission.

The Future of Adolescence:
Lengthening Ladders to Adulthood

BY REED LARSON

Navigating the social and economic complexities of adult life requires more savvy and education than ever.

The life stage of adolescence is a crucial link in the future of society. It is a period when young people either become prepared for and enthusiastic about taking over adult roles, or they rebel against the expectations and responsibilities of adulthood. When things go right, adolescents enter adulthood with new energy and ideas that revitalize society and its institutions.

As we move into the twenty-first century, this life stage is changing rapidly across the world due to globalization, shifting job markets, and transformations in the family, among other things. It is crucial to learn how these changes affect young people's preparedness for the social and economic complexities of the adult world. The Study Group on Adolescence in the 21st Century, composed of a consortium of international scholars, examined the various contours of adolescents' preparation for the years ahead. The Group found that, although the demands on adolescents and the hazards they face in reaching adulthood are increasing, many young people are rising to the challenge.

A Raised Bar for Adulthood

What we expect of young people is extraordinary. First, we expect them to attend school for 12 to 18 years or longer without any guarantee that this education will match what they will need for career success. We ask them to make a leap of trust based on the assumption that the skills they are learning will be relevant when they eventually enter adulthood. Furthermore, we expect them to study without financial remuneration, accept a generic identity defined by their student role, and delay starting a family while in school. These circumstances put young people in a kind of limbo status for years.

As society evolves, this period of limbo continues to lengthen. Young people around the world are being expected to delay entry into adulthood ever longer. This is happening, in large part, because the platform one needs to reach for successful adulthood is getting higher. An information society requires that young people learn more to become full members.

In postindustrial societies, we expect people to attend school until they're at least 22 years old—with no guarantee that their studies will lead to future employment, says author Reed Larson.

Education tops the list of new demands for adulthood, as more and more jobs, including manufacturing and service jobs, require literacy, numeracy, and computer skills. Brains are increasingly valued over brawn: In the United States, entry-level wages for people with only a high-school education have fallen by more than 20% since the 1970s. Job prospects are bleaker than ever for youths who do not continue their education after high school, and while there are exceptions—like the teenager who starts a basement computer business and becomes a multimillionaire—working a string of low-paying service jobs with no medical insurance is a much more common scenario for those with limited education.

The growing need for literacy skills in adult life extends beyond the workplace. Literacy is required to navigate complex insurance papers, retirement packages, legal regulations, and countless other complicated bureaucracies that are part of everyday life. Adults must be literate just to keep up with their own health care. Whereas 40 years ago patients were simply told what to do by their doctors, today patients are expected to be partners in their health management and to keep up with ever-changing research on diet, exercise, and disease prevention and treatment.

In addition to literacy, adolescents need to develop more versatile interpersonal skills to navigate the different worlds of home, work, and school—worlds of increasing complexity and diversity. Adult relationships are becoming less scripted and more transient, and teens need to develop skills for negotiating more *ad hoc* associations. Adults also must be able to operate in more-diverse social worlds. On the job, around the neighborhood, even within families, there is an increased likelihood that young people will need to know how to relate with people from different cultural and religious backgrounds. In developing the knowledge and vernaculars to move smoothly and communicate effectively across various social worlds, adolescents will need to acquire skills to change language, posture, tone, and negotiation strategies to adapt to multiple milieus. The adolescent who is able to function in only one world is increasingly ill-prepared for adult life.

Obstacles to Adulthood

As the platform of adulthood rises, the ladders required to get there lengthen. These boosted demands and longer ladders can increase the precariousness of adolescence, since a longer climb to adulthood creates new disadvantages for those who lack the financial means, emotional support, or mental capacity to keep climbing.

At work, at home, and at play, the human landscape increasingly features the co-mingling of individuals from different cultural, religious, and economic backgrounds. It is crucial for teens to develop social skills that will enable them to be comfortable and effective communicating with a variety of people in multiple milieus, suggests the author.

Acquiring advanced education and opportunities for learning diverse life skills often requires family wealth. In the United States, for example, annual college tuition generally ranges from $16,000 to $36,000—a full year's salary for many parents. Even when tuition is covered by grants and scholarships, families must have sufficient wealth to be able to forgo the income their college-bound children would otherwise provide; many poor families, especially in developing countries, cannot afford this sacrifice. By contrast, middle- and upper-class youths throughout the world are gaining access to new resources, such as after-school programs, camps, tutors, travel opportunities,

computers and new technologies, which will prepare them for both the literacy and life skills of modern adulthood.

Education and Earnings in the United States

High School	$1.2 million
Bachelor's	$2.1 million
Master's	$2.5 million
Ph.D.	$3.4 million
Professional	$4.4 million

Average lifetime work earnings by educational degree, based on 1999 earnings projected over a typical adult work life from age 25 to 64.

Source: U.S. Census Bureau

Girls are at a particular disadvantage in many nations, facing sex discrimination as an obstacle to obtaining even basic education and social skills. In the Middle East and South Asia, girls are more likely to be pulled from school at an early age and are thus less likely to develop critical literacy skills. Across most of the world, girls face more demands for work in the home and restrictions on movement that constrain their opportunities to gain direct experience with diverse social worlds. As rates of divorce and abandonment rise worldwide, so do the risks for young women who fail to obtain skills to function independently. As they reach adulthood, uneducated women are increasingly vulnerable to poverty and exploitation.

Even academically skilled youths from middle-class families are subject to new perils on the climb to adulthood. The rapidly changing job market makes it difficult to predict what opportunities will be available when these adolescents finally seek employment. Entire sectors can disappear on short notice when industries move their operations abroad or close shop altogether.

High school and college curricula in the United States, many critics argue, provide a poor fit to the job market. Schools in many developing countries in South Asia and Africa are using curricula that have changed little since they were colonies of Western nations, focusing on memorization rather than critical thinking and on areas such as classics rather than marketable skills in computer technology or business. The result is growing numbers of youths who are educated but unemployed.

Backlash against Limbo

It is also the case that a longer climb to adulthood, resulting in a longer period of limbo, can increase the stress experienced by adolescents. Even worse, it can lead to behaviors that arrest their process of preparation. In the United States, the experience of stress among young people has been steadily increasing. In 1999, 30% of college freshmen reported being "frequently overwhelmed," up from 16% in 1985.

The lengthening of ladders, then, increases the risk that more youths will "fall off." Adolescents who, for whatever reason, do not continue in education increasingly find themselves stuck in a low-paying and unstable labor pool.

Young people tend to live in the present moment and find immediate attractions much more appealing than long-term goals—especially when the achievement of those goals is abstract and being pushed further and further away. There is increasing possibility that adolescents will respond to the high-pressure, competitive worlds they are being asked to take on by turning off or turning away.

Societies must be concerned with a major unknown: whether young people, as a group, might rebel against the increasing demands placed upon them and the longer period of limbo they must endure. This result is increasingly probable as adolescents are spending more time with peers than they did in the past, which is creating distinct youth cultures in many societies. These youth cultures might become vehicles of mass resistance to adult society, like the hippie culture of the 1960s.

In New Zealand, Maori adolescents have drawn on American rap and hip-hop culture to resist assimilation into the mainstream. The attraction of radical Islam to many youths reflects a reaction against the competition and materialism of the new global world. In some cases these adolescents' resistance may lead to their joining militant groups, while in others it may simply mean that they enter adulthood unprepared to hold a job and raise a family.

However, we should not be too alarmist. Resistance is most likely when the ladders to adulthood are uninviting, poorly marked, and when the outcomes are uncertain—all things we can do something about. There is also a strong likelihood that the new youth cultures in the twenty-first century will lead society in positive directions. Often youth movements are inspired by pursuit of core human values: compassion, authenticity, and renewal of meaning. It is possible that generational "revolt" will pull societies away from the frantic lifestyles, shallow materialism, and divisive competitiveness that are accompanying globalization. It should be kept in mind that youths in most cases are a positive force.

Rising to the Challenge

The Study Group found that youths in most parts of the world report being optimistic about their lives and that, despite the greater demands and longer ladders, the majority of young people are rising to the challenge. Rates of illiteracy among 15-year-olds have fallen from 37% to 20% since 1970, UNESCO statistics show. Rates of high school and college graduation across most nations continue to climb. And there is little question that many young women have more versatile skills for taking care of themselves and navigating public environments today than 50 years ago. In the United States, teenage rates of pregnancy and violence have fallen substantially across the last decade, indicating that fewer teens are getting off track.

The most convincing scientific evidence of the increasing abilities of youth comes from IQ test scores. New Zealand political scientist James Flynn gathered intelligence test scores of young people over the last 70 years. Because new norms for the

tests are established every few years, the publicly reported scores have shown little change. Once Flynn went back to the unadjusted scores, however, he found the IQs of young people rose dramatically over this period: The average IQ of a young adult today is 20 points higher than in 1940. There is no way to pinpoint what accounts for this increase, but it seems likely that youths' abilities have grown as they have responded to the increased complexity of modern life.

The general decrease in family size also contributes to youths' better preparedness for adulthood. Smaller families mean that parents can devote more attention and resources to each child. Parents in many parts of the world are adopting a more responsive and communicative parenting style, which research shows facilitates development of interpersonal skills and enhances mental health.

Other new supports and opportunities have also brightened the outlook for adolescents. Young people receive better health care than they did 50 years ago; consequently, youths around the world are much less likely to die from disease. The Internet provides an important new vehicle for some young people (though as yet a very small percentage of the world's youth) to access a wealth of information. Via the Net, adolescents can also run businesses, participate in social movements, and develop relationships; they are less handicapped by traditional barriers of age.

As a result of these opportunities and their own initiative, the current generation of youth is smarter, more mature, and more socially versatile than any generation in human history. They are better able to function in multiple worlds, collaborate in teams, and solve unstructured problems. We must not underestimate the ways in which adolescents in all parts of the world and of all social classes may draw on their youthful reservoirs of energy and optimism to forge fresh directions and develop new skills.

However, it would be a mistake to be too sanguine. Adolescence in the twenty-first century provides many opportunities for youths to make wrong turns or just become turned off, never to realize their true potential. In order to keep adolescents on the right track, society needs to provide more diverse kinds of ladders for people with different learning styles and socioeconomic backgrounds, regardless of sex or ethnicity. Many jobs involve skills that do not correspond to those tested in school, and we need to provide avenues for them to receive non-aca-demic opportunities to grow and shine—internships, job skills workshops, even art classes, to name a few.

There should also be way stations along the climb that allow young people to rest, gather themselves, and consider alternatives. The success of government, business, the arts, and private life in 2050 and beyond depends on how well we nurture and inspire the next generation to take over and give their best.

About the Author

Reed Larson leads the Study Group on Adolescence in the 21st Century, which was sponsored by the Society for Research on Adolescence and the International Society for Behavioral Development. He is a professor in the Department of Human and Community Development at the University of Illinois, 1105 West Nevada Street, Urbana, Illinois 61801. E-mail larsonR@uiuc.edu.

For more information on the Study Group, visit its Web site, www. s-r-a.org/studygroup.html.

UNIT 2
Puberty and Biology

Unit Selections

Key Points to Consider

- Do you think that adolescence is an important developmental and physiological period for individuals? For example, is it more important than infancy or late adulthood? Why?

- Is there a landmark in adolescence that is more important than any other? For example, is puberty the most important developmental milestone for adolescents?

- Are there psychological consequences of late or early maturation during adolescence?

- Why is adolescence a developmental stage where the likelihood of psychopathology occurring is greater than other stages?

 **Links: www.dushkin.com/online/**
These sites are annotated in the World Wide Web pages.

Biological Changes in Adolescence
http://inside.bard.edu/academic/specialproj/darling/adolesce.htm

After arguing with his parents, Randy, a 14-year-old, is sulking in his room. They are upset because he refuses to work on the oral report he is supposed to give in English class tomorrow. He cannot tell them the embarrassing reason why he does not want to do the assignment. He told his parents that the report was on a stupid topic, and he refused to do it. In reality, Randy is worried that his voice will crack, and worse yet, that he will get an erection while standing up in front of the whole class. He is afraid that everyone will notice.

The physical changes accompanying the onset of puberty are usually the first clear indicators that a child is entering the period of adolescence. The changes can be a source of both pride and humiliation for the developing adolescent. These physiological changes are regulated by a structure in the brain known as the hypothalamus. The hypothalamus is responsible for stimulating increased production of hormones that control development of the primary and secondary sex characteristics. Primary sex characteristics include physical changes in the reproductive system. Examples include growth of the ovaries and testicles. Secondary sex characteristics are physical changes not directly involved in reproduction. Examples include voice changes, height increases, growth of facial hair in males, and breast development in females.

The hypothalamus signals the pituitary gland which in turn stimulates the gonads to produce hormones (androgens and estrogens) .The hypothalamus then detects the level of sex hormones present in the bloodstream and either calls for more or less hormone production. During childhood, the hypothalamus is very sensitive to sex hormones and keeps production at a low level. For some reason that is not yet completely known, the hypothalamus changes its sensitivity to the sex hormones in adolescence. As a result of this, significantly greater quantities of sex hormones are needed before the hypothalamus signals the pituitary gland to shut down production. The thyroid and adrenal glands also play a role in the development of secondary sex characteristics. Randy appears to be in the middle of these changes.

The physiological changes themselves occur over a 5 to 6 year span. Girls generally start to undergo puberty 18 to 24 months before boys, with the typical onset at age 10 or 11 .The earliest pubertal changes in girls are breast budding, height spurt, and sparse pubic hair. Experiencing a first menstrual cycle is a midpubertal event, with the average age of menarche in the United States currently being 12 years old. For boys, initial signs of puberty are that the testicles begin to increase in size and the height spurt begins. Facial hair, deepening voice, and first ejaculation occur later.

The sequence of pubertal changes is fairly constant across individuals; however, the timing of puberty varies greatly from one person to the next. Some adolescents, such as Randy, are out of step with their peers because they mature early, whereas others are late-maturers. The advantages and disadvantages of early versus late maturation have been the subject of much research, so a few readings touch on this topic. One conclusion is that early maturation is correlated with earlier involvement in risk-taking behaviors like alcohol use and sexual activity. In extreme cases, biological disorders result in delayed or precocious puberty but there are new medications for treating these conditions.

The onset of puberty is affected by diet, exercise, and genetic history. Largely due to improved nutrition and to better control of illnesses, puberty occurs 3 to 4 years earlier in the twenty-first century than it did 150 years ago. Adolescents today also grow several inches taller and weigh more. A visit to historical homes will show that the doorways and beds were much smaller in previous centuries. This trend toward earlier maturation is a worldwide phenomenon that has presumably reached a leveling off point. As Randy's story illustrates, adolescents experience psychological and social challenges related to puberty. For example, sexual arousal increases and the teenager must learn how to handle sexual situations. Likewise, gender-typical behavior is more expected by others observing the youth. The adolescent must also incorporate bodily changes into his or her self-image. Concerns about physical appearance become a major preoccupation and play a significant role in self-esteem at this time. These issues are addressed in this unit. In particular, the readings examine body image concerns as they relate to males versus females and early versus late maturers.

Parents and other adults are sometimes not generally forthcoming in their talks with adolescents about the changes they will be experiencing. This contributes to adolescents' anxiety about their bodies and how "normal" they are. On the other hand, other cultures employ rites of passage to mark entrance into manhood or womanhood. Many such rites of passage involve physical markings on the adolescent, such as circumcision or body tattooing

Specifically, the first article in this unit addresses the developmental markers of puberty in adolescence. The article critiques the measures and samples used in pubertal research and concludes that no single measure best captures these maturational changes. Along the same lines, the second article from *Fathering Magazine* discusses whether early or late maturation is beneficial. The article essentially concludes that neither is advantageous but that parents and their changing adolescents can cope better with these changes than they are now.

The third article in this unit discusses neurological maturation in adolescence. Surely if hormones are changing, so too is the brain changing. Continuing this subject, the fourth article discusses neurological changes and the problems inherent in these changes; adolescence is a key time for psychopathology, such as schizophrenia, to develop.

The final two selections in this unit discuss health and body image. The first article by Jennifer O'Dea describes a study of teens and their eating and exercise habits. The participants in the study reported that when they practice healthy habits they do so to enhance their endurance and performance in sporting events. For those participants who don't practice healthier life styles, the article also explores barriers to good teen health. The final essay in this unit pertains to adolescent body image. In part, this was what Randy was worried about. Body image is very important to most adolescents because it is closely tied to self-esteem or self-worth. The article would be incomplete if it did not provide information on how teens can improve their own feelings about themselves.

Vicky Kasala/Getty Images

Developmental markers in adolescence

Implications for Studies of Pubertal Processes

Lorah D. Dorn; Ronald E. Dahl; Douglas E. Williamson; Boris Birmaher;
David Axelson; James Perel; Stacy D. Stull; Neal D. Ryan

There is inconsistency in the outcome measures of biological and psychosocial studies using measures of puberty as a predictor. For example, some studies show that maturational timing may have differential influences (positive, negative, or no effect) depending on the specific disorder, dimension of measure, and gender. Other studies have suggested that some effects may be more directly linked to pubertal stage or hormone concentrations rather than timing per se. This study outlines several conceptual and methodological issues that may be relevant to addressing these inconsistencies, in the context of examining data from a study of maturational hormones obtained from a unique longitudinal cohort of 24 girls (age 10.0 [+ or -] 1.6 years) and 36 boys (age 10.4 [+ or -] 1.6 years) in the early part of puberty, where the developmental trajectory of these hormones were tracked annually in 65% of the sample. We explored the contributions of measures of pubertal growth and sociodemographic factors on hormone concentrations. In brief, it appears that no single measure best captures the maturational process during puberty and suggests that multiple processes are occurring in parallel. Several conceptual and methodological implications are discussed that may guide investigators in interpreting existing studies of pubertal timing and behavior as well as in conducting future studies.

INTRODUCTION

There is considerable evidence that describes the period of adolescence (specifically puberty) as tumultuous for some but not for all (Offer, 1987) and that it may also be a period of vulnerability for some (Dorn & Chrousos, 1997; Graber & Brooks-Gunn, 1996; Graber et al., 1996). Much of this work has focused on the role that pubertal development or pubertal timing has played on affective and behavioral changes during the adolescent period. Other studies report on the effect of timing of puberty on specific physiological disorders. Importantly, there is little consistency in what this research tells us about timing of

puberty. Specifically, in studies regarding the importance of timing of puberty, some show that early maturation has a more positive effect for boys than girls (Faust, 1960; Jones, & Bayley 1950; Mussen & Jones, 1957; Stolz & Stolz, 1944) and later maturation in boys was more negative, including lower achievement (Dubas, Graber, & Petersen, 1991; Petersen & Crockett, 1987), lower self-esteem or confidence, and less happiness (Simmons et al., 1979). Alternatively, early maturation in girls has been related to more depressive or internalizing symptoms (Ge et al., 2001a) and early maturation in girls and later maturation in boys was related to more depressed mood and psychopathology (Graber et al., 1997; Siegel et al., 1999). Others show that early maturation in boys results in more reporting of external hostile feelings (Ge et al., 2001b), more psychopathology (Susman et al., 1985), more health-risky behaviors (Orr & Ingersoll, 1995) and to a greater likelihood of associating with deviant peers, especially when living in a disadvantaged neighborhood (Ge et al., 2002). Further, early maturation in both boys and girls is linked to problem behavior (Flannery et al., 1993; Tschann et al., 1994) and suicide attempts (Wichstrom, 2000). Clearly, studies describing the role of puberty on affective and behavioral changes show inconsistencies. Studies examining physiological processes have described early timing of puberty as a risk factor for breast cancer (Apter & Vihko, 1985; Key, 1999; Magnusson et al., 1999), polycystic ovary syndrome and insulin resistance (Dunaif, 1999; Ibanez et al., 1993, 1992; Oppenheimer et al., 1995), and testicular cancer (Weir et al., 1998) and late timing of puberty as a risk for lower bone density and/or osteoporosis (Ito et al., 1995; Johnell et al., 1995). There is inconsistency among the biological studies as well. For example, Parker et al. (1999) report no increased risk for breast cancer with early menarche, a measure used to define pubertal timing.

In reviewing the pubertal timing and pubertal status literature, it is evident that a variety of measures of puberty have been utilized across studies, that no doubt contributes to the inconsistencies in findings. In the discussion section of many of these studies, underlying hormone concentrations are implicated in the affective or behavior problems, as well as in the biological disorders (e.g., breast or testicular cancer), regardless of how puberty was measured. That is, various measures of physical growth and development are used as a proxy for pubertal stage, or pubertal stage itself is used, but measured in different ways. Importantly, all of these methods and measures are designed to reflect the underlying process of hormonal change.

In this paper we take a multiassessment systematic approach for examining puberty by utilizing both descriptive sociodemographic and physiologic assessments that may be relevant to pubertal maturation. Our data set is from a large, unique, longitudinal cohort of normal, healthy boys and girls in the early part of puberty. Specifically, stratified by gender, we first explore the contribution of various measures of pubertal growth (e.g., pubertal stage, height, weight), as well as sociodemographic factors, to maturational hormone concentrations. Second, we provide an integrated discussion of these findings and how they may assist investigators in designing and interpreting studies that examine puberty or timing of puberty and its impact upon specific psychological and biological constructs of adolescence. This paper will not answer the question of what is the best pubertal measure to use in research on adolescence. In fact, the paper may raise more questions about research on puberty. However, we hope that the paper will provide information to investigators regarding important correlates or confounds of measures of puberty that may have an impact upon study findings. Perhaps then we can come to a more definitive conclusion regarding the true effects of puberty and timing of puberty on adolescent psychological and biological issues.

To examine the above questions we used a data set that is unique in several ways. First, the data were collected cross-sectionally and longitudinally from children and adolescents (ages 8-16 years) that represent all five stages of pubertal development as indexed by a physical examination (Marshall & Tanner, 1969, 1970). Subjects were seen at annual intervals for up to 6 years (range 1-6 years; mean = 2.6 [+ or -] 1.6). There were 25 participants seen for one visit, 7 for two visits, 5 for three visits, 16 for four visits, 4 for five visits, and 3 for 6 visits. Second, multiple measures of puberty were used in the study and include height and weight, pubertal staging by physical examination, and serum maturational hormones. Hormones included adrenal androgens that change throughout puberty (during adrenarche and gonadarche), as well as gonadal steroids that change in gonadarche. Third, we had a relatively large sample of normal, healthy children and adolescents. Finally, research criteria psychiatric screens were conducted on all adolescents as well as first-degree relatives. Adolescents did not meet criteria for any psychiatric disorder and family members did not meet criteria for any affective disorders. Thus, we eliminated the potential confound of affective psychopathology on maturational hormones; that is, moods and behavior influencing hormones. To our knowledge, no other data set contains such information.

SUBJECTS AND METHODS

Design and Subjects

Pre- and early-pubertal children were enrolled in a longitudinal study designed to examine psychobiological aspects of early onset depression (Ryan et al., 1992, 1994). The subjects in this report represent only the normal, healthy children and adolescents who served as controls to the depressed subjects. The control group children were recruited from newspaper advertisements, recruitment flyers, and word of mouth in the community. Normal controls were seen for annual visits for psychological testing and biological measures. Sixty subjects were included, representing those having maturational hormones measured. A total of 156 observations are represented in our data analysis. Twenty-four girls, age 10.0 ([+ or -] 1.6 years), and 36 boys, age 10.4 ([+ or -] 1.6 years) were included. The number of observations at each pubertal stage (genital) for boys included stage 1 (n = 15), stage 2 (n = 53), stage 3 (n = 10), stage 4 (n = 12), and stage 5 (n = 6). For girls, breast stage, stage 1 (n = 23), stage 2 (n = 14), stage 3 (n = 8), stage 4 (n = 9), stage 5 (n = 5). Of the 156 observations, 103 (66%) had an identical pubic hair stage to their genital or breast stage. Six of those differing in stage had a pubic hair stage greater than breast or genital and the remainder had pubic hair stage less than breast or genital stage. The majority of subjects were Caucasian (88%). Socioeconomic status was determined using the Hollingshead 4-factor score. Sociodemographic and physiologic characteristics of the sample are included in Table I. All subjects in the normal comparison group of the study could not meet criteria for any lifetime psychiatric diagnosis (see Procedures section) and were at low risk for mood disorders, which was based on

Table I. Descriptive Characteristics of 60 Normal Healthy Children and Adolescents

Gender		
Female	24	
Male	36	
Race		
White	53	
Non-White	7	
Age (years)	10.25 [+ or -] 1.6	Range (6.6-13.5)
SES	49.2 [+ or -] 11.55	Range (30.5-66)
BMI	17.9 [+ or -] 3.3	Range (13.0-31.8)

Note. SES = socioeconomic status based on 4-factor Hollingshead Scale; BMI = body mass index.

having no mood disorder in any first-degree relatives and fewer than 20% present in second-degree relatives. Other exclusionary criteria for the normal controls included (1) medications for the last two weeks other than acetaminophen, (2) significant medical illness, (3) body weight greater than 150% of ideal or severe growth failure (weight or height less than 3% on the National Health Statistics Curve), (4) IQ of less than 70, and (5) Tanner III or greater of pubertal development at entry.

Procedures

The study was approved by the Institutional Review Board of the University of Pittsburgh. All subjects were informed of the study requirements and procedures. Parents or guardians provided written informed consent and each child provided assent. All subjects were paid for their time for participating in the study.

To determine eligibility based on psychiatric status, children and parents were interviewed separately using the Schedule for Affective Disorders and Schizophrenia for School Age Children—Epidemiologic Version (K-SADS-E) (Orvaschel & Puig-Antich 1987). The interviews were administered by trained clinicians, blind to the subject's clinical status. In the normal comparison group, children and adolescents were excluded if there was evidence of any probable or definite lifetime psychiatric disorder. The final diagnosis, or lack of diagnosis in this case, was made by a child psychiatrist after confirming presence or absence of any symptoms with the child and parents and reviewing other information obtained during the screening process. Interrater reliability for all diagnoses for our studies has been k [greater than or equal to] 0.70.

To determine familial loading for mood disorders, first- and second-degree relatives were interviewed with the K-SADS-E, for those 6-18 years of age and the schedule for Affective Disorders and Schizophrenia Lifetime Version (SADS-L) (Endicott & Spitzer, 1978) for adult relatives. Those adult relatives unavailable for direct interview were assessed indirectly using

a modified version of the Family History Interview (Weissman et al., 1997) with the child's parent(s) and other available relatives serving as informant(s). All life time diagnoses among relatives were made according to the best-estimate procedure (Leckman et al., 1982) based on DSM-III-R criteria.

Subjects participating in the study required outpatient assessments as well as a 3-day and 3-night assessment in the Child Sleep Laboratory. Parents were allowed to accompany their child for the overnight visits if so desired. Family and friends were allowed to visit freely. The environment was a comfortable dorm-like setting and offered movies, games, computer activities, and individual interactions with staff. Subjects reported the environment to be very pleasant and comfortable and they enjoyed their experience. Research procedures included psychological tests as well as measures of endocrine and sleep profiles.

MEASURES

Pubertal Stage

Tanner criteria (Marshall & Tanner, 1969, 1970) were used to determine breast, genital and pubic hair stage of the subjects. Across the longitudinal study, children were classified as Tanner 1 or 2 (pre- and early-pubertal), 3, 4, or 5. Physical examinations were completed by physicians or nurses trained in the procedures. The percentage of interrater agreement for our group has been [greater than or equal to] 90%.

Body Mass Index (BMI)

BMI was obtained by computing weight in kilograms divided by height squared in meters.

Maturational Hormone Concentrations

One blood sample for all maturational hormones was obtained between 8:30 and 9:30 a.m. from an indwelling catheter during Day 2 of the 3-day stay. Samples were assayed in duplicate by the same endocrine laboratory. If the coefficient of variation between a subject's duplicates was greater than 5% the sample was retested.

Dehydroepiandrosterone (DHEA) was measured by a competitive double antibody, [sup.125]I radioimmunoassay developed by Diagnostic Systems Laboratories (445 Medical Center Blvd., Webster, Texas 77598). The limit of detection for this method is 0.5 ng/mL. The coefficient of variation for duplicates ranged from 0.03 to 4.80% (mean 1.38%). Interassay variation ranged from 7.29% (mean 2.47 ng/mL) to 14.00% (mean of 0.50 ng/mL).

Dehydroepiandrosterone sulfate (DHEAS) was measured using the Diagnostic Products solid phase [sup.125]I radioimmunoassay. Level of detection is 6.0 ng/mL. The intraassay coefficient of variation ranged from 0.03 to 4.80% with a mean of

1.57%. Interassay variation ranged from 8.69% at 3.61 ng/mL to 7.70% at 130.64 ng/mL.

Androstenedione levels are measured on a 50-[micro]L plasma sample and are tested in duplicate. The method used is the solid phase radioimmunoassay procedure by Diagnostic Systems Laboratories (445 Medical Center Blvd., Webster, Texas 77598). The limit of detection for this method is 0.10 ng/mL androstenedione. Subjects' duplicates with coefficient of variation (CV) exceeding 5% are retested. The range for the intraassay variation of subjects' sample duplicates was 0.00-4.79% CV with a mean percent CV of 1.63. Interassay variation ranged from 11.26% CV (mean of 5.49 ng/mL) to 17.71% CV (mean of 0.35 ng/mL).

Testosterone (T) was measured using the solid phase radioimmunoassay procedure by Diagnostic Systems Laboratories (445 Medical Center Blvd., Webster, Texas 77598). The limit of detection was 0.10 ng/mL. The range for the intraassay coefficient of variation has been from 0 to 4.87% with a mean of 1.53%. Interassay variation has ranged from 3.85% (mean 0.52 ng/mL) to 14.63% (mean 4.51 ng/mL).

Estradiol (E2) was measured by a modified version of the double antibody [sup.125]I radioimmunoassay procedure developed by Diagnostic Products Corporation (5700 West 96th St., Los Angeles, CA 90045). To increase the sensitivity of the assay a lower calibrator (2.5 pg/mL) is prepared and a sequential incubation of the antibody and radio-labeled antigen is used. The limit of detection for this method is 4 pg/mL. The range for the intraassay variation has been 0.01-4.89% with a mean of 1.0%. Interassay variation has ranged from 12.04% (mean 4.07 pg/ml) to 17.54% (mean 171.00 pg/mL).

STATISTICAL METHODS

To explore the relation between sociodemographic (age, gender) and physiologic characteristics (Tanner Breast/Genital, Tanner Pubic Hair, BMI) and each of the maturational hormones, random effects regression models were used, with the individual subject modeled as a random effect. This method takes advantage of multiple observations within an individual and thus captures within-person variability as they develop across time. This method also takes full advantage of data collected across time when a balanced data set is not available (e.g., when there is missing data). For statistical significance testing, log likelihood ratio chi-squares were used. Significant variables in the log likelihood ratio chi-squares were then entered into a stepwise regression equation where the most significant variable was entered first. Analyses were run separately by gender. All significance testing was done with the alpha two-tailed set at 0.05.

RESULTS

Table II reports the means and standard deviations by gender and pubertal stage (breast or genital) of all the hormones. Table III summarizes the percent variance of the hormone concentrations accounted for by sociodemographic and physiological variables.

Table II. Means ([+ or -] SD (1)) of Maturational Hormones by Pubertal Stage (Breast or Genital) and Gender

	Boys					
	Stage 1		2		3	
DHEA (ng/mL)	1.24	(0.55)	2.77	(1.49)	3.05	(1.52)
DHEAS (ng/mL)	31.29	(20.18)	72.66	(53.88)	110.7	(74.24)
[[DELTA] .sub.4]A (ng/mL)	0.44	(36)	0.64	(0.30)	0.76	(0.36)
T (ng/mL)	0.15	(0.13)	0.53	(0.95)	1.53	(1.28)
[E.sub.2] (pg/mL)	0.12	(0.36)	2.39	(7.91)	0.29	(0.58)

	Boys				Girls	
	4		5		Stage 1	
DHEA (ng/mL)	4.10	(2.72)	3.72	(0.89)	1.64	(1.07)
DHEAS (ng/mL)	133.27	(84.35)	125.19	(26.89)	25.08	(17.35)
[[DELTA] .sub.4]A (ng/mL)	1.36	(60)	1.56	(56.00)	0.60	(0.49)
T (ng/mL)	3.03	(1.41)	4.87	(0.96)	0.09	(0.10)
[E.sub.2] (pg/mL)	5.81	(5.94)	3.64	(2.53)	0.50	(2.18)

	Girls					
	2		3		4	
DHEA (ng/mL)	2.13	(1.06)	3.63	(1.28)	3.64	(1.98)
DHEAS (ng/mL)	36.69	(28.18)	66.56	(25.57)	66.72	(34.35)
[[DELTA] .sub.4]A (ng/mL)	0.97	(0.83)	1.52	(0.47)	1.69	(0.74)
T (ng/mL)	0.27	(0.22)	0.38	(0.13)	0.48	(0.12)
[E.sub.2] (pg/mL)	13.18	(10.38)	18.99	(14.13)	35.93	(35.22)

	Girls	
	5	
DHEA (ng/mL)	4.58	(1.51)
DHEAS (ng/mL)	121.79	(66.72)
[[DELTA] .sub.4]A (ng/mL)	2.26	(0.87)
T (ng/mL)	0.59	(0.23)
[E.sub.2] (pg/mL)	100.39	(98.1)

Note. Standard deviation (SD), Dehydroepiandrosterone (DHEA), Dehydroepiandrosterone sulfate (DHEAS), androstenedione ([[DELTA] .sub.4]A), testosterone (T), estradiol ([E.sub.2]).

Analyses Examining the Contribution of Physiological and Sociodemographic Variables in Boys

DHEA

Using the random effects model for DHEA in boys, univariate analyses showed all of the sociodemographic and physiologic variables were significantly ($p < 0.001$) related to the hormone concentration. In the stepwise forward regression analysis, chronological age ([chi square] = 21.4, p [greater than or equal to] 0.001) was the only variable to enter the equation, accounting for 30.1% of the variance. Older boys had higher concentrations of DHEA.

Table III. Maturational Hormones: Forward Stepping Model for all Sociodemographic/Physiologic

Characteristics Random Effects Models within Normals

	Tanner BG	Tanner PH	Age
Females			
DHEA			28.9
DHEAS	43.6%		
Androstenedione			59.3%
Testosterone	56.9%		
Estradiol	67.9% (a)		2.2%
Males			
DHEA			30.1%
DHEAS			34.5%
Androstenedione	5.5%		43.2% (a)
Testosterone	62.7% (a)	1.7%	4.0% (b)
Estradiol	6.9% (b)		

	BMI	Overall variance
Females		
DHEA		
DHEAS		
Androstenedione		
Testosterone		
Estradiol		70.1%
Males		
DHEA		
DHEAS		
Androstenedione		48.7%
Testosterone		68.4%
Estradiol	28.6% (a)	35.5%

(a) Entered first.

(b) Entered second.

DHEAS

Similar to DHEA, all of the univariate analyses all of the sociodemographic and physiologic variables were significantly (p < 0.001) related to DHEAS in boys. Again, chronological age was the only variable to enter in the stepwise forward regression analysis ([chi square] = 180.8, p [less than or equal to] 0.001) accounting for 34.5% of the variance in DHEAS. Older boys had higher concentrations of DHEAS.

Androstenedione

For boys, using the random effects models for androstenedione, univariate analyses showed that each variable was significantly (p < 0.001) related to the hormone concentration. In the stepwise forward regression analyses, chronological age ([chi square] = 120.7, p < 0.001) entered the equation, accounting for 43.2% of the variance followed by Tanner Stage Genital ([chi square] = 9.7, p < 0.005), accounting for 5.5% of the variance.

Older boys with more advanced genital stage had higher concentrations of androstenedione. The model accounted for 48.7% of the variance in androstenedione.

Testosterone

Similar to androstenedione, univariate analyses showed that all of the sociodemographic and physiologic variables were significantly (p < 0.001) related to testosterone concentration in the random effects model. In the stepwise forward regression analysis, Tanner Stage Genital was first to enter ([chi square] = 9.4, p [less than or equal to] 0.005), followed by chronological age ([chi square] = 11.7, p. [less than or equal to] 0.001), and Tanner Stage Pubic Hair ([chi square] = 7.1, p [less than or equal to] 0.01), accounting for 62.7, 4.0, and 1.7% of the variance of testosterone, respectively. Older boys with more advanced genital and pubic hair stage had higher concentrations of T. The model accounted for 68.4% of the variance of concentration of T.

Estradiol

For boys, using the random effects models for estradiol, univariate analyses showed that each variable was significantly (p [less than or equal to] 0.001) related to the hormone concentration. In the stepwise forward regression analysis, BMI ([chi square] = 26.1, p [less than or equal to] 0.001) entered the equation first, accounting for 28.6% of the variance followed by Tanner genital stage ([chi square] = 8.4, p [less than or equal to] 0.005), accounting for 6.9% of the variance. Boys with a higher BMI and more advanced genital stage had higher concentrations of estradiol. The model accounted for 35.5% of the variance in estradiol.

Analyses Examining the Contribution of Physiological and Soeiodemographie Variables in Girls

DHEA

Using the random effects model for DHEA in girls, univariate analyses showed that all of the sociodemographic and physiologic variables were significantly (p < 0.001) related to the hormone concentration. In the stepwise forward regression analysis, chronological age ([chi square] = 25.9, p [less than or equal to] 0.0001) was the only variable to enter the equation, accounting for 28.9% of the variance. Older girls had higher concentrations of DHEA.

DHEAS

Similarly to DHEA, univariate analyses showed that all of the sociodemographic and physiologic variables were significantly (p < 0.001) related to DHEAS in girls. Tanner Stage Breast was the only variable to enter in the stepwise forward regression analysis ([chi square] = 84.4, p [less than or equal to] 0.0001), accounting for 43.6% of the variance in DHEAS. Girls at higher breast stage had higher concentrations of DHEAS.

Androstenedione

For girls, using the random effects models for androstenedione, each variable was significantly (p [less than or equal to] 0.001) related to the hormone concentration. In the stepwise forward regression analyses, chronological age ([chi square] = 38.8, p < 0.0001) was the only variable to enter the equation, accounting for 59.3% of the variance in androstenedione. Older girls had higher concentrations of androstenedione.

Testosterone

Similar to androstenedione, univariate analyses showed that all of the sociodemographic and physiologic variables were significantly (p < 0.001) related to testosterone concentration in the random effects model for girls. In the stepwise forward regression analysis, Tanner Stage Breast was the only variable to enter ([chi square] = 106.3, p [less than or equal to] 0.001), accounting for 56.9% of the variance in testosterone. Girls with more advanced breast stage had higher concentrations of T.

Estradiol

For girls, using the random effects models for estradiol, each variable was significantly (p [less than or equal to] 0.001) related to the hormone concentration. In the stepwise forward regression analysis, Tanner Stage Breast ([chi square] = 28.3, p [less than or equal to] 0.001) entered the equation first, accounting for 67.9% of the variance followed by chronological age ([chi square] = 4.0, p [less than or equal to] 0.05), accounting for 2.2% of the variance. Girls with a more advanced breast stage who were older, had higher concentrations of estradiol. The model accounted for 70.1% of the variance in estradiol.

COMMENT

Discussion of Findings

We present one of the first papers that has tested the contribution of numerous sociodemographic or physiologic variables to adrenal and gonadal hormones in a psychiatrically "clean" sample. There were numerous significant correlates accounting for as much as 70% of the variance in the hormone concentration. These are variables that may in turn, contribute to variance in explaining behavioral or biological variables used in research studies in adolescence. Oftentimes these variables are not accounted for in statistical models and our findings speak to the importance of inclusion of such variables in data-analytic strategies. Alternatively, one should also consider that 100% of the variance was not explained by the correlates that we selected in our model. Other sociodemographic or physiologic variables may contribute variance or perhaps, a psychological variable would contribute variance. Our study did include a psychiatrically clean sample and thus, variance accounted for by some psychopathology may not be evident in our study. These same analyses conducted in a psychiatric sample may yield different results.

Our descriptive statistics (Table II) showing hormone trajectories by pubertal stage and gender corroborate the few studies that are reported in earlier literature (Biro et al., 1995; de Peretti & Forest, 1978; Lee et al., 1976; Lee & Migeon, 1975; Nottelmann et al., 1987; Sizonenko et al., 1976). A typical developmental trajectory of each hormone by stage is evident along with the expected gender differences, where maturation in girls is earlier than boys. Importantly, the variability in hormone concentrations is noted by the wide range of concentrations both within and between stages. It is important to note that in virtually all of these studies cited above, the figures do not represent a longitudinal study. (For exception see Lee & Migeon, 1975; Lee et al., 1976; Sizonenko et al., 1976).

With the exception of DHEAS in girls, chronological age was the strongest predictor of the three adrenal androgens (DHEA, DHEAS, antrostenedione) in boys and girls, accounting for as much as 59% of the variance of the hormone concentration. This may be expected for the adrenal androgens since their initial rise is in adrenarche (approximately ages 6-8), the earliest part of puberty, and some of our subjects were in early adrenarche. Breast and genital development is not present in early adrenarche since there is no gonadal axis activation. Similarly in early adrenarche there is no pubic hair development as the concentrations of adrenal androgens are too low to influence those target tissues. This may be why Tanner stage was not a significant statistical predictor with the adrenal androgens beyond the variance accounted for by age, in most cases. Additionally, age and Tanner stage are highly correlated. Also, age may be a strong statistical predictor because it represents both biological and psychosocial constructs. For example, biologically, age reflects the advancement of pubertal growth and development, including hormones and brain development. Age also reflects psychosocial maturation. Both biological and psychosocial development could influence hormone concentrations either directly or indirectly. Wohwill (Wohwill, 1973) describes age "… as merely a marker of time." That is, age may represent many processes that an individual undergoes. Thus, it may be difficult to disentangle what age truly represents. Other studies have shown age to be highly correlated with many markers of pubertal development and with hormone concentrations (Brooks-Gunn & Warren, 1989; Nottelmann et al., 1987). Tanner stage for breast development was a significant statistical predictor for DHEAS in girls. Since girls tend to mature earlier than boys, breast stage may indicate that girls were further along in the pubertal process and, thus, had higher concentrations of adrenal androgens as they entered and progressed into gonadarche.

Pubertal stage also was a strong statistical predictor for testosterone in boys and testosterone and estradiol in girls. In girls, breast stage accounted for as much as 68% of the variance in these gonadal steroids. This is congruent with the endocrine physiology of T and [E.sub.2] since the target tissues for these hormones are primarily genital and breast tissue. On the basis of endocrine physiology and the fact that pubic hair stage did not enter in the regressions may mean that making a composite score of breast (or genital) development and pubic hair development is not appropriate or representative for some questions examined in research studies on puberty. This technique of combining breast/genital and pubic hair stages has often been utilized in the literature without providing a rationale for doing so or without examining the differences that each stage may individually provide.

Body mass index was a significant statistical predictor of a hormone concentration in only one instance; that is, for estradiol in boys. BMI accounted for 28.6% of the variance. Estrogen in boys is generally from peripheral conversion in adipose tissue, which may contribute to the correlation with BMI. BMI increases throughout puberty but at different times depending upon gender. It may be that BMI would have accounted for variance in hormone concentrations had our sample been older and at higher stages of puberty.

Tanner Stage of genital development did account for approximately 7% of the variance in estradiol, which may reflect the rising concentrations across pubertal stage. In the case of boys, a researcher may come to an erroneous conclusion if one hypothesizes that concentrations of estradiol reflect pubertal stage or age and, thus, measures the external markers of puberty rather than estradiol. In our sample of boys, BMI would be a better measure. Furthermore, in biobehavioral studies one may need to control for BMI since it may have indirect effects on psychosocial variables as well. For example, body size as indexed by BMI may contribute to self-esteem. If one has a higher than normal BMI it can mean that one is overweight, and being overweight may influence self-esteem.

Our findings support the strong intercorrelations of various sociodemographic and physiologic variables with hormone concentrations. Our data cannot resolve all the issues regarding sociodemographic and physiologic contributions to maturational hormones. It is important to note that participants in our study represent the early part of pubertal development (e.g., most observations were made when participants were at early- or mid-puberty). Developmental markers of hormone concentrations used in our analyses may have varied if there were more observations at the later stages of pubertal development. Additionally, our sample was primarily Caucasian and thus could not be generalized to other racial groups. These data suggest that there are important sociodemographic variables and measures of growth and development that are strongly related to hormone concentrations. These, however, do not indicate causation from our analyses. Such variables should be accounted for in statistical analyses. Knowing the endocrinology of puberty may guide in the selection of variables to measure that reflect the pubertal process in the particular age group under study. Alternatively, multiple measures may be necessary to reflect the true process of puberty. The rationale for the selection of variables to measure puberty must be made on the basis of the underlying theoretical framework and the questions to be addressed. This task is not simple. Early on, Brooks-Gunn and Petersen (1984) acknowledged the complexities and difficulties in conceptual-

izing and defining puberty for studies with adolescents. The challenge for investigators is to clearly determine the necessary measures of puberty for their study and to clarify the meaning of these measures with respect to the questions or hypotheses of the study.

REFERENCES

Apter, D., and Vihko, R. (1985). Premenarcheal endocrine changes in relation to age at menarche. Clin. Endocrinol. 22: 753-760.

Biro, F. M., Lucky, A. W., Huster, G. A., and Morrison, J. A. (1995). Pubertal staging in boys. J. Pediatr 127(1): 100-102.

Brooks-Gunn, J., and Petersen, A. C. (1984). Problems in studying and defining pubertal events. J. Youth Adolesc. 13(3): 181-196.

Brooks-Gunn, J., and Warren, M. F. (1989). Biological and social contributions to negative affect in young adolescent girls. Child. Dev. 60: 40-55.

de Peretti, E., and Forest, M. (1978). Pattern of plasma dehydroepiandrosterone sulfate levels in humans from birth to adulthood: Evidence for testicular production. J. Clin. Endocrinol. Metab. 47(3): 572-577.

Dorn, L. D., and Chrousos, G. P. (1997). Neurobiology of stress: Understanding regulation of affect during female biological transitions. Semin. Reprod. Endocrinol. 15(1): 29-45.

Dubas, J. S., Graber, J. A., and Petersen, A. C. (1991). The effects of pubertal development on achievement during adolescence. Am. o Educ. 99: 444-460.

Dunaif, A. (1999). Insulin action in the polycystic ovary syndrome. Endocrinol. Metab. Clin. North Am. 28(2): 341-359.

Endicott, J., and Spitzer, R. L. (1978). A diagnostic interview: The schedule for affective disorders and schizophrenia. Arch. Gen. Psychiatry 35(7): 837-844.

Faust, M. S. (1960). Developmental maturity as a determinant in prestige of adolescent girls. Child Dev. 31: 173-184.

Flannery, D. J., Rowe, D. C., and Gulley, B. L. (1993). Impact of pubertal status, timing and age on adolescent sexual experience and delinquency. J. Adolesc. Res. 8: 21-40.

Ge, X., Brody, G. H., Conger, R. D., Simons, R. L., and Murry, V. M. (2002). Contextual amplification of pubertal transmission effects on deviant peer affiliation and externalizing behavior among African-American children. Dev. Psychol. 38(1): 42-54.

Ge, X., Conger, R. D., and Elder, G. H., Jr. (2001a). Pubertal transition, stressful life events and the emergence of gender differences in adolescent depressive symptoms. Dev. Psychol. 37: 404-417.

Ge, X., Conger, R. D., and Elder, G. H., Jr. (2001b). The relation between puberty and psychological distress in adolescent boys. J. Res. Adolesc. 11: 49-70.

Graber, J. A., and Brooks-Gunn, J. (1996). Transitions and turning points: Navigating the passage from childhood through adolescence. Dev. Psychol. 32(4): 768-776.

Graber, J. A., Brooks-Gunn, J., and Petersen, A. C. (1996). Adolescent transitions in context. In Graber, J. A., Brooks-Gunn, J., and Petersen, A. C. (eds.), Transitions Through Adolescence: Interpersonal Domains and Context. Erlbaum, Mahwah, New Jersey, pp. 369-383.

Graber, J. A., Lewinsohn, P. M., Seeley, J. R., and Brooks-Gunn, J. (1997). Is psychopathology associated with the timing of pubertal development? J. Am. Acad. Child Adolesc. Psychiatry 36(12): 1768-1776.

Ibanex, L., Potau, N., Virdis, R., Zampolli, M., Terzi, C., Fussinye, M., Carrascosa, A., and Vicens-Calvet, E. (1993). Postpubertal outcome in girls diagnosed of premature pubarche during childhood: Increased frequency of functional ovarian hyperandrogenism. J. Clin. Endocrinol. Metab. 76(6): 1599-1603.

Ibanez, L., Virdis, R., Potau, N., Zampolli, M., Ghizzoni, L., Albisu, M. A., Carrascoca, A., Bernasconi, S., and Vicens-Calvet, E.

(1992). Natural history of premature pubarche: An anxological study. J. Clin. Endocrinol. Metab. 74(2): 254-257.

Ito, M., Yamada, M., Hayashi, K., Ohki, M., Uetani, M., and Nakamura, T. (1995). Relation of early menarche to high bone mineral density. Calcif. Tissue Int. 57(1): 11-14.

Johnell, O., Bullberga, B., Kanis, J. A., Allander, E., Elffors, L., Dequeker, J., Dilsen, G., Gennari, C., Lopes, V. A., and Lyritis, G. (1995). Risk factors for hip fracture in European women: The MEDOS Study. Mediterranean Osteoporosis Study. J. Bone Miner Res. 10(11): 1802-1815.

Jones, M. C., and Bayley, N. (1950). Physical maturing among boys as related to behavior. J. Educ. Psychol. 41: 129-148.

Key, T. J. (1999). Serum oestradiol and breast cancer risk. Endocr. Relat. Cancer: 6: 175-180.

Leckman, J., Sholomskas, D., Thompson, W., Belanger, A., and Weissman, M. (1982). Best estimate of lifetime psychiatric diagnosis: A methodological study. Arch. Gen. Psychiatry 39(8): 879-883.

Lee, P. A., and Migeon, C. J. (1975). Puberty in boys: Correlation of plasma levels of gonadotropins (LH, FSH): androgens (testosterone, androstenedione, dehydroepiandrosterone and its sulfate), estrogens (estrone and estradiol) and progestins (progesterone and 17-hydroxyprogesterone). J. Clin. Endocrinol. Metab. 41: 556-562.

Lee, P. A., Xenakis, T., Winer, J., and Matsenbaugh, S. (1976). Puberty in girls: Correlation of serum levels of gonadotropins, prolactin, androgens, estrogens, and progestins with physical changes. J. Clin. Endocrinol. Metab. 43: 775-784.

Magnusson, C. M., Persson, I. R., Baron, J. A., Ekbom, A., Bergstrom, R., and Adami, H. O. (1999). The role of reproductive factors and use of oral contraceptives in the aetiology of breast cancer in women aged 50 to 74 years. Int. J. Cancer 80(2): 231-236.

Marshall, W. A., and Tanner, J. (1970). Variations in the pattern of pubertal change in boys. Arch. Dis. Child 45: 13-23.

Marshall, W. A., and Tanner, J. M. (1969). Variations in pattern of pubertal changes in girls. Arch. Dis. Child 44: 291-303.

Mussen, P. H., and Jones, M. C. (1957). Self-conceptions, motivations, and interpersonal attitudes of late- and early-maturing boys. Child Dev. 28: 243-256.

Nottelmann, E. D., Susman, E. J., Inoff-Germain, G. E., et al., (1987). Developmental processes in early adolescence: Relations between adolescent adjustment problems and chronologic age, pubertal stage, and puberty-related hormone levels. J. Pediatr. 110: 473-480.

Offer, D. (1987). In defense of adolescents. JAMA 257: 3407-3408.

Oppenheimer, E., Linder, B., Saenger, P., and DiMartino-Nardi, J. (1995). Decreased insulin sensitivity in prepubertal girls with premature adrenarche and acanthosis nigrans. J. Clin. Endocrinol. Metab. 80: 614-618.

Orr, D. P., and Ingersoll, G. (1995). The contribution of level of cognitive complexity and pubertal timing to behavioral risk in young adolescents. Pediatrics 95(4): 528-533.

Orvaschel, H., and Puig-Antich, J. (1987). Schedule for Affective Disorders and Schizophrenia for School-age Children (6-18). Epidemiologic Version, K-SADS-E, Fourth Version.

Parker, R. G., Rees, K., Leung, K. M., and Legoretta, A. P. (1999). Expression of risk factors for breast cancer in women younger than 49. Am. J. Clin. Oncol. 22: 178-179.

Petersen, A. C., and Crockett, L. J. (1987). Biological correlates of spatial ability and mathematical performance. Ann. N. Y. Acad. Sci. 69-86.

Ryan, N. D., Birmaher, B., Perel., J. M., Dalai, R. E. Meyer, V., Al-Shabbout, J., Iyengar, S., and Puig-Antich, J. (1992). Neuroendocrine response to L-5-hydroxytryptophan challenge in prepubertal major depression. Arch. Gen. Psychiatry 49:843-851.

Ryan, N. D., Dahl, R. E., Birmaher, B., Williamson, D. E., Iyengar, S., Nelson, B., Puig-Antich, J., and Perel, J. M. (1994). Stimulatory tests of growth hormone secretion in prepubertal major depression: Depressed versus normal children. J. Am. Acad. Child Adolesc. Psychiatry 33(6): 824-833.

Siegel, J. M., Yancey, A., Aneshensel, C. S., and Schuler, R. (1999). Body image, perceived pubertal timing and adolescent mental health. J. Adolesc. Health 25: 155-165.

Simmons, R., Blyth, A., Van Cleave, E., and Bush, D. (1979). Entry into early adolescence: The impact of school structure, puberty, and early dating on self-esteem. Am. Sociol. Rev. 44(6): 948-967.

Sizonenko, P., Paunier, L., and Carmignac, D. (1976). Hormonal changes during puberty. IV: Longitudinal study of adrenal androgen secretions. Horm. Res. 7(4-5): 288-302.

Stolz, H. R., and Stolz, L. M. (1944). Adolescent problems related to somatic variation. Yearbook of the National Committee for the Study of Education, Vol. 43. Chicago, University of Chicago Press, pp. 80-99.

Susman, E. J., Nottelmann, E. D., Inoff, G. E., Dorn, L. D., Cutler, G. B., Jr., Loriaux, D. L., and Chrousos, G. E. (1985). The relationship of relative hormone levels and physical development and social-emotional behavior in young adolescents. J. Youth Adolesc. 14: 245-264.

Tschann, J. M., Adler, N. E., Irwin, C. E., Jr., Millstein, S. G., Turner, R. A., and Kegeles, S. M. (1994). Initiation of substance use in early adolescence: The roles of pubertal timing and emotional distress. Health Psychol. 13: 326-333.

Weir, H. K., Kreiger, N., and Marrett, L. D. (1998). Age at puberty and risk of testicular germ cell cancer. Cancer Causes Control. 9(3): 253-258.

Weissman, M., Warner, V., Wickramarame, E, Morean, D., and Olfson, M. (1997). Offspring of depressed parents: 10 years later. Arch. Gen. Psychiatry 54: 932-940.

Wichstrom, L. (2000). Predictors of adolescent suicide attempts: A nationally representative longitudinal study of Norwegian adolescents. J. Am. Acad. Child Adolesc. Psychiatry 39(5): 603-610.

Wohwill, J. F. (1973). The age variable in psychological research. The Study of Behavioral Development. Academic Press, New York.

Lorah D. Dorn, (1) Ronald E. Dahl, (2) Douglas E. Williamson, (3) Boris Birmaher, (4) David Axeison, (5) James Perel, (6) Stacy D. Stull, (7) and Neal D. Ryan (8)

(1) Associate Professor, in the School of Nursing and Department of Psychiatry, University of Pittsburgh. Received PhD in Human Development and Family Studies at The Pennsylvania State University. Research interests primarily focus on the influence of hormones and physiological changes during puberty upon health and developmental outcomes in adolescents. To whom correspondence should be addressed at the University of Pittsburgh, 3500 Victoria St., 440 Victoria Building, Pittsburgh, Pennsylvania 15261; e-mail: 1dd001@pitt.edu.

(2) Professor of Psychiatry and Pediatrics at the University of Pittsburgh School of Medicine. Received MD from the University of Pittsburgh and completed a Research Fellowship in Clinical Neuroendocrinology at the Western Psychiatric Institute and Clinic. Is Board Certified in Pediatrics and Sleep Medicine. Research interests and areas of expertise include the development of sleep, neuroendocrine regulation, and psychiatric disorders in children and adolescents.

(3) Assistant Professor of Psychiatry and Epidemiology at the University of Pittsburgh. Received PhD in Psychiatric Epidemiology from the University of Pittsburgh. Has conducted extensive research studying the familial-genetic and psychosocial/stress risk factors for depression in children and adolescents. Currently involved in projects examining the heritability of anxious traits in macaques as well as research examining the effect of being exposed to specific environments for the subsequent development of depression in children and adolescents.

(4) Associate Professor of Child and Adolescent Psychiatry at the University of Pittsburgh School of Medicine. Received MD, Medicine and Surgery, at Valle College of Medicine (Cali, Columbia) and

completed a Clinical Fellowship in Biological Psychiatry at Albert Einstein College of Medicine, a fellowship in Child Psychiatry at Columbia Presbyterian Medical Center and New York Psychiatric Institute, and a Research Fellowship at Columbia Presbyterian Medical Center and New York Psychiatric Institute. Area of interest includes the psychobiology of mood disorders and anxiety disorders in children and adolescents.

(5) Assistant Professor of Child and Adolescent Psychiatry at the University of Pittsburgh School of Medicine. Received MD at Duke University and completed a combined residency in General and Child Psychiatry and a Post-Doctoral Research Fellowship in Child and Adolescent Mood Disorders at the University of Pittsburgh Western Psychiatric Institute and Clinic. Area of interest includes the assessment and pharmacological treatment of pediatric affective disorders.

(6) Professor of Psychiatry, Pharmacology and Graduate Neurosciences at the University of Pittsburgh, and Director of the Clinical Pharmacology Program and Pediatric Neuroendocrine/Neurochemistry Laboratory at the Western Psychiatric Institute and Clinic. Has extensive experience in neuroendocrine assessment studies of pediatric and adolescent populations of psychiatric patients.

(7) Research Principal Scientist in the Women's Behavioral Health Care Program at Western Psychiatric Institute and Clinic. Conducts research in peripartum and postpartum depression. Has developed, adapted, and validated methodologies for small volumes of biological samples for hormone assays. Her extensive experience and data interpretation have contributed to a significant number of research publications from this project.

(8) Joaquim Puig-Antich Professor in Child and Adolescent Psychiatry at the University of Pittsburgh, School of Medicine. Received his MD from Yale University. Career has been devoted to the study of the pharmacological treatment and psychobiological correlates of child and adolescent depression and anxiety.

From *Journal of Youth and Adolescence*, October 2003, pp. 315-324. © 2003 by Kluwer Academic Publishers. Reprinted with permission.

Early Puberty

Because of the changing age at which today's children begin puberty, many parents want to learn more about how puberty normally progresses. Parents are often too late in seeking help for a child with precocious puberty, and aren't sure whether "early" has become "normal" puberty. Often, questions arise because a suggestion has been made to accelerate or delay the rate of puberty in a child whose body is perceived to be changing into that of an adult too early (or too late).

The sexualization of childhood: Adrenarche (androgen secretion by the adrenal glands) precedes the onset of true central puberty. In girls, Herman-Giddens, et al found puberty to be occurring at a much earlier age than just a few years ago.[1] Adolescent boys seem to be completing puberty at the usual age, but in younger boys (eight to twelve years of age), sexual characteristics are evident at a profoundly earlier age (Tanner stage 2 in up to 58.2% of nine-year-old boys versus 0.62% a few years ago).[2] This change to an earlier puberty is quite literally the sexualization of childhood in a physical sense. The worst disruption of normal pubertal timing occurs in those population groups at the bottom of the economic scale, exploding the once popular myth that early puberty results from "good nutrition."

The visible markers of sexual maturation are a slow and lagging indicator of high sex hormone levels in the bloodstream. In order to morph a child's body into one with adult sexual markers, internally produced sex steroids must usually build at heightened levels for several years. This buildup of adult sex hormones in a child's blood occurs long before the first outward signs are recognized by the untrained eye of parents. Because of this time lag parents usually underestimate the brewing steroid power that lies behind the first visible changes of pubescence.

Whether due to the effect of endocrine disrupters (chemicals in our environment) or other causes, early or late puberty can be emotionally difficult. Yet the issues here are not just ones of convenience. There are genuine health concerns, and most parents of children with early puberty are so late in seeking treatment that irreversible damage is done to their child's health.

The damage caused by early puberty is not just physical. Young children lack the socialization and self restraint that we expect of older children. No matter what you tell them, young children tend to judge things by the concept that whatever FEELS good, IS good. A young child filled with adult levels of

sex hormones easily becomes involved in sexually charged situations that an older and more emotionally mature adolescent would avoid.

Health effects associated with early puberty in girls:

1. greater lifelong risk of breast cancer and PCOS (polycystic ovary syndrome)
2. age inappropriate behavior, skin acne, hirsutism
3. greater risk of becoming willingly involved in incest and other illicit sexual encounters by attracting the attention of older males, fertile young girls may also be more at risk of becoming the victim of a forced sexual encounter
4. premature risk of pregnancy and sexually transmitted disease (STD).

In addition, many of the risks that boys face (listed below) also apply to girls.

Assessment of pubertal status

In girls, the formation of breast buds is normally the earliest indicator of sexual maturation. In the absence of breast buds, early pubic hair may be a sign of adrenarche rather than true puberty.

Health effects associated with early puberty in boys:

1. greater lifelong risk of testicular cancer problems due to lack of self-control: the combination of testosterone and social immaturity may make it difficult or impossible for the child to control his own behavior
2. greatly increased risks of academic failure/expulsion, incarceration, alcohol and other drug abuse, accident, suicide
3. age inappropriate sexual behavior leads to illicit sexual involvements with other children and adults
4. increased legal and medical risks, including paternity/child support liabilities, STDs

Anecdotal evidence links high androgen levels in young boys to attention deficit disorder ADD/ADHD and in the most extreme cases (such as full adult sex hormone levels in a boy less than ten years old): very early puberty will produce a tall child who abruptly ceases growth before reaching adult height; this condition is untreatable once the bone growth plates close. Particularly in boys, very early puberty should always be investigated carefully, as it sometimes indicates the presence of a brain tumor or other serious disease. In addition, many of the risks that girls face (listed previously) also apply to boys.

Assessment of pubertal status

In boys, an increase in testicular volume is normally the earliest indicator of sexual maturation, though in the absence of testicular enlargement, the first traces of pubic hair indicate adrenarche, which is soon followed by true puberty.

In mail to FatherMag.com, parents complain of doctors who try to put a "they're just growing up early" spin on early puberty. By delaying treatment, or by withholding medical treatment from all but the most extreme cases, some medical professionals may leave parents with psychotherapy as the only means to help their children cope with the excesses of early puberty.

Once a sympathetic physician is found, treatment may still be delayed by a long sequence of testing and case assessment.

Meanwhile, irreversible changes are left to advance in children who are years away from being ready to cope with adult sexual characteristics. These problems have lead to the concept of minidosing for children with signs of early adrenarche to neutralize adult sex hormones and maintain the natural timing of puberty. Minidosing (using small amounts of the compounds traditionally used to treat adrenal hyperplasia) must be applied early, before the sex organs are triggered into starting the production of hormones that will lead to full central puberty and adult sexual characteristics. Many parents are unprepared to recognize the signs of early adrenarche, and so do not realize that adult hormones are rising until is too late to prevent the onset of premature puberty.

References

Herman-Giddens ME, Slora EJ, Wasserman RC, et al. Secondary sexual characteristics and menses in young girls seen in office practice: a study from the Pediatric Research in Office Settings network. Pediatrics. 1997;99:505-512. Herman-Giddens ME, Wang L, Koch G. Secondary sexual characteristics in boys: estimates from the National Health and Nutrition Examination Survey III, 1988-1994. Arch Pediatr Adolesc Med. 2001;155:1022-1028

Adolescent Neurodevelopment and Psychopathology

Elaine F. Walker

Department of Psychology, Emory University, Atlanta, Georgia

Adolescence is a high-risk period for the onset of psychopathology. The occurrence of depression increases markedly in the years following the onset of puberty, and most individuals who are eventually diagnosed with a psychotic disorder show a marked rise in adjustment problems during adolescence. It is well established that puberty involves increases in the secretion of gonadal hormones. More recently, research has shown that stress hormones show a similar normative rise following puberty. Accumulating findings indicate that the postpubescent period is also characterized by significant neurodevelopment; there are changes in brain structure and function that are partially a consequence of hormonal factors. Researchers are now challenged to elucidate the neural mechanisms relating postpubertal neurodevelopment with the elevations in risk for psychopathology that characterize adolescence. One plausible mechanism is the effect of hormones on gene expression. The normal neuromaturational processes observed in adolescence partially reflect the effect of gonadal hormones on the expression of genes that control brain development. Hormone surges following puberty may also trigger the expression of genes that code for brain abnormalities that give rise to mental disorders.

The notion that adolescence is a period of storm and stress has been highly controversial among psychological theorists (Cote, 1994). The debate was sparked by Margaret Mead's contention that Western culture generated a stereotype of tumultuous adolescence—one that did not apply to non-Western societies. But the controversy has gradually subsided, and the weight of the empirical literature does suggest that adolescence is a period of heightened anxiety and stress across many cultural contexts. The data also indicate that a substantial number of teenagers experience adjustment problems and dysphoria (Arnett, 1999). Although in most cases these difficulties do not persist into adulthood, for a subgroup the problems escalate, reflecting the prodromal (precursor) stage of serious mental illness. There is now a growing body of evidence that the onset of puberty marks the entry into a sensitive developmental period with respect to the neural circuits involved in mental health and illness (Benes, 1999). The developmental changes associated with adolescence are reflected in behavior, endocrinology, and brain structure.

ADOLESCENCE AND BEHAVIORAL ADJUSTMENT

Adolescence is also associated with a rise in a variety of adjustment problems. There is a precipitous increase in self-reported negative emotional experiences, and in rates of risk taking, substance abuse, and clinical depression (Arnett, 1999; Spear, 2000). Although social and cultural factors undoubtedly contribute to these problems, the fact that similar developmental trends are observed in diverse cultures suggests that biological factors also play a role.

The onset of depression during adolescence is especially pernicious because it is linked with a poorer long-term prognosis. That is, adolescents who manifest clinical depression are much more likely to have a chronic course with repeated episodes than are individuals who first experience depression in adulthood. Although the postpubertal rise in depression is observed in both sexes, it is most pronounced among girls (Hankin et al., 1998; Silberg et al., 1999). Further, girls who show an early onset of puberty manifest the highest rates of mood disorders.

It is noteworthy that there is some evidence that the rate of adolescent depression has increased in recent cohorts of youth. The onset of puberty is also occurring earlier in recent cohorts, and this could be related to the escalation in adolescent mood disorders.

Although psychotic disorders, such as schizophrenia, usually have their onset in the early 20s, the subclinical signs are typically apparent during the teenage years (Walker, Baum, & Diforio, 1998). In fact, the majority of individuals who are eventually diagnosed with schizophrenia and other psychotic illnesses show a steep increase in adjustment problems through adolescence. Social withdrawal, anxiety, academic difficulties, and thought problems become more common with each year between the ages of 12 and 18 in this group.

As with teenage depression, there are sex differences in the prodromal course of psychotic disorders. Boys who are subsequently diagnosed with schizophrenia show more severe adjustment problems than do girls. The prodromal phase for boys is also characterized by more disruptive behavior. Sex differences persist through the early course of schizophrenia; females tend to be diagnosed with the illness 2 to 3 years later than males, and they have a more favorable long-term prognosis. It has been suggested that these differences are due to hormones, with estrogen serving to delay the onset and ameliorate the course of the illness. Specifically, the activity of the neurotransmitter dopamine, which has been implicated in the neuropathology of schizophrenia, is dampened by estrogen.

Some childhood-onset mental disorders undergo a change in clinical expression during adolescence. For example, children with Tourette's syndrome often experience an amelioration of symptoms after the onset of puberty. In contrast, many forms of epilepsy have their onset following puberty. Again, these developmental trends suggest that brain maturation has implications for vulnerability to various neuropsychiatric syndromes.

One of the most fascinating findings from behavioral genetic studies is that the heritability of some behavioral propensities and mental disorders increases with age. In other words, the proportion of the variance accounted for by genetic factors rises, particularly during adolescence. This holds for cognitive and personality traits, as well as clinical depression (Silberg et al., 1999). The reason for the increase in heritability is not known; however, as I discuss later, hormones may exert a major influence.

ADOLESCENT NEURODEVELOPMENT

Brain Changes During Adolescence

New technologies for studying the brain in vivo have quickened the pace of research on brain development in humans. As a result, significant postpubertal brain development has now been documented. In general, these changes entail a maturation and refinement of neural cir-

cuitry. There are normative maturational changes in the volume of several brain regions, including the frontal and temporal cortex, amygdala, and hippocampus (Giedd et al., 1996, 1999; Sowell & Jernigan, 1998). Specifically, limbic structures, including the hippocampus and amygdala, tend to show an increase in volume. The limbic system is a group of interconnected brain structures that play an important role in human emotion. Also, gray matter volume in some areas of the cortex decreases through adolescence. The gray matter is the outer layer of the cortex where the cell bodies of neurons are concentrated. In addition, there is protracted maturation of fiber pathways in the white matter throughout childhood and adolescence. The white matter of the brain contains neural fibers that are covered with myelin, and the maturation of these pathways includes increased myelination of the hippocampus and associated limbic regions, and increased white matter density in fiber tracts that connect regions of the cortex with each other and with the spinal cord. The age-related changes in white matter density may reflect increases in axon diameter or myelination.

Frontal brain activity, as measured with functional MRI (magnetic resonance imaging) and electrophysiology, is enhanced during adolescence (Casey, Giedd, & Thomas, 2000; Rubia et al., 2000). This increased activation is assumed to contribute to advances in higher-level cognitive processes. For example, abstract reasoning and attentional capacities improve following puberty and into young adulthood. Interest in social activities and interpersonal awareness also increases (Spear, 2000). It is likely that these normative changes in cognitive capacities and behavior, as well as risk for certain forms of psychopathology, are a consequence of changes in the brain that are linked with sexual maturation.

Hormonal and Neurotransmitter Changes

There are well-established developmental changes in activity of what is called the hypothalamic-pituitary-gonadal (HPG) axis as the child advances through puberty. The HPG axis is the neural system that controls the rise in sex hormones (e.g., estrogen and testosterone). These maturational processes result from the genetic program that prepares the organism for reproduction.

More recently, researchers have documented adolescent changes in the secretion of thyroid and adrenal hormones. Most relevant to the issue of adolescent "stress and storm" is the increased activation of another neural system, the hypothalamic-pituitary-adrenal (HPA) axis, during the teenage years. The HPA axis, which comprises the hypothalamus, pituitary, and adrenal gland, plays a central role in the biological stress response. The HPA axis subserves a cascade of biochemical events: The hypothalamus releases corticotropin-releasing hormone, which activates pituitary secretion of adreno-corticotropin hormone, which, in turn, stimulates the adrenal gland to release glucocorticoids, most notably cortisol in primates. Studies of humans have revealed a gradual rise in cortisol levels beginning in early adolescence (see the Recommended Reading). These and other findings have led some researchers to conclude that adolescence is a period of heightened stress sensitivity (Kiess et al., 1995; Spear, 2000).

Levels of neurotransmitters also change with the onset of puberty. There appears to be a generalized decrease in serotonin, whereas dopamine activity increases in some cortical regions. Certain enzymes that play a role in the synthesis and degradation of neurotransmitters also increase during the teenage years. It has been hypothesized that the increased risk for the onset of psychosis during adolescence and early adulthood may be due to the elevation in dopamine activity.

Hormones and the Brain: Potential Neural Mechanisms in Adolescent-Onset Psychopathology

When researchers examine the relation between gonadal hormone levels and behavior in youth, they typically find only a modest linear association. This is consistent with the assumption that hormonal effects on behavior are mediated by changes in brain structure and function. Thus, hormones trigger changes in brain structure and function that, in turn, influence behavior. There is also evidence of threshold effects of hormones, so, rising hormones may have no effect on behavior until they exceed a certain level. As a result, the relations between baseline circulating levels of hormones and behavior are likely to be nonlinear.

Hormones play a pivotal role in neuromaturation. They have organizational as well as activational effects on the brain. In other words, they affect the brain's structural development as well as its immediate functional properties. The organizational effects of gonadal hormones are pronounced during the prenatal period, when sexually dimorphic aspects of the central nervous system arise. Then later, during puberty, gonadal hormones play a role in brain maturation, and, in turn, influence cognition, mood, and behavior.

It has been shown that the behavioral influences exerted by gonadal and adrenal hormones are partially mediated by their effects on gene expression (i.e., the activation of the gene's program; McEwen, 1994; Watson & Gametchu, 1999). There are hormone receptors on the surface of neurons as well as inside the cell body. In general, it appears that the surface receptors mediate short-term effects on behavior. These are referred to as *nongenomic* effects. The hormone receptors that reside in a cell's nucleus are responsible for hormones' *genomic* effects. These effects can be long term because they can permanently alter the brain. When hormones bind to receptors inside the nucleus, they can increase gene expression by changing the expression of messenger RNA

that codes for specific proteins. These proteins, in turn, influence neuronal structure and function, including neuronal growth, neurotransmitter synthesis, and receptor density and sensitivity. For example, in rodents, stress hormones change the expression of genes that code for the production of brain growth factors, which are substances that can induce neuronal development in the hippocampus. Hormones are also capable of augmenting the expression of genes that affect the survival of neurons. Thus, cell death (apoptosis) may result from abnormal levels of hormones.

Research with rodents has shown that hormones can trigger the expression of genes that control postpubertal maturational processes. Thus, some of the normative brain changes observed in human adolescents are assumed to result from the effects of hormones on the expression of genes that govern maturational processes such as the proliferation and elimination of neuronal processes. This raises the possibility that the hormonal changes occurring during adolescence may also be capable of triggering genes that contribute to vulnerability for mental disorders. The postpubescent increase in heritability for behavioral traits and disorders suggests that hormonal maturation results in the expression of genes that were previously silent. If the individual possesses genes that code for aberrant brain function, and gonadal or adrenal hormones trigger the expression of these "vulnerability" genes, then signs of behavioral disorder may first become apparent in adolescence. For example, the rise in hormones during puberty may result in the expression of a gene that codes for abnormal dopamine neurotransmission. This, in turn, may give rise to the brain abnormality that confers susceptibility to schizophrenia. Similarly, vulnerability to depression might result if hormone surges trigger the expression of a gene that leads to a defect in one of the neurotransmitter systems involved in this illness, such as the serotonin system.

Hormonal deficiency may also be involved in neurodevelopmental abnormality. It is plausible that insufficient levels of gonadal or adrenal hormones lead to the failure of expression of genes that are critical for adolescent brain maturation, resulting in psychopathology. In this connection, it has been suggested that schizophrenia involves a deficit in the pruning of neural connections that is normally triggered by puberty. In other words, deficient elimination of neural processes may result in faulty neuronal interconnections.

Finally, adjustment problems may arise during adolescence when there is a preexisting abnormality in a brain region that comes "on line" during this period. Thus, genetically programmed brain maturation could lead to maladaptive behavior if one or more components of a newly emerging circuit is defective. In this way, a previously "silent" brain lesion could begin to negatively influence behavior after the onset of puberty.

FUTURE RESEARCH DIRECTIONS

Our understanding of adolescent development has increased dramatically. The convergence of advances in neuroimaging, molecular genetics, and endocrinology has elucidated the nature of adolescent neurodevelopment. At the same time, developmental research on various forms of psychopathology has demonstrated that adolescence is a pivotal period for the onset of certain symptoms and syndromes.

But there is still much to be learned about both normal and abnormal neuromaturation. It is generally agreed that normal developmental changes in hormones arise from genetic programs that govern the maturation of the HPA and HPG axes. But we have little information on the temporal ordering of the changes in hormones, brain structure, and behavior in humans. To what extent are adolescent changes in brain structure and activity driven by hormonal changes? Further, what direct and indirect effects do hormones and brain structure have on behavior? Answering questions such as these will require comprehensive, longitudinal studies of normal adolescent development. The optimal approach will be one that combines measures of behavior with biological indices, such as hormonal activity and brain structure. Data from repeated assessments beginning before pubescence and extending to the postpubescent years will allow investigators to chart the temporal course for each measure and determine the temporal ordering of maturational events. Taking this line of investigation to the molecular level will involve studies of gene expression. Such work is now well underway with animals, and advances in technology may soon make it possible to pursue this kind of research with humans.

In addition to charting the course of normal neurodevelopmental processes, investigators should give high priority to longitudinal research on the development of at-risk adolescents, such as those at genetic risk for psychopathology, or those who are manifesting excessive adjustment problems following the onset of puberty. One salient set of questions concerns the role of hormonal and brain changes in the emergence of mental disorder. Does the emergence of psychopathology parallel maturational changes in hormones or brain characteristics? Taking this question to the molecular level raises questions about the effect of hormones on the expression of vulnerability genes that result in aberrant neurodevelopment. Do hormones trigger the expression of genes that lead to depression or schizophrenia? If the answer is "yes," a host of intriguing questions about prevention will ensue. Of course, before we can explore the factors that trigger the expression of vulnerability genes, we must be able to identify such genes. To date, genetic research has not identified a specific gene or set of genes that leads to any particular form of psychopathology, but there are some extremely promising leads.

Acknowledgments

This work was supported by Research Scientist Development Award No. K01 MH00876 from the National Institute of Mental Health.

Note

1. Address correspondence to Elaine F. Walker, Department of Psychology, Emory University, Atlanta, GA 30322; e-mail: psyefw@emory.edu.

References

Arnett, J. (1999). Adolescent storm and stress, reconsidered. *American Psychologist, 54*, 317–326.

Benes, F. (1999). Neurodevelopmental approach to the study of mental illness. *Developmental Neuropsychology, 16*, 359–360.

Casey, B., Giedd, J., & Thomas, K. (2000). Structural and functional brain development and its relation to cognitive development. *Biological Psychology, 54*, 241–257.

Cote, J. (1994). *Adolescent storm and stress.* Hillsdale, NJ: Erlbaum.

Giedd, J., Jeffries, N., Blumenthal, J., Castellanos, F., Vaituzis, A., Fernandez, T., Hamburger, S., Liu, H., Nelson, J., Bedwell, J., Tran, L., Lenane, M., Nicolson, R., & Rapoport, J. (1999). Childhood-onset schizophrenia: Progressive brain changes during adolescence. *Biologicall Psychiatry, 46*, 892–898.

Giedd, J., Vaituzis, A., Hamburger, S., Lange, N., Rajapakse, J., Kaysen, D., Vauss, Y.C., & Rapoport, J. (1996). Quantitative MRI of the temporal lobe, amygdala, and hippocampus in normal human development: Ages 4–18 years. *Journal of Comparative Neurology, 366*, 223–230.

Hankin, B., Abramson, L., Moffitt, T., Silva, P., McGee, R., & Angell, K. (1998). Development of depression from preadolescence to young adulthood: Emerging gender differences in a 10-year longitudinal study. *Journal of Abnormal Psychology, 107*, 128–140.

Kiess, W., Meidert, A., Dressendorfer, R., Scheiver, K., Kessler, U., & Konig, A. (1995). Salivary cortisol levels throughout childhood and adolescence. *Pediatric Research, 37*, 502–506.

McEwen, B. (1994). Steroid hormone actions on the brain: When is the genome involved? *Hormones & Behavior, 28*, 396–405.

Rubia, K., Overmeyer, S., Taylor, E., Brammer, M., Williams, S., Simmons, A., Andrew, C., & Bullmore, E. (2000). Functional frontalisation with age: Mapping neurodevelopmental trajectories with fMRI. *Neuroscience & Biobehavioral Review, 24*, 13–19.

Silberg, J., Pickles, A., Rutter, M., Hewitt, J., Simonoff, E., Maes, H., Carbonneau, R., Murrelle, L., Foley, D., & Eaves, L. (1999). The influence of genetic factors and life stress on depression among adolescent girls. *Archives of General Psychiatry, 56*, 225–232.

Sowell, E., & Jernigan, T. (1998). Further MRI evidence of late brain maturation: Limbic volume increases and changing asymmetries during childhood and adolescence. *Developmental Neuropsychology, 14*, 599–617.

Spear, L.P. (2000). The adolescent brain and age-related behavioral manifestations. *Neuroscience & Biobehavioral Reviews, 24*, 417–463.

Walker, E., Baum, K., & Diforio, D. (1998). Developmental changes in the behavioral expression of the vulnerability for schizophrenia. In M. Lenzenweger & R. Dworkin (Eds.), *Origins and development of schizophrenia* (pp. 469–492). Washington, DC: American Psychological Association Press.

Watson, C., & Gametchu, B. (1999). Membrane-initiated steroid actions and the proteins that mediate them. *Proceedings of the Society for Experimental Biology & Medicine, 220*, 9–19.

Why do kids eat healthful food?

Perceived benefits of and barriers to healthful eating and physical activity among children and adolescents.

Jennifer A. O'Dea

The goal was to have children and adolescents identify and rank the major perceived benefits of and barriers to healthful eating and physical activity and to suggest strategies for overcoming barriers. Semistructured, in-depth focus groups were undertaken using standardized questions and prompts. Students in grades 2 through 11 (ages 7 through 17; N=213) from 34 randomly selected schools participated in 38 focus groups. Major benefits of healthful eating included improvements to cognitive and physical performance, fitness, endurance, psychological benefits, physical sensation (feeling good physically), and production of energy. Barriers included convenience, taste, and social factors. Benefits of physical activity included social benefits, enhancement of psychological status, physical sensation, and sports performance. Barriers included a preference for indoor activities, lack of energy and motivation, time constraints, and social factors. Suggested strategies for overcoming barriers included support from parents and school staff, better planning, time management, self-motivation, education, restructuring the physical environment, and greater variety of physical activities. J Am Diet Assoc. 2003; 103: 497-501.

Health education theories (1-2) suggest that health behaviors are influenced in part by the perceived benefits of and barriers to a specified action. Social learning theory (3) emphasizes the importance of understanding personal beliefs and motivations underlying different behaviors, and the need to emphasize short-term and tangible benefits of behaviors. Obtaining a detailed understanding of the perceived benefits of and barriers to healthful eating and physical activity among children and adolescents forms the first step in designing appropriate dietary counseling and would be very valuable in the planning of health and nutrition education treatment and prevention programs, particularly obesity prevention programs.

There is a paucity of published studies about children's and adolescent's perceived benefits of healthful eating together with their perceived barriers to these practices. Several studies (4-8) have explored barriers to healthful eating, typically asking children and adolescents why they do not eat healthful foods and drinks, but few have investigated why they do eat healthful foods or what factors motivate this behavior.

Barriers to healthful eating, identified in previous studies, include a lack of sense of urgency about personal health; undesirable taste, appearance and smell of healthful food; lack of time; limited availability of choice; and convenience (5-8).

The major goal of this study was to answer the question, "Why do children and adolescents eat healthful foods and engage in physical activity?"

METHODS

The focus groups included 213 school students (51% female) from school grades 2 through 11 in 34 schools representing all states and territories of Australia and including a representative mix of ethnicity and socioeconomic status. Forty school principals were invited to participate, and two declined because of time constraints. Participants were randomly selected from class lists and given parental consent forms to return (98.3% response rate). A total of 38 focus group discussions were conducted, each lasting 20 to 30 minutes. A total of 15.8 hours of tape-recorded interviews were obtained and transcribed verbatim to produce a manuscript. The data were then analyzed using content analysis (9-12), which involved the systematic examination of the transcripts to identify and group emergent clusters and themes, and then code, classify, and develop major categories of themes.

RESULTS

Healthful foods were frequently defined by grade 3 through 11 students as fruits, vegetables, juice, pasta, rice, milk, and cheese, and less frequently as bread, cereals, meat, chicken, and water.

The most important benefits of healthful eating (Table 1) were enhancement of cognitive function, physical performance, psychological factors, and physical sensation, and production of energy. These five themes were consistently described by both sexes from all school grades and ethnic groups.

Older participants in grades 6 through 11 were able to clearly articulate the "refreshing" effect of healthful foods, particularly fruits and vegetables, as they related to the enhanced function of the body, mind, and psyche. Participants commonly used descriptive words such as "clean" "refresh," "feeling good," and "revived." Contrasting themes about the benefits of healthful eating included descriptions about the adverse effects of "junk foods" (defined as candy, chocolate, soda, fast foods, fried foods), which were described as slowing down the mind and body, draining the body of energy, making the body and mind feel "slow" and "heavy," and "clogging up the system." Eating "junk foods" was accompanied by guilt that contrasted with the psychological benefits of healthful eating, including personal pride, self-reward, and a sense of accomplishment and self-efficacy.

An overlapping theme was the clearly articulated link between healthful eating and physical performance. Participants clearly reported that the benefits of healthful eating enabled physical fitness, endurance, and physical well-being, whereas the impact of "junk food" reversed the beneficial physical effects and caused a "draining of energy" and subsequently resulted in more physical inactivity.

The benefits of healthful eating to appearance, weight control, immunity, longevity, and future health were articulated by males and females of all ages, but were ranked as moderately important, well below the importance of the other benefits.

The major barriers to healthful eating are given in Table 1. The theme of parental control over the food supply was notable, with the vast majority of participants of all ages indicating that they eat what is available and allowable at home, at school, and at friends' homes. Advertising for "junk foods" and price were identified as minor barriers.

Participants in grades 5 through 11 were able to suggest strategies for overcoming the barriers to healthful eating, but younger children could not. The major strategies included the following:

- Parental support, as described above;
- Planning to eat more healthful foods and drinks—carrying healthful foods to school; not taking money to school; reducing the availability of 'junk food" at home, school, and community; increasing the availability of healthful foods at home and school to reduce boredom and to motivate interest;
- Cognitive strategies—using self-motivation strategies to remind oneself of the many benefits of healthful eating and the undesirable short-term impact of "junk foods"; and
- Educational strategies—-increasing information and education about food and nutrition; increasing advertising of healthful foods to make them more appealing; receiving personal advice from a doctor or dietitian about healthful eating habits.

The major benefits of and barriers to physical activity are given in Table 2. Minor benefits included health protection (eg, heart health, bone strength, weight control).

The theme of feeling tired, sluggish, and lazy was clearly linked to the consumption of "junk food." Minor barriers included disinterest in current physical education activities, teasing, self-consciousness, lack of transport, and unsuitable outdoor environment.

Suggested strategies to increase physical activity were identified by participants in grades 5 through 11. These included the following:

- Planning/organization—making arrangements to play with friends, becoming involved in a team, prioritizing physical activity as important and fun;
- Increase variety and excitement of physical activity—participants, particularly teenagers, indicated boredom with existing physical education programs and expressed interest in new and unusual activities such as aerobics, martial arts, Tai Bo, yoga, archery, hiking, rock climbing, and water sports;
- Parental support and involvement—participants of all ages indicated that they would like to do outdoor games and activities with parents and they would like their parents to encourage them to become involved in various physical activities;
- Time management—participants of all ages indicated that they needed to rearrange the amount of time spent on homework, chores, part-time work, and family activities to make time for physical activities; and
- Restructure physical environment—female adolescents indicated that they would like female-ori-

Table 1

Major reported perceived benefits of and barriers to healthful eating identified by children and adolescents[a]

Major benefits (in descending order of importance)	Typical comments
Cognitive function/cognitive performance	
Enhanced concentration and mental function. Mental alertness/mental activity. Improved school performance.	"After eating healthy, it just cleans out the system and you focus better ... I focus better on school work and everything." (11th-grade female)[b]
Physical sensation	
Feel good physically. Feel "fresh and clean" physically, not "clogged up".	"I feel good ... I feel more refreshed ... lighter ... cleaner ... I feel cleaner on the inside." (9th-grade female) "Eating healthy foods is like taking a shower." (8th-grade male)
Psychological benefits	
Self reward—have done something good for self. Cleans, refreshes, and clears mental function. Enhances self-esteem. Reduces guilt and anxiety.	"It's just a personal achievement ... it's my personal feeling like I've done something for myself ..." (8th-grade male) "I like feeling that I've done something good for myself, feeling good about myself ... not feeling guilty." (11th-grade female)
Physical performance	
Enhanced fitness and sports performance. Enhanced strength, energy, endurance.	"It helps me run ... it can make me do things like run ... skip ... jump ... hop ... walk a long way." (3rd-grade female) "It keeps you fit ... like I've got heaps of energy and I eat healthy foods if I want energy ..." (6th-grade male)
Increases production of energy	
"Creates" energy. Sustains energy and endurance. Regulates energy throughout the day.	"... I eat a salad and I feel ... fresh and I feel like going out and doing stuff ... but if I sit there and pig out on junk food, I feel like a blob ... I can't move ..." (9th-grade female) "Every time I eat fruit, I feel revived ... it's energizing." (7th-grade male)

Major barriers to healthful eating (in descending order of importance)	Typical comments
Convenience of less healthful alternatives	
Availability of "less healthful" alternatives. Easy and quick preparation of "less healthful" alternatives. Time costs involved in healthful foods.	... and when I get home from school, I think 'I should eat some fruits,' but then I see the chips ... they're easier ... it just feels like the easier thing to do." (6th-grade male)
Internal/physiologic preference	
Prefer taste of "less healthful" alternatives. Satiety of "less healthful" alternatives. Cravings for "less healthful" alternatives. Healthful food "looks and smells dull and boring."	"The sugar is ... a tasty food and sometimes healthy food is kind of yucky and smelly..." (3rd-grade female) "Temptation for all those nutty chocolate things ..." (5th-grade female)
Social reinforcement	
Peer pressure. Parental control over food. Lack of parental/school support and modeling.	"My parents buy the food ... I think it's the availability of food that's around at the time ..." (11th-grade male) "We have lots of junk food ... my dad's into junk food ..." (5th-grade female)
Reward driven/mood enhancement	
Treating oneself with unhealthful alternatives. Eating when bored/emotional eating. Relieve stress with less healthful alternatives. Less healthful alternatives improve mood and are more fun/exciting.	"Sometimes it all depends on your mood ... if I'm feeling depressed, I just feel like eating chocolate ..." (11th-grade female) "Sometimes I just have to have some junk food ... it makes me feel better ..." (9th-grade male)

[a] Results in Table 1 were obtained by using the following semistructured focus group questions and prompts: What does healthy eating do for you? How? What stops you from having healthy foods and drinks? How? Why? Can you vote on which benefit/barrier is most important or has the greatest effect on you?

[b] Approximate age ranges (in years) for school grade levels: 3rd grade=8 to 9; 4th=9 to 10; 5th=10 to 11; 6th=11 to 12; 7th=12 to 13; 8th=13 to 14; 9th=14 to 15; 10th=15 to 16; 11th=16 to 17; 12th=17 to 18.

Table 2

Major reported, perceived benefits of and barriers to physical activity among children and adolescents[a]

Major benefits (in descending order of importance)	Typical comments
Social benefits	
Fun/enjoyment. Socializing with friends. Enjoyment of teamwork, team identity. Fitness aids other areas of life (eg, coping). Development of life skills. Parental approval.	"It's fun ... just playing with your friends." (4th-grade male) [b] "At physical culture ... I just have all these friends that I've known for a long time and to have a social group outside of school ... it just makes me feel better." (9th-grade female) "It's the social part of it that's most important ... having friends in the team is really important so that you have fun and you learn to get on with people ... and the life skills help with the social side." (11th-grade male)
Psychologic enhancement	
Sense of achievement, pride, self-esteem, confidence. Enhanced mood. Develop discipline. Sense of balance in life. Reduces guilt. Enjoyment of challenges and goals, excitement, adrenaline rush.	"You feel better physically and it increases your self-esteem ... because you know you're doing something good for your body ..." (11th-grade female) "Feelings about yourself ... in the mind ... the feeling that you've done something good for yourself ... feeling good about yourself ... not feeling guilty ..." (9th-grade female)
Physical sensation (feeling good physically)	
Feel refreshed, "cleansed." Enjoy sensation of movement. Creation of energy, reduces fatigue. Sensation of well-being, strength, and fitness. Enhanced sleep.	"When you're dancing ... you're sweaty but you don't care ... you just keep on going and then when you go out you feel so good ... you feel so health ..." (11th-grade male) "It makes me feel good ... afterwards my body just feels better..."(9th-grade female) "It uses my energy so I'm not restless in the night and I get good sleep." (6th-grade male)
Sports performance	
Improved sports performance. Skill development. Improved coordination, agility, flexibility, reflexes. Improved fitness, strength, endurance.	"It keeps you being able to play well for the whole game ..." (8th-grade male) "Being able to turn and breathe after you run ..." (10th-grade female)
Cognitive benefits	
Clears mind and thinking. Enhances concentration and brain function.	"It clears my mind for studying ...if I go for a run I can come back and be sharper ...better concentration ..." (11th-grade male)
Coping strategy	
Stress relief, relaxation, distraction from worries, mental break. Outlet for aggression, frustration, and anger. Physical break.	"You get your mind off school, like all the pressures of school ... you just forget about it ... so that's relief." (9th-grade male) "If I'm really, really angry, I can go outside and go for a big walk ..." (11th-grade female) "Sometime I just need to go and punch the punching bag and kick it and it makes me feel heaps ..." (8th-grade female)
Preference for indoor activities	
Prefer to watch television, videos, play on computer. Prefer to play with toys, games, books, music indoors.	"I'm stuck to the television somethimes ... lots of movies ..." (3rd-grade female)
Low energy level	
Feeling tired, lazy, and sluggish. "Junk food" snacks drain energy. Lack of energy.	"I just can't move ... I just don't feel like moving ... I feel tired or I feel lazy ..." (6th-grade male) "Junk food makes you slow-down ... really lazy ... you don't feel like doing anything ..." (3rd-grade female)
Time constraints	
Homework, jobs consume spare time. Other plans, commitments consume time.	"Sometimes I just don't have time because I've got school and I've got homework or I've got to go to work ..." (11th-grade female)
Social factors	
Peer pressure—friends are involved in sedentary activities. Parental control/preferences. Lack of parental support. Lack of playmates or suitable playmates. Teasing/bullying from peers. Criticism from others (peers, teachers).	"... it's like my social life as well ... I just like to go and hang around with friends ... sit and talk ..." (9th-grade female) ...if I want to play with my best friend ... my mom has to drive me there ..." (5th-grade female)"... I hate physical education with boys ... they hog the gear and they laugh at you and tease you ..." (9th-grade female)
Motivation	
Low level of self-motivation. Low level of motivation from others. Low perceived rewards.	"... I'd do more stuff it I had someone to do it with me ... because you'd motivate each other ..." (10th-grade male)

[a] Results in Table 2 were obtained by using the following semistructured focus group questions and prompts: What does physical activity do for you? How? What stops you from being physically active? Why? Can you vote on which benefit/barrier is most important or has the greatest effect on you?

[b] Approximate age ranges (in years for school grade levels: 3rd grade = 8 to 9; 4th =9 to 10; 5th = 10 to 11; 6th = 11 to 12; 7th = 12 to 13; 8th = 13 to 14; 9th = 14 to 15; 10th = 15 to 16; 11th = 16; 11th = 16 to 17; 12th = 17 to 18.

ented sports and activities taught by female teachers in private facilities. They suggested having doors on private showers and changing rooms, and self-selected physical education uniforms.

Children of all ages expressed the need for parents and teachers to help with these strategies.

DISCUSSION

This study presents rich new data on a somewhat neglected area of research, namely, the specific benefits children and adolescents obtain from healthful eating and physical activity.

The study results suggest that the greatest motivator of healthful eating among children and adolescents in grades 5 through 11 is the desire to create a "cleansed," "refreshed," and "energized" mind, body, and emotional state. Participants of both sexes and all ages and ethnicities consistently reported having experienced short-term mental, physical, and psychological benefits from healthful eating as well as similar benefits from physical activity. In agreement with previous findings (5-7), motivating factors of less importance were health protection, benefits to appearance, and weight control, although these benefits were certainly not considered unimportant.

The strong social, psychological, and cognitive benefits of physical activity reported by participants add to the paucity of literature on this topic (13-16) and have the potential to help clinicians, educators, administrators, and parents better understand the strongest motivating factors behind children's health behaviors.

Overlapping themes between the benefits of healthful eating and physical activity included beliefs that both food and exercise have a "cleansing" effect on the body, mind, and emotional state and that "junk food" has the reverse effect. Children and adolescents report that the combination of healthful eating and physical activity confers many benefits to schoolwork by enhancing clear thinking, concentration, sleep, stress control, and energy. Findings about barriers concur with those of previous studies (48, 13-16) with the expansion of themes and addition of a new barrier related to parental control, parental expectations, lack of parental and school support, and lack of role modeling.

Results clearly show that children and adolescents are looking to their parents and teachers to encourage, support, and enable them to be involved in more healthful behaviors.

APPLICATIONS

The combination of these findings, applied within appropriate theoretical frameworks, could be a powerful way of motivating children to seek the health benefits that they identify as most important. In particular, the finding that children and adolescents believe that healthful eating and physical activity confer many interrelated cognitive, physical, and psychological benefits is a new and interesting result that has vast implications for motivating children and adolescents in clinical, community, and educational settings.

This research was supported by a Kellogg Australia Nutrition Research Grant.

Many thanks to the school staff and students who participated in this national research study.

References

1. Ajzen I, Fishbein M. Understanding Attitudes and Predicting Social Behaviour. Englewood Cliffs, NJ: Prentice-Hall; 1980.
2. Ajzen I. The Theory of Planned Behaviour. Organizational Behaviour and Human Decision Processes. 1991;50:179-211.
3. Bandura A. Social Foundations of Thought and Action: A Social Cognitive Theory. Englewood Cliffs, NJ: Prentice-Hall; 1966.
4. Ling A. Perceived benefits and barriers of increased fruit and vegetable consumption: Validation of a decisional balance scale. J Nutr Ed. 2001;33:257-265.
5. Gracey D, Stanley N, Burke V, Corti B, Beilin LJ. Nutritional knowledge, beliefs, and behaviours in teenage school students. Health Ed Res. 1996;11:187-204.
6. Neumark-Sztainer D, Story M, Perry C, Casey MA. Factors influencing food choices of adolescents: Findings from focus group discussions with adolescents. J Am Diet Assoc. 1999;99:929-934,937.
7. California Project Lean. Food on the Run Campaign. Key informant interviews with students, experts and LEAN regional coordinators about healthful eating and physical activity in multicultural youth. Sacramento, CA: Food on the Run Campaign; 1998.
8. Glanz K, Basil M, Maibach E, Goldberg J, Snyder D. Why Americans eat what they do: Taste, nutrition, cost, convenience and weight control concerns as influences on food consumption. J Am Diet Assoc. 1998;98:1118-1126.
9. Miles MB, Huberman AM. Qualitative Data Analysis: An Expanded Sourcebook. Thousand Oaks, CA: Sage; 1994.
10. Pope C, Maya N. Reaching the parts other methods cannot reach: An introduction to qualitative methods in health and health service research. BMJ. 1995;311:42-45.
11. Britten N. Qualitative interviews in medical research. BMJ. 1995;311:251-253.
12. Mays N, Pope N. Rigour and qualitative research. BMJ. 1995;311:109-112.
13. Heath GW, Pratt M, Warren CW, Kann L. Physical activity patterns in American high school students: Results from the 1990 youth risk behavior survey. Arch Pediatr Adolesc Med. 1994;148:1131-1136.
14. Thompson JL, Davis SM, Gittlesohn J, Going S, Becenti A, Metcalfe L, Stone 2, Harnack L, Ring K. Patterns of physical activity among American Indian children: An assessment of barriers and support. J Community Health. 2001;26:423-445.
15. Wu TY, Pender N. Determinants of physical activity among Taiwanese adolescents: An application of the health promotion model. Res Nurs Health. 2002;25:25-36.
16. Leslie J, Yancy A, McCarthy W, Albert S, Wert C, Miles 0, James J. Development and implementation of a school-based nutrition and fitness promotion program for ethnically diverse middle-school girls. J Am Diet Assoc. 1999;99:967-970.

J A. O'Dea is a faculty member, Department of Education, University of Sydney, Australia, and a visiting scholar, Center for Weight and Health, Department of Nutritional Sciences, University of California, Berkeley, CA. Address correspondence to: Jennifer A. O'Dea, MPH, PhD, RD, University of Sydney, Faculty of Education, ASS, NSW 2006, Australia. E-mail: j.o'dea@edfac.usyd.edu.au

Body Image: How do you see yourself?

**How you feel about your body has a big impact on your health.
Learn to like the person you see in the mirror!**

Kathiann M. Kowalski

Brianna slipped quietly out of the house before dawn. She had lost 30 pounds by dieting, but now the weight was creeping back. She decided to try non-stop exercising for three days. Brianna wasn't thinking about missing school or even being alone by herself on the street. She would start walking and just keep going.

Fifteen hours later, Brianna walked into a police station. Her feet ached, and her sweat-pants were covered with burrs from wandering through a park. She was exhausted, scared, and hungry.

A poor body image had led to Brianna's eating disorder and depression. Her grand exercise plan failed, but it had one good outcome. Brianna finally got help dealing with her problem.

What You See and Feel

Body image is the way you see your body and how you feel about it. People with a healthy body image view themselves realistically and like their physical selves. People with a poor body image feel dissatisfied with their bodies, regardless of whether they are objectively healthy.

Different factors influence a teen's body image. "Certainly the media are setting standards for how girls and boys should look, defining what is beautiful in our culture," says Mimi Nichter. When the University of Arizona professor interviewed girls for her book, Fat Talk: What Girls and Their Parents Say About Dieting, most girls chose a "Barbie-doll" look: tall, thin, and large-breasted.

That same image pervades many ads on television and in magazines. When it comes to males, the media emphasize a tall, lean, muscular look. "People are paid to create an image or an illusion," says Sarah Stinson, head of the eating disorders program at Fairview Red Wing Health Services in Minnesota.

Only about 2 percent of women are as thin as most models, says the National Eating Disorders Association. Models work full-time with exercise trainers, makeup artists, and others to maintain their appearance. At photo shoots, clips and weights mold clothes to flatter a model's body. Once images are shot, computer artists take over. They airbrush pictures to remove any flaws. They can even change the shape of the bodies in the pictures. Thus, the standard media images of beauty often aren't true to life.

Faced with such unrealistic ideals, most teens feel worse about their bodies after reading teen fashion magazines. For those who felt unaccepted or unappreciated in their social environment—up to one-third of girls in one study—the effects lasted longer, according to Eric Stice at the University of Texas at Austin.

"From my perspective," says Stice, "this study is very damning for the mass media." In real life, he adds, most boys think a starved waif look is ugly for girls. And most girls don't like seeing mega-muscles on guys.

Peer pressure also influences a teen's body image. "Teasing can be very painful," says Nichter. "Kids seem to remember that for a very long time."

Frequently talking about weight can wear down someone's body image too. "I guess I started thinking I was fat at the start of high school," says Brianna. "Girls talk about it all the time at school—who's on diets. I would compare myself to other people, and I guess I thought I was fat."

"The majority of young women feel insecure," says Stinson. "What's happening is they're projecting those insecurities on each other, and you're getting this very competitive environment."

Families factor in too. When Brianna was little, her father sometimes commented on her eating a lot. Her brother sometimes called her a "fat pig." In other families, parents may tell a boy to eat so he grows up "big and strong." Or they may wistfully say that a daughter has "such a pretty face"—implying that the rest of her body is ugly.

Growing Pains

Young people internalize those messages. In a study by the Centers for Disease Control and Prevention (CDC), around 30 percent of students thought they were overweight. In reality, less than 14 percent of students were "at risk for becoming overweight." (The term refers to students whose body mass index was above the 85th percentile.)

Yet the 14 percent figure is also a problem. Nearly one-third of students get little or no physical activity, reports the CDC. Higher weight and a sedentary lifestyle increase the risks for diabetes, heart disease, and other health problems. Meanwhile, young people at the higher ranges of the weight scale often feel more frustrated by the gap between what they see in the mirror and what they see in the media.

Puberty complicates things. Girls get taller and gain an average of 25 pounds. They need the added fat for breast development and to enable them to conceive and carry babies as adults.

"Young women don't believe that they should gain fat," says Stinson. "They're terrified of it and don't understand the healthy role of natural body fat in development."

Boys get taller and more muscular as their bodies mature. That's generally consistent with our culture's ideal for males. But not all boys mature at the same rate. And not everyone gains muscle like the images featured in sports and fitness magazines.

When Problems Arise

When teens have a poor body image, self-esteem dips. Relationships suffer too. Conversations with friends may center on dieting and exercise, to the exclusion of other topics. Teens focus more on how they look than on what they want to accomplish in life. Instead of bonding with each other, teens often become competitive. That fuels feelings of isolation.

In the worst cases, eating disorders and other unhealthy behaviors develop. Eating disorders are more common among females than males. Yet the National Eating Disorders Association says about 10 percent of patients are male. (Besides a poor body image, other factors are often to blame. These include feelings of being out of control and, in some cases, a history of physical or sexual abuse.)

Brianna had anorexia nervosa. She did not eat enough to maintain a normal weight for her height. Besides looking very thin, she felt weak and had dizzy spells. Because girls need a certain level of body fat to menstruate, she stopped getting her period regularly. With her immune system weakened, Brianna came down with pneumonia during her sophomore year. Plus, Brianna recalls, "I lost hair. And I was cold all the time."

In addition to these problems, anorexia can cause loss of bone density, dehydration, and downy hair on the skin. When the heart muscle weakens and blood pressure drops too low, fatal heart failure can happen. By experimenting with diet pills, Brianna added to that risk. Even "natural" weight loss products can over-stimulate the heart and cause heart attacks.

Binge eating disorder involves frequent episodes of uncontrolled eating, without regard to physical hunger or fullness. Patients suffer from guilt, shame, or disgust with their behavior. They often gain weight, which adds to any body image problems.

A person with bulimia experiences cycles of binging and purging. Even if a patient's weight stays normal, frequent vomiting causes decaying tooth enamel, swollen glands, a sore throat, and a puffy face. If patients take laxatives, they risk damage to their digestive systems and suffer from nutrient deficiencies.

Exercise bulimia compensates for eating with excessive physical activity. In her junior year of high school, actress Jamie Lynn Sigler exercised every day for hours. Her weight dropped to 90 pounds.

"As time went on, it began to take over my life and interfere with other things that were important to me," Jamie recalled, "like hanging out with my friends, my family, dance and theatre, and even my health." When she began thinking about suicide, Jamie finally confided in her parents. The book Wise Girl: What I've Learned About Life, Love, and Loss tells the story of her recovery.

Body dysmorphia, a distorted body image, can also lead to excessive bodybuilding, especially among boys. Some also abuse steroids—drugs that unnaturally mimic the hormone testosterone to spur muscle growth. Risks of steroid abuse include possible outbreaks of violence during use and depression after cycling off the drugs, plus other physical and psychological consequences.

"When you have an eating disorder, you really don't want to talk about it," said Sigler. "You get very defensive. You isolate yourself a lot." If you're concerned about a friend, keep telling that person, "I'm here for you when you're ready to talk about it."

Building a Healthier Body Image

A doctor specializing in eating disorders gave Brianna a thorough check-up and prescribed medicine to help her clinical depression. Brianna also meets regularly with a psychologist, who has given her strategies to build a healthier body image.

"She had me write a list of things I like about myself," says Brianna. "When I start comparing myself to people, I think of one of those things rather than thinking, 'Oh, she looks so good and I look so bad.'" Among other things, Brianna is very intelligent. She is a hard worker. She is great at ballet. She plays the flute beautifully. And she likes her pretty blonde hair and blue eyes.

Dance class can still be a challenge, since the other advanced students are very thin. Brianna is learning to accept that people have different body shapes: ectomorphic, mesomorphic, and endomorphic. Ectomorphic people are very thin. Mesomorphic people are muscular. Endomorphic people tend to carry more fat. Many people's bodies mix these characteristics. Thus, one part of the body may be muscular, while another part may gain fat easily.

Brianna also met with a dietitian. When she was constantly dieting, she skipped meals. By nighttime she was so hungry that she might eat half a box of cereal. Now she's eating regular meals and including a reasonable amount of fat. She feels healthier and stronger. Now that she's eating regular meals again, she socializes more with other students at lunchtime too.

Another helpful strategy is to change the pattern of "fat talk" among friends. Sometimes teens join in the talk as a way to fit in. Other times, "I feel fat" can be code for other feelings that young people feel uncomfortable talking about: loneliness, disappointment, anger, insecurity, and so on. If teens encourage each other to talk about what's really bothering them, they can break the cycle of putting their bodies down. Clearer communication also frees teens to help each other deal with problems constructively.

Taking Charge

The media emphasize unrealistic standards of beauty. But, says Stinson, "You don't have to buy into these messages." She encourages young people to become activists: Write letters to companies praising ads that show normal teens with different body shapes and sizes. Conversely, send complaints and boycott companies that exploit young people by sexualizing them or glorifying thinness.

Don't fall prey to the dieting industry either.

Even "natural" weight-loss pills can contain stimulants that cause serious health problems. And despite "money-back guarantees," diet gizmos and gimmicks don't work. If any one did work, would Americans continue to spend $40 billion a year on books, diet programs, pills, gadgets, and everything else the dieting industry produces?

You can help educate other young people about having a healthy body image. In Minnesota, teen members of Red Wing GO GIRLS! make frequent presentations to help other young people develop a positive body image. By teaching others, the teens have become role models who are very proud of their own bodies.

Your Body, Your Health

"It's not your weight that determines your health," says Stinson. "It's your lifestyle." Here are some tips for a healthy lifestyle:

- Eat a variety of foods when you're physically hungry. Refer to the U.S. Department of Agriculture's Food Guide Pyramid www.nal.usda.gov:8001/py/pmap.htm).
- Don't forget the calcium: The Food and Drug Administration (FDA) recommends four servings of calcium-rich foods a day for teens.

- Enjoy regular physical activities. Aim for at least 30 minutes a day most days of the week. Set realistic goals for yourself, and have a good time. The more your body can do, the better you'll feel about it.

Brianna is enjoying dance more now. She also has joined her school's swim team and enjoys the camaraderie with her teammates. When the team members feel tired after a practice, it's a good feeling. "As long as you're healthy and active, and your body is doing everything it's supposed to do, there's nothing wrong with your body shape," she says.

Based on her experience, Brianna adds this message to teens: "You're OK the way you are. Think of the many great things you are—you're like no one else. Just don't ever try to compare yourself with anyone because it's not worth it. You have to be yourself."

Reality Check: Show YOUR Appreciation

Real life heroes aren't people who stand around looking good. They're people who accomplish things and share their talents with others. In fact, you may be surprised about the things other people admire in you.

Try the following exercise:

1. Sit down with a group of classmates. Let each person take turns telling every other person something positive that they sincerely appreciate about the other person. The positive thing must be something other than physical appearance.
2. When group members hear something positive about themselves, they must look directly at the speaker and say thank you. No mumbling allowed!
3. Promise aloud to go for a week without commenting at all on anyone's weight or physical appearance. Enforce the agreement among yourselves.
4. For an added challenge, avoid looking at yourself in the mirror for two days. Talk with classmates about how hard or easy it was.

How WEIGHT CHANGES Can Affect You

If you think losing 10 or even 20 pounds will make life wonderful, think again. The standard media images of beauty are not realistic. Even if you lost weight, you probably still would not match that ideal.

Initially, people who lose weight often feel proud of themselves. When many people hit a plateau, they feel frustrated. Weight levels off, despite continued dieting. The body naturally resists losing more than a small percentage of its weight too quickly. The metabolism slows down.

The National Eating Disorders Association says that 95 percent of people who diet gain back the weight within one to five years. That yo-yo effect places physical stress on the body. Gaining the weight back can further damage self-esteem.

More important, weight loss won't make all of life's problems go away. Dating and other social encounters can still be rocky. Family relationships can still be perplexing. School and work remain challenging.

Before you try to lose any weight, talk to your doctor or a dietitian. Body mass index (BMI) varies tremendously. Health professionals usually recommend weight loss only for people at the high end of the range. (BMI equals weight in pounds divided by height in inches, divided by height in inches again, multiplied by 703.)

Instead of going on a diet, many health professionals stress a healthy lifestyle. That includes a reasonable amount of enjoyable physical activity. It also includes healthy eating behaviors. Instead of wolfing down food on the run, for example, try slowing down and enjoying what you're eating. You can also learn to make smart nutrition choices by watching serving sizes and keeping the USDA's Food Guide Pyramid in mind.

From *Current Health 2*, Vol. 29, No. 7, March 2003, pp. 6-12. © 2003 by Weekly Reader Corporation. Reprinted with permission.

UNIT 3
Cognitive Growth and Education

Unit Selections

Key Points to Consider

- Should schools be the focal point of a teen's attention?

- Why does school violence occur and what can we do to prevent it?

- What types of students have problems that make school transitions difficult for them?

- Is it fair to students to administer standardized tests? How are test scores utilized in the first place? Why are girls' scores higher on such tests?

- Do you know students who cheat in school? Why do they cheat? How can schools prevent academic dishonesty?

- What factors, social or otherwise, detract from academic performance? How can educators and parents focus adolescents on their studies?

 **Links: www.dushkin.com/online/**
These sites are annotated in the World Wide Web pages.

At-Risk Children and Youth
http://www.ncrel.org/sdrs/areas/at0cont.htm

PhotoLink/Getty Images

Adolescence entails changes in cognitive capacities that are just as monumental as the biological changes. Whereas children tend to be more literal, more tied to reality and to the familiar—adolescents are more abstract, systematic, and logical. Adolescents can appreciate metaphor and sarcasm, they can easily think about things that do not exist, they can test abstract ideas against reality, and they can readily conceive of multiple possibilities. Many of these improvements in thinking ability contribute to conflicts with adults as adolescents become better able to argue a point or take a stand. They are better at planning out their case and at anticipating counterarguments. They are also more likely to question the way things are because they can now conceive of alternate possibilities.

The study of the cognitive changes that occur in adolescence has largely been based on the work of the Swiss psychologist, Jean Piaget, and his colleague Barbel Inhelder. Piaget and Inhelder described the adolescent as reasoning at the *formal operational stage*. Children from the approximate ages of 7 to 11 years old were described as being in the "*concrete operational*" stage. Although not all researchers agree with Piaget and Inhelder that changes in adolescent cognitive abilities represent true stage-related changes, they do agree that adolescent thought is characteristically more logical, abstract, and hypothetical than that of children. Recognize, though, that having certain mental capacities does not mean that adolescents, or even adults for that matter, will always reason at their rational best!

Piaget's views on cognitive development have been very influential, particularly in the field of education. Awareness of the cognitive abilities and shortcomings of adolescents can make their behaviors more comprehensible to parents, teachers, counselors, and other professionals who work with them. Similarly, as Piaget suggested, schools need to take the developmental abilities and needs of adolescents into account in planning programs and designing curricula. In addition, Piaget's general philosophy was that learning must be *active*. Others in the field of education, however, caution that there are other important issues left unaddressed by Piaget. For example, the U.S. has an elevated school dropout rate, so we need to find alternatives for keeping disaffected and alienated youth in school.

Building on the work of Piaget and Inhelder, David Elkind has argued that the newly emerging formal operational cognitive abilities of adolescents lead to some troublesome consequences. For one thing, adolescents tend to over intellectualize. They often make things too complex and fail to see the obvious, a phenomenon that Elkind calls *pseudostupidity*. Teachers often bear the brunt of this as adolescents overanalyze every word of a multiple-choice question. Elkind also maintains that much of the extreme self-consciousness of adolescents occurs because they construct an *imaginary audience*. Formal operations make it possible for adolescents to think about other people's thoughts. Adolescents lose perspective and think that others are constantly watching them and thinking about them. A related mistake is that adolescents are likely to believe that everyone shares their concerns and knows their thoughts. This belief, that one is at the center of attention, further leads to the development of what Elkind calls the *personal fable*. Namely, if everyone is paying so much attention to me I must be special and invulnerable. Bad things won't happen to me. I won't get in a car crash. I won't get pregnant. These phenomena—pseudostupidity, the imaginary audience, and the personal fable—diminish as adolescents' cognitive abilities mature and as they develop friendships in which intimacies are shared. Peer interaction helps adolescents see that they are not as unique as they thought, nor are they the focus of everyone else's attention.

The first subsection of this unit consequently pertains to school issues. The first article discusses school alienation, class cutting,

45

and violence. The authors, Fallis and Opotow, contend that schools do not see the above issues systemically. Rather, schools focus on individual students and on punishment. Only when schools take student concerns into account will schools become environments that stimulate attendance, interest, and harmony. The second article addresses one of these topics in more detail—school violence. School violence by disenchanted youth has peaked in the U.S. Schools need to promote a sense of belonging or a sense of community if disaffected and potentially violent students are to become members of the school community.

One point at which school problems are somewhat predictable is during school transitions, especially from junior high to high school. These transitions may be even more difficult for disabled students who can be stigmatized by and estranged from other students. How schools can create smoother, less stressful transitions for disabled and other students is the focus of the fourth article in this unit.

Finally, the last essay in the subsection on schools describes the role of technology in today's schools. Many schools have become so media-oriented that teachers, parents, and administrators may wonder whether the traditional classroom will survive. The authors of this essay predict that the conventional classroom as we know it is certain to survive for a long time.

The second subsection of this unit pertains to measuring and explaining academic performance. While developmentalists in the Piagetian tradition focus on the ways in which the thought processes of children and adolescents differ, other researchers have taken a different tack—a psychometric approach. In this approach, the emphasis is on quantifying cognitive abilities such as verbal ability, mathematical ability, and general intelligence (IQ). The measurement of intelligence, as well as the very definition of intelligence, has been controversial for decades. A classic question is whether intelligence is best conceptualized as a general capacity that underlies many diverse abilities or as a set of specific abilities. Traditional IQ tests focus on abilities that relate to success in school and ignore abilities such as those that tap creativity, mechanical aptitude, or practical intelligence.

The role of genetic versus environmental contributions to intelligence has also been controversial. At the turn of the century the predominant view was that intelligence was essentially inherited and was little influenced by experience. Today, the consensus is that an individual's intelligence is very much a product of both nature and nurture. Even greater controversy centers on the role that heredity versus the environment plays in explaining racial, ethnic, and gender differences in performance on various cognitive tests such as IQ tests.

Adolescents clearly have larger vocabularies, more mathematical knowledge, better spatial ability, etc., than children. Their memories are better because they process information more efficiently and use memory strategies more effectively. Adolescents possess a greater general knowledge base than children, which enables adolescents to link new concepts to existing ideas. Stated another way, *psychometric intelligence may well increase with age*. On the other hand, because of comparisons to age peers, the relative performance of adolescents on aptitude tests *remains fairly stable*. A 9-year-old child's outstanding performance on an IQ test, for example, is fairly predictive that the same individual's IQ score at age 15 will be better than the score of most peers.

Performance on standardized tests, IQ or otherwise (e.g. achievement tests), is often used to place junior high and high school students in ability tracks, a practice that increasingly is questioned. Similarly, standardized test results compared across schools are being used to measure a school's educational effectiveness. These types of issues are addressed in the following set of articles.

The first article on measurement presents a general overview of standardized testing, a multi-million dollar industry. Because testing not only measures the students' performance but the school's performance as well, teachers must make a choice about whether to teach to the test or teach to the school's curriculum and to preordained learning goals. Along the same lines of reasoning, the prevalence of such tests and their use to measure all kinds of performance in schools has ratcheted up the pressure for students to perform well. We thus have witnessed a surge in academic dishonesty or cheating among students. The next article examines cheating in high school and how it can be curbed.

Our schools do not exist in a vacuum. There are other factors that affect how adolescents perform in school. For instance, today's students have a choice of subjects and learning methods outside of school. Television and the internet come to mind as easy (and highly controversial) resources for all manner of adolescent learning. The third article in this series scrutinizes television. The authors, Thompson and Austin, review the literature on TV viewing and school performance. They conclude that there is a link between viewing and poor performance. It is unclear, however, whether too much TV viewing results in poor academic achievement or whether poor academic achievement produces too much television watching.

The last article in this unit discusses why girls outperform boys in school. For example, girls enroll in college in larger numbers and are likely to outscore boys on standardized tests. The article adopts the stance that schools can do more to make these situations equitable for boys.

Are Students Failing School or are Schools Failing Students?

Class cutting in high school. (Youth Confronting Public Institutions)

R. Kirk Fallis; Susan Opotow

In many urban public high schools today, students navigate their day by selectively cutting class leading to course failure and dropping out. Collaborative, qualitative research conducted with urban high school students indicates that cutting results from disengagement and alienation that students label "boredom." Focus group data (N = 160 in 8 groups) indicate that class cutting has not only an individual component that schools address, but also a systemic, conflictual component that schools do not address. These unaddressed, intransigent conflicts can foster moral exclusion and structural violence. These data suggest that rather than relying on standard punitive approaches, schools can respond to class cutting more effectively by taking students' concerns seriously, working collaboratively with students, and engaging in institutional self-scrutiny.

Class cutting (also called "skipping" or "ditching") is selective class attendance that occurs when a student comes to school, is marked present, but fails to attend particular classes without a legitimate reason. Decades ago cutting was a rare escapade for ordinarily compliant students or chronic behavior for a handful of students labeled "loafers" or "losers." Now, however, class cutting is neither rare nor characteristic only of miscreants. In many high schools today, particularly urban public schools that predominantly serve low-income students, more students navigate their school day by selectively cutting class than do not (Opotow, 1994; Opotow, Fortune, Baxter & Sanon, 1998). While it is tempting to view students who cut class as deficient in their academic capability, intelligence, motivation, or values, teachers dispute this stereotype and describe students who cut class as intellectually and academically similar to their regularly-attending peers (Opotow, 1995a).

This paper describes the prevalence of class cutting, the way schools address it, and student perceptions of class cutting. Although class cutting seems prosaic rather than violent, our qualitative data indicate that class cutting is symptomatic of intransigent institutional conflict which, in turn, is fertile ground for moral exclusion (Opotow, 1990) in which some kinds of people are seen as outside the boundaries for fairness and, ultimately, for structural violence (Galtung, 1969) in which harm is gradual, chronic, and invisible. While class cutting has an individual component, it must also be acknowledged as an institutional issue with costly consequences for students.

Class Cutting

Students "cut" when they utilize breaks in the school day to selectively skip class. They do so to avoid classes they dislike, see as too hard or too easy, or for which they are unprepared; to avoid particular peers or teachers with whom they are engaged in conflict; to attend to personal matters; as well as for a variety of other reasons. While missing one class can be inconsequential, with even a few cuts, students lose a sense of continuity, class work becomes difficult to follow, homework becomes difficult to complete, and tests become difficult to pass. To cope, students cut test days. As grades suffer and students fail class, their academic progress slows. Students then become discouraged and drop out (Opotow, 1994; Khaminwa, Fallis, & Opotow, 1999). Overage students (16 or 17 years of age) can be discharged or transferred to an alternative program or to a high school equivalency program where low retention statistics suggest they may not graduate (Hoyle, 1993; Fine, 1991).

Class cutting is a slippery slope; once begun, the academic damage it does is difficult to reverse. In sequential courses, critical pieces of information needed to understand new material are missed, and students who return to class can face a cold welcome from overburdened teachers (Opotow, 1994, 1995a). Ultimately, short-term stress reduction gained by class cutting can lead to greater stress from academic difficulties. Rather than innocuous, cutting is the slow-motion process of dropping out made class-by-class and day-by-day in students' daily lives.

Prevalence

Although class cutting is particularly common in urban public high schools (National Center for Education Statistics, 1996), it is also problematic outside urban centers, occurs in schools throughout the world, and begins as early as fifth grade and continues into college (Lynn, 1995; Mulvany, 1989; Wyatt, 1992). Aggregate data on class cutting are scarce. Few empirical studies compare the characteristics of schools with high levels of cutting with those that have lower levels (but see Hofmann, 1991), but research suggests that students attending large urban schools have higher rates of class cutting than students in smaller schools (Bryk & Driscoll, 1988; Fine & Somerville, 1998), and that cutting has increased over the past two decades. In 1984, one-third of the students at an urban high school in the northwest United States cut at least one class a day (Duckworth & deJung, 1989), while ten years later, data from three large cities (Boston, Chicago, and New York) indicate that two-thirds of students at some schools cut at least one class a day (Boston Public Schools, 1999; Opotow, Fortune, Baxter, & Sanon, 1998; Roderick, 1997). System-wide effects of class cutting are evident in increases in within-grade retention, delayed graduation, and transfers and discharges of students (cf. New York City Board of Education, 1993, 1997; Hoyle, 1993). Thus, in many schools, particularly large, urban high schools, class cutting has become an acceptable modus vivendi for a substantial proportion of students and has proven itself an intransigent problem that is unresponsive to standard methods of intervention (Mulvany, 1989).

Intervention

Cutting interventions often begin with the classroom teacher who decides whether a student's absence is excused and the kind of follow-up that is indicated. If the absence is unexcused, a teacher might call home and/or notify administrators, deans, or guidance counselors. Many schools also utilize computerized flagging procedures to identify students who have accumulated a spec-ified number of class absences over a given period. Regardless of specific procedures schools utilize to identify cutting, it is universally viewed as a disciplinary offense that triggers a variety of responses: parental notification, lowering of a course grade, failing a course, detention, suspension, and retention in grade. Staff and students report, however, that interventions designed to deter cutting—no matter how strict—are rarely effective. Some yield immediate but not sustained results; others are effective with some students but not all (Opotow, 1995a).

Surprisingly, given high proportion of students who cut class, schools do not identify cutting as a priority. Staff almost exclusively described cutting as an individual's problem and were unable to quantify cutting prevalence at their school or compare their school with others (Fallis, 2000). A staff member at one school said: "You see cutting itself is seen—it is not looked on—it is considered—ahhh—well, how can I say it?—it is almost like a pest—like a pesty thing. It is not considered that serious until there are other factors involved" (Fallis). A staff member at another school said: "But it is funny you talk about cutting, because cutting—we have so many other serious issues. Cutting is kind of overlooked" (Fallis, 2000). Not only can cutting be overlooked in schools, but responses to cutting tend to overlook students' understanding of class cutting. This paper focuses on students' perspectives and concerns to understand them and suggest their importance for practice.

Student Perspectives on Class Cutting

Methods

We studied class cutting in two cities in northeastern United States. Our primary research site in each city was a large urban public school (S1 = 3000 students; S2 = 1000 students). In each school, more than half the students were free-lunch eligible indicating low family incomes. Both schools had high dropout rates (22-42%), and although each school had considerable religious, ethnic, and national diversity, students were predominantly Black and Latino (94-98%).

In this paper, we report on data collected and analyzed collaboratively with two student researchers from S2 over a four-year period. In the first year the student researchers analyzed 10 interviews collected at S1. In the years that followed, student researchers collected qualitative data in focus groups (160 students in 8 groups) in which students described their perspectives on and reasons for class cutting. In this context, focus groups offer a number of benefits: they foster a collaborative atmosphere, students' comments create positive feedback loops, and students push themselves toward a deeper understanding of the issues at hand. This "spiraling effect" (Kahan, 2001) of focus groups is appropriately reported as products of the group rather than as comments attributed to particular individuals as would be the case for more individually-focused methods such as interviews.

Participants for focus groups were recruited by teachers in their schools and participation was voluntary. Student participants attended public high schools throughout the city, ranged from freshmen to seniors, and were members of ethnic and racial minority groups mirroring the demographics of cooperating schools. Student participants were told that our research examined students' views on class cutting. Following focus group sessions, student researchers worked collaboratively with university-based researchers to identify themes that emerged in focus group data. In reporting our findings we distinguish comments by student researchers Fredo Sanon and Maurice Baxter that emerged in post-focus group analytic discussions ("student researchers") from comments made by student participants in the focus groups ("students").

"Layered" collaborative research. Qualitative data analysis, the most labor-intensive of our research activities, evolved as taped discussions of puzzling or revealing statements in focus group transcripts. Because our topic garnered the interest of educators struggling with class cutting, we were periodically asked to present our research findings. Such dissemination efforts became part of our research process. In preparing for dissemination opportunities at conferences, for school committees, and in graduate education courses, the research process came alive. These dissemination opportunities challenged student researchers to become conceptually clear about their work. They prompted urgent, focused discussions (which were audio-taped) in which student researchers specified what they learned from their data and why it was important.

We describe this collaborative and cyclical research process as layered because each research activity—collecting, analyzing, and presenting research findings—led to new questions, additional data collection, analysis, presentations, and so on. Layering enabled the student researchers to acquire research and speaking skills while maintaining their interest during the slow process of qualitative analysis. Revisiting their data and findings, students' analyses became increasingly complex as they became aware of diverse perspectives and were able to identify contradictions in their own thinking around complex individual-institutional issues. Student researchers spoke with increasing clarity of what it meant to be a student in a large urban public school. Asked, "What was the research like?" Fredo Sanon said:

> It's like what we've been talking about. We were always talking about how cutting class did this or that. But when we started doing the surveys and the presentations we found out how and why. And it was real. It was there. Instead of us listening to what students

in the transcripts were feeling, we got to feel it. I guess the research has helped us to come to understand a reality. It makes you understand that it is not just you—that there are other things going on.

Student-centered research. The student-centered research approach we utilized is more time consuming than qualitative analytic methods that center on the skills and knowledge of a social scientist. However, student researchers' knowledge proved to be a valuable resource. They were able to connect the research to the daily realities of urban students and their analyses yielded insight into subtle contextual issues that would have otherwise remained hidden in the data. Instead of viewing high school students as subjects, we worked alongside them. This approach is a paradigm shift that is consistent with a research methodology advocated by Kurt Lewin (1948): "we should consider action, research, and training as a triangle that should be kept together." Thus, to understand complex organizational life in schools, our research became a process "in which knowledge-getting and knowledge-giving are an integrated process, and one that is valuable to all parties involved" (Friedlander and Brown, 1974; also see Cooperrider and Srivastva, 2000). Fredo Sanon described his engagement in the repetitive process of conducting research: "You got to learn a lot of things. We talked about some interesting topics. We really got into discussions and broke down why kids cut class. We were really committed. We wanted to know why." Students' commitment to knowing why provided us with the opportunity to understand class cutting as symptomatic of structural violence that claims so many students while remaining ineffectively addressed by urban public high schools.

Findings: Class Cutting and Boredom

In focus groups, students described class cutting as a reaction to educational structures that are sterile, bureaucratic, disrespectful of student's pedagogical preferences or goals, and that do not value student contributions. They also identified student, teacher, and staff burnout and the labeling of students as losers as additional causes of cutting (Sanon, Baxter, Fortune, & Opotow, 2001). A short-cut students use to label these alienating aspects of school is "boring."

Although the Oxford English Dictionary (1989) defines "boring" as tedious, wearying, and dull, it was only after talking with student researchers about boring for more than a year that we realized students use "boring" to mean this and more. For students, boring connotes a one-way, tops-down, unengaged relationship with a teacher whose pedagogy feels disrespectful because it is not designed to tempt, engage, or include students. In addition, for students, boring connotes something missing in their education, conveys a deep sense of disappointment, and casts class cutting as a coping mechanism for classes that fail to engage. Fredo Sanon said:

> Boredom is one person doing most of the talking. You are not doing anything. A lot of kids that we talked to said that the teacher makes it boring. Because if you know you are not getting good grades in that class and you know there is a chance you might fail then you're going to get bored because you don't want to do that work. I'm not going to do the work if I am going to fail anyway.

A student described classes as boring if they wold not help her be productive now or in the future:

> Well, for me, it's like the learning. There's only like a few classes I actually care about. Everything else is, like, pointless, because I'll never use it in my life ... If my teacher's not teaching me anything, then I'm gonna go to work. I'm not gonna sit here and waste my time and twiddle my thumbs when I could be doing something more productive.

Boredom and school. In addition to seeing boredom at the individual level as the failure to meet an individual's pedagogical preferences or aspirations, students see boredom also at the institutional level, as the way things are done in schools, such as high staff turnover or excessive teacher absence:

> I do not go to that class. I cut that class everyday because it's like—okay the teacher's not there and we're just gonna sit here and watch TV and read the newspaper. I can do that at home ... [or] if your teacher's not concerned about learning, you're not learning anything in that class, it's like a waste of your time. Why are you going to be there?

Students also see cutting as a coping response to lockstep pedagogy that does not work for everyone. Students see themselves as distinct and having their own motivators and skills. For some students, grades and doing homework are motivating; others care less about school or are more easily discouraged. One student said: "If the class is boring, I'm going to try only to a certain extent. If the class is real boring, I'm just going to say 'Forget it. Just give me the homework.'"

Students also noted that boredom in some classes resulted from the teacher's tendency to focus on a struggling student and ignore those who hunger for more: "They will cater to the people who don't learn, eh, who won't learn. They won't cater to everybody else." Another student said she cut because "every single day

we're learning the same thing." She described her frustration with the painfully slow pace as a dialogue with her teacher: "Why can't you teach me something else?" "Because, oh, that other kid didn't learn it." "There's 35 kids in the room and one kid didn't learn anything; and you make us stay there and watch this kid learn?"

In addition to boredom resulting from a curriculum that does not challenge or interest students, students who want to engage can be further challenged by peers who have become disengaged, fallen behind, and become disruptive. Student researcher Maurice Baxter said: "It's not all the teachers' fault. Some students just act up so bad that the teachers after awhile just don't even care. The students who do want to learn, they just miss out on that." Fredo Sanon described boredom and disengagement as elicited and shaped by institutional culture:

> That's learned behavior. That's something that, you know what I'm saying, is instilled in you ... Kids who used to care are gonna stop caring because, it's like— "Well, I'm in this environment and nobody else cares, so ... What am I gonna do?" You adapt to the environment. And if your teachers are just like, "forget it," you're like, "forget it" too. "I don't want to be here. I'm leaving."

Boredom and resources. At the societal level, students were keenly aware that pedagogical resources differed between schools and school systems. Comparing her school with an elite public high school, one student said: "That's another reason why people cut. 'Cause we don't have any, you know what I'm saying, anything—no reason to keep us here." She described attending a school that lacks resources not only as boring but also as a trap:

> You know, it's like going to the job where you work and you hate your job. Every chance you get to leave that job, you will leave. And there's nothing that we can do ... The difference between us going to school and having a job is you can quit the job and find another job. This school— we cannot go anywhere else. The only other school that offers things like that in [city] is [school]. And if you didn't get in in the seventh grade, then you know what I'm saying, all hope is lost for you unless you go to private school. But if your parents can't afford private school ... then you get stuck going to a school like this and you're just not learning.

Another student commented that his school, unlike suburban public schools, does not offer course selection that he might need or enjoy, such as courses on specific aspects of literature, language choices in addition to Spanish, and advanced placement. One student, comparing what he sees in the media with his own educational reality, stated:

> You see TV and, like, do these schools really exist? Because we don't have them here. It's like—it's not like a real high school. We don't even have pep-rallies. We don't have homecoming. We don't have an honor society. They don't have anything in this school.

The lack of elective choices, extra-curricular activities results in school environments that students see as sterile, uninviting, and boring.

Discussion: Class Cutting as Conflict, Exclusion, and Violence

In these data, when students state that teachers, counselors, or administrators "don't care" and that students cut class because they prefer to "do something more productive," they appear to be fobbing off blame for cutting on others. Rather than taken as a serious institutional critique, students' explanations about class cutting can be dismissed as self-serving, one-sided, shortsighted, and immature (cf. Roman, 1996). Yet, our analyses suggest that students' reasons for class cutting are thoughtful. In contrast to school personnel who tend to blame students and individualize the problem, students express a complex view that locates responsibility for class cutting in both individual behavior and its wider institutional context. Students described what they wanted and felt they deserved—caring and knowledgeable teachers they can count on to be there, a safe and individually-attuned learning environment, and resources that entice them. But they noted also that students have responsibilities. Reflecting on these data, Maurice Baxter said "kids have to motivate themselves instead of putting all the blame on teachers. It is a fifty-fifty thing from where I stand." Yet in spite of students' ability to articulate concerns connected with class cutting, their perceptions were largely ignored at the institutional and system level in interventions designed to deter cutting. This failure to take students' views seriously suggests that class cutting is behavior emerging from unaddressed intransigent conflicts, which have led to moral exclusion and structural violence.

Intransigent Conflict

Students describe class cutting as emerging in the context of conflicts, many of which concern institutional issues. Conflicts "exist whenever incompatible activities occur... An action that is incompatible with another action prevents, obstructs, interferes, injures, or in some way makes the latter less likely or less effective" (Deutsch, 1973).

School staff describe class cutting as occasionally leading to conflict involving students, parents, and the school, yet they also dismiss cutting as a "pesty thing" (Fallis, 2000). In class cutting some conflicts were overt but many remained latent and unaddressed.

Dropping out among minority youth has been connected to latent conflict also (cf. MacLeod, 1995). Michael Apple (1996) describes, "student rejection of so much of the content and form of day to day educational life bears on the almost unconscious realization that ... schooling will not enable them to go much further than they already are" (Bourdieu and Passeron, 1990; Gison & Ogbu, 1991). Edwin Farrell (1990) describes student dozing as latent conflict, echoing students' descriptions of cutting as disengagement:

> One major manifestation of resistance, in behavioral terms, is dozing. Putting your head down on the desk is a visual signal. It is difficult to believe, because of the numbers who do it, that it can be attributed to depression or fatigue. The fact that my [student researcher] used it to define boredom to me implies that the behavior has a shared meaning for this population. It is socially constructed just as boredom is. And because it is passive resistance, there is often teacher compliance.

As we have discussed, class cutting has proven robust as an institutional problem. Intransigent conflicts that resist standard solutions are often characterized by misdiagnoses that miss deeper issues such as the basic need for consistency, security, respect, justice, and a sense of personal control (Burton, 1990; Fisher, 1997). Because what is at stake remains unaddressed, the conflicts persist and fluctuate in intensity. When interventions are ill-conceived or are not anchored within an empirical and theoretical foundation that can show the logical sequence of steps from identifying the conflict to achieving its resolution, they can increase frustration, deepen conflict, and lead to destructive outcomes (Rothman, 1997; Rouhana, 1995). In the long run, avoiding, renaming, and denying conflict rather than addressing it is rarely effective; often it leads to higher overall costs to institutions and individuals (Costantino & Merchant, 1996).

When school staff approach class cutting at the behavioral, manifest level or in an ad hoc, freewheeling way that overlooks or oversimplifies deeper, unaddressed issues, they may not only fail to stem class cutting, but can also exacerbate negative conflict dynamics and even cause harm. In the context of class cutting, focusing on individuals is not an inherently problematic approach; it can be warranted and helpful. However, focusing exclusively on individuals biases the intervention by protecting interests of the organization and those with institutional power while excluding the perspective of those with low power (Rouhana & Korper, 1996). Describing cutting at the individual level as a "discipline issue" means that institutional self-scrutiny is not warranted because institutional responsibility is not implicated.

Within institutions, admitting responsibility for harmful outcomes can be difficult because it threatens the core identity of school professionals who see their personal and institutional goals as promoting student well-being (Hicks, 1999; see also Janeway, 1980; Pratto & Walker, 2001). Therefore, conventional approaches to class cutting that locate blame exclusively in students protect the institution and its staff from scrutiny. Students, lacking voices and institutional influence, are the perfect repository for blame. Thus, for school staff it may not be enough to want to do good. It may even not be enough to have success at interventions on the level of individual symptoms. At the very minimum, school staff need to look more closely at structural contexts that give rise to the intransigent conflicts that foster cutting. Conflicts, when recognized and addressed, can promote constructive change, but conflicts can also be destructive. Destructive conflicts are those that foster moral exclusion and rationalize harms that others experience.

Moral Exclusion

Moral exclusion is viewing some kinds of people as outside one's boundary for fairness or "scope of justice" (Deutsch, 1974) so that considerations of fairness do not apply to them, they are not seen as worthy of effort or sacrifice, and they are not seen as entitled to community resources (Opotow, 1987, 1990, 1995b). Harm experienced by those who are morally excluded does not elicit remorse or a sense of injustice. Instead it is rationalized, normalized, and viewed as the way things are or ought to be. Thus, moral exclusion is a theory that describes how negative social categorizations give rise to moral justifications and allow those outside the scope of justice to be harmed. In its severe form moral exclusion justifies human rights violations and mass murder. In its mild form moral exclusion justifies disparate access to opportunity and resources. Whether mild or severe, moral exclusion fosters viewing those outside the scope of justice as psychologically distant, unworthy of constructive obligations, expendable, undeserving, and eligible for processes and outcomes that would be unacceptable for those within our scope of justice (Opotow, 2001).

In class cutting we see subtle forms of moral exclusion when students who cut class are depicted as deserving harsh outcomes. When students are caught cutting class, admonished, and persist, their fate—including failure, transfer, expulsion, and long-term negative outcomes—can be seen as the student's own doing. A school staff member, recognizing the systemic problems faced by his largely African American student body, nonetheless said of students who "fall by the wayside" as the result of cutting: "Schools can not be everything to all kids. And they try to be—I think you have to have the, pardon my French, the balls to do what you tell them you're going to do. So if you cut you will get suspended" (Fallis, 2000). Moral exclusion was also evident in the tendency of staff members to talk about students who cut class negatively and to frame students simplistically as "good" or "bad." One teacher said, "You as the class room teacher know in the first week or second week of class who is going to be good or who is going to be bad and who is going to pass" (Fallis, 2000). This kind of thinking was also generalized from individuals to the student body as a whole. In explaining the make-up of his school, a staff member, sensitive to the institutional challenges his students faced, nevertheless disparaged them, saying: "I know what my particular situation is, we have, we're not getting the best at my school. Neither the best nor the brightest." At another school, too, a staff member stated "crack babies or the drug addicted babies—these are the kids that are at my school now" (Fallis, 2000).

Students are painfully aware that they are struggling against these negative categorizations and they intrude on their interactions with school staff. One student said,

> A lot of teachers do make it seem like they do not like you. I mean they may not want it to come out that way, but a lot of teachers do make it seem like "I don't like you. You don't have to come to my class"—I mean they don't say it to you but the way they talk to you, you can see it. The way a teacher talks to one kid and then the way he talks to you. I have one teacher who will talk to one student with a soft tone, and then he talks to me he feels that he must bring some force deep inside of his voice, to make him sound all tough. I will think in my head, "Why are you putting this front up? Why are you acting this way …?"

Another student expressed skepticism about his institutions' interest in addressing class cutting constructively: "Nah, they would be like, oh you know, 'stupid kids' or 'they don't want to learn'—[or the administration] will go like, 'oh, just a bunch of Black kids. They don't want to learn nothing.'"

Several students who had discussed class cutting with peers reflected on the marginality and invisibility of students who cut class:

- S1: We went around asking questions, because there were a lot of kids just hanging out. Hanging out in the hall. Literally hanging out. They were, I think, it was like on the 3rd floor especially.

- S2: [We] knew where the hiding places were.
- S3: They were like cockroaches; they did not care if anybody passed by.
- S1: If someone told them to move, they would just move to another area.
- S3: Even the teachers would not pay attention to them anymore.
- S2: Because they knew they were just going to go someplace else and it was just a waste of time.
- S1: And the teachers just didn't care.
- S3: Then they thought our interviewing them was just a joke, they were making fun, they were laughing, saying stupid comments—"Because we feel like it"; "Because the teacher does not give them work"—Which was a lie.

Not only were the students situated so that they were physically invisible to school staff, but they also internalized their invisibility. In hiding and joking, they concealed their desire for engagement in their schooling.

Framing class cutting with moral exclusion helps us understand how schools—trusted social institutions—can become locations of systemic violence in which a large proportion of students can be viewed as deserving invisibility, failure, and expulsion without eliciting a sense of injustice. Students are first seen as behaviorally, then as cognitively, and finally as morally deficient and therefore outside the scope of justice and, ultimately, the cause of their own debilitation. Moral exclusion, which flourishes in overt and latent conflict, can itself foster structural violence.

Structural Violence

The mismatch between the high prevalence and long-term costs of cutting for student and the ineffective, diffuse, and individually-focused responses of schools suggests that structural violence is a useful lens to understand class cutting. In contrast to direct violence which is committed by and on particular people, structural violence is gradual, chronic harm that occurs because of the way things are done, whose voice is heard or ignored, and who gets resources or goes without (Galtung, 1969). Structural violence debases people by treating them as irrelevant, but is difficult to isolate and examine. It remains invisible because responsibility for outcomes is diffused or denied by the way that institutions structure process and outcomes.

In class cutting, we see that injurious short- and long-term outcomes that accrue to students: (a) are not inflicted by any particular person; (b) are small, cumulative, hidden and institutionalized as the way cutting is and is not addressed; (c) occur for a substantial numbers of students who attend large public high schools in low-income urban communities; (d) are viewed as result of ill-considered student behavior rather than institutional process.

We also see that: (e) issues and complaints by students are dismissed as groundless griping; and (f) in spite of the prevalence of class cutting and its injurious effect on students, responses are ineffective, maintain an individual focus, and blame the victim.

Conclusions

Implications for Moral Exclusion Theory

Our analysis suggests that moral exclusion is the alchemy that transforms intransigent, unaddressed conflict into structural violence. It does so by facilitating a critical figure-ground shift that situates responsibility for negative outcomes in victims rather than in those with institutional resources and power. In class cutting this shift is evident when the outcomes of unnamed and unaddressed conflicts fall more heavily on those who are relatively powerless in an institutional/political hierarchy. The full weight of dysfunctional institutional systems is then borne by the strata least able to influence those systems or even give voice to their negative impacts.

Our analysis of class cutting also reveals that violence results from both exclusion and inclusion. Violence can result from processes that exclude students from school justified by class cutting. While acknowledging that students are minors, young, and making shortsighted, counter-productive decisions, standard school interventions nevertheless treat students as competent, warranting such institutional consequences as transfer and expulsion. Violence also occurs as a consequence of inclusion of students in an institutional context in which they have no choice, in which they are exposed to forces over which they have no control, and as a result, have little chance of gaining what they want and need on their own terms. Thus, in schools that students find alienating and insensitive to their needs and goals, they have two choices. They can endure a dysfunctional system, succumb to systemic pressures, and suffer institutional systems that may psychologically debase. Or, as an alternative, they can take actions which may grant relief in the short term, such as cutting or dropping out, but suffer such long term consequences as decreased educational attainment and career opportunities. While either of these negative options are occurring, the complicity of the organization and its institutional processes that debase—clearly part of students' problems with schooling that leads to cutting—eludes scrutiny.

Implications for School Policy

Class cutting is an intransigent problem and capable of defying standard school interventions. In class cutting, we see structural violence flourishing when schools seek to preserve their sense of efficacy and worthiness by situating their problem in low-power individuals. Although

53

small schools have the potential to positively transform educational environments (cf. Fine & Somerville, 1998), they are not the daily reality of most urban high school students. It is not the size of small schools that yields benefits to students, per se, but the opportunities they can offer students for engagement.

Our data and analysis suggest that, rather than getting tough and investing time and money in punitive interventions and security systems, school can approach class cutting with a stronger knowledge base by fostering student voice and engagement. When viewed as student critique and feedback, class cutting can be an opportunity to elicit student input to better understand students' experiences, perspectives, and hopes; to engage students as active members of the school community; and to utilize students' class attending choices to guide institutional change. Schools would benefit from student guidance in the design of institutional interventions. As these data indicate, when students lack the opportunity to participate, offer their perspective, and have it acted upon, they may find themselves faced with institutional conditions they find untenable. When schools fail to engage students in constructive forms of conflict resolution they miss an opportunity to teach students appropriate and useful methods for dealing with conflict in institutional life.

In contrast, when young people are provided with opportunities to expand their conflict coping repertoires and negotiation skills, they will be able to deal with life circumstances in ways that facilitate their physical and psychological health and well-being rather than being debilitated by circumstances (Frydenberg, 1997). Designing school processes and structures is an opportunity to elicit students' participation, encourage students to air their feelings and describe their experiences, and for students to understand that they have been heard and have something to contribute. This will not only help them learn how to express themselves effectively but it will also give them opportunities to relate to the school staff in creative and constructive ways. Inclusion, however, needs to be significant, and neither illusory nor superficial. Students understand when they have real, transformative voice or only expressive voice and the appearance of participation (cf. Sampson, 1993).

The collaborative, long-term research method that emerged in our efforts to understand class cutting models the approach we suggest schools take. Maurice Baxter captures the way that the tedium and effort of research—similar to schoolwork—can promote engagement, discovery, learning, conceptual integration, connection, respect, and personal growth:

> We were doing the same thing over and over. But in some way it always changed and we ended up somewhere different. Every time we talked we came up with some more elaboration or more detail. Every time we came in we had

something different. We did get a lot out of the research: the patience, the reviewing things, just learning things, working with people, accepting other people's views, respecting their views, and trying to get one bigger or better view—trying to pull it all together.

References

Apple, M. W. (1996). Cultural politics and education. New York: Teachers College Press. Boston Public Schools. (1999). Boston Public Schools, Year Report 1999. Boston: Boston Public School Committee.

Bourdieu, P., & Passeron, J. C. (1990). Reproduction in education, society, and culture. London: Sage Press.

Bryk, A., & Driscoll, M. (1988). The high school as community: Contextual influences and consequences for students and teachers. Madison, WI: National Center on Effective Secondary Schools.

Burton, J. (1990). Conflict: Resolution and prevention. New York: St. Martin's Press.

Cooperrider, D. L., & Srivastva, S. (2000). Appreciative inquiry in organizational life. In D. L. Cooperrider, P. F. Sorenson, Jr., D. Whitney, & T. F. Yaeger (Eds.), Appreciative inquiry: Rethinking human organization toward a positive theory of change (pp. 55-97). Champaign, IL: Stipes Publishing.

Costantino, C. A., & Merchant, C. S. (1996). Designing conflict management systems. San Francisco, CA: Jossey-Bass.

Deutsch, M. (1973). The resolution of conflict. New Haven, CT: Yale University Press.

Deutsch, M. (1974). Awakening the sense of injustice. In M. Lerner & M. Ross (Eds.), The quest for justice: Myth, reality, ideal. Canada: Holt, Rinehart, & Winston.

Duckworth, K., & deJung, J. (1989). Inhibiting class cutting among high school students. High School Journal, 72(4), 188-195.

Fallis, R. K. (2000). An analysis of social influence in class cutting: Student-counselor negotiations. Master's project, University of Massachusetts Boston, Boston, MA.

Farrell, E. (1990). Hanging in and dropping-out: Voices of at risk high school students. New York: Teachers College Press.

Fine, M. (1991). Framing dropouts: Notes on the politics of an urban high school. Albany: SUNY Press.

Fine, M., & Somerville, J. (1998). Small schools big imagination: A creative look at urban public schools. Chicago: Cross City Campaign for Urban School Reform.

Fisher, R. J. (1997). Interactive conflict resolution. Syracuse, NY: Syracuse University Press.

Friedlander, F., & Brown, L. (1974). Organization development. Annual Review of Psychology, 25, 313-341.

Frydenberg, E. (1997). Adolescent coping: Theoretical and research perspectives. London: Routledge.

Galtung, J. (1969). Violence, peace and peace research. Journal of Peace Research, 3, 167-191.

Gison, M. A., & Ogbu, J. U. (1991). Minority status and schooling. New York: Garland.

Hicks, D. (1999, June 22). How functional aspects of identity become dysfunctional in protracted conflict. Unpublished paper presented at the 12th annual conference of the International Association for Conflict Management, San Sebastian-Donostia, Spain.

Hofmann, W. P. (1991). The effects of computerized attendance systems on teacher attendance with-itness and student attendance. (Doctoral Dissertation, University of Miami, Florida, 1991). Dissertation Abstracts International #AAT 9214822.

Hoyle, J. R. (1993). Our children: Dropouts, pushouts, and burnouts. People and Education, 1(1) 26-41.

Janeway, E. (1980). Powers of the weak. New York: Knopf.

Kahan, P. (2001). Focus groups as a tool for policy analysis. Analyses of Social Issues and Public Policy, 1(1), 129-146.

Khaminwa, A., Fallis, R. K., & Opotow, S. (1999). Cutting in high schools. Australian Journal of Guidance Counseling, 9(1), 193-204.

Kipnis, D. (1976). The powerholders. Chicago: University of Chicago Press.

Lewin, K. (1948). Action research and minority problems. In G. W. Lewin (Ed.), Resolving social conflicts. New York: Harper and Row.

Lynn, P. (1995). The 1993 Leavers: The Scottish School Leavers' survey. Edinburgh: Scottish Office Education Department.

MacLeod, J. (1995). Ain't no makin' it: Aspirations and attainment in a low income neighborhood. San Francisco, CA: Westview Press.

Mulvany, J. (1989). Social control processes, activities and ideologies: The case of non-attendance in Melbourne. Australian and New Zealand Journal of Sociology, 25(2), 222-238.

National Center for Education Statistics (NCES). (1996). NELS:88, National longitudinal study: 1988-1994; Data files and electronic codebook system. Third follow-up. Washington, DC: U.S. Department of Education.

New York City Board of Education. (1993). The cohort report: Four-year results for the class of 1992 and follow-ups for the classes of 1989, 1990, and 1991 and the 1991-1992 annual dropout rate. New York: Division of Planning, Research, and Development, Board of Education of the City of New York.

New York City Board of Education. (1997). The class of 1997: Four year longitudinal report and 1996-1997 event dropout rates. New York: Division of Assessment and Accountability, Board of Education of the City of New York.

Opotow, S. (1987). Limits of fairness: An experimental examination of antecedents of the scope of justice. (Doctoral dissertation, Columbia University, 1987). Dissertation Abstracts International, DAI-B 48/08.

Opotow, S. (1990). Moral exclusion and injustice: An introduction. Journal of Social Issues, 46(1), 1-20.

Opotow, S. (1994, August). "Breaking out": Class cutting in an inner-city high school. Paper presented at the annual meeting of the American Psychological Association, Los Angeles, CA.

Opotow, S. (1995a, August). The "cutting" epidemic: How high school teachers respond and adapt. Paper presented at the annual meeting of the American Psychological Association, New York.

Opotow, S. (1995b). Drawing the line: Social categorization and moral exclusion. In J. Z. Rubin & B. B. Bunker (Eds.), Conflict, cooperation, and justice (pp. 347-369). San Francisco, CA: Jossey-Bass.

Opotow, S. (2001). Social injustice. In D. J. Christie, R. V. Wagner, & D. D. Winer (Eds.), Peace, conflict, and violence: Peace psychology for the 21st century (pp. 102-109). Upper Saddle River, NJ: Prentice Hall.

Opotow, S., Fortune, L., Baxter, M., & Sanon, F. (1998, June). Conflict, coping, and class cutting: Perspectives of urban high school students. Paper presented at the biannual meeting of the Society for the Psychological Study of Social Issues, Ann Arbor, MI.

Pratto, F., & Walker, A. (2001). Dominance in disguise. In A. Y. Lee-Chai & J. A. Bargh (Eds.), The use and abuse of power: Multiple perspectives on the causes of corruption. Philadelphia, PA: Psychology Press.

Roderick, M. (1997, July). Habits hard to break: A new look at truancy in Chicago's public high schools. Chicago: Consortium on Chicago School Research.

Roman, L. G. (1996). Spectacle in the dark: Youth as transgression, display, and repression. Educational Theory, 46(1), 1-22.

Rothman, J. (1997). Resolving identity-based conflict in nations, organizations, and communities. San Francisco, CA: Jossey Bass.

Rouhana, N. N. (1995). Unofficial third-party intervention in international conflict: Between legitimacy and disarray. Negotiation Journal, 11(3), 255-271.

Rouhana, N. N., & Korper, S. K. (1996). Dealing with dilemmas posed by power asymmetry in intergroup conflict. Negotiation Journal, 12(4), 353-366.

Sampson, E. E. (1993). Identity politics: Challenges to psychology's understanding. American Psychologist, 48(12), 1219-1230.

Sanon, F., Baxter, M., Fortune, L., & Opotow, S. (2001). Class cutting: Perspectives of urban high school students. In J. Shultz & A. Cook-Sather (Eds.), Student voices: Middle and high school students' perspectives on school and schooling. Lanham, MD: Rowman & Littlefield.

Simpson, J. A., & Weiner, E. S. C. (Eds.). (1989). Oxford English dictionary (2nd ed.). Oxford, UK: Oxford University.

Wyatt, G. (1992). Skipping class: An analysis of absenteeism among first year college students. Teaching Sociology, 20(3), 201-207.

KIRK FALLIS is a graduate student in the International Studies Program at the Golden Gate University School of Law. He has practiced law in Toronto, Canada, where he was called to the bar in 1992. He holds a certificate from the Canadian International Institute of Negotiation. He completed the master's degree in the Graduate Program in Dispute Resolution at the University of Massachusetts Boston, has participated in the Program for the Instruction of Lawyers at Harvard, the Program on Negotiation at Radcliffe College, and has served as a mediator in community programs in Toronto, Ontario, and in Boston. His research focuses on power asymmetries and implicit negotiations in organizational conflicts.

SUSAN OPOTOW is an associate professor in the Graduate Programs in Dispute Resolution at the University of Massachusetts Boston. She received her PhD from Columbia University in social and organizational psychology. Her research examines social psychological conditions justifying moral exclusion to understand the conditions that allow us to see others as outside the scope of justice and as eligible for exploitation and harm. Her work describes the implications of moral exclusion in schooling, environmental conflict, and public policy debates over fairness, such as affirmative action. She is associate editor of Peace and Conflict: Journal of Peace Psychology, and was issue editor for two issues of Journal of Social Issues, one on "Moral Exclusion and Injustice" (1990) and the other on "Green Justice: Conceptions of Fairness and the Natural World" (1994, with Susan Clayton). She edited, also, an issue of Social Justice Research on "Affirmative Action and Social Justice" (1992).

From *Journal of Social Issues*, Vol. 59, No. 1, Spring 2003. © 2003 by Blackwell Publishers, Ltd. Reprinted with permission.

Sense of Belonging to School

Can Schools Make a Difference?

Xin Ma

There has been renewed public concern about students' sense of belonging to school (sense of school membership) following the recent waves of school violence in North America. Goodenow and Grady (1993) defined sense of belonging as the extent to which students feel personally accepted, respected, included, and supported in the school social environment. Maslow (1962) stated that the need of belonging has to be satisfied before other needs can be fulfilled. (Finn's (1989) identification-participation model indicates that unless students identify well with their schools (i.e., feel welcomed, respected, and valued), their education participation always will be limited. Applying the principles of affective psychology, Combs (1982) stated that successful student learning depends on four highly affective variables, one of which is the feeling of belonging or being cared for. In "The Discipline of Hope," M. Scherer (1998), editor of Educational Leadership, highlighted H. Kohl's (personal communication, 1998) emphasis on the critical importance of fostering a sense of belonging and love of learning in public education.

Students' sense of (or lack of) belonging to school has social consequences beyond recent tragedies of school violence. In a review of empirical studies on the growth and nature of juvenile gangs, Burnett and Walz (1994) concluded that gang-related problems increase when students do not have a sense of belonging to their school. A school district superintendent who interviewed gang members to determine their views about school reported that encouraging a sense of belonging to school was a major prevention and intervention strategy (Reep, 1996). In a phenomenological study in which Omizo, Omizo, and Honda (1997) interviewed boys about their gang membership, the authors revealed major themes such as sense of belonging, self-esteem, and protection.

Results of case studies indicate that sense of belonging is a direct cause of dropping out of high school (Fine, 1991). In an ethnographic study of culturally diverse adolescents identified as potential school dropouts, Schlosser (1992) reported that those whose teachers emphasized sense of belonging were more likely, compared with those whose teachers did not emphasize belonging, to ac-

cept their teachers' education values and to continue in school. On the basis of a review of an eclectic body of literature, Kagan (1990) developed a research model to determine whether treatment, behavior, perception, and cognition differ between students at risk of dropping out of high school and those not at risk. One major component of the model is that sense of belonging to school, which distinguishes students with and without risk, enhances commitment to schooling. Wang, Haertel, and Walberg (1998) described the roles of educators in promoting children's educational resilience (e.g., their demonstration of remarkable academic achievement despite conditions that put them at risk of academic failure such as family poverty, physical illness, parent divorce, substance abuse, and frequent relocation); sense of belonging was presented as an important ingredient in any educational program for children at risk of academic failure.

Sense of belonging to school appears essential to many educational processes and schooling outcomes. Goodenow (1991) investigated the relationship between students' sense of belonging in their classes and measures related to motivation, student effort, and academic achievement. Multiple regression analysis of 612 students in Grades 5 to 8 revealed that sense of belonging in a class was related to students' expectations of academic success, intrinsic interests in academic work, and course grades and to teachers' ratings of students' academic effort. A survey of 301 students in two multiethnic urban junior high schools with African American, European American, and Hispanic American students (each ethnic group comprising about one third of the participants) was designed to examine the correlation between sense of belonging and measures of motivation and achievement. Multiple regression analysis showed that even after controls for the impact of the immediate peer group's values, a student's sense of belonging still had a statistically significant impact on motivation as well as on engaged and persistent effort in difficult academic work (Goodenow & Grady, 1993). Gonzalez and Padilla (1997) identified high achievers and low achievers from among 2,169 Mexican American students in three high schools; multiple regression analysis showed that sense of belonging to school was the only statistically significant predictor of student academic grades.

Goff and Goddard (1999) studied the relationship between terminal core values and delinquency, substance use, and sexual behavior among 544 high school students. Results of analysis of variance indicated that students who valued self-respect, sense of belonging, and sense of accomplishment exhibited (statistically) significantly lower frequency of delinquent behavior and substance use. Romero and Roberts (1998) conducted a school-based survey in a large metropolitan area that included 3,071 students of African, European, Mexican, and Vietnamese descents; results of multiple regression analysis indicated that a stronger sense of belonging to one's racial-ethnic group was associated with more positive attitudes toward other racial-ethnic groups. Wendel, Hoke, and Joedel (1994) surveyed 70 outstanding middle school administrators and found from descriptive analyses that the ability of school administrators to create students' sense of belonging was essential for a successful school operation.

A student's sense of belonging to school develops in a school social environment. In a philosophical examination of issues related to sense of belonging, Edwards (1995) advocated that school administrators ensure that teachers must feel a sense of belonging to school so that they, in turn, can help their students feel a sense of belonging. In a position paper, Routt (1996) asserted that students perceive teachers who are attentive, respectful, and helpful as caring and concerned about their social and academic well being, which gives the students a sense of belonging and fosters their academic engagement. Kester (1994) conducted an action research (researchers and teachers collaborated on research design and process) to examine whether African American students in a multiage classroom with the same teacher for 3 years had a stronger connection to their school than students in other classrooms had. He reported that school structure and peer influence can interact to affect students' sense of belonging to school. Reviews of research literature suggest consistently that small high schools are in a better position than large schools to create a stronger sense of belonging (Cawelti, 1995; Cotton, 1996; Raywid, 1996). The researchers reported that attendance at small schools resulted in better student involvement, better interpersonal relationships, and easier management of individual and cooperative practices.

Using individual and focus-group interviews, Williams and Downing (1998) investigated the characteristics of classroom membership perceived by 51 middle school students from two school districts (one urban and one rural). Results of qualitative data analysis showed that having friends in class, interacting with peers, participating in class activities, and obtaining good grades indicated membership or sense of belonging. Children from four elementary schools participated in a survey study intended to improve their self-esteem through adult role-model intervention. One of the major descriptive data analyses indicated that a student's sense of belonging can be affected by the labels placed on the student (Greenberg, 1995).

Students' sense of belonging to school is a critical research topic in education because it constitutes a construct that is distinctly different from other constructs often discussed in education research, such as school climate and social support (Goodenow, 1991). Albert (1991) conceptualized sense of belonging in three Cs (connect, capable, and contribute). The first C emphasizes that students need to connect with one another by cooperative learning and with teachers by their greeting and encouraging the students. The second C emphasizes that teachers need to help students feel capable, by modified tasks and assignments that teachers design to provide students with successful learning experiences. The third C emphasizes that students need to contribute to their school by performing duties (e.g., being line leaders and lunch card collectors) that teachers assign to provide them with opportunities to feel valued.

Research Questions

There is widespread research evidence that sense of belonging to school is critical to the success of public education (see Scherer, 1998). A recent increase in the occurrences of serious school violence has put a heavier emphasis on educators to develop students' sense of belonging. The National School Safety Center reported that about one crime in every 6 (bullying, fighting, carrying weapons, and gang activities) occurs when school is in session (Kum-Walks, 1996). In contrast, empirical studies have lingered behind in advancing working knowledge for educators on students' sense of belonging. Most existing empirical studies have focused on documenting the educational benefit of a strong sense of belonging. There is a lack of empirical studies on the development of sense of belonging in a school social environment, particularly on what schools can do to shape and enhance students' sense of belonging. Specifically, little research evidence exists on how school context and climate affect students' sense of belonging. Unfortunately, most educators need adequate working knowledge in that aspect of sense of belonging. That aspect of school context and climate is also necessary to formulate any theories of students' sense of belonging to school. The present study is a direct response to that limitation.

Using survey data that describe students in Grades 6 and 8, I addressed the following three research questions:

1. Is there any variation in students' sense of belonging to school among students and schools in Grades 6 and 8? Specifically, to what extent are students or schools responsible for the variation in sense of belonging? Are schools equally effective (or successful) in developing students' sense of belonging (to

what extent do schools vary in affecting students' sense of belonging)?

2. If there is variation in sense of belonging among students, then what student characteristics are responsible for it? Specifically, are there individual differences related to gender, socioeconomic status (SES), native status, number of parents, number of siblings, academic achievement, self-esteem, and general health in students' sense of belonging in Grades 6 and 8?

3. If there is variation in sense of belonging among schools, then what school characteristics are responsible for it? Specifically, do students in schools with advantaged context (school size and school mean SES) have a better sense of belonging than do students in schools with disadvantaged context in Grades 6 and 8? Do students in schools with a positive climate (academic press, disciplinary climate, and parental involvement) have a better sense of belonging than do students in schools with a negative climate in Grades 6 and 8?

The two grade levels involved in this study were ideal for the examination of sense of belonging. Goodenow (1991) found that the beginning of secondary education is the most critical stage for the development of sense of belonging because students at this stage are in transition from childhood to adolescence (see also Eccles & Midgley, 1989).

Method

Setting and Data Sources

New Brunswick is the largest of Canada's three maritime provinces, located below Quebec and beside Maine. With an area about 73,440 kilometers in a roughly rectangular shape, the population of New Brunswick was about 757,000 people in 2000. The province is largely rural, and has a relatively homogenous population with few visible minorities. Most of the people live along the Atlantic Coast and in the St. John River valleys. About 33% of the population speaks French; New Brunswick is the only official bilingual province in Canada.

There are two provincially funded public education systems in New Brunswick. The Anglophone system has 12 school districts (English is the instructional language), and the Francophone system has 6 school districts (French is the instructional language). Both systems are governed by a parent-based structure, consisting of parent advisory councils at the school and district levels and two provincial boards (one Anglophone and one Francophone). Education is a provincial jurisdiction in Canada (i.e., provinces have total control of their education policies and practices). The Curriculum Development Branch in the provincial Department of Education sets goals and objectives of education. Specifically, administrators develop and implement curricula in all subject areas, recommend print and nonprint instructional resources, and suggest the purchase of equipment to support the prescribed curricula. Both school systems use the same provincial curricula but different languages for instruction.

Data used in the present study were collected in 1996 for the New Brunswick School Climate Study (NBSCS). All of the students in Grades 6 and 8 from the Anglophone school system participated in the NBSCS (6,883 Grade 6 students from 148 schools and 6,868 Grade 8 students from 92 schools). Therefore, the two data sets represent populations of students rather than samples of students. Students completed four achievement tests (mathematics, science, reading, and writing) and a student questionnaire.

The present study is a secondary data analysis in which I used the NBSCS database. Although the data were collected 7 years ago, they were suitable for this study because the NBSCS is the latest large-scale education survey available that contains comprehensive measures on students and their schools. In addition, there were no dramatic educational changes in the past 7 years in New Brunswick (e.g., curriculum and instruction remained largely the same). Therefore, the NBSCS data, although somewhat dated, can still be relevant for one to examine, for example, students' sense of belonging to school. At least, the present study can provide a historical profile for future senior high school students on their state of sense of belonging to school when they started middle school. This research also can offer useful information for investigations on students' sense of belonging that are now underway.

Measures

Students' sense of belonging to school was the outcome (dependent) variable. Explanatory (independent) variables were classified into student and school characteristics. Student characteristics included gender, SES, native status, number of parents, number of siblings, academic achievement, self-esteem, and general health. School characteristics were classified into school context variables, including size and mean SES; and school climate variables, including academic press, disciplinary climate, and parent involvement. Table 1 describes outcome, student-level, and school-level variables.

The NBSCS staff developed scales measuring sense of belonging, academic press, disciplinary climate, and parental involvement based on a theoretical schema on schooling process (see Willms, 1992). This schema contains constitutive definitions for these (and other) constructs and the operational guidance on the selection of measures for each construct. Other scales were borrowed directly from existing scales. The Self-Esteem subscale was taken from the Self-Description Questionnaire 1 (SDQ1; Marsh, 1992), and the General Health Scale was developed by the World Health Organization. I intended that these practices (developing scales on the basis of a

TABLE 1 Basic Statistics on the Anglophone and Francophone School Systems in New Brunswick

School system	Anglophone system	Francophone System
Student enrollment	86,555	38,387
Education staff	5,218	2,358
Support staff	2,539	1,280
Student-teacher ratio	16.5	
Average class size	23.4	
Graduation rate	0.86	
Dropout rate	0.03	

Note. Separate statistics were not available on student-teacher ratio, average class size, graduation rate, and dropout rate. Data source: New Brunswick Department of Education.

theoretical schema and borrowing scales from existing, popular, and well-documented scales) would reach an adequate match between constitutive and operational definitions. Researchers commonly used a 5-point scale to promote larger variance for statistical analysis.

At the student level, sense of belonging to school measured the extent to which students felt personally accepted, respected, included, and supported in the school social environment. Cronbach's alphas were .68 in Grade 6 and .73 in Grade 8. Gender was coded as 1= girls and 0 = boys, therefore, gender effects as reported later were female effects. In a similar logic, native status was coded as 1 = native and 0 = other; number of parents was coded as 1 = single parent and 0 = both parents. Self-esteem measured global attitudes toward self in academic and nonacademic areas. Cronbach's alphas were .87 in Grade 6 and .88 in Grade 8. The General Health Scale measured children's general physical and mental wellness. Cronbach's alphas were .77 in Grade 6 and .76 in Grade 8.

I used regular provincial achievement tests in mathematics, science, reading, and writing as academic achievement measures. A panel of curriculum specialists and experienced teachers developed the achievement tests on the basis of provincial curricula in the four school subjects. The reading test had 35 items in Grade 6 and 50 items in Grade 8; it measured reading comprehension of fiction and nonfiction passages. Two writing samples that were collected from each student in Grades 6 and 8 over a period of time were rated by a panel of teachers on a 6-point scale (unratable, weak, marginal, acceptable, competent, and superior). Student categorical writing scores were transformed to a continuous scale with a mean of 0 and a standard deviation of 1 (see Mosteller & Tukey, 1977). Mathematics and science achievement tests were administered to students in Grade 6 only. The mathematics test had 39 items that measured computation, concep-

tual understanding, and application in the areas of numeration, geometry, measurement, and data management. The science test had 33 items that measured knowledge and understanding of scientific concepts and processes. In the present study, the variable, academic achievement, was an average measure of academic achievement in Grades 6 and 8, respectively.

At the school level, school context variables included school size (in terms of student enrollment in Grades 6 and 8) and school mean SES (aggregated from student SES within each school). School climate variables included academic press, disciplinary climate, and parent involvement (aggregated from student responses within each school). Academic press measured the extent to which teachers and peers valued academic success and held high academic expectation (Cronbach's [alpha]s = .61 in Grade 6 and .65 in Grade 8); disciplinary climate measured the extent to which students complied with school rules of conduct (Cronbach's [alpha]s = .77 in Grades 6 and 8); and parent involvement measured the extent to which parents were involved in their children's education (Cronbach's [alpha]s = .77 in Grade 6 and .79 in Grade 8). For the purpose of data analysis, continuous variables at student and school levels were standardized (M = 0; SD = 1). There were a few dichotomous variables at the student level that were centered around their grand means.

"Reliability may be thought of as a special type of correlation that measures consistency of observations and scores" (Sax, 1997), and a correlation measure can be considered an effect-size index (see Cohen, 1988). These statistical properties allow one to evaluate roughly the adequacy in terms of reliability on scales used in the present study (see Table 1). The range of effect-size indices was between .61 and .88. According to Cohen, an effect-size index above .50 can be considered large in the behavioral sciences. Therefore, from the perspective of behavioral sciences, scales in this study appeared to be reliable.

Statistical Procedure

I used hierarchical linear modeling (HLM) techniques in which students were nested within schools for data analysis (see Bryk & Raudenbush, 1992). The use of HLM corresponded to the three research questions addressed previously in this study. HLM allowed me to partition the total variance in sense of belonging into within-school and between-school variances to address the first research question. Furthermore, HLM estimated student and school effects on sense of belonging simultaneously with adjustment for sampling and measurement errors to address the second and third research questions.

I developed two-level HLM models in which students were nested within schools. At the first (student) level, sense of belonging was regressed on gender, SES, native status, number of parents, number of siblings, academic achievement, self-esteem, and general health. The intercept of that regression represented an average measure of sense of belonging within each school, adjusted for student characteristics in that school. A slope of the regression associated with an explanatory variable represented the relationship between sense of belonging and the particular variable in that school. At the second (school) level, school average measures of sense of belonging were regressed on school context (school size and school mean SES) and climate (academic press, disciplinary climate, and parent involvement) variables. The slopes from the student-level model were fixed because my primary purpose in this study was to explain variation in sense of belonging among students and schools (see Thum & Bryk, 1997).

I performed the statistical procedure described in the preceding paragraphs for each grade level; specifically, I tested two HLM models. The null model contained only the outcome measure, without any explanatory variables at either the student or school level. The null model parti-

tioned the total variance in sense of belonging into within-schools and between-schools components (for the first research question). The full model contained student-level and school-level variables that modeled within-school and between-school variations in sense of belonging (for the second and third research questions). With the results from Grades 6 and 8, I made a cross-sectional comparison to describe any pattern of change in students' sense of belonging.

Assumptions for the HLM models developed in this study were that (a) residuals at the student and school levels have a normal distribution with a population mean of zero and constant variance (σ^2 at student level and τ at the school level) and (b) residuals at the school level are independent between schools. I examined those assumptions on the basis of the six-question procedure outlined in Snijders and Bosker (1999); no serious violation of HLM assumptions was detected. I removed a few extreme cases to improve the models (e.g., small schools with fewer than five students).

TABLE 2. Descriptive Statistics for Outcome and Explanatory Variables at the Student and School Levels

Variable	Grade 6		Grade 8	
	M	SD	M	SD
Sense of belonging (outcome variable)	3.76	0.81	3.79	0.79
Student characteristics (student-level explanatory variables)				
Gender (girls = 1, boys = 0)	0.49	0.50	0.55	0.83
Socioeconomic status (SES)	0.00	1.00	0.00	1.00
Native status (Native = 1, Others = 0)	0.01	0.10		
Number of parents (single parent = 1, both parents = 0)	0.14	0.34	0.16	0.37
Number of siblings	1.99	1.46	2.00	1.48
Academic achievement	0.00	1.00	0.00	1.00
Self-esteem	3.78	0.61	3.77	0.69
General health	4.06	0.68	4.1	0.65
School characteristics (school-level explanatory variables)				
School mean SES	0.00	1.00	0.00	1.00
School size	39.71	30.73	67.91	56.23
Academic press	3.72	0.16	3.58	0.15
Disciplinary climate	2.96	0.30	2.86	0.26
Parent involvement	2.27	0.17	1.90	0.12

Note. Calculations were based on 6,883 students from 148 schools in Grade 6 and 6,868 students from 92 schools in Grade 8. Native status was not available in Grade 8. SES and academic achievement were standardized variables at the student level. School mean SES was a standardized variable at the school level. Effect sizes were 0.04 for sense of belonging, 0.02 for self-esteem, 0.06 for general health, 0.90 for academic press, 0.36 for disciplinary climate, and 2.55 for parent involvement.

Results

Table 2 shows means and standard deviations of outcome and explanatory variables (at both student and school levels) in Grades 6 and 8. To compare the results between the two grade levels, I calculated average group standard deviation effect sizes for the major student-level and school-level variables (Abrami, Cholmsky, & Cordon, 2001). For a two-group comparison, an effect is small if half of its effect size is 0.10, medium if 0.25, and large if 0.40 (Cohen, 1988). At the student level, differences between the two grade levels in sense of belonging, self-esteem, and general health were all extremely small. At the school level, differences in academic press and parent involvement were large, whereas differences in disciplinary climate were small, between the two grade levels. The differences in school means were all in favor of Grade 6. Overall, school-level characteristics varied much more across the two grade levels than student-level characteristics.

Table 3 shows the proportion of variance in students' sense of belonging within and between schools. In Grades 6 and 8, about 96% of the variance in sense of belonging was attributable to the students. Although schools differed systematically in students' sense of belonging, they were responsible for only 4% of its variance (in both grades). I introduced student-level variables and school-level variables to explain the variations among students and schools.

Results of HLM models for students in Grades 6 and 8 are shown in Table 4. To illustrate the practical significance of an effect and to compare effects across the two grade levels, I needed a common metric. I used effect size (SD) unit in the present study, as advocated by Lee and Loeb (2000). In behavioral sciences, Rosenthal and Rosnow (1984) classified effect sizes more than 0.5 standard deviation as large, effect sizes between 0.3 and 0.5 standard deviation as moderate, and effect sizes less than 0.3 standard deviation as small.

Grade 6 girls demonstrated a more positive and statistically significant sense of belonging than did Grade 6 boys (effect size [ES] = 0.47 SD). According to Rosenthal and Rosnow (1984), that result was a practically moderate effect. Students with a lower level of academic achievement showed a more positive and statistically significant sense of belonging than did students with a higher level of academic achievement. However, with an effect size of 0.04 SD, the effect of academic achievement was practically small (or unimportant). Students with higher self-esteem reported a more positive and statistically significant sense of belonging than did students with lower self-esteem (ES = 0.72 SD, a practically large effect). Students with better general health demonstrated a more positive and statistically significant sense of belonging than did students with worse general health (ES = 0.44 SD, a practically moderate effect).

TABLE 3. Proportion of Variance in Sense of Belonging Within and Between Schools

Variable	Grade 6	Grade 8
Within schools	0.96	0.96
Between schools	0.04	0.04

The effect sizes were estimated with other variables in the statistically controlled model. In other words, each effect size represented a pure effect of its associated variable. The effect sizes were examined with other variables in the model being statistically controlled. In the case of students' sense of belonging in Grade 6, the cumulative effect of gender, self-esteem, and general health was highly significant, both statistically and practically. Therefore, student-level characteristics played a critical role in sense of belonging to school.

Grade 8 girls demonstrated a more positive statistically significant sense of belonging than did Grade 8 boys, but the effect size was much smaller than that in Grade 6 (0.11 SD vs. 0.47 SD, respectively). SES became a statistically significant predictor of students' sense of belonging (ES = 0.07 SD, a practically small effect). Students with a higher level of academic achievement showed a more positive statistically significant sense of belonging than did students with a lower level of academic achievement (ES = 0.06 SD, a practically small effect). Students with higher self-esteem showed a more positive statistically significant sense of belonging than did students with lower self-esteem (ES = 0.51 SD, a practically large effect). Students with better general health reported a more positive statistically significant sense of belonging than did students with worse general health (ES = 0.34 SD, a practically moderate effect). Finally, the cumulative effect of self-esteem and general health was significant both statistically and practically in Grade 8, indicating that student-level characteristics continued to play an important role in sense of belonging to school.

A comparison of effects between Grades 6 and 8 shows that gender differences (in favor of girls) in sense of belonging were practically moderate in Grade 6 but practically small in Grade 8. Effects of student's self-esteem were practically large on their sense of belonging in Grades 6 and 8. Students' general health showed a practically moderate effect on their sense of belonging in both Grades 6 and 8. Students' SES had no statistically significant effect on their sense of belonging in Grade 6, but a practically small effect in Grade 8. Self-esteem, gender, and general health were the most important predictors of sense of belonging in Grade 6, whereas self-esteem and general health were the most important predictors in Grade 8. Overall, as students progressed through junior high school, effects of student characteristics became smaller. This finding also could be observed from a comparison of cumulative effects between the two grade levels.

Although there were not many statistically significant predictors at the school level, the effects of statistically significant predictors at that level were practically large. In Grade 6, students in schools with higher academic press demonstrated a more positive statistically significant sense of belonging than did students in schools with lower academic press (ES = 6.26 SD, a practically large effect). In Grade 8, students in schools with a better disciplinary climate reported a more positive statistically significant sense of belonging than did students in schools with a worse disciplinary climate (ES = 5.70 SD, a practically large effect). Overall, school effects were not consistent in terms of statistically significant predictors of students' sense of belonging, but they were practically large across the two grade levels.

The bottom panel of Table 4 shows the proportion of variance accounted for at the student and school levels. The model explained 36% of the variance in sense of belonging among students in Grade 6 and 27% in Grade 8. The model accounted for 61% of the variance in sense of belonging among schools in Grade 6, and 65% in Grade 8. Although the percentages of variance explained were sufficient at the school level, those at the student level were low. That finding implied that other student-level characteristics were responsible for the majority of the variance in sense of belonging at the student level. A category of student-level characteristics was the interaction of a student with peers and teachers. Although the characteristics were not obtained, they might be important predictors of sense of belonging. Presumably, this interaction directly affects the extent to which the student feels accepted, respected, included, and supported in the school community.

Using cross-sectional data (at the middle school level), I highlighted the finding that discrepancies in student's sense of belonging to school were mainly within schools (between students) rather than between schools. I also attempted to explain differences among students and schools in sense of belonging with some student and school characteristics. As one of the most important findings in this study, I unveiled an empirical relationship between students' self-esteem and their sense of belonging. Self-esteem was the single most important predictor of sense of belonging, with fairly consistent effects across Grades 6 and 8.

The aforementioned finding implies that students' attitude toward themselves is transferable to their attitude toward school. Students who had a greater feeling of worthiness appeared to feel more comfortable in their schools than did those students who felt less worth. Beyond the data available in the present study, one may speculate that higher confidence in one's ability (e.g., academic, athletic, and social) may promote more active participation in school activities that often makes one feel that he or she is valued. However, low self-esteem, or doubt about one's ability, may alienate one from participation in school activities. Alienation may be the major reason for students' lack of sense of belonging to school. The rela-

TABLE 4. Hierarchical Linear Modeling Results of Student and School Effects on Sense of Belonging

Variable	Grade 6		Grade 8	
	Effect	SE	Effect	SE
Effects of student characteristics				
Gender	0.294 *	0.021	0.081 *	0.013
Socioeconomic status (SES)			0.046 *	0.011
Academic achievement	-0.023 *	0.011	0.044 *	0.011
Self-esteem	0.446 *	0.011	0.361 *	0.012
General health	0.274 *	0.011	0.243 *	0.011
Effects of school characteristics				
Academic press	0.094 *	0.016		
Disciplinary climate			0.075 *	0.019
Proportion of variance explained				
Within schools	0.36		0.27	
Between schools	0.61		0.65	

Note. SE = standard error. At the student level, Native status, number of parents, and number of siblings are not statistically significant in Grades 6 and 8. At the school level, school mean SES, school size, and parent involvement are not statistically significant in Grades 6 and 8.

* $p < .05$.

tionship between self-esteem and sense of belonging may be circular, with each enhancing the other.

The next important predictor of sense of belonging at the student level was general health. This finding seemed to convey a similar story about participation and alienation. Students with good health may have had more "capital" to participate in academic, athletic, and social activities in school than did students with poor health.

The theme of participation in school activities as it relates to students' sense of belonging to school was inferred in the present study not only by the most statistically significant predictors such as self-esteem and general health but also by predictors that were not statistically significant, including SES (practically unimportant in Grade 8 although statistically significant), native status, number of parents, and number of siblings. One may have noticed that these predictors all describe individual background characteristics and thus did not directly determine participation in school activities. Overall, perhaps the most important contribution of this study to the research literature is that it helps propose the research hypothesis that students' participation in school activities may be the key to their sense of belonging to school.

My findings also help dismiss some misperceptions that have long existed among the public. For example, many educators and administrators believe that native students are far more negative in their sense of belonging to school than are non-native students. In the present study, however, the predictor, native status, was not statistically significant. Therefore, if native students had a negative sense of belonging, then the problem appeared to be associated with their self-esteem and health status (which again brings the discussion to the issue of participation). Stated differently, once students' self-esteem and health status were taken into account, native students did not necessarily have more negative sense of belonging to school than did their non-native counterparts.

Similarly, the misperception exists that low-SES students tend to misunderstand the values of education; thus, they have a negative attitude toward school. In the present study, SES was not statistically significant in Grade 6 and was practically unimportant, although statistically significant, in Grade 8. In comparison with self-esteem and health status, SES was trivial in its effect on sense of belonging. In general, many misperceptions about sense of belonging's being associated with gender, SES, native status, number of parents, and number of siblings may well be dismissed in the presence of self-esteem and health status.

Because schools, in comparison with students, varied in a secondary way, it is perhaps not surprising that few school-level variables played important roles in explaining students' sense of belonging. Still, this study has shown some large school effects. In both Grades 6 and 8, school context variables (school size and school mean SES) were not statistically significant, whereas some school climate variables (academic press, disciplinary climate, and parent involvement) showed statistically significant effects. Therefore, school climate was more important than school context for students' sense of belonging to school. That finding highlights the fact that teachers can play a critical role in shaping students' sense of belonging because, unlike school context characteristics, school climate characteristics are usually under the direct control of school staff.

Another major finding at the school level was that school climate effects were not consistent in type (academic press was statistically significant in Grade 6; disciplinary climate was statistically significant in Grade 8) but were similar in magnitude. For the sixth graders, peers' and teachers' care for and concern about their academic wellness seemed to make them feel at home in school. One should understand that finding together with the one from the student level that showed a small effect of academic achievement on sense of belonging. Therefore, the academic achievement that students attain is not critical for their sense of belonging to school; what matters to their sense of belonging is the presence of caring peers and teachers, along with a lot of attention to their schoolwork and academic success. That conclusion adds to the research a "rare" finding that academic press has effects not only on students' cognitive wellness, such as

their academic success, but also on students' affective wellness, such as their sense of belonging.

For the eighth graders, however, the school disciplinary environment shaped their sense of belonging to school. An unsafe school is not a desirable place to be for most students. In this study, items descriptive of disciplinary climate were mostly about students' perceptions of disciplinary rules in school. Therefore, if students perceived school disciplinary rules as unfair, they developed a negative sense of belonging, even though their school disciplinary climate may not necessarily have been negative.

In sum, this study suggests (a) that students' sense of belonging to school is influenced more by their mental and physical conditions but less by their individual and family characteristics and (b) that students' sense of belonging to school is influenced by school climate characteristics rather than school context characteristics. Findings from the school level do indicate that teachers and administrators are in a powerful position to influence students' sense of belonging to school (the large school effect sizes suggest that schools can make a difference in students' sense of belonging to school). School climate that makes students feel that they are cared for, safe, and treated fairly is conducive to their developing a positive sense of belonging to school. Therefore, the practice of communal schools in which, among other things, interpersonal relationships are emphasized to create affective bonds among all school members (see Lee & Smith, 1995) may be instrumental in developing students' positive sense of belonging to school.

REFERENCES

Abrami, P. C., Cholmsky, R., & Cordon, R. (2001). Statistical analysis for the social sciences. Needham Heights, MA: Allyn & Bacon.

Albert, L. (1991). Cooperative discipline. Circle Pines, MN: American Guidance Service.

Bryk, A. S., & Raudenbush, S. W. (1992). Hierarchical linear models. Newbury Park, CA: Sage.

Burnett, G., & Walz, G. (1994). Gangs in the schools (Rep. No. EDO-CG-94-28). Greensboro, NC: ERIC Clearinghouse on Counseling and Student Services.

Cawelti, G. (1995). The missing focus of high school restructuring. School Administrator, 52(11), 12 16.

Cohen, J. (1988). Statistical power analysis for the behavioral sciences (2nd ed.). Hillsdale, NJ: Erlbaum.

Combs, A. (1982). Affective education or none at all. Educational Leadership, 39, 495–497.

Cotton, K. (1996). Affective and social benefits of small scale schooling (Rep. No. EDO-RC-96-5). Charleston, WV: ERIC Clearinghouse on Rural Education and Small Schools.

Eccles, J., & Midgley, C. (1989). Stage-environmental fit: Developmentally appropriate classrooms for young adolescents. In C. Ames & R. Ames (Eds.), Research on motivation in education: Goals and cognitions (pp. 215–286). San Diego, CA: Academic Press.

Edwards, D. (1995). The school counselor's role in helping teachers and students. Elementary School Guidance and Counseling, 29, 191–197.

Fine, M. (1991). Framing dropouts. Albany, NY: SUN Press.

Finn, J. (1989). Withdrawing from school. Review of Educational Research, 59, 117–142.

Goff, B. G., & Goddard, H. W. (1999). Terminal core values associated with adolescent problem behavior. Adolescence, 34, 47–60.

Gonzalez, R., & Padilla, A. M. (1997). The academic resilience of Mexican American high school students. Hispanic Journal of Behavioral Sciences, 19, 301–317.

Goodenow, C. (1991, April). The sense of belonging and its relationships to academic motivation among pre- and early adolescent students. Paper presented at the annual meeting of the American Educational Research Association, Chicago.

Goodenow, C., & Grady, K. (1993). The relationship of school belonging and friends' values to academic motivation among urban adolescent students. The Journal of Experimental Education, 62, 60–71.

Greenberg, R. N. (1995). Self-esteem enhancement through adult role-model intervention. Unpublished master's thesis, Saint Xavier University, Palatine, IL.

Kagan, D. (1990). How schools alienate students at risk: A model for examining proximal classroom variables. Educational Psychologist, 25, 105–125.

Kester, V. M. (1994). Factors that affect African American students' bonding to middle school. Elementary School Journal, 95, 63–73.

Kum-Walks, D. A. (1996). Responses to school violence by schools and students (Doctoral dissertation. Claremont Graduate University. 1996). Dissertation Abstracts International, 57, 4303A.

Lee, V. E., & Loeb, S. (2000). School size in Chicago elementary schools: Effects on teachers' attitudes and students' achievement. American Educational Research Journal, 37, 3–32.

Lee, V. E., & Smith, J. B. (1995). Effects of high school restructuring and size on early gains in achievement and engagement. Sociology of Education, 68, 241–270.

Marsh, H. W. (1992). Self Description Questionnaire (SDQ) I: A theoretical and empirical basis for the measurement of multiple dimensions of preadolescent self-concept. Macarthur, New South Wales, Australia: University of Western Sydney.

Maslow, A. (1962). Toward a psychology of belonging. Princeton, NJ: Van Nostrand.

Mosteller, F., & Tukey, J. W. (1977). Data analysis and regression. Reading, MA: Addison-Wesley.

Omizo, M. M., Omizo, S. A., & Honda, M. R. (1997). A phenomenological study with youth gang members: Results and implications for school counsellors. Professional School Counseling, 1, 39–42.

Raywid, M. A. (1996). Downsizing schools in big cities (Rep. No. EPO-UD-96-1). Columbia University, NY: ERIC Clearinghouse on Urban Education.

Reep, B. B. (1996). Lessons from the gang. School Administrator, 53(2), 26–29.

Romero, A. J., & Roberts, R. E. (1998). Perception of discrimination and ethnocultural variables in a diverse group of adolescents. Journal of Adolescence, 21, 641–656.

Rosenthal, R., & Rosnow, R. L. (1984). Essentials of behavioral research: Methods and data analysis. New York: McGraw-Hill.

Routt, M. L. (1996). Early experiences that foster connectedness. Dimensions of Early Childhood, 24, 17–21.

Sax, G. (1997). Principles of educational and psychological measurement and evaluation (4th ed.). Belmont, CA: Wadsworth.

Scherer, M. (1998). The discipline of hope: A conversation with Herb Kohl. Educational Leadership, 56(1), 8–13.

Schlosser, L. K. (1992). Teacher distance and student disengagement: School lives on the margin. Journal of Teacher Education. 43, 128–140.

Snijders, T. A. B., & Bosker, R. J. (1999). Multilevel analysis. Thousand Oaks, CA: Sage.

Thum, Y. M., & Bryk, A. S. (1997). Value-added productivity indicators: The Dallas system. In J. Millman (Ed.), Grading teachers, grading schools: Is student achievement a valid evaluation measure? (pp. 100–109). Thousand Oaks, CA: Corwin.

Wang, M. C., Haertel, G. D., & Walberg, H. J. (1998). Building educational resilience. Fastback, 43.

Wendel, F. C., Hoke, F. A., & Joekel, R. T. (1994). The search for success. Middle School Journal, 25(3), 48–50.

Williams, L. J., & Downing, J. E. (1998). Membership and belonging in inclusive classrooms: What do middle school students have to say? Journal of the Association for Persons With Severe Handicaps, 23, 98–110.

Willms, J. D. (1992). Monitoring school performance: A guide for educators. London: Falmer.

XIN MA is associate professor, Education Department, University of Alberta, Canada. His research interests include school effects, policy research, program evaluation, mathematics education, and statistical methods.

From Journal of Educational Research, Vol. 96, No. 6, July/August 2003. © 2003. Reprinted with permission of the Helen Dwight Reid Educational Foundation. Published by Heldref Publications, 1319 Eighteenth St., NW, Washington, DC 20036-1802.

Challenges and Suggestions for Safe Schools

Katherine T. Bucher; M. Lee Manning

In this article we look at challenges to safe schools and offer eight suggestions for ensuring the safety of students and educators. School violence includes unacceptable social behavior ranging from aggression that threatens or harms others (and the highly publicized acts of mass bloodshed) to bullying, threats (Hoang 2001), sexual harassment, gang violence, extortion, and other forms of intimidation (McEvoy 1999). It involves criminal acts in schools, inhibits development and learning, and harms the school's climate (Furlong and Morrison 2000). At least 10 percent of our nation's schools are unsafe (Walker and Eaton-Walker 2000). Also, the gravity of youth violence has increased in recent years. Although today's students may not be any more likely than yesterday's to experience violence, the violence they do experience more often results in serious injury (Kingery, Coggeshall, and Alford 1999). Confronted by increasing incidence of violent behavior in schools, educators are being asked to make schools safer (Sugai et al. 2000).

Many middle and secondary school students experience a variety of forms of violence—pushing, bullying, shoving, grabbing, slapping, verbal insults, and threats—that make their lives in school miserable. Of twelve students who stay home on any given day, one stays home due to fear (Harris 2000). Incidents of school violence are disturbing:

- Nearly 8 percent of students nationally reported having been threatened or injured with a weapon on school property during the prior twelve months (Leone et al. 2001).
- Slightly over 1 percent of students reported that they had been physically assaulted (Verdugo 1999).
- The odds that a student will be threatened or injured with a weapon in school are approximately one in fifteen, and the odds of getting into a physical fight are approximately one in eight (Reddy et al. 2001).
- Student surveys indicate that behaviors such as carrying a weapon at school are significantly more widespread than surveys of school administrators suggest (Doggeshall and Kingery 2001).
- Males reported much higher rates than females of weapon-carrying in schools (11 percent to 2.8 percent).
- Fourteen percent of students reported being in a physical fight at school during the past twelve months.
- Over 7 percent of students nationally reported having been threatened or injured with a weapon on school property during the past twelve months (Leone et al. 2000).

Suggestions for Promoting School Safety

National concern over school violence has led to federal, state, and local efforts to address the issue by creating new laws and policies, such as zero-tolerance, conducting targeted and random searches of students and their property, using metal detectors, and launching violence prevention education programs (Yell and Rozalski 2000). Educators should also consider the following eight suggestions for ensuring school safety.

Suggestion 1

Look for school conditions that might cause or contribute to school violence and aggression. For example, overcrowded or poorly supervised schools, and school communities with less tolerance for individual differences in abilities and attitudes have more aggressive and antisocial behavior (Furlong, Bates, and Smith 2001). Harris maintains that school authorities often condone "structural" violence, which results from an overemphasis on competition, the use of tracking which lowers self-esteem, and dictatorial administrators who make students resentful of authorities (Harris 2000). How adults perceive adolescents can also contribute to violence. In one study (Hedin, Hannes, and Saito 1985), two-thirds of the students believed that significant adults in their lives perceived them negatively.

Braaten (1999) also found that students believed that adults neither valued nor trusted them and did not treat them with respect. Other conditions that can lead to violence include insensitivity toward multicultural factors, student alienation, rejection of at-risk students by teachers and peers, and student anger and resentment at school routines and demands for conformity.

Suggestion 2

Make a commitment to civility and a positive school culture and climate. A safe school has a positive climate where people are trusted, respected, and involved. They work cooperatively; intolerance does not exist, nor are students harassed or threatened. Students feel that adults care for them as a group and as individuals. High expectations exist so that students are successful both academically and socially (Erb 2000). Some schools have unnecessarily harsh and punitive disciplinary practices that create a climate conducive to school violence (Hyman and Snook 2000). Educators can increase respect for authority by not disciplining students with peers present. Also, they can make punishments consistent and appropriate for the severity of the infractions (Kingery, Coggeshall, and Alford 1999).

A climate of emotional and verbal violence can be as damaging as physical violence. In fact, a lack of respect and constructive communication forms the foundation of violence and should be treated assertively (Plucker 2000). When educators focus on cognitive development and ignore affective domains, problems can result. Some students do not learn constructive and productive use of leisure time, to maintain a healthy lifestyle, or to practice personal hygiene (Scott 1998). Other students use violence to distinguish themselves from others and to express disgust toward mainstream school culture (Kostinsky, Bixler, and Kettl 2001).

Educators must teach young people how to behave and to address the sources of violence in their lives, and they must help them to recover from violence (Harris 2000). Students need to feel they belong to have opportunities to make real choices, to realize that effective communication can prevent violence, and to know the consequences of their actions (Plucker 2000). School uniforms can cultivate a sense of belonging and make it easy to distinguish between students and nonstudents (Schneider 2001a).

Educators can encourage civility by

1. focusing educational efforts on both cognitive and affective domains;
2. changing the school day from the traditional "periods" to a more flexible schedule;
3. providing times for students to socialize, eat a healthy lunch, and practice hygiene;
4. teaching students how to use their leisure time productively and acceptably;
5. providing age-appropriate discussions on drug abuse, sex, and violence;
6. structuring the school day to lessen emotional and physiological stress; and
7. teaching students how to think and act in restrooms, hallways, locker rooms, and lunchrooms (Scott 1998).

Suggestion 3

Take advantage of environmental design and technological innovations that contribute to students' and educators' safety. The physical school environment affects student behavior. In fact, violence occurs at predictable school locations—generally unsupervised ones (Astor, Meyer, and Behre 1999).

New schools should incorporate architectural designs that reduce the likelihood of school crime and vandalism and eliminate unnecessary student conflict due to overcrowding, inappropriate congregating, and brushing against one another in narrow school spaces. Existing schools can be improved by architectural retrofitting. In neither case does the school have to look and feel like a fortress (Walker and Eaton-Walker 2000).

In the wake of recent school shootings, an industry of school safety products has quickly developed (Reddy et al. 2001). Security-oriented measures and products include ID systems for students, staff, and visitors; cameras in key locations (e.g., behind shrubbery and walls that limit visibility); and metal detectors (Erb 2000). "Smart" cards have become a common means of access control. Issued to staff, they can instantly be canceled in case of card loss or theft. In addition, relatively inexpensive metal-detector wands can be used by security personnel or other staff to check for weapons. After hours or in controlled areas, alarms can detect intruders, signal emergency personnel for immediate help, and allow staff to use emergency "panic" buttons. Closed circuit television cameras can identify suspects after the fact. Unfortunately, although they can deter some criminal activity, cameras may be targeted by vandals (Schneider 2001b).

Uniformed police officers may make the school more secure, but they do little to make individual students feel safe (Dodd 2000). Still, police officers or school security managers trained in crime prevention through environmental design can examine a school's physical environment and recommend modifications to prevent or reduce violence (Hoang 2001). They can also work with students before violence occurs by coaching sports, serving as good listeners, and working with outside agencies to provide students with positive support instead of waiting for something bad to happen. Still, recent events have made clear that the presence of officers does not prevent all violence (Erb 2000).

Suggestion 4

Identify early warning signs of violence, while recognizing the dangers of student profiling. As concern about the safety of America's public schools increases, Furlong, Bates, and Smith (2001), referring mainly to school psychologists, indicated that school personnel have been asked to render professional judgments about potentially dangerous behaviors.

Undoubtedly, educators should know early warning signs—emotional and behavioral indicators that signal the potential for dangerous or violent behavior. However, educators must remember that, although such signs might indicate a problem, they do not necessarily pinpoint a violent student. Early warning signs of violence include social withdrawal, excessive feelings of isolation and being alone, excessive feelings of rejection, being a victim of violence, feeling picked on and persecuted, low school interest and poor academic performance, expression of violence in writings and drawings, uncontrolled anger, patterns of impulsive and chronic hitting and intimidating, a history of discipline problems, a history of violent and aggressive behavior, intolerance for differences and prejudicial attitudes, drug and alcohol use, affiliation with gangs, inappropriate access to firearms, and serious threats of violence (U.S. Department of Education 1998).

Unfortunately, educators often have difficulty identifying violence-prone students. Bender, Shubert, and McLaughlin (2001) used the term "invisible kids" to describe students generally unknown by many school personnel prior to incidents of violence. These quiet and shy students had not demonstrated overt problem behaviors in schools. Therefore, teachers were less likely to know them (Bender, Shubert, and McLaughlin 2001).

Educators can use profiling checklists to predict an individual student's potential for violent behaviors. However, while some people see student profiling as a promising tool, others perceive it as an ill-conceived response to school violence (Lumsden 2000). They believe that the use of profiles is inefficient and ineffective, carries considerable risk of false positives (e.g., many youths who demonstrate the profile are not violence risks), and has the potential to stigmatize students and deprive them of their civil liberties (Reddy et al. 2001).

Suggestion 5

Have written intervention plans for ensuring safety and for responding to violence. Walker and Eaton-Walker (2000) called for written school safety plans. Unfortunately, some administrators might be hesitant to draw up a written safety plan that could imply that the school is unsafe. Still, since the public knows schools' safety records, taking action is better than ignoring potential violence.

School intervention plans should be developed in cooperation with students, parents/guardians, and the community and school. The plans should include specific principles that research or expert experience shows contribute to success. The written prevention and response plan should contain

- descriptions of the early warning signs of potentially violent behavior and procedures for identifying dangerous students;

- descriptions of effective prevention practices that the school has undertaken to build responsive interventions;
- descriptions of intervention strategies that the school community can use to help students who are at risk of behavioral problems and more intensive, individualized interventions for students with severe behavioral problems or mental health needs; and
- a crisis intervention plan that includes immediate responses for imminent warning signs and violent behavior, as well as a contingency plan to be used in the aftermath of a tragedy (U.S. Department of Education 1998).

When planning a written safe schools plan, educators should consider three fundamental principles. First, the plan should be based on a public health model so that schools can systematically address the needs of all students, including those with academic, emotional, and behavioral problems. Second, approaches that emphasize punishment and control have been demonstrated to be ineffective. Third, effective, written, schoolwide prevention plans are comprehensive, involve a broad range of services and initiatives, and extend supports over a sufficient period of time (Leone et al. 2000).

Suggestion 6

Efforts to make schools safe should include collaborative relationships among administrators, teachers, students, parents, law enforcement officers, and various social service personnel (Stader 2000). Calling for "collaborative conversations," Dodd (2000) suggests that educators should view behavioral situations as problems to be resolved rather than actions to be punished and should ask disrupting students to help resolve problems. Such an approach will result in the student's being less likely to feel misunderstood or unfairly treated. To promote this collaboration with students, both administrators and educators can

- provide leadership toward promoting student responsibility for safer schools;
- coordinate student courts that are trained by local justice system experts;
- provide conflict resolution materials as well as appropriate training;
- develop a buddy system that assigns current students to newcomers to ease the transition;
- plan a school beautification campaign for the school and neighborhood using students as the work crew;
- provide a student tip line as an anonymous, nonthreatening way for students to report school crime (National School Safety Center 1999).

Suggestion 7

Build on zero-tolerance policies, but do not rely on them to solve all school problems. Zero-tolerance policies resulted from Congress's passing the Gun-Free Schools Act of 1994, which requires states to legislate zero-tolerance laws or risk losing federal funding (McAndrews 2001). Almost all schools have zero-tolerance policies for firearms (94 percent) and other weapons (91 percent). Eighty-seven percent of schools have zero-tolerance policies for alcohol, and 88 percent for drugs. Seventy-nine percent of schools have zero-tolerance policies for violence and tobacco (McAndrews 2001).

As school officials implement zero-tolerance policies, they must ensure that their approach is fundamentally fair and legally defensible (Essex 2000). Unfortunately, the development of zero tolerance has caused some administrators to treat all behaviors, minor and major, with equal severity. These increasingly broad interpretations of zero tolerance have resulted in a "near epidemic" (Skiba and Peterson 1999) of suspensions and expulsions for seemingly trivial reasons.

In light of litigation and controversy regarding zero tolerance, educators must keep several things in mind. First, zero tolerance should not be used solely to rid the school of troubled students. Second, administrators, teachers, parents, and community leaders should be involved in the formulation of zero-tolerance policies. Actual policies should guarantee students' constitutional rights. Zero-tolerance policies should not be seen as a "cure-all" (Essex 2000) for student misconduct. School officials should consider the student's history of behavior at school and the seriousness of the offense prior to determining punishment (Essex 2000).

Educators need to recognize that little evidence exists that zero tolerance actually makes schools safer. In fact, these policies might only give schools and communities a false sense of security (Skiba and Peterson 1999; Stader 2000). The policy has the potential to alienate students who are actually crying out for help through their negative behavior (Arman 2000).

Suggestion 8

Implement conflict resolution programs to help students see alternatives to violence. When schools develop conflict resolution programs, they create an environment that fosters the development of resiliency by helping students preserve relationships, showing youth how to control their own behavior, and offering a way to resolve conflicts peacefully. Students who learn negotiation and resolution procedures in school have more positive attitudes about conflict and are more likely to seek nonviolent remedies for conflicts in their lives. These results are even stronger when there is whole-school involvement in conflict resolution activities and academic integration of peace-making themes into school content (Harris 2000).

To develop a conflict resolution program, educators should

1. consider several conflict resolution approaches to determine the one that best meets students' and educators' needs;

2. never underestimate students' abilities and motivation to engage in conflict resolution;

3. maintain objectivity—let students know that decisions about causes and solutions have not already been reached;

4. be prepared to teach the purpose, goals, and steps of conflict resolution rather than assume students will know;

5. model how conflicts can be constructive and can lead to better understandings of others as well as oneself.

Conclusion

Educators have long dealt with behavior problems such as students' talking out of turn, goofing off, fighting, and bullying, however, educators in some schools struggle to deal with threats of violence and aggression. The safe schools movement represents an effort of educators, parents, and the community to provide students with safe havens in which to learn. Although far from exhaustive, these suggestions can help educators create a learning environment that is physically and psychologically safe for all students.

REFERENCES

Arman, J. F. 2000. In the wake of tragedy at Columbine High School. Professional School Counseling 3(3): 218-20.

Astor, R. A., H. A. Meyer, and W. J. Behre. 1999. Unowned places and times: Maps and interviews about violence in high schools. American Educational Research Journal 36(1): 3-42.

Bender, W. N., T. H. Shubert, and P. J. McLaughlin. 2001. Invisible kids: Preventing school violence by identifying kids in trouble. Intervention in School and Clinic 37(2): 105-11.

Braaten, S. 1999. Youth violence and aggression: "Why?" or, should we be asking, "Why not?" Preventing School Failure 44(1): 32-36.

Coggeshall, M. B., and P. M. Kingely. 2001. Cross-survey analysis of school violence and disorder. Psychology in the Schools 38(2): 117-26.

Dodd, A. W. 2000. Making schools safe for all students: Why schools need to teach more than the 3 R's. NASSP Bulletin 84(614): 25-31.

Erb, T. 2000. Interview with Gerald Bourgeois: Voice of experience on school safety. Middle School Journal 31(5): 5-11.

Essex, N. L. 2000. Zero tolerance approach to school violence: Is it going too far? American Secondary Education 29(2): 37-40.

Furlong, M. J., M. P. Bates, and D. C. Smith. 2001. Predicting school weapon possession: A secondary analysis of the youth risk behavior surveillance survey. Psychology in the Schools 38(2): 127-39.

Furlong, M. I., and G. Morrison. 2000. The school in school violence: Definitions and facts. Journal of Emotional and Behavioral Disorders 8(2): 71-99.

Harris, I. M. 2000. Peace-building responses to school violence. NASSP Bulletin 84(614): 5-24.

Hedin, D., K. Hannes, and R. Saito. 1985. Minnesota youth poll. Youth look at themselves and the world, Minneapolis: Center for Youth Development and Research, University of Minnesota.

Hoang, F. Q. 2001. Addressing school violence. The FBI Law Enforcement Bulletin 70(8): 18-27.

Hyman, I. A., and P. A. Snook. 2000. Dangerous schools and what you can do about them. Phi Delta Kappan 81(7): 488-93.

Kingery, P. M., M. B. Coggeshall, and A. A. Alford. 1999. Weapon carrying by youth. Education and Urban Society 31(3): 309-33

Kostinsky, S., E. O. Bixler, and P. A. Ketti. 2001. Threats of school violence in Pennsylvania after media coverage of the Columbine High School massacre: Examining the role of imitation. Archives of Pediatrics and Adolescent Medicine 155(9): 994-1008.

Leone, P. E., M. J. Mayer, K. Malmgren, and S. M. Meisel. 2000. School violence and disruption: Rhetoric, reality, and reasonable balance. Focus on Exceptional Children 33(1): 1-20.

----2001. School violence and disruption: Rhetoric, reality, and reasonable balance. Counseling and Human Development 33(8): 1-20.

Lumsden, L. 2000. Profiling students for violence. ERIC Digest 139. University of Oregon: College of Education.

McAndrews, T. 2001. Zero-tolerance policies. ERIC Digest 146. University of Oregon: College of Education.

McEvoy, A. 1999. The relevance of theory to the safe schools movement. Education and Urban Society 31(3): 275-85.

National School Safety Center. 1999. Working together to create safe schools. Westlake Village, CA National School Safety Center.

Plucker, J. A. 2000. Positive approaches to preventing school violence: Peace building in schools and communities. NASSP Bulletin 84(614): 1-4.

Reddy, M., R. Borum, J. Berglund, B. Vossekuil, R. Fein, and W. Modzeleski. 2001. Evaluating risk for targeted violence in schools: Comparing risk assessment, threat assessment, and other approaches. Psychology in the Schools 38(2): 157-72.

Schneider, T. 2001a. Safer schools through environmental design. ERIC Digest 144. University of Oregon: College of Education.

----. 2001b. Newer technologies for school security. ERIC Digest 145. University of Oregon: College of Education.

Scott, V. 1998. Breaking the cycle of incivility. High School Magazine 6(1): 4-7.

Skiba, R., and R. Peterson. 1999. The dark side of zero tolerance. Phi Delta Kappan 80(5): 372-76.

Stader, D. L. 2000. Preempting threats with sound school policy. NASSP Bulletin 84(617): 68-72.

Sugai, G., J. R. Sprague, R. H. Homer, and H. M. Walker. 2000. Preventing school violence: The use of office discipline referrals to assess and monitor school-wide discipline interventions. Journal of Emotional and Behavioral Disorders 8(2): 94-100.

U.S. Department of Education. 1998. Early warning timely response: A guide to safe schools. Washington, DC: U.S. Department of Education.

Verdugo, R. R. 1999. Safe schools: Theory, data, and practices. Education and Urban Society 31(3): 267-74.

Walker, H. M., and J. Eaton-Walker. 2000. Key questions about school safety: Critical issues and recommended solutions. NASSP Bulletin 84(614): 46-55.

Yell, M. L., and M. E. Rozalski. 2000. Searching for safe schools: Legal issues in the prevention of school violence. Journal of Emotional and Behavioral Disorders 8(3): 187-207.

Katherine T. Bucher and M. Lee Manning are professors in the Department of Curriculum and Instruction at Old Dominion University, in Norfolk, Virginia.

From *The Clearing House*, Vol. 76, No. 3, January/February 2003. © 2003. Reprinted with permission of the Helen Dwight Reid Educational Foundation. Published by Heldref Publications, 1319 Eighteenth St., NW, Washington, DC 20036-1802.

Best Practices in Transition Programs

Nicole M. Deschenes; Hewitt B. Clark

Although the Individuals with Disabilities Education Act (IDEA) has provided a national mandate to help high school students with disabilities grow into independent adults, youth with emotional and behavioral difficulties continue to experience considerable problems transitioning into adulthood. Their adjustment into socially acceptable adult roles has been examined in a number of follow-up and follow-along studies.[1-3] These studies consistently show that many of these young people achieve only a few of the critical post-school outcomes identified by Will, Halpern and others:

- High school completion. In numerous studies, students who have experienced emotional and/or behavioral difficulties have been found to have the highest high school dropout rates among all exceptionalities.

- Postsecondary or vocational education. Only 7 to 26 percent of the youth who do graduate go on to enter postsecondary education and training.

- Employment. These youth are more likely to be unemployed, under-employed, or employed in lower-skilled jobs than any other group of the same age. The earnings of these young people are slightly more than minimum wage and often in less than full-time employment, placing them in poverty.

- Independent living. Many of these young adults are unable to attain a level of financial self-sufficiency necessary to live independently. Therefore, they are at great risk of homelessness and dependency on public assistance once they leave the school system.

- Social adjustment. Finally, youth with emotional and behavioral difficulties are more likely to experience substance abuse, unplanned adolescent pregnancy, involvement with the criminal justice system, psychiatric disorders, and poor work, marital and occupational adjust-

ment than other groups. These youth are more than twice as likely as youth with other disabilities to be living in a correctional facility, a halfway house, a drug treatment center or "on the street" as they transition to adulthood.

The complex challenges of the transition process of these young people and their unique needs pose a major challenge to parents, practitioners, administrators and policy makers. It also presents a compelling argument for designing transition systems around a solid framework of promising strategies that facilitate the vocational, social and community transition of these young people.

To identify the best practices in transition programs for youth with emotional and behavioral difficulties, Clark and Stewart[4] conducted a survey of more than 250 transition programs across North America, visiting some of them in order to examine their values and practices. Although the transition programs studied presented a wide range of supports and services, common crucial features were identified leading to the development of six guidelines that seem to drive the development and operation of quality transition systems.[5,6]

Transition to Independence Process (TIP) system guidelines

1. Person-centered planning is driven by the young person's interests, strengths and cultural and familial values.

Improved community outcomes for young people in transition stem from an informal and flexible planning process driven by the young person's interests, strengths, and cultural and familial values; a process that allows for the formulation of the individual's goals. In model programs, staff encourages youth to take an active role in planning their transition to work and adult community life and allowing them to make decisions regarding their futures. For example, young people served by these programs often determined who would participate in their transition processes. Family members, friends, co-workers, therapists, church-members and others were invited to come together to create a circle of friends to help these young people reach their goals. In addition, the young person's skills, strengths, preferences, cultural values, limitations and personal goals were used to guide students to educational opportunities as well as pre-employment experiences and employment. This focus clearly increased the interest, involvement and self-determination for the young people.

For example, at one of the programs we visited, Jose, a 17-year-old, strong, tall, Hispanic young man, had not been in school since he was arrested three months before. Jose had been in and out of a variety of out-of-home placements since he was eight years old. Released to a foster home in his hometown of San Antonio, Jose had been mandated by the judge to return to school and keep out of trouble. Throughout his multiple placements and incarcerations, Jose had always managed to keep a ten-speed bicycle he had purchased three years ago with money given to him by his Aunt Rosie. Jose had maintained his bicycle in excellent condition despite the miles he had put on it.

A transition facilitator at Jose's new school worked with him on identifying his interests and skills and on expressing them during his transition-planning meeting. His team was very supportive of his interest in mechanics. With the team's encouragement, Jose joined a school-to-work program that taught him skills in small engines repair. The transition facilitator also helped him find an after-school job opportunity that required these new skills and helped him prepare for the interview. Now, along with his school activities, Jose works at a bicycle shop in his neighborhood.

2. Services and supports must be tailored for each youth individually and must encompass all transition domains.

An array of individualized services and supports is essential during the transition from school to employment and independent community living. The supports and services provided by the model programs visited were comprehensive in scope, encompassing the four different transition domains of employment, educational opportunities, living situation and community-life adjustment. A comprehensive array of community-based service and support options within each of these domains was provided to accommodate the strengths, needs and life circumstances of each young person.

For example, in the employment domain, the model programs accessed a range of work opportunities with varying levels of support, including practicum and paid work experience, transitional employment, supported employment and competitive employment (e.g., employment in a large hotel or in a park with a co-worker identi-

fied as a training mentor). Similarly, in the domain of community-life adjustment, supports and services were provided in different settings by various supportive individuals, including the youth's natural support system. For example, a live-in aunt taught her nephew how to cook at home, a teacher helped her students establish an Internet users' group and a case manager helped a young person obtain the necessary financial means to move into an apartment. These supports and services were most effective when they were flexible, individualized and reflected the changing needs of the young person.

3. Services and supports need to be coordinated to provide continuity from the young person's perspective.

Continuity of supports across child and adult systems is essential during the transition to adult living, especially when a young person turns 18 and must begin to access adult services. To ensure access to required community resources and the creation of opportunities across all of the transition domains, collaborative linkages must be established at the young person's level and at the system level. For example, in some programs that were visited, transition facilitators or case managers assigned to transitional youth were employed half-time in children's mental health and halftime in adult mental health services giving them the authority to work in both arenas. In other communities, regional and state-level interdepartmental teams were formed to coordinate available resources and to resolve issues related to specific individuals (e.g., eligibility criteria).

Continuity is, however, best achieved from the young person's perspective when the program focused on establishing the young person as his or her own "life manager," teaching self-advocacy and related skills that allowed him or her to function as independently as possible. In conjunction to this focus is the development of reliable natural support systems. In many cases, these supports are found to be the only ones that continued after managed care had pulled its funding.

4. A safety net of support is provided by the young person's team.

Another crucial feature identified in some of the model programs was their unconditional safety net of support. Kaleidoscope, a youth development program in Chicago, was one such program that exemplified this no eject/no reject policy. The program service providers offered an unconditional commitment to transitional youth by accepting referrals based on the community's determination of who was to be admitted and by unfailingly adjusting services and supports based on the current and future changing needs of each individual. They never denied services to these youth and never rejected them under any circumstances. Kaleidoscope did not punitively discharge any of the youth involved in their transitional program. Although a few youth did decide to leave the program on their own, and others left due to contingencies such as criminal convictions that involved prison terms, administrators and staff at Kaleidoscope "stuck with" the youth they served "no matter what." This commitment is a powerful expression by staff of their hopefulness and a positive affirmation of the young person's worth and merit.

5. Achieving greater independence requires the enhancement of the young person's competencies.

Although vocational training and career development often predominate in transition programs, other community life skills are necessary to successfully transition into independent adult living. Such skills, including problem solving, communication, daily living, money management, personal hygiene, housekeeping, emotional/behavioral self-management, recreational and social development are integrated into numerous curricula on the market, offering models and strategies for teaching **these** relevant and meaningful life skills. These approaches, however, often do not account for the diversity of individual needs of transitional youth. To avoid this deficit, model programs provided youth with concrete actions and practice opportunities in real-life community environments, such as integrated worksites, apartments and shopping malls, to teach these important skills most effectively and functionally.

Effective transitions to the world of work and adult community life were clearly enhanced in programs that helped youth acquire community-relevant skills. It was important for these youth to learn how to function in the mainstream of the community alongside regular students, community members and co-workers. In the model programs visited, such environments included practicum experiences in a competitive work environment, school-sponsored work experiences, community-based instruction, apartment living and after-work social activities with co-workers. In several of the model programs visited, transition facilitators actually helped transitional youth establish themselves in the community. They helped them select the apartment, furnish it and obtain necessary kitchen appliances, hygiene supplies and cleaning materials. As the young person moved into the apartment, the transition facilitators taught and reinforced such skills as budgeting, shopping, cooking, cleaning and getting along with neighbors.

Community businesses and industries were tremendous partners in the transition programs when youth were ready to enter the labor market. Often the businesses' unique needs were met by these interested young people. For example, at the Marriott Foundation for people with disabilities, a school-to-work program, employer representatives worked closely with youth that had experienced difficulties in order to place and support them in corporate-sponsored internships. Such internships provide the young people with work experiences that helped them gain the skills and experience necessary to seek competitive employment later in life.

This approach to teaching relevant and meaningful community living skills is very important for these students who often have had poor experiences related to traditional classroom instruction. Students involved in these activities also appreciate being able to earn high school credits toward graduation while acquiring these relevant community-based experiences.

6. The TIP system must be outcome-driven.

Finally, all of the programs visited exhibited an outcome orientation that emphasized three features: youth outcomes, system responsiveness and system effectiveness. Limited resources, new legislative mandates and changing views about the needs for ongoing services for youth during transition all indicate the need for increased evaluation of programs and youth outcomes. Service providers who were interested in and responsive to evaluation data seemed to be more effective than those who were not involved in monitoring outcomes.

For example, the school attended by Jose, the young man previously described in this article, went the extra mile to track outcomes. Not only did this program monitor Jose's outcomes closely (he only partially met his academic goals, but was successful in achieving each of his employment and independent living goals), the program also aggregated such outcomes data on a regular basis to determine how the program was doing overall. These data on goal completion were tracked across all four transition domains.

Conclusion

To "make it" as adults is particularly difficult for youth with emotional and behavioral challenges. Many of these youth encounter economic hardship, instability and dependence when they leave the school to enter the world of employment and independent living. The consequences of being set adrift during this transition can be tragic if these young people are left without social or independent living skills and community support. To be effective, professionals and community members must continue to address the complex, multiple and interrelated needs of this population across the four transition domains of employment, educational opportunities, living situation, and community-life adjustment.

Transition systems based on the six TIP guidelines identified above will clearly be more effective in addressing these youths' needs than those that are not. However, adopting best practices alone may not be enough to ensure successful transitions. Greater collaboration among all required supportive resources and services also needs to occur. Finally, research and development efforts must continue to be undertaken in order to address critical issues faced by youth and young adults in their crucial transitions from school to adult living. These systemic developments, in conjunction with best practices, may be what are required to ensure more successful transitions of these young people.

Nicole Deschenes and Hewitt B. Clark are affiliated with the Department of Child and Family Studies at the Florida Mental Health Institute at the University of South Florida. Deschenes can be reached at (813) 974-4493 or by e-mail: deschene@mirage.fmhi.usf.edu. Clark can be reached at (813) 974-6409 or by e-mail: clark@mirage.fmhi.usf.edu.

References

1. Will M: OSERS Programming for the Transition of Youth with Disabilities: Bridges from School to Working Life. Washington, DC: Office of Special Education and Rehabilitative Services, 1984.

2. Halpern A: Transition: a look at the foundations. Exceptional Children 1985; 57:479-486.

3. Davis M, Vander Stoep A: The Transition to Adulthood Among Adolescents Who Have Serious Emotional Disturbance. Report prepared for the National Resource Center on Homelessness and Mental Illness Policy Research Associates, Delmar, NY, 1996.

4. Clark HB, Stewart ES: Transition into employment, education, and independent living: a survey of programs serving youth and young adults with emotional/behavioral disorders. In Kutash K, Liberton CJ, Algarin A, et al. (eds.): Proceedings of the Fifth Annual Conference on a System of Care for Children's Mental Health: Expanding the Research Base. Tampa: University of South Florida, 1992.

5. Clark HB, Foster-Johnson L: Serving youth in transition to adulthood. In Stroul BA (Ed.) Children's Mental Health. Creating Systems of Care in a Changing Society, 533-551. Baltimore: Paul H. Brookes Publishing Co., 1996.

6. Clark, HB, Deschenes N, Jones J: A framework for the development and operation of a transition system. In Clark HB, Davis M (Eds.) Transition to Adulthood. A Resource for Assisting Young People with Emotional or Behavioral Difficulties. Baltimore: Paul H. Brooks Publishing Co., 2000.

From *The Brown University Child and Adolescent Behavior Letter,* Vol. 17, No. 6, June 2001. © 2001 by Manisses Communications Group. Reprinted with permission.

Technology in the Classroom

How it is Changing (And not Changing) Learning

"The history of computer technology in the classroom demonstrates an amazing lack of vision." —*Alan November*, educational technology expert and consultant.

Thirty years ago, the "multimedia center" in any given public school housed the books, the movie and slide projectors, and the tape recorders. Language learning was "interactive" in labs where dutiful students sat in sound-deadening booths, bulky headphones strapped to their head, repeating foreign words and phrases playing off scratchy vinyl records. Current definitions of "interactive multimedia" would surely have been marked wrong on the weekly vocabulary quizzes of the day.

Fast forward 20 years to the advent of digital audio, video and graphics—and the software tools that combined them into user-friendly multimedia games and encyclopedias. In the early 1990s, technology gurus predicted a new kind of learning. Educators had been developing multisensory teaching techniques—teaching the same idea through a variety of stimuli and at one's own pace to help reach more learners in more ways—and the shiny CD-ROMs packed with interactive multimedia information took on the reflected light of a holy grail. Finally, it seemed, teachers and students stood at the brink of an important breakthrough in access to and control of information.

In his 1988 book Odyssey, then-Apple CEO John Sculley speculated about a future learning tool he called a "Knowledge Navigator." "Grab the handles and drive into the future. Document scanning, speech and handwriting recognition replace keyboards for data input," the text enthused. Did it actually go down like that? Well, yes and no. what some called a navigator morphed into the "Information Superhighway," and efforts to bring high technology to bear on interactive learning took a giant step onto the World Wide Web.

Interactive learning differs from traditional classroom learning in some essential ways. First, it is driven primarily by the learner, not the teacher. Online or in an interactive computer-based format, learners explore at their own pace and on their own schedule. Second, they move through information in paths that make sense to them, not just to the teacher. The paths they choose are intuitive, driven by interest rather than by topic or syllabus. Just as important, interactive learning can be multisensory, offering a mix of text, image, sound and video.

What is the impact of this new learning paradigm on the traditional classroom? How can today's school stay ahead of rapidly changing technology that is hard to predict and even harder to direct? And, what is the role of the traditional classroom in a world of distance learning and wireless, Web-enabled personal digital assistants (PDAs)?

For the architect, there are practical matters to attend to. According to Tom Spies, senior vice president and director of the Education Studio at CS&D Architects, a Baltimore-based architectural firm, "with the advent of the e-mail accounts we see in private schools that every kid has access to the Internet—and they want to get to it all the time. So, we are putting more computers in public places." As schools require their students to have laptops, "one issue is making sure that there is enough room (designed) for the laptop and a notebook to be open on the table at the same time." In most independent school populations, there is a computer at home, and much of the research and writing is done there. "Schools need to provide output devices, such as plotters, good printers and binders," he says. Of course, this also means designing convenient locations for such "service bureau" functions into new school planning.

Like many states, Maryland in the mid-90s launched a statewide initiative to get schools wired, connected to the Internet and outfitted with computers. "The governor's initiative to wire Maryland's schools was really the first phase," says Spies. "Today, in both private and public schools, it's hard to find a classroom without access to computers." The next step, he says, will focus on classroom applications. And the state is funneling money into software development and teacher training.

"My own personal experience is that I see a lot of classrooms with a lot of dark screens," says Spies. He says many students "only use computers for word processing" and to e-mail back and forth to classmates and teachers. "The way curriculum is set up a lot of computers are not used," he concedes. "When a new invention like a computer comes along, it is often used in an old way. It takes a while for the uses of a new invention to be discovered." Technology use too often mimics traditional classroom exercises, relegating costly computer gear to the role of glorified paper. What about the computer's unique ability to create collaborations with others at great distances, or its information gathering and publishing power? What about its exquisite skill at crunching numbers and collecting data? What if more schools used the computer as a platform to compile real data and provide research information with real-world applications?

Enter Alan November, a nationally known educational consultant who helps schools and school districts define how new technologies can be applied in useful ways. According to November, it's high time high tech was used right in educational settings: "First we had the computer lab, but it was down the hall, not in the classroom. Then we moved computers into classrooms, but teachers kept giving the same assignments as they always gave. At best, we got the same results; at worst, we get worse results because so much time was spent on system maintenance. Now we have the Internet. Unfortunately, it is too often seen as a one-way wire going out to find information. We are bolting technology into an industrial version of education where the teacher controls the information." His vision of computer use in schools amounts to a kind of "authentic" curriculum that fundamentally "raises our expectations of learning."

Further, he says, "If I ran an independent school, I would use the Internet and reality-based projects to have students build relationships with alumni."

His goal would be to have alumni mentor work with the student on the big problems, and have teachers working with students to set schedules, make sure work is getting done, feed the student necessary skills and make sure they are learning. "Schools are dying to strengthen relationships with alumni," he says. What better way than through sustained contact with current students?

He advocates creating environments where students can make noise and work in teams to get things done. "We need many smaller spaces for four to six kids," he says, "because all of the sound and video and conferencing that is possible can be distracting." He also predicts that the traditional blackboard will soon be replaced by large flat panel displays, where teachers and students can share the results of work done in collaboration with other schools, students and teachers. In November's mind, the "whole concept of rows and furniture has to evolve to accommodate more collaboration." He predicts that in some schools, "the walls will fold back—even the hallway walls—so that kids can put on authentic presentations for large groups of peers." There also need to be more room sizes to accommodate more varied groups. "Not the traditional classroom size," he insists. "Mix it up for larger and smaller groups."

"I would stop buying desktop computers altogether," he continues, "because most students in the future will be using Palm-like devices." Palms, Visors and other PDAs, represent two converging trends in technology: miniaturization and wireless communication. These trends may actually have the effect of minimizing the significance of architectural change in schools, because they do away with the need for designing computer labs, special desks, wiring and fiber optic cabling systems, and the like.

But that is still in the future. "Because wireless and battery technologies are not quite there yet," says Spies, "we provide boxes in the floor every five or six ft., which will soon become dinosaurs as (wireless and battery) technologies come online."

November believes there should be an online learning facility in every school, with a facilitator. "You need to teach information literacy," he says. "Students don't understand why (Internet) search engines return different results. They don't understand the structure of the Internet and how to deconstruct its layers." To do that, "every kid must understand how to build a Website and how to tear it apart." That demands a place to conduct such study, and it requires teacher education. So, while schools continue to grapple with the adaptation of computers and the Internet to architectural design, they must also integrate technology more fully into the curriculum.

Will the traditional classroom ever disappear? "No teacher I work with has ever said that the computer will replace the classroom," says Spies. "The socialization that comes through interaction at school and the sharing of ideas will continue to be mediated through classrooms." November agrees and adds, "parents don't want kids at home all the time. Kids don't want to be with parents. I don't think the classroom will ever go away. It's like the library: you always need someone to help. We'll always need teachers to raise expectations, to help kids manage their learning more."

From *School Planning and Management*, Vol. 41, No. 3, March 2002, pp. 43-45. © 2002 by Peter Li Education Group. Reprinted with permission.

The New Cheating Epidemic

More (and younger) kids are taking the easy way out to get good grades in school. Even worse, parents are actually helping students get away with it. Redbook reports on this troubling trend—and tells you how to keep your children honest.

Anne Marie Chaker

While grading essays, Eileen Theim, a teacher in Bethesda, Maryland, came across some lines in a seventh grader's assignment that sounded suspiciously eloquent. After a quick search online, Theim found the phrase in question—a professional writer's web-site. When Theim confronted the student about the stolen lines, "the student said, 'Oh, OK,' as if she didn't know it was wrong," Theim recalls. Asked to redo the essay, the student chose to merely cut the lines she'd lifted and resubmit it.

If you think that this student was the exception and that most kids wouldn't dream of cheating on schoolwork, you're in for a surprise. Recent studies show that the majority of students cheat. In a survey by the Josephson Institute of Ethics, 74 percent of high schoolers say they've cheated on an exam at least once; this is up 13 percent from a decade ago. And 59 percent of middle schoolers admit to the same crime, according to a study conducted at Rutgers University in New Jersey. Even younger kids are cheating, according to one teacher's experiment in Rigby, Idaho: When the teacher, Sharon Jones, asked second and fifth graders to grade their own tests, all but three kids cheated to get the reward she'd promised high scores: a candy bar.

Making matters worse is that teachers and parents are allowing—even helping—kids to cheat, seeing it as the only way for them to survive and stay sane in these high-stakes, fast-paced times. Under more pressure to keep test scores up than ever, schools are sometimes abandoning their ethics to meet their goals. And parents, pained at the sight of their kids in tears or up late slaving over homework, are increasingly willing to finish those assignments themselves.

But what, exactly, is driving so many students, at such early ages, to cheat? And why are adults—their alleged role models—letting them get away with this deceit? Redbook reveals this disturbing trend and how you can encourage your kids to stay honest.

New High-Tech Hicks

We're all familiar with the usual ways kids cheat, from crib sheets written on sneakers to coughing codes between classmates. But these days, cheating has gone high tech. Pagers can transmit test answers without telltale whispers; websites such as school sucks.com hawk custom-written term papers on any topic. Ken Rodoff, a high school teacher in Springfield, Pennsylvania, was recently introduced to the powers of a laser printer when he uncovered a student's thumbnail-size crib sheet, printed in a font just large enough to read. "I have to admit it, it was impressive," he says. Though he failed that student, he doubts he's spotting every cheat sheet. "They're so small," he says.

These tech-savvy scams make it easier than ever for students to slide phony work by teachers, who are often unaware that cheating is going on—or just don't care. "Ninety-eight percent of cheaters don't get caught, and only half of those caught are punished," estimates Michael Josephson, president of the Josephson Institute, a Marina del Rey, California, research institute.

Sadly, it's the honest students who sometimes get the short end of the stick. "Once, an eleventh grader arrived at my after-school book club crying," says one school librarian. "She said that earlier that week, students in her history class had gotten a hold of their exam before they had to take it." But the girl had refused to look at it, and her grade ended up being lower than those of the cheaters. Even so, she refused to rat out her peers. The girl's teacher felt that little could be done, since she couldn't tell who'd cheated. "Here was a girl who was trying to do the right thing," says the librarian. But she was paddling against the current, which allowed others to thrive while she faltered.

Students in Crisis

Why are so many kids becoming cheaters? Largely because the pressure they're under to succeed is more intense than ever—

and hits them as early as primary school. "These days getting on the honor roll or into elite secondary schools is increasingly difficult. I've seen third graders with private tutors," says John Dacey, Ph.D., an author of Your Anxious Child. Plus, the growing importance of extracurricular activities as a way to stand out to admissions boards is forcing students to spread themselves thin. Combine all this with the fact that young kids often lack the judgment or self-control to enable them to do the right thing, and some are bound to take the easy way out by copying their neighbors' test answers. "Kids are starving for some free time," says Dacey. "They'll do what it takes to get some hours to themselves."

One reason this pressure to excel starts early is standardized tests, now taken as often as once a year starting in kindergarten in some states, says Kevin Welner, a director of the Education and the Public Interest Center at the University of Colorado in Boulder. Kids who don't perform well may be held back, shuttled into less advanced curricula, or denied entrance into selective middle and high schools.

For Maria Vidal de Haymes, 40, this emphasis on standardized tests rather than on a school's curriculum convinced her to pull her seventh-grade son out of a Chicago public school at the end of the term and enroll him in a private school. "The better public high schools in this area pretty much only accept kids who score above the 95th percentile on the Iowa Test of Basic Skills [a standardized test]," she says. "These tests are demoralizing for kids, especially when their friends make it into good high schools and they don't. Parents with seventh and eighth graders are all panicking."

And as if high-stakes tests didn't produce enough anxiety, kids are doing nearly twice as much homework as they did 20 years ago, according to a study by the University of Michigan in Ann Arbor. Given these time constraints, Dianna Ewton, 40, empathized when her ninth-grade daughter confessed that she's copied friends' homework. "I gave her hell, but I can see why she did it," she says. "Her field hockey practice lasts until 5:30, and she also volunteers at the YMCA, babysits, and plays flute in the school band." Copying, she concludes, is her daughter's attempt to make ends meet.

School for Scandal

Perhaps most shocking, teachers themselves are cheating as well. Last October teachers and principals in 14 Chicago-area elementary schools were investigated for helping students answer questions on the Iowa tests, which are mandatory for students in the third, sixth, and eighth grades. So far, a substitute teacher and teacher's aide have been dismissed. What's more, some teachers claimed that their supervisors had told them to cheat on the tests to jack up the scores; one teacher claimed she'd lost her job after refusing to do it.

What drove these schools into such shady territory? A fear that low standardized test scores will have dire consequences for the school itself. "Last year alone, three Chicago schools were shut down as a result of their students' overall performance on the

test," says the Chicago Teachers Union President Deborah Lynch. And President Bush's January 2001 signing of the No Child Left Behind Act ratchets up the pressure even more, requiring annual standardized testing of all students in third through eighth grade. High poverty schools that get federal funding and don't show an adequate yearly progress five years in a row face a state-government takeover. "This doesn't give schools much time at all to improve," says Melanie Mitchell, assistant director of the Keenan Institute for Ethics at Duke University. "I wouldn't be surprised if it tempts some schools to cheat."

Parents Who Help too Much

With the stakes so high, even parents don't always play fair when it comes to their child's education. While most adults wouldn't approve of kids' copying each other's homework, more than one in five parents say they've done part of a child's homework assignment themselves, according to a study by Public Agenda, a research firm in New York.

AnneLise Wilhelmsen, 41, of Los Alamitos, California, freely admits she's had a hand in doing her fourth-grade son's homework. In particular, she recalls watching her 9-year-old son struggle to complete a geography assignment. When she realized he couldn't get it done in time, she lent a hand. "Strictly speaking, this may have been cheating, but it was the right decision for this boy on this specific day," she says. "It [excessive homework] cuts into family time. It cuts into our children's opportunity to be children."

Etta Kralovec, an author of The End of Homework: How Homework Disrupts Families, Overburdens Children and Limits Learning, doesn't blame parents for helping so much. "Parents don't want to, but they also don't want their child to get bad grades or to have a meltdown trying to get everything done," she says. Another reason some parents do homework is so that they can spend more quality time with their kids. "We're increasingly protective of family time," Kralovec says. So much so, in fact, that at one school in Piscataway, New Jersey, parents staged protests decrying the amount of homework their kids received. The school now has "homework caps" limiting the amount of homework teachers can assign.

While schools often justify heavy homework loads by claiming that they boost standardized-test scores, this doesn't hold true for elementary school students, says Harris Cooper, professor of educational psychology at the University of Missouri in Columbia. "Younger kids don't have the cognitive skills or the attention span to benefit from long periods of study," Cooper explains. Some experts even say it's detrimental to young kids, who get frustrated and lose interest in subjects they once adored.

Why Cheating Goes Unpunished

Teachers say some forms of cheating are easier to spot than others. For instance, spotting homework that's benefited from a parent's "help" is a no-brainer. Some parents make it even more obvious by turning in assignments in their own handwriting. But calling parents on their rule-bending is often more trouble than it's worth. One New York middle school teacher says she argues with parents over grades on homework they've helped with "on a weekly basis." "They'll demand that I change the grade from a C to an A," she says. "I usually say, 'You get an A, but your kid gets a C.'" But more often than not, this teacher's principal recommends that she inflate the grade, and she does. "I'm an untenured teacher," she points out. "What else am I supposed to do?"

Christine Pelton, a former tenth-grade biology teacher at Piper High School in Kansas, knows all too well the consequences of standing up to irate parents. In December 2001, she found out that 28 of her students had cut and pasted essays off websites. She gave those students zeros, causing many to fail the course. A parental uproar ensued. "I got phone calls in the middle of the night from people cursing," she says. After the superintendent and the school board forced her to pass the students, she resigned in disgust. The superintendent and some board members have since left the district. "But I got a lot of respect from students," she says. "They said they were glad someone had finally stood up to the students who cheated."

How to Cheat-Proof Your Child

While containing such widespread cheating may seem daunting, parents can do so in various ways, starting in their own homes. Even before kids head off to kindergarten, you should have a talk with them, telling them that cheating is wrong and won't be tolerated (for tips on this topic, refer to "How to Talk to Your Child About Cheating").

But since even honest kids will be tempted to cheat if everyone else is getting away with it, parents also have to push for school-wide reform. The best place to do this is at a school board meeting. "Parents often make the mistake of approaching teachers," says Kralovec. But, surprisingly, teachers won't be able to do much; only principals and school boards have the power to put an end to rampant cheating, through changes in school policy (to find out when your local school board meets, inquire at the school principal's office).

What kinds of policies should parents request? For starters, ask that the board prohibit teachers from giving the same test to students in different periods of the same class, or from year to year. This measure will keep students from passing tests around to their peers who may be taking them later. You can also request that teachers keep a close eye on students during tests.

But teaching students to behave ethically on their own is a far more important and challenging goal for schools, says Don Mc-Cabe, founder of the Center for Academic Integrity. To this end, parents can ask the school board to write and enforce an honor code delineating what constitutes cheating and how students will be penalized if caught doing so. Having clear guidelines that are explained to students regularly goes a long way toward keeping students in line. Students and parents should receive a copy of this code at the beginning of every school year; after big tests, students should sign a waiver stating that they haven't cheated and are aware of the consequences if they do. These regular reminders will also discourage cheating.

Heavy homework loads may also be part of the problem. To keep your kids from feeling so pressed for time that they copy pals' assignments, ask the school board to make some homework nongraded (especially for younger kids) and to establish homework caps. Ron Bolandi, a school superintendent in Tewksbury, New Jersey, has implemented these policies, and while it's too early to tell how they will affect the incidence of cheating, Bolandi knows one thing for sure: "Students love it," he says. "They say now they can stop staying up until 3 a.m. doing homework and have a life."

How to Talk to Your Child About Cheating

Acknoweldge the pressure he's under. Lecturing your child about cheating by simply saying "Don't do it" will create a you-versus-him dynamic that will likely cause him to stop listening to you. Instead say, "I know you're incredibly busy and stressed about school, and that it must be tempting to cheat. But it's still not right." This lets him know you're on his side without conveying that cheating's OK.

Don't say "You'll get caught." Too many kids get away with cheating for you to be able to convince your child that this is true. Instead appeal to his sense of morality by asking him, "How would you feel if someone cheated off you in your favorite class—and got the better grade?" It'll be much harder for him to cheat if he visualizes what it's like to be in the victim's shoes, says Caroline Watts, a psychologist at Children's Hospital in Boston.

Reassure him that grades don't matter that much. Kids often think that their getting high marks means more to you than their doing the right thing. Emphasize that this isn't the case by saying, "I'd be much, much more disappointed in you if you cheated than if you failed a test."

Is Your Child Cheating?

4 ways to find out if your kid earned his grades the honest way.

1. Even if you swear your child isn't cheating, it's good to check in with him regularly to establish that you're monitoring his work to see what he's learned. If you know that your child had a big exam, for example, ask him. "So what were some of the questions on that test you took today?" If he can't remember any, it may mean he copied off someone else, filling in the answers without really reading the questions.

2. Look in on your child frequently while he's doing homework, asking him if he needs any help. If he never has questions, is reluctant to … show you what he's working on, or refuses to work in the same room with you, it may suggest he's doing something you wouldn't approve of, such as exchanging answers with his friends.

3. Ask to see his resources—books, encyclopedias, etc.—for written assignments. If he can't provide them, it may mean he has pasted his essay off the Web or gotten it from someone else.

4. Read his written assignments. If a word he uses seems too sophisticated for someone his age, ask him to define it. If he can't explain it—or the overall point of his essay, for that matter—it may spell trouble.

Once You Know the Score

If your child fails three or more of these measures, there's a very good chance he's cheating. What then? While alerting his teacher and making your child face the consequences at school may seem the right things to do, Michael Josephson of the Josephson Institute usually recommends against this plan. "It may destroy any trust your child has in you," points out Josephson. "The important issue is that the child should be punished at home in a way that conveys that this is not acceptable." You should also address the underlying situation that led your child to cheat. If, for example, he's spread too thin by all his activities, suggest cutting a few of the less important ones so he'll have time to finish his schoolwork without cutting corners.

Television Viewing and Academic Achievement Revisited

Franklin T. Thompson; William P. Austin

The purpose of this paper is to provide readers with a summary of the literature from the last 25 years regarding the impact of television viewing on student achievement and necessary behaviors for school success. Although the overall picture is muddled, the following initial conclusions are offered: (1) moderate levels of viewing are better than high levels or no viewing at all, (b) the type of programming is more critical than the intrinsic qualities of the medium itself, (c) high informational viewing generally correlates positively with achievement, while low informational viewing correlates negatively, (d) once IQ, SES, and other mediating factors are accounted for, the relationship weakens, (e) it is not clear at this time whether negative television viewing causes or is caused by low levels of achievement, and (f) because cultural and socioeconomic differences and responses to TV viewing exist, educators must view each case on a situational basis. Intervention strategies for educators and parents are included.

Introduction:

Given the central role popular media plays in the lives of our children, it is important to have an understanding of the impact television viewing has on academic achievement and school performance. Parents and teachers alike ask the question of how much television viewing is too much. Few people would argue that an investigation of children's TV viewing habits could help parents better understand how youth occupy their free time. In addition, there has been growing concern over the relationship between the media and rising violence and other antisocial behaviors among youth.

The relationships between TV viewing and academic achievement, age, home environment, and other variables are complex, multidimensional, and inconclusive (Bachen, et al., 1982; Beentjes & Van der Voort, 1988; Broome & Fuller, 1993; Razel, 2001). The purpose of this paper is to provide readers with a summary of the literature from the last 25 years regarding the impact of television viewing on student achievement and necessary behaviors for school success. Although the general picture from research is somewhat muddled, an initial understanding of the question can be achieved, nonetheless. It is hoped that this review of literature will provide a basis to implement sound educational policy and family practice.

A Summary of Television Effects Research:

More than half of U.S. students watch more than three hours of television per day on weekdays, and 60% of parents rarely or never limit their child's television viewing habits (Levine & Levine, 1996). The average television weekly viewing time is approximately 27 hours per week, while the average reading time is 8.1; a 3 to 1 ratio (Angle, 1981). Studies (Levine & Levine, 1996; Wells & Blendinger, 1997) support the finding that children watch too much TV and read too little. It has been argued that a negative side effect of high levels of viewing might include the promotion of "unintelligent consumerism" and a physically and intellectually passive dependency among our youth (Levine & Levine, 1996).

Viewing habits typically increase throughout elementary school years, and decrease during high school years. The years right before and after adolescence are the most opportune times to shape TV viewing habits (Clark, et al., 1978). Individuals in lower income brackets and with lower educational levels watch more television (Housden, 1991; Mediamark Research Inc, 1996). Adolescents who view television during late night hours average more television viewing than do other adolescents (Potter, 1987). African American youth tend to watch more TV than their white counterparts (Caldas & Bankston, 1999). Teens who are in the lowest per week viewing category are more likely to continue their education by enrolling in college (Corporation for Public Broadcast, 1993).

Some of the studies reviewed found no significant relationship at all (Gortmaker, Salter, Walker & Dietz, 1990b; Hagborg, 1995; Shastri & Mohite, 1997). A few studies (Felter, 1984; Kohr, 1979) uncovered a large and significant negative relationship, while most others (Angle, 1981; Clark, et al., 1978; Cooper & Valentine, 1999; Dornsbusch, 1986; Gorman & Yu, 1990; Patrick, 1991; Tymms, 1997) found smaller, yet significant negative relationships. Naturally, parents' failure to provide guidelines for television viewing has a lot to do with the attitudes and values of today's children (Clark, et al., 1978; Levine & Levine, 1996; Sharman, 1979).

Patrick (1991) discovered that higher school social studies achievement is associated with "limited television viewing." Felter (1984) reported that achievement scores in reading, math, and written expression were "sharply lower" among students who viewed more than six hours of television per day. Researchers (Dornbusch, 1986; Potter, 1987) have stated that a negative relationship does not begin to manifest itself until a child exceeds a 10 or more hour per week threshold, with the strongest negative relationship observed for 30 or more hours of viewing. Razel (2001) reported a curvilinear relationship for each age group up to 20 years. Each category had an optimal range of viewing times that allowed for a positive impact up to a certain amount, and a negative impact after a point of saturation. The fact that pre-second grade children possessed a larger positive relationship than older children might be a reflection of the quality of programming targeted at the younger group. According to the analysis, optimal viewing time decreased with age, which provided for an overall negative relationship when age group was not disaggregated. The author is careful to report the findings as preliminary.

The impact of television on social adjustment and youth behavior is also not fully understood. Tentative findings are that high amounts of television viewing are associated with relatively poor social skills and peer relations among some youth populations (Clark, et al., 1978; Levine & Levine, 1996). In one study (Sharman, 1979), there was a relationship between low self-esteem and heavy viewing of cartoons, which is often viewed as a form of escapist behavior. When total hours of all types of programming were considered, however, the relationship was not significant. Another study (Anderson, Huston, Schmitt, Linebarger & Wright, 2001) found that preschoolers, male subjects in particular, who had an opportunity to view educational TV behaved less aggressively as adolescents.

For a short time during the 1980's, the television industry responded positively to criticism about violence on TV, but the 1990's saw a rise in the amount of negative portrayals (Levine & Levine, 1996). Some writers (McVey, 1999; Minow & LaMay, 1995; Plagens, 1991; Sager, 1994; Stroman, 1991) have found that heavy amounts of childhood television viewing which promoted violence was associated with adult participation in violent crimes. Negative impacts might include the promotion of increased violence, teenage pregnancy, sexual

perversion, disrespect for adults, and the stereotyping of low-status minorities and women. It is quite likely, however, that adults underestimate children's abilities to separate themselves from the violence, negativity, and the unrealistic problem solving messages of contemporary programming (Broome & Fuller, 1993). Generally speaking, it appears the effects of TV on violent behaviors of youth are largely dependent on situational factors, however.

Research to date has not successfully disentangled the relationship between TV viewing and reading scores (Beentjes & Van der Voort, 1988; Wober, 1992). We know that formal schooling is not the only variable that impacts reading ability (Bachen, et al., 1982). Preliminary findings are that positive television viewing has the potential to enhance reading comprehension skills for younger children (Razel, 2001; Van den Broek, 2001), and can be associated with higher grades and the reading of more books (Anderson, Huston, Schmitt, Linebarger & Wright, 2001). However, IQ is a confounding variable that must be considered in all future research. Once IQ, SES, and other mediating factors are accounted for, the relationship between TV viewing and achievement weakens (Angle, 1981; Gortmaker, 1990a; Hornik, 1981; Potter, 1987).

Race and class differences exist, but more research is needed to clear up a clouded picture. Low teacher expectation, noninvolvement of parents in the child's homework, and high levels of TV viewing appear to work together to produce academic failure for minority students (Viadero & Johnston, 2000a, 2000b). We do know that there is greater usage of television by lower socioeconomic families and inner-city minorities compared to suburban dwellers and whites (Clark, et al., 1978). On the other hand, Gorman and Yu (1990) found a negative relationship between science achievement and high viewer behavior of white students, and were unable to find a relationship for black and Hispanic students. Caldas and Bankston (1999) posit that black youth utilize higher TV viewing habits and relationships among friends who possess a "television culture" as a means to offset the negative impact of homes and neighborhoods higher in incidences of single parent and dysfunctional family settings. Once family structure is accounted for, however, black patterns became similar to that of whites.

Gender roles can play a small but important role in understanding the relationship. In one study (Sharman, 1979), children of lesser-educated fathers watched more entertainment television and exhibited more before school and unsupervised viewing behaviors. Children of higher educated fathers viewed less before school and unsupervised television, and watched more documentaries and less entertainment programming. Henggeler and Cohen (1991) found that a father's dissatisfaction with his marriage and a mother's stress level and related symptomatology were associated with high levels of child television viewing.

Many writers (Angle, 1981; Bachen, et al., 1982; Bianculli, 1992; Eastman, 2001; Levine & Levine, 1996; Razel, 2001) have demonstrated that not all television is harmful to children; television can yield positive, as well as negative results. Children from lower classes potentially benefit if viewing is done in moderate doses, as opposed to large doses or no amounts at all

(Housden, 1991; Levine & Levine, 1996). Benefits for pre-school aged children are best realized if viewing doesn't exceed 3 hours a day (Razel, 2001). Interestingly, a few teenagers surveyed claimed TV offered a "wall of sound" that helped them block out distractive and uninviting home environments. This provided them a more conducive environment to complete homework assignments (Wober, 1992).

Whether television's information enriches, impoverishes, or has no effect on student achievement is partially dependent on the content and quality of the programming instead of intrinsic qualities of the medium itself (Caldas & Bankston, 1999; St. Peters, Fitch, Huston, Wright & Eakins, 1991; Razel, 2001). If students are exposed to programs with high informational content (i.e., news programs or documentaries) students have a better opportunity to increase their knowledge and skills (Housden, 1991; Memory, 1992). If most of the viewing is of the low informational content variety (i.e., shorter fast-action shows, cartoons, music videos, soap operas) an opportunity for a detrimental academic impact is increased (Geist, 2000; Potter, 1987).

The role television should or should not play as an official part of the school's curriculum is a debate that is decades old. Kohr (1979) performed an analysis of data collected from 90,000 fifth, eighth, and eleventh graders from 750 schools and found no significant individual student level differences, but discovered a strong negative relationship at the school level. One longitudinal study (Anderson, Huston, Schmitt, Linebarger & Wright, 2001) found that adolescents who watched educational programs as preschoolers had a positive effect on their grades, behavior, creativity, and social behavior during later years. Another study (Wright, Austin, Aletha, Murphy, St. Peters, Pinon & Kotler, 2001) found that viewing of child-audience informative programs between ages 2 and 3 predicted higher academic performance of low-income children. Others are not as optimistic about the long-range benefits of children's educational TV shows such as Sesame Street. Some contend that the learning involved has the potential to reinforce trivial cognitive skills and produce distractible learners with short attention spans (Levine & Levine, 1996; Neuman, 1995).

A common explanation for the negative relationship between television viewing and achievement is the displacement hypothesis. In short, viewing displaces activities that are educationally more valuable (Hagborg, 1995). Neuman (1995) identifies two additional theories readily endorsed by researchers: (a) the information processing theory—television trains students to process information in a different manner than what schools require, and (b) the short-term gratification theory—television programming promotes short attention spans and quick-fix, magical answers that are non-conducive to high levels of school success. A combination of all three theories most likely mirrors reality in contemporary society.

General Discussion:

There are many gaps in the literature. The impact of parental control, social class, race, and peer pressure is not fully under-

stood. The inability to disentangle multiple variables has plagued the television effects on literature (Levine & Levine, 1995). Some studies show a correlation with one population, but not for others. Methodological problems have been noted, namely the reliance on cross-sectional rather than longitudinal approaches (Gortmaker & Salter, 1990a), the underutilization of social context (Caldas & Bankston, 1999), and the failure to account for the influence of IQ and other mediating factors (Angle, 1981; Hornik, 1981; Potter, 1987).

Since the effects of television viewing are not monolithic, care must be taken to consider various socioeconomic and environmental factors as well as the reasons for viewing. Clearly, program content is a more important consideration than qualities of the medium itself. An area that needs more attention is the impact school-supported television viewing has on achievement. Many educators use television quite extensively in their teaching practices, and would greatly benefit in knowing more about how to offset negative influences. At this point in time, it is not clear whether television viewing causes or is caused by low levels of achievement (Potter, 1987; Razel, 2001).

In summary, the research appears to be saying that high levels of unsupervised mindless television viewing, especially when it is done in lieu of daily reading or other academic stimulation, can have the potential to exert harmful effects on achievement. The utilization of informational television, both in and out of the classroom, can have a positive impact on student achievement if properly channeled. Moderate levels of meaningful and supervised television viewing may be better for children than too much or no viewing at all.

Implications for Parents and Educators:

Findings on the effects of television viewing on academic achievement, study habits, negative behavior, and social skills are largely inconclusive and situational based. Although what we don't know about the impact of television viewing on youth is more than what we do know, we are able, nonetheless, to construct a preliminary intervention approach. Because cultural and socioeconomic differences and responses to TV viewing exist, educators and parents must view each case on a situational basis. Ways in which society can mitigate potential negative effects has begun to surface.

Starting at the core of remediation, parents must become more involved in monitoring the quality and quantity of their children's television viewing habits (Viadero & Johnson, 2000a). We must not be afraid to make a TV plan with our children based on the following suggestions (Broome & Fuller, 1993; Eastman, 2001; Moss, 1998): Parents should require that homework and chores be completed before children partake in the pleasures of recreational TV. They must demand that children engage themselves in individual reading and family socialization time away from the television set. It is prudent to mandate that children include so many hours of informational programming into their viewing diet. Children under four years of age should have little or no exposure to violence. Look for shows based on children's books. A certain amount of viewing should be done together as a family. It is recommended that TV time be turned into thinking time. Talking and thinking about TV helps reduce its negative impact. The utilization of one's VCR and video rentals to prescreen what is viewed is wise.

Classic movies and informational shows can serve to bring families together. Parents who come home late from work might find it helpful to have teenagers report on the specific content of their television viewing before they are allowed special privileges. It also may not hurt to have young children keep TV logs of their viewing, and provide summaries or drawings of what is good and not so good about various television shows as a way to earn reward tokens. Parents may want to keep an atlas and reference books near so that children can look up places they hear on the news. Point out how various school subjects are often incorporated into TV shows. Use commercials to clarify questions. Explain how TV sometimes promotes stereotypes. Help children understand that the messages behind commercials are mostly profit driven. Lastly, parents might consider discussing with their children the pros and cons of values promoted by today's pop media. Research suggests that after clarifying values, people feel more energetic, more critical in their thinking, and are more likely to follow through on decisions (Alexander, 2000).

Likewise, educators must find ways to make television an educational resource instead of an enemy (Broome & Fuller, 1993). Schools would do better by embracing the medium and promoting homework via television. Classroom teachers might encourage students to (a) supplement their learning with viewing documentaries that corroborate subject matter found in textbooks, (b) provide updated statistics through current events reporting, (c) write reports on television programs about history, (d) contrast how a single event is reported by two different news stations, (e) critique informational shows for accuracy and objectivity, (f) report on television interviewing strategies and techniques, and (g) encourage greater reading comprehension and ability through the viewing of TV performing arts presentations (Memory, 1992).

In addition, Levine & Levine (1996) suggest the following suggestions for classroom teachers and administrators to consider:

1. Utilize a "window of opportunity" component that considers age appropriateness and child development theory;
2. Utilize policies and practices that draw on literature about risk factors and validated strategies that change high-risk behaviors;
3. Attack academic problems within a holistic environmental and "family systems" approach; and
4. Encourage activities and lesson plans that teach very young children how to differentiate between fact and fiction.

More conclusive research is needed to back up the preliminary findings of this report. Although some of the suggestions offered in this paper are obvious, failure to abide by them is far too common. Too often, there exists a parenting mindset of omission that ends up having monumental repercussions for a whole generation of youth. Since children find ways to watch TV regardless of adult supervision, it is best to teach and train them in the proper usage of a medium that could help them prepare for better school and career advancement.

References

Alexander, T. (2000). Adjustment and human relations: A lamp along the way. Upper Saddle River, NJ: Prentice Hall, p. 232

Anderson, D. R., Huston, A. C., Schmitt, K. L., Linebarger, D. L., and Wright, J. C. (2001). Early childhood television viewing and adolescent behavior: The recontact study. Monographs of the Society for Research in Child Development, 66 (1),1-147.

Angle, B. D. (1981). The relationship between children's televiewing and the variables of reading attitude, reading achievement, book reading, and IQ in a sample of fifth grade children (Doctoral dissertation, University of Akron, 1981). ProQuest Dissertation abstracts, DAI-A 41/08. (Order No. AAC 8102796)

Bachen, C. M., Hornby, M. C., Roberts, D. F., Hernandez-Ramos, P. E. (1982). Television viewing behavior and the development of reading skills: Survey evidence (Report No. CS-006573). New York, N.Y.: Annual Meeting of the American Educational Research Association. (ERIC Document Reproduction Services No. ED214150)

Beentjes, B. J. (1988). Television's impact on children's reading skills: A review of research. Reading Research Quarterly, 23, 389-413.

Bianculli, D. (1992). Teleliteracy: Taking television seriously. New York, NY: Continuum.

Broome, J., and Fuller, L. (1993). What you need to know about children and television. PTA Today, 18 (7), 7-9.

Caldas, S. J., and Bankston, C. (1999). Black and white TV: Race, television viewing, and academic achievement. Sociological Spectrum, 19 (1), 39-62.

Clark, R. E., Comstock, G., Door, A., Hornik, R., Levie, H., Medrich, E., Salomon, G. (1978). Schooling and leisure time uses of television (Report No. IR-005841). San Diego, California: San Diego Conference on Television and Learning. (ERIC Document Reproduction Services No. ED152317)

Cooper, H., and Valentine, J. (1999). The relationship between five after-school activities and academic achievement. Journal of Educational Psychology, 91 (2), 369-378.

Corporation for Public Broadcasting (1993). How television impacts kids and learning: Lessons from the youth monitor (Report No. IR018198). Washington, DC: Corporation for Public Broadcasting Research Notes - No. 65 (ERIC Documentation Reproduction Service No. ED402909)

Dornsbusch, S. (1986). Helping your kid make the grade (Report No. PS-016104). Reston, Virginia: National Association of Secondary Principals. (ERIC Document Reproduction Services No. ED275406)

Eastman, W. (2001). Media culture and media violence: Making the television work for young children, early childhood educators, and parents. (Report No. PS-029467). Athens, Greece: Third World Forum on Early Care and Education. (ERIC Document Reproduction Services No. ED453916

Felter, M. (1984). Television viewing and school achievement. Journal of Communications, 34 (2), 104-118.

Geist, E. A. (2000). The effect of network and public television programs on four and five year olds' ability to attend to educational tasks. Journal of Instructional Psychology, 27 (4), 250-262.

Glanz, Jeffrey. (2002). Finding Your Leadership Style. Alexandria, Virginia. Association for Supervision and Curriculum Development.

Gorman, S., and Yu, C. C. (1990). Science achievement and home environment: National assessment of educational progress 198501986 (Report No. TM-016266). Boston, MA: Annual Meeting of the American Educational Research Association. (ERIC Document Reproduction Services No. ED330702)

Gortmaker, S. L., Salter, C. A., Walker, D. K., and Dietz, W. H. (1990a). A kind word for TV. Wilson Quarterly, 15 (3), 18.

Gortmaker, S. L., Salter, C. A., Walker, D. K., and Dietz, W. H. (1990b). The impact of television on mental aptitude and achievement: A longitudinal study. Public Opinion Quarterly, 54, 594-604.

Hagborg, W. J. (1995). High school television viewing time: A study of school performance and adjustment. Child Study Journal, 25, 155167.

Henggeler, S., and Cohen, R. (1991). Family stress as a link in the association between television viewing and achievement. Child Study Journal 21 (1), 11-20.

Hornik, R. (1981). Out-of-school television and schooling. Hypothesis and methods. Review of Educational Research, 51, 193-214.

Housden, T. (1991). Television viewing habits of San Juan students related to achievement (Report No. PS-020611). San Juan, CA: San Juan School District Television News. (ERIC Document Reproductive Service No. ED345874)

Kohr, R. L. (1979). The relationship of homework and television viewing to cognitive and noncognitive student outcomes (Report No. IR007608). San Francisco, California: Annual Meeting of the National Council for Measurement in Education. (ERIC Document Reproduction Services No. ED175441)

Levine, D. U., and Levine R. F. (1996). Society and Education (9th ed.). Boston, MA: Allyn and Bacon, pp. 121-124.

Mediamark Research Inc. (1996). Multimedia audiences: Summary. New York, NY: MRI Publishers.

Memory, D. M. (1992). Encouraging the switch to informational television. Clearing House, 65 (5), 302-306.

McVey, M. D. (1999). Violence on television: How teachers can help parents affect positive change. Journal of Early Education and Family Review, 7 (2), 36-45.

Minow, N. N., and LaMay, C. L. (1995). Abandoned in the wasteland. New York: Hill and Wang, pp. 121-122.

Moss, J. (1998). Making the most of television: Tips for parents of young viewers-brochure (Report No. CS-510817). Newark, DE: International Reading Association. (ERIC Document Reproduction Services No. ED462723)

Neuman, S. B. (1995). Literacy in the television age: The myth of the TV effect (2nd ed.). Greenwich, CT: Albex Publishing.

Patrick, J. J. (1991). Achievement of knowledge by high school students in core subjects of the social studies (Report No. SO-021176). Bloomington, Indiana: ERIC Clearinghouse for Social Studies/Social Science Education. (ERIC Document Reproduction Services No. ED329486)

Plagens, P. (1991). Violence in our culture. Newsweek, 117(13): 46-52, pp. 121, 175.

Potter, W. J. (1987). Does television hinder academic achievement among adolescents? Human Communications Journal, 14 (1), 27-46.

Razel, M. (2001). The complex model of television viewing and educational achievement. Journal of Educational Research, 94 (6), 371-380.

Sager, M. (1994). The temple of doom. GQ, 64 (1): 1220136. p. 121.

Sharman, K. J. (1979). Children's television behavior: Its antecedents and relationship to school performance (Report No. IR-007850). Melbourne, Australia: Australian Council for Educational Research - Hawthorn. (ERIC Document Reproduction Services No. ED 179-190)

Shastri, J., and Mohite, E. (1997). Television viewing pattern of primary school children and its relationship to academic performance and cognitive skills. International Journal of Early Years Education, 5 (2), 152-160.

St. Peters, M., Fitch, M., Huston, A. C., Wright, J. C., and Eakins, D. J. (1991). Television and families: What do young children watch with their parents? Child Development, 62 1409-1423.

Strotman C. A. (1991). Television's role in the socialization of African American children and adolescents. Journal of Negro Education, 60 (3): 314-326, pp. 121-122.

Tymms, E. (1997). Science in primary schools: An investigation into differences in the attainment and attitudes of pupils across schools. Research in Science Technological Education, 15 (2), 149-159.

Van den Broek, P.(2001). The role of television viewing in the development of reading comprehension (Report No. CS-014521). Washington, DC: Office of Educational Research and Improvement. (ERIC Document Reproductive Service No. ED458552)

Viadero, D., and Johnston, R. C. (2000a). Lifting minority achievement: Complex answers. Education Week, 19 (30), 1-4.

Viadero, D., and Johnston, R. C. (2000b). Lags in minority achievement defy traditional explanations. Education Week, 19 (28), 1-4.

Wells, L., and Blendinger (1997). Action research: How children in the fifth grade spend their time outside of school (Report No. CG-028241). Memphis, TN: Annual Meeting of the MidSouth Educational Research Association, November. (ERIC Document Reproduction Service No. ED415465)

Wober, J. M. (1992). Text in a texture of television: Children's homework experience. Journal of Educational Television, 18 (1), 2335.

Wright, J. C., Auston, A. C., Murphy, K. C., St. Peters, M., Pinon, R. S., and Kotler, J. (2001). The relations of early television viewing to school readiness and vocabulary of children from low-income families: The Early window project. Child Development, 72 (5), 1347-1366.

Studies Reveal Strengths, Weaknesses

Improving Rates of High School Graduation and College Completion for Low-Income and Minority Students

Bill Hemmer

An in-depth analysis of high school and college graduation data shows that only one in three eighth graders in 1988 earned an Associate's degree 12 years later.

At the same time, a new national study of public perceptions of our education system shows that most Americans recognize that a college degree is critical for economic success, yet most people also believe that our education system, particularly high schools, is failing to prepare young people for higher education.

The Boston-based Jobs for the Future (JFF) today released the two reports, conducted for JFF by the Parthenon Group and Lake Snell Perry & Associates (LSPA), at "Double the Numbers," a national conference focused on improving the rates of college success for youth who are underrepresented in postsecondary education. More than 400 education leaders, public officials, and policymakers are participating in this conference, which is exploring ways to "plug the leaks" in the so-called education pipeline and improve the high school-to-college transition rates, especially for lower-income and minority youth.

According to the national public opinion survey, Americans are aware of the barriers to success that students encounter in high school and college, yet many people also underestimate the challenges that young people—including lower-income and minority youth—face in attempting to earn a college degree. The results show near universal agreement that the high number of students who fail to graduate from high school and complete a college degree is a major problem for the national economy.

"The United States faces the daunting task of improving a major pipeline that is seriously limited," said Hilary Pennington, CEO of Jobs for the Future. "This pipeline is not in a foreign nation. It is our education system, which wastes human potential at an alarming rate."

At a news event in Washington, DC, Pennington and other experts called on states and the federal government to take a number of steps to improve high school graduation, college enrollment, and completion rates, especially for low-income, minority students.

Based on the reports, JFF issued recommendations for federal and state policies that would "double the numbers" of young people who complete college or earn another postsecondary credential:

- Align expectation, curricula, and assessments with those of postsecondary institutions.
- Provide all students with opportunities and support to take and succeed in advanced courses.
- Connect students to the world beyond the high school walls by internships, community service, and work experience.
- Set up data systems that track students over time and hold postsecondary and secondary institutions accountable for how well they help students complete a recognized postsecondary credential by age 26.
- Eliminate boundaries between high school and college. For example, early college high schools, middle college high schools, and dropout recovery programs at community colleges permit students to accelerate their route to higher education and earn college credit at the same time.
- Offer incentives that reward secondary and postsecondary institutions when students successfully progress to and through college.

"The nation can no longer focus on high school reform as a standalone endeavor and regularly ignore as many as half of the young people who drop out of the education system before earning high school and college degrees," says Pennington. "And we're spending millions of dollars and substantial political capital building high school exit exams that ignore the next part of the pipeline: how to ensure that students gain the credentials and the education required for career jobs and college-level studies."

The research by the Parthenon Group examined the return that states and the nation would gain on investments designed to increase the number of students attending college. Doubling the numbers offers potential economic, as well as social and civic benefits. Economic benefits include increased tax revenues; social and civic benefits include reduction in unemployment and increased voter participation rates.

The JFF/LSPA opinion survey shows that Americans are optimistic about many of the initiatives already in use nationwide to prepare all students for high school and college success: for example, smaller high schools, need-based aid, and scholarship programs. According to the poll, Americans believe cost is the most important impediment faced by students—especially from lower-income families—in the pursuit of a college degree.

The Gates Millennium Scholars (GMS)—supported by the Bill & Melinda Gates Foundation and administered by the United Negro College Fund—is an example of a scholarship program that helps qualified minority youth attend the higher education institution of their choice. Early analysis of the program shows that GMS scholarship recipients are more likely than non-recipients to attend and stay in a four-year or private college.

"Qualified students, regardless of the race, ethnicity, or financial background, should not have to trim their ambitions and be denied the opportunity to attend college," said Tom Vander Ark, executive director of education at the Bill & Melinda Gates Foundation. "Gates Millennium Scholars are showing that when financial and other barriers are removed, students from the most challenging backgrounds can achieve, attend college, and prepare to become leaders in a range of professions and our communities."

But cost is not the only obstacle, the poll says. A majority of Americans believes that high schools need to do more to prepare students for college. They want to see better high school teachers in the classroom. Moreover, they feel it is important for guidance counselors to do more to help students understand the value of college and to help them choose and apply to colleges that are right for them.

According to the JFF/Parthenon Group research, the barriers to college entrance and success are especially great for low-income families and other underrepresented youth, including minorities and immigrants who are learning English. For example, only 19 percent of lower-income families complete an Associate's degree or higher, compared to 76 percent of high-income families.

All states have room for improvement in overall degree attainment. However, the nature of the problem varies across states, driving the need for tailored solution sets to address state-specific challenges along the higher education pipeline. The emphasis in some states might be focused on high school graduation rates, while others might address post-secondary access and attainment issues.

According to the report, if the United States is to address anticipated shortages of 12 million highly skilled workers by 2020, we must radically change how we educate and support low-income students and minority students, who comprise the fastest-growing segments of the youth population. This requires transforming how we prepare young people for college, breaking down the barriers that separate schools and postsecondary education, and developing new incentives for individuals to attend college and for institutions to enroll and retain students.

The public opinion study found near universal agreement that the high number of students who fail to go from high school to complete a college degree is a major problem facing the nation. Moreover, most people appreciate that this problem threatens not only the economic well-being of students who leave school without a college (or even a high school) degree but also the potential of the U.S. economy as a whole.

References

National partners in the "Double the Numbers" conference include the Bill & Melinda Gates Foundation, Carnegie Corporation of New York, the Ford Foundation, and the W.K. Kellogg Foundation.

The national public opinion survey of 1,010 Americans age 18 and older was conducted by Lake Snell Perry & Associates in September through October 5, 2003. It included oversamples of African Americans and Hispanics. Altogether, 639 non-Hispanic whites, 161 non-Hispanic African Americans, and 171 Hispanics were surveyed. For results based on total sample, oversampled groups were weighted to reflect their true representative proportion.

GIRLS RULE

Jodi Wilgoren

In the latest round of the battle of the sexes, girls seem to be winning—performing better in school and enrolling in college at a higher rate than boys. Have boys been left behind?

At Whitefish Bay High School, in a village north of Milwaukee on the shore of Lake Michigan, all four officers of the student council are female. So is the editor of the school newspaper, the Tower Times. And the two news editors.

Each spring at graduation, the school, which has about 900 students, honors the 10 seniors with the highest grade point averages. Last year, nine were girls. Whitefish Bay had nine semifinalists for the prestigious National Merit Scholarships, based on college-board scores; eight were girls.

The senior class president is female, the senior class vice president is female, the junior class president is female, and so is the junior class vice president. Freshman class officers? Girl, girl, girl. Only the sophomores are led by someone with a Y chromosome.

"This jock got it," explains Jon Schweitzer, a member of the Whitefish Bay Class of '03. "He's a nice guy, kind of smart. Everybody likes him. Then, with the vice president, everybody got serious and chose a girl who knows what she's doing. When I want to talk to somebody about stuff, I talk to the vice president."

As the bumper stickers say, girls rule.

Less than a decade ago, educators, researchers, and policy makers set off alarm bells in schoolhouses across the country, warning that America's educational system was shortchanging girls. They worried that girls sat ignored in class while boys called out; that female students were lagging in science and math; that young women suffered withering self-esteem, depression, and eating disorders. Take Our Daughters to Work Day was born, along with a federal law in 1994 that categorized girls as an "underserved population."

Now, the roles are being reversed, with a new round of research raising troubling questions about boys' achievements, extracurricular activities, and attitudes toward education. A spate of school shootings over the last several years spawned a discipline crackdown that largely targets young men. As enrollment in the nation's colleges and universities has flip-flopped—56 percent of today's students are female—the latest skirmish in the educational gender wars casts boys as the underdogs.

"The idea that schools and society grind girls down has given rise to an array of laws and policies intended to curtail the advantage boys have and to redress the harm done to girls," Christina Hoff Sommers, a philosopher, writes in her recent book, The War Against Boys. "That girls are treated as the second sex in school and consequently suffer, that boys are accorded privileges and consequently benefit—these are things everyone is presumed to know. But they are not true."

Indeed, a Department of Education report released last spring shows that girls are less likely to repeat a grade than boys, less likely to be classified as having a learning disability, and less likely to have teachers call home reporting problems with schoolwork or behavior. Girls get better grades, and their parents are more likely to describe them as being near the top of their class.

Girls have outperformed boys on standardized tests in reading and writing for decades, and, in recent years, they have been catching up on math and science exams, the report shows. In 1998, female high school graduates were just as likely as their male peers to have taken upper-level math like trigonometry and calculus, and more likely to have enrolled in biology and chemistry; in higher education, 56 percent of graduate students in 1996 were women, compared with 39 percent in 1970. A separate survey of college freshmen in 1999, by researchers at UCLA, shows that young women spent more time than young men doing volunteer work and participating in student clubs.

"The large gaps in educational attainment that once existed between men and women have significantly decreased or been eliminated altogether," the Department of Education report says. "Females are now doing as well or better than males."

WHERE ARE THE GUYS?

This new gender gap yawns even wider in poor, minority communities. Sixty-three percent of African-American college students are female; five times as many black women pursue master's degrees as do black men. At Frederick Douglass Academy, a public school in New York City where 80 percent of the students are black and 19 percent are Hispanic, enrollment is 60 percent female—except in advanced placement classes, where it is more like 80 percent.

"When you go to a graduation ceremony, you don't see too many males," says the school's principal, Gregory Hodge. "When you go to Rikers Island [a city jail], that's where they are."

Thus a new era of affirmative action has begun: Invited to send a student to Capitol Hill as a congressional page, Hodge started going down the honor roll, then considered everyone with an 85 average, but says, "We had to scrape the bottom of the barrel to get a boy candidate." Some private colleges have begun sending out extra mailings to recruit young men, and others are even giving admissions preference to marginal male applicants.

"I think generally the guys have the same potential, but the girls work harder," says Katie Panciera, 17, a senior from Berea, Kentucky. "The guys think they can get it without working, and the girls know they have to work."

BEYOND GIRLS VS. BOYS

The publication of Sommers's book, and other writings highlighting boys' problems, are, in part, a backlash against the feminist focus on girls' experiences that dominated the discussion in the early 1990s. Many researchers are trying to redefine the debate not as a battle of the sexes, pitting girls' interests against boys', but as an exploration of gender in the classroom that could benefit both sexes. All children suffer from stereotyping, they say, and teachers should employ a variety of methods to accommodate various learning styles.

I know some guys who dropped out because people were telling them they're stupid. And they felt humiliated because the girls were smarter. — JOSUE OLIVAS, 17

"The only way to really understand girls is to understand boys," says William S. Pollack, director of the Center for Men and Young Men in Belmont, Massachusetts. "And the only way to understand boys is to understand girls."

Experts say both sexes continue to have separate struggles. Boys are more likely to be shunted into special education, and feared as violent outcasts rather than nurtured. Yet girls attempt suicide more often. Girls have better grades overall, but boys continue to have the edge in calculus, physics, and computers,

not to mention sports, where male athletes tend to command more attention and respect (see "Leveling the Playing Field,"). Outside of school, men continue to earn more than women for similar work, yet men are slipping in every category of higher education. "Gender and issues of gender equity are not a matter of either-or, or a zero sum game, girls against the boys, boys against the girls," says Barrie Thorne, a sociologist at the University of California, Berkeley. "There are as many differences among girls and among boys as there are between them."

BATTLES OF THE SEXES

As these generals try to push beyond the gender wars, the soldiers—male and female students—see the battles taking shape in their own schools.

Lauren Westbrook, 16, a sophomore at John Burroughs High School in St. Louis, Missouri, says girls skip classes as often as guys, but are less likely to get caught. At the same time, she says, boys openly defy the closed-campus policy by carrying Burger King bags nonchalantly down the hallway, while girls sneak in the back door.

At Stafford High in Fredericksburg, Virginia, senior Zaahira Wyne, 15 (she skipped two grades), is in a special program called Commonwealth Governor's School, which includes advanced courses in English, math, science, and social studies. Of the 19 pupils in her class, 6 are boys.

THE FEMALE WORK ETHIC

Matt McKinstry, 18, a senior at Greenon High in Springfield, Ohio, notices it after school, in the pool. There are more girls than guys on the swim team, he says. And they're better. "They're more dedicated to the sport," he says. "The girls who are really dedicated are some of the best swimmers I've seen, boys or girls."

That work ethic shows up in class, too.

"On homework, for instance, you don't get the right answers and a lot of guys will blow it off, saying, 'Well, I'll just understand it later,'" Matt says. "If girls don't get the right answers for the homework, they constantly plug away."

In Scarsdale, New York, a wealthy suburb of New York City known for its stellar schools, teachers and administrators established a gender-equity committee in the early 1990s. After years of workshops focused on the problems girls face, a social studies teacher, David Greene, checked his grade book and found girls outperforming boys on tests and papers. He compared notes with others, and discovered a half-grade gender gap, with girls in the lead.

Students have examined this and other issues in a course called Sexual Politics, where they deconstruct their favorite children's books using a gender lens, and conduct surveys on issues like sexual harassment (43 percent of female students said they had been harassed, compared with 35 percent of males).

"I really didn't understand all these roles. I thought it was just everyday life, until we started discussing it in class," says Matt Capone, 18, a senior who is captain of Scarsdale's football team. "A lot of times men are treated unfairly, and a lot of times women are treated unfairly, it really depends on the places you are with the different teachers."

"My eyes have really been opened."

TEACHING OBJECTIVES

To help students critically evaluate a question that touches their lives every day—how the two sexes fare in school. They should understand the strides girls are making in the classroom, and why some experts now fear that girls' success comes at the expense of boys.

Discussion Questions:

• Do you believe that schools treat boys and girls equally?

• Are new programs needed to help more boys achieve excellence in school? If so, what programs should they be?

• Are you aware of school-safety initiatives that focus on male students?

• Given that all individuals differ, do you believe the experts quoted in the article place too much emphasis on gender?

CLASSROOM STRATEGIES

Discussion: Students should address the following issues:

• Why do some people believe that schools have traditionally shortchanged girls?

• Have students heard that science and math are "boy" subjects, while literature and the arts are "girl" subjects? Is this true?

• What accounts for the rise in girls' school performance? Do programs like Take Your Daughter to Work Day build the self-esteem that breeds success?

Research: You might have students test some of the theories offered in this article. Ask other teachers and/or the school administration to share this information with one or two student researchers: (1) the gender breakdown in Advanced Placement (AP) science and math classes and literature and language classes. (2) any noticeable change in these gender balances over the last 5 to 10 years. Students can use the data to construct a graph illustrating the differences. (If yours is an all-boys or all-girls school, students may explore instead the school's rationale for single-sex status, and whether it has changed over the years.)

Cooperative Learning: Direct students to page 13 and Scarsdale High School's Sexual Politics course. Assign students to write a syllabus for such a course. What activities or information would teach students about sex discrimination and understanding and respecting the differences between the sexes?

TEACHING OBJECTIVES

To help students understand the paucity of women in the top ranks of government and business, and why Title IX, the federal law meant to bring gender equality to school sports, has yet to finish the job.

Discussion Questions:

• Suppose you are a school superintendent. A principal in your district complains that there is not enough money in the budget to fund sports programs for both boys and girls. What would you tell the principal to do to comply with Title IX?

• Should companies strive to have a certain percentage of women in their executive ranks? Or should they ignore gender and just hire the best people?

CLASSROOM STRATEGIES

Critical Thinking: Some critics say data on women's pay and executive jobs do not demonstrate discrimination, but merely reflect the fact that qualified women have come to high-level government and business jobs relatively recently. How would students support and rebut this argument?

The article says that many school districts are in disagreement about their compliance with Title IX. Ask students what criteria they believe school officials should employ in trying to determine whether or not a school is complying with Title IX.

Sports Survey: Students can interview coaches and others who are knowledgeable about sports in their school. How many boys and girls play sports? What percent of the total do girls represent? Have the numbers of male and female athletes risen or fallen over the last 5 or 10 years?

Tough Choice: Suppose a wealthy alumnus bequeaths $5,000 to your school with the stipulation that the money be used to buy football uniforms. Should the school (a) reject the bequest; (b) accept it; (c) try to get the estate to comply with Title IX rules; (d) raise an equal amount to fund girls' sports; (e) put girls on the football team?

JODI WILGOREN is a national education correspondent for The New York Times, based in New York. Additional reporting by CHRIS TAUBER.

UNIT 4

Identity and Socioemotional Development

Unit Selections

Key Points to Consider

• What is Erikson's theory of development? Does he suggest that adolescence is a particularly stormy period?

• How does globalization affect today's teenagers?

• What is self-esteem? Why is it a particularly important concept in adolescence?

• What is emotional intelligence; how can we foster it in the classroom?

• Do you think males and females respond differently to the tribulations of adolescence? Why?

Links: www.dushkin.com/online/
These sites are annotated in the World Wide Web pages.

ADOL: Adolescence Directory On-Line
http://education.indiana.edu/cas/adol/adol.html

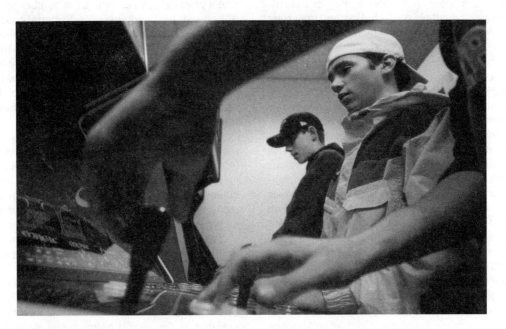

Keith Brofsky/Getty Images

Facing her mirror, Rosa sat in her room and pondered who she was. Was she more like her father or more like her mother? Was she one of the popular kids at school? When she goes off to college in two years, will she change or remain the same? And if asked, would she tell strangers that she was Latino or American? Rosa is facing a crisis of identity and pondering many of the same questions other adolescents ask themselves.

Each age period is associated with developmental tasks. A major aspect of psychosocial development for adolescents is the formation of a coherent personal identity. Erik Erikson referred to this as the *adolescent identity crisis*. Identity formation is a normative event, but it represents a turning point in human development that has consequences for later psychosocial skills.

Children's identities often represent an identification with parents and significant others. Adolescents reflect on their identity and come to some sense of who they are and who they are not. Identity formation involves an examination of personal likes and dislikes; political, religious, and moral values; occupational interests, as well as gender roles and sexual behaviors. Adolescents such as Rosa must also form an integrated sense of their own personality across the various roles they engage in (e.g., son or daughter, student, boyfriend or girlfriend, part-time worker, etc.).

To aid in the identity formation process, Erikson advocated that adolescents be given license to explore alternative roles and values. He believed that such a moratorium period would allow adolescents to make commitments that reflect true personal choices. James Marcia elaborated on Erikson's ideas about identity formation. He described four identity statuses that depend on the degree of exploration an adolescent engages in and whether the adolescent makes choices or commitments to certain paths. Adolescents who are actively searching and evaluating options are said to be in *moratorium*, as Erikson described. An identity-achieved status eventually is expected to follow this moratorium period. Other adolescents adopt values and life roles without experiencing a period of questioning. These adolescents are called *identity-foreclosed* as they essentially conform to parental expectations for themselves. Conformity to parents is not automatically a sign of identity foreclosure, however. *Identity-achieved individuals* often make choices that fit parental values and expectations but they do so only after some self-reflection. As a result, they are more invested in their choices and more self-confident. Finally, Marcia describes some adolescents as *identity-diffused*. These adolescents have not undergone a period of questioning and exploration, nor have they made clear ideological, occupational, or personal commitments. Identity-diffusion is expected in early adolescence, but it is seen as developmentally immature in college-age adolescents. Rosa, then, may be facing identity choices at just about the right time.

Erikson also proposed some differences in male and female identity development. Females were presumed to delay full identity development until the formation of an intimate relationship (that is, marriage). Interpersonal issues were seen as more paramount in female identity development with the occupational domain being more relevant for male identity development. Recent research indicates that there are fewer gender differences in identity development than may have been true of earlier generations when Erikson did his work (1950s). Modern psychologist Carol Gilligan maintains that moral decision making is another area of gender differences. She argues that females' moral values and moral judgments reflect more concern for interpersonal relationships and for caring about others. Males, she says, have a legalistic outlook which is less compassionate and more focused on the abstract application of rules. Unfortunately, Gilligan's ideas have not been fully tested to date.

An area that has received recent attention is how identity development may differ for minority individuals, such as Rosa. In addition to ideological, occupational, sexual, and interpersonal commitments, ethnicity is a salient component that must be integrated into a person's identity. Adolescents may or may not identify with their respective ethnic group but instead may reject their own ethnicity. Jean Phinney has articulated several phases characteristic of ethnic identity development. Her suggested stages parallel Marcia's identity statuses. Similar to identity foreclosure, some minority adolescents adopt the values of the dominant culture and possess an unexamined ethnic identity. Others are in moratorium and are wrestling with conflicts between the dominant culture and their own culture, a bit like Rosa. Finally, adolescents with an achieved ethnic identity feel an emotional attachment to their ethnic group and come to some resolution integrating ethnic group values with the dominant culture's values.

Whether male or female, minority or majority, identity issues have implications for emotional health, self-concept, and self-esteem. Adolescents' self-concepts become more and more abstract as they begin to think of themselves in terms of personality traits. They compare themselves to others in order to evaluate their own characteristics and abilities. They often construct an ideal self that is difficult to live up to. The abstract nature of their self-concept means that self-evaluation is more removed from concrete, observable behaviors and, thus, subject to distortion. Adolescents just like Rosa who are struggling with identity issues are also likely to undergo fluctuations in their self-concept as they explore alternative roles, values, and personalities.

Another important aspect of identity is *self-esteem*, which reflects how good one feels about oneself. The essential question is, "Am I okay?" Self-esteem is at a low point in early adolescence relative to other age periods. In adolescence, more dimensions contribute to self-esteem than is the case in childhood. Global self-esteem measures are often less informative, because adolescents' self-esteem varies in different domains (e.g., physical attractiveness, peer acceptance, academic competence, and athletic competence). Research by Susan Harter and her colleagues indicates that feeling good about one's physical appearance is the number one predictor of overall self-esteem in adolescents. Pubertal changes heighten concern about body image and appearance. Females compared to males are even more concerned about their looks and are much more likely to have a negative body image. Contrary to most expectations, recent studies show that self-esteem in African Americans is comparable to that of Caucasian Americans. Little work on self-esteem has been done in other minority populations.

The articles in this subunit elaborate on some of these themes. The first article again utilizes Erikson's theory of identity formation in adolescence. The article offers an excellent overview to commence this unit. The next article discusses adolescents who have matured in a multicultural world so may hold multiple self-identities. The advantages and disadvantages of a multicultural identity are shared with the reader.

The third article pertains to self-esteem. Baldwin and Hoffman discuss what self-esteem is and whether it changes drastically during and after the adolescent era. Some of the factors that make self-esteem dynamic in adolescence are reviewed as well. A companion article describes why some students face socioemotional problems in school and how such students can be assisted in developing better social skills. Finally, the topic of gender identity is reviewed. Thorne and McLean, in an interesting article, share their research on the role of threatening events in identity formation. The authors contend that life-threatening events, in part, shape adolescents' self-definitions. The memories of such events may or may not differ depending on the type of incident and the adolescent's gender.

Introduction: Identity Development Through Adulthood

Jane Kroger

Psychology Department
University of Tromsø

The problem of adulthood is how to *take care* of those to whom one finds oneself committed as one emerges from the identity period, and to whom one now owes *their* identity.

—Erikson, 1968

The process of identity development through adulthood has been a topic of growing interest among identity researchers over the past 15 years. Erikson's (1963, 1968) seminal writings on the identity formation task of adolescence have certainly inspired a wealth of theoretical and research writings on processes and contents associated with initial identity resolutions made toward the end of adolescence. Identity as formed in adolescence, according to Erikson, involves finding an optimal balance between identity and role confusion; this resolution provides the initial framework through which the biological, psychological, and social demands of adult life are encountered. Marcia's (1966; Marcia, Waterman, Matteson, Archer, & Orlofsky, 1993) elaborations of Erikson's bipolar task of adolescence have been popular in understanding identity processes and contents over adolescence and young adulthood. Researchers using Marcia's identity status paradigm (Marcia, 1966, 1967) have now produced several hundred publications and many valuable insights regarding the identity formation process of adolescence.

Erikson (1968) noted, however, that "the process described [identity development] is always changing and developing: at its best, it is a process of increasing differentiation". How then, may identity development proceed beyond adolescence? In his well-known epigenetic diagram of the psychosocial stages, Erikson illustrated the precursors of the identity versus role-confusion task of adolescence, both in terms of its components appearing in earlier psychosocial tasks and the contributions of earlier task resolutions toward identity versus role-confusion issues of adolescence. However, he has remained silent on the ways in which identity components may change and be changed by the psychosocial task demands of adult development. Whitbourne (1986a, 1986b) and Josselson (1987) were among the first researchers to draw attention to identity processes beyond the years of adolescence, noting considerable changes in identity processes and commitments beyond the initial resolutions of late adolescence. An adult form of Marcia's

(1966) identity status interview by Archer and Waterman (1993) has provided further possibilities for extending identity status concepts into adult life. However, many questions arise as one attempts to consider the contours of identity beyond its formative years in adolescence. What dimensions of identity are likely to change over the course of adult life, and what drives identity changes? Are the processes of exploration and commitment, so vital to initial identity resolutions of adolescence, still relevant to identity revisions that may be made during adult life? Are Marcia's (1966, 1967) identity statuses still relevant in describing various modes of identity resolution during adult life? These and further issues are considered in the articles of this special issue.

Articles for this special issue of *Identity: An International Journal of Theory and Research* grew from an invited symposium, "Identity Development Through Adulthood," presented at the International Congress of Psychology in Stockholm, Sweden, July 2000. Presenters had been requested by the symposium organizer to offer an overview of their previous research programs and to present some of their current thinking on issues related to identity development during the adult years of life. Initial conference papers were elaborated, reviewed, and again expanded to appear as articles for this special issue. We thank the many reviewers who provided invaluable assistance in helping these articles reach their present form.

James Marcia and colleagues (e.g., Bradley & Marcia, 1998; Hearn et al., 2001; Orlofsky, Marcia, & Lesser, 1973) have worked over the past three and a half decades to develop measures of identity, intimacy, generativity, and integrity. All of these measures have adopted a "status approach" in specifying qualitatively different styles by which individuals may resolve the various psychosocial tasks of adult life. In the opening article, Marcia provides an overview of these measures and proposes possible developmental linkages between the identity statuses of late adolescence and the different statuses of intimacy, generativity, and integrity, respectively, during adult life. Marcia also suggests a conical pattern for ongoing identity development throughout adult life, and illustrates this model as well as movement through other adult psychosocial stages via clinical case histories. Marcia's contribution to this special issue vividly illustrates the complexities of identity development beyond its first resolution in adolescence.

Susan Whitbourne, Joel Sneed, and Karyn Skultety wrote the second article, which reviews Whitbourne's previous studies of identity assimilation, accommodation, and balance processes in adult development, and presents a study designed to explore the relationship between various defense mechanisms and self-esteem and identity experiences during adult life. Whitbourne and colleagues (e.g., Whitbourne & Collins, 1998) had developed and refined an Identity and Experiences Scale that measures the extent to which individuals use identity assimilation (e.g., minimizing the importance of change), accommodation (e.g., feeling overwhelmed by the change), or balance (e.g., using the change as an impetus for growth) in adjusting to some selected, specific changes of aging. The study presented in their article seeks to clarify unanticipated gender differences in identity experience and self-esteem from previous research, and their research proposes very different identity processes for adult men and women, providing a thoughtful attempt to understand rather complex and unanticipated results in identity processes among women.

Janet Strayer offers a third contribution, which focuses on the role of emotions in identity development, particularly during adult life. Strayer's previous research (e.g., Roberts & Strayer, 1996; Strayer, 1993) addressed the role of emotions in human development. This article focuses on the role of emotions for identity processes of exploration and commitment as well as for identity outcomes in terms of Marcia's (1966) identity statuses. Strayer emphasizes how negative emotions, which she considers to be a force for change, may help to further identity development during adulthood. Tension, notes Strayer, is an inevitable concomitant of identity consciousness. She offers suggestions for linking emotional development to stability and change of adulthood identity, and then provides examples from statements from the life of Ingmar Bergman to illustrate how events must be emotionally salient to evoke identity exploration and change during adult life. In conclusion, Strayer offers some unique insights into the Eriksonian identity virtue of fidelity and its changing contours throughout further Eriksonian psychosocial tasks of adulthood.

I (Kroger, this issue) present the fourth article, in which I focus on issues of identity processes and contents during the years of late adulthood. My interests in late adulthood stem from a recently completed book (Kroger, 2000) in which I examine identity-related research focusing on adult life. The dearth of identity literature pertaining to late adulthood inspired this article. I begin my contribution to this special issue by noting the many parallels between late adolescence and late adulthood, and provide a review of the scant research available on themes of identity continuity and content pertaining to the latter time period. I proceed to describe a small, qualitative investigation I undertook with 14 late-life adults. The investigation was designed to explore possible identity revision (exploration) and maintenance (commitment) processes during the early and older years of late adulthood. Rather different identity process and content themes prevailed within each of these two age groups.

Patricia Raskin offers a final commentary on the four manuscripts and overviews some of her own research on gender differences in identity development during mid-adulthood. In her commentary, Raskin notes that a diverse number of themes are covered by the articles, reflecting the great need to further explore and explain many phenomena associated with identity continuity and change during adult life. She also focuses on the need to consider contextual issues and cues in understanding the individual and life stage, the role of loss as an aspect of identity formation, and the importance of gender differences to the nature of identity development and revision throughout adult life.

Lastly, all authors contribute a final statement on future research directions for the study of identity in the years beyond its initial resolution during adolescence.

Contributors to this special issue wish to encourage further identity research during and beyond the years of adolescence and hope that the focus of this special issue may be a step toward that end.

ACKNOWLEDGMENT

Production of this special issue was supported by a grant from the Norwegian Research Council 144459/300.

REFERENCES

Archer, S. L., & Waterman, A. S. (1993). Identity status interview: Adult form. In J. E. Marcia, A. S. Waterman, D. R. Matteson, S. L. Archer, & J. L. Orlofsky (Eds.), *Ego identity: A handbook for psychosocial research* (pp. 318–333). New York: Springer-Verlag.

Bradley, C. L., & Marcia, J. E. (1998). Generativity-stagnation: A five category model. *Journal of Personality, 66*, 39–64.

Erikson, E. H. (1963). *Childhood and society* (2nd ed.). New York: Norton.

Erikson, E. H. (1968). *Identity: Youth and crises.* New York: Norton.

Hearn, S., Saulnier, G., Strayer, J., Glenham, M., Koopman, R., & Marcia, J. E. (2001). *Integrity, identity and beyond: Development of a measure of Erikson's eighth stage.* Manuscript submitted for publication.

Josselson, R. (9187). *Finding herself: Pathways to identity development in women.* San Francisco: Jossey-Bass.

Kroeger, J. (2000). *Identity development: Adolescence through adulthood.* Newbury Park, CA: Sage.

Marcia, J. E. (1966). Development and validation of ego identity status. *Journal of Personality and Social Psychology, 3*, 551–558.

Marcia, J. E. (1967). Ego identity status: Relationship to self-esteem, "general maladjustment," and authoritarianism. *Journal of Personality, 3*, 118–133.

Marcia, J. E., Waterman, A. S., Matteson, D. R., Archer, S. L., & Orlofsky, J. L. (Eds.). (1993). *Ego identity: A handbook for psychosocial research.* New York: Springer-Verlag.

Orlofsky, J. L., Marcia, J. E., & Lesser, I. (1973). Ego identity status and intimacy versus isolation crisis in young adulthood. *Journal of Personality and Social Psychology, 3*, 415–423.

Roberts, W., & Strayer, J. (1996). Emotional expressiveness, empathy, and prosocial behavior. *Child Development, 60*, 140–177.

Strayer, J. (1993). Children's concordant emotions and cognitions in response to observed emotions. *Child Development, 64*, 188–201.

Whitbourne, S. K. (1986a). *Adult development.* New York: Praeger.

Whitbourne, S. K. (1986b). *The me I know: A study of adult identity.* New York: Springer-Verlag.

Whitbourne, S. K., & Collins, K. C. (1998). Identity and physical changes in later adulthood: Theoretical and clinical implications. *Psychotherapy, 35*, 519–530.

Coming of Age in a Multicultural World

Globalization and Adolescent Cultural Identity Formation

Lene Arnett Jensen
Catholic University of America

The aim of this article is to explore implications of globalization for adolescent cultural identity formation. The thesis is that adolescents increasingly form multicultural identities because they grow up knowing diverse cultural beliefs and behaviors. First, ways that adolescents increasingly have exposure to different cultures are illustrated with ethnographic and cross-cultural work. Then, 3 emerging research issues are raised: (a) the extent to which it is important whether a multicultural identity is based on first-hand versus indirect (media-based) interactions with diverse peoples, (b) how cultural identity formation may take diverse developmental paths depending on the particular cultures involved, and (c) gains and losses that occur when persons form a multicultural identity rather than an identity based primarily on one cultural tradition. Finally, the article suggests using multiple methods that are sensitive to different perspectives in research on globalization and adolescent identity formation.

Contemporary adolescents are coming of age in a world that is considerably more multicultural than the world in which their parents and grandparents grew up. Due to the processes of globalization, adolescents increasingly have knowledge of and interactions with people from diverse cultures. The flow across cultures of ideas, goods, and people is not new, but the current extent and speed of globalization are unprecedented. With increasing migrations, worldwide media disseminations, multinational corporations, tourism travel, and so forth, diverse peoples interact with one another more than ever (Friedman, 2000; Giddens, 2000; Hermans & Kempen, 1998; Sassen, 1998).

My aim in this article is to explore implications of globalization for adolescent cultural identity formation. I will argue that developing a cultural identity in the course of adolescence has become more complex. Adolescents seldom grow up knowing of only one culture but increasingly have interactions with people from diverse cultures, either first-hand or indirectly through different media. Increasingly, then, adolescents forge multicultural identities.

There are many issues to address on the topic of globalization and adolescent identity formation. My aim here is to draw attention to some of the emerging issues. Writings that specifically address adolescent psychology in light of globalization are still few (e.g., Arnett, 2002; Larson, 2002). I will draw on writings on globalization as well as writings from related areas on ethnic and immigrant identity formation (e.g., Berry, 1997; Phinney, 1990).

In the following, I will start by defining the term *cultural identity* and discuss why globalization may be particularly salient for adolescent cultural identity formation. Then, I will provide a few examples illustrating how adolescents increasingly grow up in a multicultural world and form multicultural identities. Next, I will discuss three issues pertaining to adolescent multicultural identity formation that would seem to be fruitful and timely areas for research:

1. The issue of the extent to which it is important whether a multicultural identity is based on first-hand versus indirect (media-based) interactions with diverse peoples.
2. The issue of how cultural identity formation may take diverse developmental paths depending on the particular cultures involved.
3. The issue of gains and losses that occur when a person forms a multicultural identity rather than an identity based primarily on one cultural tradition.

Finally, I will end on a brief methodological note, raising the issue of using culturally sensitive and valid methods when studying cultural identity formation.

A Definition of Cultural Identity

What is a cultural identity? Forming a cultural identity involves taking on worldview beliefs and engaging in behavioral practices that unite people within a community (Shweder et al., 1999). Typically a worldview provides answers to four questions: Who am I? Where am I? Why do people suffer? What is the remedy for suffering? (Walsh & Middleton, 1984). Thus, worldview beliefs often pertain to conceptions of human nature, the relation of the individual to others in society, and moral and religious ideals.

Worldview beliefs find expression in and are passed on from generation to generation through a variety of everyday practices (such as behaviors pertaining to eating, dressing, sleeping, work, and recreation) as well as practices marking life course transitions (such as graduating from school, marriage, and having children). One's cultural identity, then, subsumes a broad range of beliefs and behaviors that one shares with members of one's community.

Cultural identity formation also in some respects intersects with the formation of identity in spheres such as religion and morality. Often religious beliefs and behaviors as well as moral beliefs and behaviors are crucial elements in peoples' understanding of their cultural identity. For example, the extent to which one values autonomy and independence, or familial duties and obligations, or adherence to spiritual precepts and practices constitute important elements in one's understanding of one's cultural identity. In fact, the globalization ethos, in many ways a Western and even American ethos, often emphasizes individual autonomy and secular values, and quite frequently these values are not easily reconciled with those of more traditional cultures emphasizing community cohesion and religious devotion. Thus challenges involved in forming an adolescent cultural identity in the face of globalization extend to aspects of one's identity formation centering specifically on moral and religious issues.

One's cultural identity, then, encompasses a broad set of worldview beliefs and behavioral practices. Half a century ago, anthropologists (Whiting & Child, 1953) described the relation between these cultural beliefs and practices as a "custom complex" consisting of "customary practice and of the beliefs, values, sanctions, rules, motives and satisfactions associated with it" (quoted in Shweder et al., 1998). Given the broadness of beliefs and practices that a

cultural identity subsumes, it in many ways includes the key areas that Erikson (1968) emphasized as central to the formation of an adolescent's identity as a whole. These key areas pertain to ideology (beliefs and values), love (personal relationships), and work. However, Erikson's focus was on how adolescents make choices about ideology, love, and work in order to arrive at an independent and unique sense of self *within* the cultural context in which they live (Erikson, 1950, 1968). Forming a cultural identity, however, involves making choices about the cultural contexts that one identifies with in the first place. Put another way, the Eriksonian identity formation task centers on deciding what distinguishes you as an individual among the members of your cultural community, whereas forming a cultural identity involves deciding on the cultural communities to which you will belong—a task that has become more complex as more and more people have exposure to multiple cultural communities with their diverse and divergent custom complexes. In fact, forming a cultural identity becomes mainly a conscious process and decision when you have exposure to more than one culture.

Researchers conducting work on ethnic identity formation in many ways address issues similar to those involved in cultural identity formation. As Phinney (1990) pointed out, there are widely discrepant definitions of ethnic identity. However, a central focus of research on ethnic identity formation is how members of ethnic and racial minority groups negotiate their identifications with their own group in the context of living among other ethnic and racial groups. One difference between research on ethnic identity formation and cultural identity formation as described here is that the former focuses on minority groups. However, cultural identity formation in the context of globalization also pertains to people who form part of a majority culture but who still have exposure to other cultures as well. For example, an Indian adolescent living in India but with exposure to the global economy and media will likely negotiate culturally diverse custom complexes in forming a cultural identity.

One important similarity between ethnic and cultural identity formation pertains to the issue of power and dominance. As diverse ethnic, racial, and cultural groups come into contact with one another there are invariably differences in power and status among those groups. This is clearly the case with respect to processes pertaining to globalization. Later in this article, I will discuss some problems and losses that arise in forming a multicultural identity in the context of globalization.

One last issue is worth mentioning with respect to defining the concept of cultural identity. Although one's cultural identity subsumes a broad range of beliefs and behaviors that one shares with members of one's community or communities, this does not entail that all members of a cultural community hold uniform beliefs and engage in identical practices. There is invariably variation within communities based on factors such as generation, gender, individual differences, religious affiliation, and social class (e.g., Jensen, 1997, 2003; Turiel & Wainryb, 2000).

Adolescence and the Saliency of Globalization

The influence of globalization on cultural identity formation may be particularly salient in adolescence. Some have argued that adolescents are the forefront of globalization (Dasen, 2000; Schlegel, 2001). Popular and media culture (television, movies, music, and the Internet) contribute to the rapid and extensive spread of ideas across cultures, and adolescents have more of an interest in popular and media culture than children or adults.

Adolescence may also be a time of life with a more pronounced openness to diverse cultural beliefs and behaviors. Adolescents have developed enough maturity to think in more complex ways about that which is new and different, and often there are many areas of life in which they have not yet settled on particular beliefs and behaviors (Arnett, 2002). Some research with immigrants to the United States indeed shows that sometimes adolescents change their beliefs and values more than adults. Nguyen and Williams (1989) in a study with Vietnamese immigrants found that adolescents' values varied with length of time in the United States whereas parents' values did not. Also, Phinney, Ong, and Madden (2000) found greater value discrepancies between adolescents and parents who have lived in the United States for a longer time, than between adolescents and parents who had immigrated more recently. Phinney et al. found this pattern for Vietnamese and Armenian immigrants. This phenomenon is also known as dissonant acculturation (Portes, 1997), when exposure to a new culture leads to more rapid change among adolescents than among adults. The research results with immigrants to the United States suggest that adolescents may be more receptive to new and foreign cultural values and beliefs as compared to adults. Thus processes of globalization may particularly influence adolescents in their cultural identity formation.

It Is a Multicultural World

The title for this article—Coming of Age in a Multicultural World—was inspired by Margaret Mead's (1928/1961) title for her well-known book, *Coming of Age in Samoa*. The focus of Mead's work on the socialization of adolescents and ways that culture influences socialization remains important. Yet, descriptions such as Mead's of adolescents coming of age within one cultural tradition are becoming a rarity. Mead spoke of "one [Samoan] girl's life [being] so much like another's in an uncomplex, uniform culture like Samoa." What is striking about much contemporary anthropological and cross-cultural work from all over the world is the way it describes the many changes that traditional societies undergo due to globalization—the ways that many societies have ceased to be "uncomplex and uniform" (e.g., Brown, Larson, & Saraswathi, 2002; Burbank, 1988; Condon, 1988; Liechty, 1995; Naito & Gielen, 2002). In the following, I will discuss a few examples from ethnographic and psychological work of the ways that globalization is changing traditional cultural beliefs, everyday practices, and life-course transitions. The intent of these examples is to provide specific qualitative illustrations of changes that occur in adolescents' custom complexes as they are exposed to diverse cultures.

The Inuit of the Canadian Arctic

The anthropologist Richard Condon (1988) provided a fascinating ethnographic description of dramatic cultural changes occurring in a relatively short period of time among the Inuit of the Canadian arctic. Just a generation ago, the Inuit were nomadic. Family groups followed the movements of fish and game. Children and adolescents assisted their parents and elders with work necessary for daily survival, and they grew up under the close protection and supervision of their families. There were few influences from the outside.

Today's Inuit children and adolescents, however, live very different lives. They reside in fixed settlements established by the Canadian government. The traditional nomadic work of ice fishing and hunting has become recreational, and Inuit children and adolescents now attend school in pursuit of skills required in a changed world. Unlike before, Inuit children and adolescents now spend much time outside of the socialization environment of the family both in school and in peer groups.

Inuit adolescents have also gained access to Western media, especially television. According to Condon (1988), the influences of television on Inuit adolescents have been striking. He had a rare opportunity to observe a variety of clear effects of the introduction of television because he studied the Inuit both before and after the introduction of television. Adolescent boys and young men avidly took up the game of hockey after being exposed to pro hockey games on TV. During the long summer nights, they play hockey for hours on end. Along with playing the sport has come a new ethos. Traditional Inuit culture discourages calling attention to individual skills and accomplishments. From watching pro hockey players, however, adolescent boys learned to be competitive and even to brag about their sports abilities. TV also seems to have brought along a new ethos for dating and relationships between girls and boys. Previously very reserved about their romantic relationships, after the introduction of TV young couples became publicly affectionate. When Condon queried adolescents about this change, they attributed it to watching the show "Happy Days."

Today, then, Inuit adolescents no longer form a cultural identity solely based on their traditional culture. Their worldview and everyday behaviors (such as dating, sports participation, and school work) reflect and express values that derive from multiple cultures. From their traditional Inuit culture, adolescents still take collectivist values. Condon (1988) wrote that young people grow up with a "pronounced sense of belonging, of being integrated into a social network." From Canadian culture and Western culture more generally, Inuit adolescents also take new values and identity ideals centering on individual expressiveness and accomplishment. Condon's ethnography reflected how Inuit adolescents form multicultural identities that incorporate diverse beliefs and practices. This is a complex task as some beliefs from the different cultures can be integrated with ease, but others are more difficult to reconcile—a point that I will elaborate on later.

An Example from India

As described earlier, cultural identity formation occurs in the context of everyday cultural practices. It also occurs in the context of practices marking life course transitions. One example of how globalization has influenced life course transitions comes from research in India, where marriage (a highly significant life course transition often culturally marking the transition into adulthood) appears to have become subject to diverse cultural interpretations. In an in-depth interview study in which Indian young and midlife adults were asked to describe a personal moral experience (i.e., a time in their life when they had faced an important decision pertaining to right and wrong), almost 50% chose to discuss the issue of whether to have a traditional arranged marriage, that is, a marriage where a person's parents and family decide who they will marry, or whether to have what Indians call a "love marriage," that is, a marriage where persons decide for themselves whom to marry (Jensen, 1998).

These two types of marriages reflect very different conceptions of individual choice, family obligations, and the purpose of marriage. Arranged marriages seem perfectly sensible within a traditional Indian worldview that emphasizes duty to family, respect for elders, and behaving according to one's station in life rather than according to individual preferences. Love marriages fit much better with the values of globalization and the West that emphasize freedom of choice and individual rights, as well as a media culture saturated with images of romance and interpersonal attraction. In the interviews, one young woman discussed her unwillingness to have an arranged marriage in the context of a changing Indian society. She said:

> I've always insisted that I've got to have the right man and I won't just be able to adjust to anyone … There have been pressures, if I can call them that, from family, but I've … not given in to it. I won't do that ever because I know the situation now … From the very beginning things foreign and imported were very glamorous to me. From those days onward [when I became familiar with things foreign], I was against having an [arranged] marriage … Arranged marriages in India are becoming obsolete, I think. Because even now in [arranged marriages], girls and boys they talk to each other. They come to know each other. Perhaps the decision may not be theirs, because in some traditional households it's not theirs. But they get to know each other. But as for me, I should [decide] and know him.

Although arranged marriages are still by far more common than love marriages in India, the research finding reflects how Indian adolescents and adults now are aware of and at times contend with values and identity conceptions that are different from the traditional Indian conceptions with respect to a life course transition as crucial as marriage (for more on globalization in India, see Verma & Saraswathi, 2002).

The findings from India and the Inuit are by no means unique or unusual. What is striking about much contemporary ethnographic and cross-cultural work is the way it describes the many changes that traditional societies undergo due to globalization. Descriptions of adolescents coming of age within one cultural tradition are becoming less and less common. Adolescents increasingly come of age in a multicultural world and they face the task of forming their identities in the context of multiple traditions. Robertson (1992) phrased it very well when writing that today's children and adolescents develop "the intensification of consciousness of the world as a whole."

Three Emerging Research Issues

With contemporary adolescents growing up in a multicultural world, many complexities of adolescent identity formation arise that merit further research. In the following, I will discuss three such issues.

First-Hand Reality
Versus Virtual Reality

One issue pertains to the agents of cultural socialization: To what extent is it important whether adolescent cultural identity formation is based on the first-hand reality of interactions with diverse peoples or based on indirect exposure to diverse cultural traditions through the virtual reality of media? Or to use Robertson's (1992) language, does it matter if an adolescent's consciousness of the world as a whole derives primarily from first-hand interactions with diverse people or from media exposure?

The classical definition of acculturation by Redfield, Linton, and Herskovitz (1936) assumed direct interactions; "acculturation comprehends those phenomena which result when groups of individuals having different cultures come into *continuous first-hand contact* [italics added] with subsequent changes in the original culture patterns of either or both groups". Increasingly numbers of adolescents indeed do experience first-hand contact with people from different cultures as a consequence of migrations and tourism. However, for many adolescents much of their exposure to cultures other than their traditional one occurs indirectly through media. Thus in a world of fast-paced and abundant media transmissions and interactions, Redfield et al.'s definitions of acculturation might fruitfully be expanded to encompass more indirect interactions occurring in virtual reality.

Arnett (2002) proposed that many adolescents in today's world of globalization develop a "local identity" based on their indigenous tradition, as well as a "global identity" based on their exposure to a global (often Western) culture conveyed through media. Television, in particular, provides exposure to new ideas, events, and people. For example, the number of televisions per 1,000 persons rose from 5 in 1970 to 255 in 1995 in East Asia, and from 70 in 1970 to 220 in 1995 in Latin America and the Pacific. The comparable figures were from 280 in 1970 to 525 in 1995 for Western industrialized countries (United Nations Development Programme, 1998). As described previously for the Inuit, television exposure can influence adolescent identity formation in important ways. (The Internet may at some point rival or even surpass

TV in providing adolescents with global access.) Friedman (2000) described how companies cater in global media to a new market of "global teens" because urban adolescents from all over the world follow similar consumption patterns. To conceptualize adolescent development that entails both a local and a global identity, Arnett suggested a need to expand the traditional use of the concept of bicultural identity. In this expanded use, the term *bicultural identity* would refer not only to acculturative processes occurring with first-hand exposure to different cultures (as for immigrants, minority groups, or workers who come in frequent contact with foreigners) but also to acculturative processes occurring with exposure to different cultures through media.

It may make a difference in identity formation whether contact occurs first-hand or through media. One possibility is that identity formation on the basis of media exposure is more *subjectivized or individualized*. Sociologists of religion have used these two concepts fruitfully to refer to the ways that people increasingly construct individual and idiosyncratic religious or spiritual belief systems as the establishment of a religious identity less frequently occurs in the context of shared practices with a community of fellow believers and more frequently as an individual process of exploration (Arnett & Jensen, 2002; Berger, 1967; Luckman, 1963).

Media, more so than first-hand interactions with others, allow the adolescent to choose what to see and hear. Also, media usage would seem to allow for more individual interpretations than first-hand interactions in which other people are more likely to co-construct experiences. Media messages are not interpreted within an immediate group context (unless, e.g., a group of adolescents watch a TV program together and talk about it). Thus when Inuit or Indian adolescents watch an American TV show or a music video, the messages they come away with may vary substantially from individual to individual. Adolescent cultural identity formation on the basis of media exposure, then, may be more subjectivized or individualized than cultural identity formation on the basis of first-hand interactions.

Clearly adolescent identity formation in the face of globalization encompasses the classic form of acculturation based on first-hand interactions as well as a more recent form of acculturation based on media exposure. The extent to which a person's cultural identity is influenced in different ways by these two types of acculturation merits further attention.

Not One, but Multiple Developmental Paths

A second research issue meriting attention pertains to the extent to which adolescent cultural identity formation may take diverse developmental paths depending on the particular cultures to which they have exposure. In a very interesting study by Phinney, Kim, Ossorio, and Vilhjalmsdottir (2002), they asked 240 adolescents to reason about vignettes describing adolescents and parents disagreeing about a variety of everyday and major issues. The vignettes pertained to issues such as doing household chores, everyone gathering for family dinner, and dating.

The research included four different ethnic groups residing in the United States and showed interesting interactions between culture and development. European American adolescents moved from assertions of autonomy in midadolescence (ages 14 and 17) to increased consideration of the views and feeling of their parents in late adolescence (ages 18 to 22). This pattern fits well with what some psychologists have described as a movement from unilaterality to mutuality in young persons' relationships with parents (Youniss & Smollar, 1985). Armenian American and Mexican American adolescents, however, moved from consideration of parents in midadolescence to self-assertion in the late adolescence. Finally, Korean American adolescents maintained a high degree of consideration for parents' point of view at all ages.

As discussed earlier, conceptions of individual autonomy and family obligations are typically important aspects of people's cultural identities. Phinney et al.'s (200) research indicated that during adolescence these conceptions appear to develop in different ways and in varying orders across cultural traditions. Thus cultural identity formation becomes more complex as adolescents have exposure to more cultures. They have to form identities in the face of cultural traditions that may hold out different end goals (such as differing emphases on the assertion of autonomy from parents and the fulfillment of responsibilities to parents) and different pathways to those end goals (such as acceptance of assertions of autonomy in midadolescence but not in late adolescence or acceptance of assertions of autonomy in late adolescence but not in midadolescence). This suggests, then, that we cannot assume a universal developmental pathway to adolescent cultural identity formation in a world of globalization.

Gains and Losses

A third research question that arises is what gains and losses occur when an adolescent forms a multicultural identity rather than an identity based primarily upon one cultural tradition. Based on a review of the immigration literature, Berry (1997) suggested that the psychological adjustments and problems accompanying acculturation can be divided into three levels, moving from minor to severe adjustment issues. These levels are helpful in thinking about adolescent multicultural identity formation. At one level, acculturation may involve "culture shedding" in which an adolescent has to leave behind or unlearn aspects of their parents' culture. Such culture shedding may entail some sense of loss, as well as some positive sense of leaving behind undesirable beliefs and practices. At a second level, acculturation may involve more serious psychological adjustment in which an adolescent experiences "culture shock" or "acculturative stress." In other words, the adolescent has difficulty forming a coherent identity in the face of culturally distinct worldviews that are difficult to reconcile. Finally, at a third level, acculturation may lead to major difficulties in the form of psychopathology.

Many factors will influence the kind of psychological adjustment experienced by adolescents who are forming multicultural identities. One notable factor that may influence the balance between gains and losses is the degree of cultural distance between the cultures to which an adolescent has exposure. Here the immigration literature suggested that the greater the cultural distance in beliefs and behaviors between cultures, the greater the psychological and social problems (Berry, 1997). Returning to the Inuit, Condon's (1988) work showed how Inuit adolescents attend school in sporadic ways because they find it boring and alienating. Perhaps the distance between the traditional Inuit nomadic ways of life and the sedentary school culture introduced by the Canadian government is too great to be smoothly bridged. In fact, Condon suggested that boredom and alienation are among the factors contributing to adolescent risk behavior, such as shoplifting and alcohol use, in contemporary Inuit society.

Arnett (2002) suggested that recent increases in adolescent problem behaviors such as substance use, prostitution, armed aggression, and suicide that have occurred in a variety of traditional cultures may in part result from processes linked to globalization and attendant identity confusion and sense of marginalization in the face of diverse cultural values that are difficult to reconcile.

Forming a multicultural identity clearly presents adolescents with psychological challenges that may be difficult to meet in a positive way. Yet, it may be worthwhile to keep in mind potential positive outcomes. Berry (1997) pointed out that with respect to immigrants (with most of the research focusing on immigrants in North America), the assumption among scholars used to be that acculturation inevitably brings social and psychological stress and problems. However, this view has changed as research has indicated that the gains and losses of immigrant acculturation are varied and complex (varying by factors such as age, gender, level of education, degree of social support, intergroup attitudes, and discrimination). Also, research indicates that children and adolescents who are first and second generation immigrants to the United States tend to do very well with respect to grades in school, physical and mental health, and avoidance of risk behavior (Fuligni, 1998).

Multicultural identity formation in adolescence, then, is likely to involve gains and losses, sometimes mostly losses, sometimes mostly gains, and sometimes both. The factors that influence the outcomes are likely to be varied and complex. Also, assessment of what constitutes gains and losses may at times be complex. Whereas some outcomes seem clearly to be either a gain or a loss, other times perceptions of what is a gain or loss may be dissonant. For example, adolescents may see shedding some parts of their parents' cultural traditions as a positive (e.g., getting rid of an outdated custom), whereas the parents and other adults of the community experience this as a loss of a valuable tradition. Clearly, we have to carry out research on psychological gains and losses entailed by adolescents forming multicultural identities in a world of globalization. This is a vast area requiring research on many factors influencing acculturation, and the research must be carried out in a way that is sensitive to divergent conceptions of what constitutes gains and losses.

Methodological Multiplicity

Earlier in this article I have discussed several issues that seem to me to merit further attention. The nature of these issues and the nature of the topic of globalization more generally point to the need for the use of research methods that are culturally appropriate. I will end by briefly discussing a few methodological points. In recent years, cultural psychologists have called for the need to reassess more common and standard methodologies when working with participants from different cultures (e.g., Shweder et al., 1998; Stigler, Shweder, & Herdt, 1990). Their advice would seem particularly apt as more and more cultures come into contact due to the processes of globalization.

In studying adolescent cultural identity formation in which different socialization agents, different cultures, different pathways to identity formation, and different conceptions of the best end goals are in play, methodological multiplicity would seem to be helpful. By this, I mean two things. First, by using more than one method we might better capture different cultural concepts, and capture these concepts as they are understood within their respective cultures. Of course in deciding on more than one method, it helps to use those that maximize cultural sensitivity and ecological validity (Briggs, 1986). Second, methodological multiplicity also entails understanding globalization from different perspectives. As mentioned previously, adolescents and

parents may not view the gains and losses of multicultural identity formation in the same ways. In fact, adolescents themselves may at times view the same outcome as both a gain and a loss. Hermans and Kempen (1998) pointed out that in the face of globalization, "self or identity can be conceived of as a dynamic multiplicity of different and even contrasting positions or voices that allow mutual dialogical relationships." Thus using methodologies that allow room for different perspectives, or voices (Gilgun, 1992; Gilligan, 1982), would be helpful.

Conclusions

Contemporary adolescents are coming of age in a multicultural world where creating a cultural identity has become complex. Often, they face the task of integrating diverse cultural beliefs and behaviors conveyed to them by multiple agents of socialization—socialization agents that at times are at odds with one another (e.g., parents and TV). The task of forming a coherent cultural identity that allows adolescents to become contributing members of society presents challenges that may be stressful or even considerably more problematic. However, adolescent cultural identity formation also presents challenges that may be met by developing new skills, the kinds of skills necessary for a multicultural world, that allow adolescents to function well psychologically and to contribute to society.

References

Arnett, J. J. (2002). The psychology of globalization. *American Psychologist, 57,* 774–783.

Arnett, J. J., & Jensen, L. A. (2002). A congregation of one: Individualized religious beliefs among emerging adults. *Journal of Adolescent Research, 17,* 454–467.

Berger, P. L. (1967). *The sacred canopy: Elements of a sociological theory of religion.* New York: Anchor.

Berry, J. W. (1997). Immigration, acculturation, and adaptation. *International Journal of Applied Psychology, 46,* 5–34.

Briggs, C. L. (1986). *Learning how to ask: A sociologuistic appraisal of the role of the interview in social science research.* Cambridge, England: Cambridge University Press.

Brown, B. B., Larson, R., & Saraswathi, T. S. (2002). *The world's youth: Adolescence in eight regions of the globe.* New York: Cambridge University Press.

Burbank, V. (1988). *Aboriginal adolescence.* New Brunswick, NJ: Rutgers University Press.

Condon, R. G. (1988). *Inuit youth: Growth and change in the Canadian Arctic.* New Brunswick, NJ: Rutgers University Press.

Dasen, P. (2000). Rapid social change and the turmoil of adolescence: A cross-cultural perspective. *International Journal of Group Tensions, 29,* 17–49.

Erikson, E. H. (1950). *Childhood and society.* New York: Norton.

Erikson, E. H. (1968). *Identitiy: Youth and crisis.* New York: Norton.

Friedman, T. L. (2000). *The Lexus and the olive tree: Understanding globalization.* New York: Anchor.

Fuligni, A. J. (1998). The adjustment of children from immigrant families. *Current Directions in Psychological Science, 7,* 99–103.

Giddens, A. (2000). *The consequences of modernity.* Cambridge: Polity Press.

Gilgun, J. F. (1992). Definitions, methodologies, and methods in qualitative family research. In J. F. Gilgun, K. Daly, & G. Handel (Eds.), *Qualitative methods in family research* (pp. 22–39). Newbury Park, CA: Sage.

Gilligan, C. F. (1982). *In a different voice: Psychological theory and women's development.* Cambridge, MA: Harvard University Press.

Hermans, H. J. M., & Kempen, H. J. G. (1998). Moving cultures: The perilous problems of cultural dichotomies in a globalizing society. *American Psychologist, 53,* 1111–1120.

Jensen, L. J. (1997). Different worldviews, different morals: America's culture war divide. *Human Development, 40,* 325–344.

Jensen, L. J. (1998). Moral divisions within countries between orthodoxy and progressivism: India and the United States. *Journal for the Scientific Study of Religion, 37,* 90–107.

Jensen, J. L. (2003). *A cultural-developmental approach to moral development.* Unpublished manuscript. Catholic University of America, Washington, DC.

Larson, R. (2002). Globalization, societal change, and new technologies: What they mean for the future of adolescence. *Journal of Research on Adolescence, 12,* 1–30.

Liechty, M. (1995). Media, markets, and modernization: Youth identities and the experience of modernity in Katmandu, Nepal. In V. Amit-Talai & H. Wulff (Eds.), *Youth cultures: A cross-cultural perspective* (pp. 166–201). New York: Routledge.

Luckman, T. (1963). *The invisible religion.* New York: Macmillan.

Mead, M. (1928/1961). *Coming of age in Samoa.* New York: Morrow Quill Paperbacks.

Naito, T., & Gielen, U. P. (2002). The changing Japanese family: A psychological portrait. In J. L. Roopmarine & U. P. Gielen (Eds.), *Families in global perspective.* Boston: Allyn & Bacon.

Nguyen, N., & Williams, H. (1989). Transitions from east to west: Vietnamese adolescents and their parents. *Journal of the American Academy of Child and Adolescent Psychiatry, 28,* 505–515.

Phinney, J. (1990). Ethnic identity in adolescents and adults: A review of research. *Psychological Bulletin, 108,* 499–514.

Phinney, J., Kim, T., Ossorio, S., & Vilhjalmsdottir, P. (2002). *Self-and other-orientation in the resolutions of adolescent-parent disagreements: Cultural and developmental differences.* Unpublished manuscript. California State University, Los Angeles.

Phinney, J., Ong, A., & Madden, T. (2000). Cultural values and intergenerational values discrepancies in immigrant and non-immigrant families. *Child Development, 71,* 528–539.

Portes, A. (1997). Immigration theory for a new century: Some problems and opportunities. *International Migrant Review, 31,* 799–825.

Redfield, R., Linton, R., & Herskovitz, M. (1936). Memorandum on the study of acculturation. *American Anthropologist, 38,* 499–514.

Robertson, R. (1992). *Globalization: Social theory and global culture.* Chicago: University of Chicago Press.

Sassen, S. (1998). *Globalization and its discontents: Essays on the mobility of people and money.* New York: The New Press.

Schlegel, A. (2001). The global spread of adolescent culture. In L. J. Crockett & R. K. Silbereisen (Eds.), *Negotiating adolescence in times of social change.* New York: Cambridge University Press.

Shweder, R. A., Goodnow, J., Hatano, G., LeVine, H., Markus, H., & Miller, P. (1998). The cultural psychology of development: One mind, many mentalities. In W. Damon (Ed.), *Handbook of child development* (pp. 865–937). New York: Wiley.

Stigler, J. W., Shweder, R. A., & Herdt, G. (1990). *Cultural psychology: Essays on comparative human development.* New York: Cambridge University Press.

Turiel, E., & Wainryb, C. (2000). Social life in cultures: Judgments, conflict, and subversion. *Child Development, 71,* 250–256.

United Nations Development Programme. (1998). *Human development report.* New York: Oxford University Press.

Verma, S., & Saraswathi, T. S. (2002). Adolescents in India: Street urchins or Silicon Valley millionaires? In B. B. Brown, R. Larson, & T. S. Saraswathi (Eds.), *The world's youth: Adolescence in eight regions of the globe* (pp. 105–140). New York: Cambridge University Press.

Walsh, B. J., & Middleton, J. R. (1984). *The transforming vision: Shaping a Christian worldview.* Downers Grove, IL: Varsity.

Whiting, J. W. M., & Child, I. (1953). *Child training and personality.* New Haven, CT: Yale University Press.

Youniss, J., & Smollar, L. (1985). *Adolescent relations with mothers, fathers, and friends.* Chicago: University of Chicago Press.

Acknowledgment

I thank Jeff Arnett as well as all of the participants in the "Beyond the Self" project for their constructive comments on this article. I would also like to extend a special thanks to Linda Wagener and Jim Furrow for organizing the project.

Requests for reprints should be sent to Lene Arnett Jensen, Life Cycle Institute, Catholic University of America, Washington, DC 20064. E-mail: JensenL@cua.edu

The Dynamics of Self-Esteem: A Growth-Curve Analysis

Scott A. Baldwin; John P. Hoffmann

Research on adolescent self-esteem has been inconsistent regarding development patterns and processes, with some scholars concluding that self-esteem is a static construct and others concluding that it is a dynamic construct. A potential source of this inconsistency is the lack of attention to intraindividual changes in self-esteem across adolescence and to gender-specific developmental patterns. Building on previous research, we use a growth-curve analysis to examine intraindividual self-esteem changes from early adolescence to early adulthood. Using 7 years of sequential data from the Family Health Study (762 subjects ages 11-16 in Year 1), we estimated a hierarchical growth-curve model that emphasized the effects of age, life events, gender, and family cohesion on self-esteem. The results indicated that age had a curvilinear relationship with self-esteem suggesting that during adolescence self-esteem is a dynamic rather than a static construct. Furthermore, changes in self-esteem during adolescence were influenced by shifts in life events and family cohesion. These processes were different for males and females, particularly during early adolescence.

Introduction

Developmental theorists often note that adolescence is a time in which youths experience substantial changes in their physical, mental, and social identities (Graber, et al., 1996; McCandless, 1970; Santrock, 1986; Sprinthall and Collins, 1984). Among the many changes experienced during adolescence are shifting self-concepts (Santrock, 1986). Santrock (1986) notes that during adolescence there is an increase in self-consciousness, which leads to adolescents beginning to develop an understanding of themselves (i.e., their self-concept). Santrock also notes that this understanding is not fixed but changes as they face different life experiences. Because self-esteem is a large part of youths' self-understanding it is likely a fluctuating, dynamic construct during adolescence (McCandless, 1970).

Early and more recent self-esteem theorists have also suggested that self-esteem is a dynamic, changing construct. For example, William James (1983) viewed self-esteem as the ratio of one's successes to one's pretensions. To increase self-esteem one must either increase one's successes or lower one's expectations. Similarly, Rosenberg (1979) referred to

self-esteem as a "positive or negative evaluation of the self." Combining these 2 perspectives, one may arrive at the following proposition: A positive evaluation of the self stems from having more success than one expected, whereas a negative evaluation stems from having fewer successes than one expected. Clearly, this interpretation suggests that one's self-esteem is not constant over time, but instead is dynamic and changes depending on one's successes and expectations. Thus, a person with high self-esteem who is successfully moving through life meeting all her expectations who is suddenly fired from a job will likely experience decreasing self-esteem. Yet, when employment is found once again, self-esteem will likely be restored.

As noted by developmental theorists, these ebbs and flows of self-esteem are probably felt most keenly during the adolescent years. Studies that address changes in adolescent self-esteem are inconsistent, however. Several studies support both adolescent development and self-esteem theories which suggest that self-esteem is a dynamic construct. Some have found that self-esteem increases during adolescence (Cairns et al., 1990; Chiam, 1987; O'Malley and Bachman, 1983), while others have shown that self-esteem declines across the adolescent years (Brown et al., 1998; Simmons and Rosenberg, 1975). Other research that is inconsistent with developmental theories of self-esteem has indicated that self-esteem remains fairly static during adolescence (Bolognini et al., 1996; Chubb et al., 1997; Nottelmann, 1987; Savin-Williams and Demo, 1984; Simmons and Blyth, 1987; Wylie, 1979). Overall, attempts to model the developmental trajectories of adolescent self-esteem have provided inconsistent evidence about whether or not self-esteem changes significantly across adolescence.

On both sides of the issue, little research has focused on changes in self-esteem that occur within individuals over time. Rather, the most common focus is on group-level changes in mean levels of self-esteem. Indeed, a search of PsychINFO revealed only 4 out of more than 18,000 articles concerning self-esteem that attempted to look at intraindividual changes (Block and Robins, 1993; Deihl et al., 1997; Hirsch and Dubois, 1991; Zimmerman et al., 1997). As Block and Robins (1993) noted, "studies of self-esteem change that focus on mean-level changes..., reveal whether variables 'behave' consistently across time rather than whether individuals are behaviorally consistent." Thus, focusing on mean-level changes may mask true changes in a youth's self-esteem, and the trajectory of self-esteem may appear to be static rather than dynamic. For example, suppose that we are interested in self-esteem change among adolescent females. It is likely that some group of these females—perhaps those who are popular in school—shows increasing self-esteem during adolescence. Yet other groups of similarly situated females may have decreasing levels of self-esteem. Over time, these increasing and decreasing trends tend to cancel each other out, resulting in no evidence of mean change (Hirsch and Dubois, 1991). The solution for previous studies has been to attempt to control for the numerous variables that may distinguish diverse groups of adolescents (e.g., Cairns et al., 1990). Yet the number of factors that may affect mean levels of self-esteem are legion, thus it is important to determine if adolescents are following similar developmental paths individually, not simply as a group (Block and Robins, 1993).

Block and Robins (1993) studied both group mean level and individual changes in self-esteem among a sample of adolescents. They found no age differences in mean levels of self-esteem. Intraindividually, however, they discovered substantial change over time—over the entire sample, 60% of the participants showed either an increase or decrease in self-esteem by at least 1 standard deviation. This result provided clear evidence of individual change even when group-level change does not appear and strongly supports the notion that self-esteem is a dynamic construct. Block and Robins's research, in particular, brings into question the conclusions from studies that have looked only at mean-level differences or changes in means over time (Block and Robins, 1993). Is an individual's level of self-esteem as consistent as the group's level as a whole, or is an individual's level of self-esteem dynamic, changing despite the consistency of their particular group?

Although several researchers (e.g., Block and Robins, 1993; Hirsch and Dubois, 1991) have elaborated this issue, there are limits to the analytic tools they used to examine their data.

These limitations have been a formidable obstacle when attempting to estimate both between-subjects and within-subjects effects (Bijlereld and van der Kamp, 1998; Duncan et al., 1999). However, advances in hierarchical growth-curve modeling have overcome some of these limitations and provide an innovative approach to estimating intraindividual changes. These growth-curve models, or random-effects models as they are often labeled, allow the researcher to evaluate longitudinal data at two levels: (1) at the intraindividual level and (2) at the interindividual level (Singer, 1998; Snijers and Bosker, 1999). Therefore, our aim in the present study was to utilize growth-curve models to provide a better understanding of changes in self-esteem during adolescence at the intraindividual level. Specifically, it was hypothesized that the results of the growth-curve models would support the conceptualization of self-esteem as a dynamic, changing construct during adolescence and early adulthood. Hence we were able to compare explicitly propositions from a developmental theory (e.g., Cairns et al., 1990) and a more static conceptualization (e.g., Nottelmann, 1987) of self-esteem among adolescents.

In addition to examining age effects on self-esteem—which give rise to change across the adolescent years—we were interested in evaluating the influences of stressful life events, family relations, and gender on the dynamics of self-esteem. The impact of both stressful life events, family relations, and gender on self-esteem have been researched extensively (e.g., Cohen et al., 1987; Dumont and Provost, 1999; Kling et al., 1999). Nevertheless, because of a lack of sufficient analytical tools, most researchers who have studied these effects on self-esteem have not evaluated individual changes over time, although we propose that developmental shifts in these variables have important effects on the dynamics of self-esteem. Self-esteem has been evaluated either cross-sectionally (e.g., Kliewer and Sandler, 1992; Siddique and D'Arcy, 1984), which suggests that self-esteem is a static construct, or longitudinally focusing on mean-level differences across groups (e.g., Brown et al., 1998; Chubb et al., 1997). Consequently, to expand upon previous research it is particularly important to evaluate how age, gender, family relations, and life events affect individuals over time. Although there are a plethora of variables that may affect self-esteem during adolescence, evidence has shown that during adolescence levels of stress increase (e.g., Hoffman et al., 1992; Petersen et al., 1991), gender becomes a more salient feature of identity (e.g., Hill and Lynch, 1983), and families play an important role in adolescent's well-being (e.g., Blaske et al., 1989). Moreover, evidence has suggested that these variables may influence changes in self-esteem (Santrock, 1986; see below). Other potential variables that might be considered do not have a consistent basis of support in models of adolescent self-esteem or in developmental research.

Stressful Life Events

Adolescence is a time of transition in which youths take on greater responsibility as members of society (Eccles et al., 1992). Accompanying this increased responsibility is the possibility that they will experience additional stressful life events (Hoffman et al., 1992; Petersen et al., 1991). Furthermore, adolescents tend to magnify the severity of stressful events (Compas et al., 1985, 1993; Larson and Asmussen, 1991). Consistent with dynamic notions of self-esteem, research has also shown that as the number of stressful life events increases, adolescent self-esteem decreases (Cohen et al., 1987; Dumont and Provost, 1999; Johnson and McCutcheon, 1980; Kroger, 1980; Youngs et al., 1990). In addition to the adverse effects of life events on self-esteem, adolescents who experience these events are often depressed, angry, frustrated, nervous, anxious, and involved in more deviant activities (Banez and Compas, 1990; Compas, 1987; Compas et al., 1988; Hoffman et al., 1992; Hoffmann and Cerbone, 1999). The literature has clearly suggested that there is a relationship between stressful life events and adolescent dysfunction, such as low self-esteem. Nevertheless, most of the studies that have assessed adolescent development and stressful life events have examined only the effect of stress on group means. Thus, the intraindividual relationship between stressful life events and self-esteem is not currently understood.

Gender

The relationship between gender and self-esteem has been well-researched. Studies have typically found that males have a higher self-esteem than females, particularly during adolescence (Block and Robins, 1993; Bolognini et al., 1996; Chubb et al., 1997; Harper and Marshall, 1991; Simmons and Rosenberg, 1975; Zimmerman et al., 1997). A recent meta-analysis of self-esteem studies has supported this conclusion. Specifically, this analysis showed a modest, yet significant difference between male and female self-esteem ($d = 0.21$; Kling et al., 1999). Kling et al. (1999) found that the average gender difference in self-esteem was greatest during middle adolescence. One potential reason for this rift is that females' ratings of their attractiveness decline during adolescence whereas boys' perceptions remain positive and fixed (Harter, 1993). Moreover, females tend to be criticized in school on an intellectual basis whereas males are criticized on a motivational basis, which potentially hampers female self-esteem (Dweck et al., 1978). Block and Robins (1993) suggested that "females are socialized to get along in society and males are socialized to get ahead." Thus, perceived failures in the social realm of life, a common occurrence in adolescence, may have a more dramatic effect on females than on males.

Kling et al. (1999) also determined that self-esteem is fairly stable during adolescence, even among females, which is inconsistent with the dynamic theories of self-esteem. Hence, the conclusion that females' self-esteem plummets during adolescence appears to be incorrect. That is, gender is thought to have a little effect on changes in self-esteem during adolescence, although it may have an influence on initial levels of self-esteem during adolescence. However, as with age and life events effects, most of the research on gender differences during adoles-

cence has compared only mean-level changes among males and females. An analysis of intraindividual differences by gender provides a clearer picture of the development of self-esteem in adolescent males and females. This is especially important given that constant mean-level differences across adolescence may mask intraindividual shifts in self-esteem that differentially affect males and females.

Family Relations

Social support has been shown to be beneficial to one's well-being and to protect individuals from the untoward effects of stress (Cohen and Willis, 1985). During adolescence, youths often desire a strong relationship with their parents and siblings (Lempers and Clark-Lempers, 1992). Furthermore, consistent with developmental theories of self-esteem, strong family relationships often have a positive effect on self-esteem over time (Roberts and Bengtson, 1996; Yabiku et al., 1999). Yet adolescents with inadequate family support suffer from poorer mental health, retarded social development, and attenuated well-being overall (Barber and Olsen, 1997; Blaske et al., 1989; Yoshikawa, 1994). Extending the results of these studies, it is likely that adolescents who experience poor family cohesion do not cope with stress effectively and thus have lower self-esteem. However, family cohesion may not necessarily buffer the effects of stress; perhaps adolescents who come from a cohesive family simply have higher self-esteem than those from a noncohesive family due to the support and love that they perceive.

Summary

In this study, the dynamics of self-esteem during the adolescent years were examined. Building on the adolescent development literature and James's and Rosenberg's conceptualizations of self-esteem, we hypothesized that self-esteem is a dynamic construct. We further hypothesized that stressful life events, gender, and family relations all contribute to the dynamics of self-esteem during adolescence. Specifically, it was hypothesized that adolescents who experience a high number of stressful life events over time report lower self-esteem. Moreover, while males report higher self-esteem on average than females, this difference was expected to vary across adolescence, becoming most dramatic during the high school years (Harter, 1993). Based on sex-based socialization research (Dweck et al., 1978), we also suspected that self-esteem among females is more sensitive to stressful life events than it is among males. Finally, it was hypothesized that family relationships have a positive impact on self-esteem change across adolescence, yet this impact is attenuated by stressful life events. Given the developmental nature of both stressful life events and family relationships, it is likely that changes in these variables predict developmental shifts in self-esteem intraindividually; that is, they influence self-esteem over time within individual respondents. This study thus provides a more accurate characterization of self-esteem among adolescents.

Methods

Participants and Procedure

To examine the hypothesis of intraindividual change in self-esteem, 7 years of data from the Family Health Study (FHS), a longitudinal survey conducted in a large, upper Midwestern U.S. metropolitan area that was designed primarily to assess how parental mental health affects adolescent behavior and development, were used. Parents were recruited in 1990 from a variety of locations associated with a major medical center that serves the metropolitan area. Additional families were recruited from the surrounding community. About 85% of those approached by study personnel agreed to participate in the study. Those who refused to participate were slightly more likely to be single parents, but other demographic characteristics (e.g., race/ethnicity, family income) did not distinguish participants from nonparticipants. Adolescents in the sample ranged in age from 10 to 16 and were 51% female and 49% male. Approximately 89% were White, with modest percentages of African Americans, Asians, Hispanics, and Native Americans. The median annual family income was about $40,000, which is close to the median income reported by the U.S. Census Bureau for this part of the United States. Additional aspects of the sample, its recruitment techniques, and health assessments of the parents are described in detail in a series of previous papers (Hoffmann et al., 2000; Hoffmann and Su, 1998; Su et al., 1997).

On an annual basis the parents and their adolescent children completed self-administered questionnaires in their homes or in other convenient locations. Trained interviewers were available to assist with the completion of the interviews. The questionnaire addressed a number of topics that are of concern to researchers interested in families and adolescents, including extensive questions about stressful life events, support systems, health statuses, drug and alcohol use, delinquency, self-esteem, and depressive symptoms. A total of 861 adolescents from 601 families participated in the first year of the survey. The study achieved an impressive follow-up rate: After 7 years of data collection, more than 95% of the adolescents, many of whom made the transition to young adulthood, continued to participate in the study.

The participants in the study ranged in age across the 7 waves from early adolescence to early adulthood (ages 11-22). The analysis was limited to those participants who were of ages 11-16 during the initial year of data collection (n = 762; mean age at Year 1 = 12.9). Thus, the sample is an accelerated longitudinal design because it consists of members of multiple birth cohorts (Duncan et al., 1999; Raudenbush and Chan, 1993). The advantage of this approach is that one may sketch a portrait of the development of self-esteem from early adolescence to early adulthood.

Measures

Self-Esteem

Self-esteem was a time-varying covariate that was measured each year by Rosenberg's Self-Esteem Scale (1979). The scale included 10 items that assessed the respondent's feelings of worth, pride, ability, respect, and satisfaction with life. Higher values indicated higher self-esteem. Each variable was standardized prior to creating an additive scale. The unstandardized version of this scale ranged from 0 to 30. The alpha coefficient for the scale was consistently greater than 0.82 across the 7 years.

Stressful Life Events

The measure of stressful life events was a time-varying covariate that was based on a variety of events reported by the respondents during the 7 years under investigation. Stressful life events are a standard measure in the stress literature and have their most consequential effects when they are uncontrollable and undesirable (Mirowsky and Ross, 1989). They were measured each year by a checklist of 16 items from the Junior High Life Experiences Survey (Swearingen and Cohen, 1984), the Family Inventory of Life Events and Life Changes (McCubbin et al., 1981), and clinical diagnoses of parental substance use disorder or effective disorder (Chassin et al., 1991; Hoffmann and Cerbone, 1999). The events included incidents that occurred in the 12 months prior to each annual survey, such as death, physical and mental illness, or accidents among family or friends; changes in school or residence; parental divorce or separation; and family financial problems. The actual number of life events reported by the respondents ranges from 0 to 10 per year, although over three-quarters of them reported no more than 3 events in any 1 year.

Stressful life events tend to be relatively independent (Newcomb and Harlow, 1986; Newcomb et al., 1981), but since one is usually interested in their aggregate effects within a measurable time period (Simmons and Blyth, 1987), they are typically conceptualized as count variables. The relative independence of these events in our study is demonstrated by the low alpha levels (between 0.44 and 0.51 across the years). The events were not weighted differentially since research has shown that weighting does not affect statistical analyses (Cohen and Willis, 1985). Unfortunately, the data did not provide an acceptable assessment of other sources of stress, such as school problems, neighborhood problems, or life hassles. Nonetheless, the study of stressful life events has a significant history in psychological research (Cohen et al., 1987; Cohen and Willis, 1985) and thus we focused on their effects.

Family Cohesion

Family cohesion was determined each year by FACES-III (Olsen et al., 1990). The measure included items such as the amount of support given by the family during difficult times, the extent that the family communicated, the time that the family spent together, and the extent to which the respondent was included in family decision making. The alpha coefficient for this measure during each year was above 0.85. As with the self-esteem scale, the family cohesion measure was a composite variable based on summing the standardized values of each constituent variable. The unstandardized scale ranged from 0 to 60. The alpha coefficient exceeded 0.89 in each year.

The demographic variables proposed as having potential effects on adolescent self-esteem are sex and income. Both were time-invariant covariates. Sex was coded as 0 for females and 1 for males. Family income was measured on a scale from 1 to 12 corresponding to increasing monetary levels. It had a mean of 4.04 (corresponding to about $40,000 per year) and a standard deviation 2.6. Family income was measured during Year 1 by the father's report if one was available; otherwise the mother's report was used. In about 65% of the cases, both the mother and father reported family income, while in the remaining 35% of the cases only the mother reported the family income. This was due to both single-mother families and families in which only the mother participated. However, we found that the correlation between mothers' and fathers' reports, when both were available, was 0.88.

Data Analysis

A hierarchical linear model was used to conduct a growth-curve analysis of self-esteem from adolescence to early adulthood (Bryk and Raudenbush, 1992; Goldstein, 1996). The general idea was to combine in a single regression equation a 2-level hierarchical model to estimate variability in these growth-curves. Level 1 of the model examined variability within individuals—how self-esteem changed over time and whether these changes were due to other time-varying covariates (i.e., was self-esteem a dynamic construct during adolescence and, if so, did the other variables affect its changes?). However, unlike a standard regression approach, the coefficients indicating the effects of these covariates were treated as random rather than fixed effects. For example, the models assessed the effects of stressful life events, measured during 7 consecutive years, on repeated measures of self-esteem, yet these effects were allowed to vary across individuals. A set of cross-level interaction terms between the time-varying and time-invariant explanatory variables were introduced in the model to determine whether these random effects depended upon fixed attributes of the respondents (Snijders and Bosker, 1999). Thus, the models estimated whether one of the fixed effects, such as sex, explained any of the intraindividual variability in the association between life events and self-esteem. Given the separation of within-individual and between-individual variability, this type of growth-curve model controls for the effects of unobserved heterogeneity that may affect self-esteem differences across adolescents (Homey et al., 1995). Hence, more precise estimates of the impact of the explanatory variables on changes in self-esteem from early adolescence to young adulthood may be obtained.

Similar to the approach used by Raudenbush and Chan (1993), individual "growth" in self-esteem (i.e., increase or decrease, through annual repeated self-report measures of self-esteem) was related to the subject's age and stressful life events. The age variable was resealed so that a 0 value equaled age 11, thus providing an interpretable intercept. The other continuous variables were centered to have a mean of 0. Level 2 of the model examined whether these parameters varied across individuals by sex and family cohesion. Although family cohesion was measured as a time-varying covariate, its associated coefficient was "fixed" to be nonrandom over time.

Thus, family cohesion was entered in the model as a varying coefficient term rather than a random coefficient (Kreft and De Leeuw, 1998). This was primarily a practical step because growth-curve models can usually accommodate only half the number of random coefficients as there are years of data (Bryk and Raudenbush, 1992). Hence in the model the number of random coefficients was exhausted by considering the intercept, age, and stressful life events. Although it is conceivable to introduce additional random effects, attempts to do so resulted in models that could not be estimated. We also considered cohort effects by introducing dummy variables that indexed the different birth cohorts in the model (Raudenbush and Chan, 1993). We found no cohort differences in the models, nor did the introduction of these dummy variables affect the other coefficients in the models. Therefore, they are omitted from further consideration.

A graph of mean-level self-esteem across all ages indicated that age had a cubic effect among males and females. In other words, average levels of self-esteem initially increased with age, then decreased during middle adolescence, especially among females (cf. Kling et al., 1999), and then increased in young adulthood. Consequently, age-squared and age-cubed terms were included in the model as fixed effects. Once again, due to limitations in the number of years of data, these two higher order terms could not be estimated as random effects. Because previous studies have indicated that male and female self-esteem develop differently during adolescence (Bolognini et al., 1996; Kling et al., 1999) and that changes in male and female self-esteem are markedly different, an age by sex interaction term was also included in the model. This cross-level interaction was used to examine the impact of sex on the time-varying effects of age.

Researchers have also often found that males and females react to stress in diverse ways (Mirowsky and Ross, 1990; Vaux and Ruggiero, 1983); thus, a stress by sex interaction term was included in the model. Finally, past studies have shown that family cohesion has a main effect on adolescent outcomes such as self-esteem and a buffering effect on the relationship between stressful life events and intrapersonal outcomes (Cohen and Wills, 1985). To investigate both of these potential relationships, family cohesion was entered into the model as a main effect and as an interaction term with life events.

Results

Preliminary Analyses

A study has shown that there are changes in mean self-esteem during adolescence and early adulthood by gender. Although this study does not address intraindividual change in adolescence, there was significant mean-level variability in self-esteem across the adolescent and early adulthood years. The study also indicates that age has a cubic effect on self-esteem for both females and males. Mean self-esteem among females increased until age 12, then dropped until age 17, and then began to rise after age 17. In contrast, mean self-esteem among males increased until age 14, then decreased until about age 16, and finally increased after age 16 (with a slight dip at age 19). Note that the patterns suggest that the changes for females were far more dramatic than for males.

Growth-Curve Models

The results of the growth-curve analyses are presented in Table I. Model 1 introduced the effects of age on self-esteem. As suggested, age had a cubic effect—initially self-esteem increased with age (Age: [beta] = 1.23, p < 0.01), followed by a decrease in self-esteem ([Age.sup.2]: [beta] = - 0.28, p < 0.01), and lastly a second increase in self-esteem ([Age.sup.3]: [beta] = 0.02, p < 0.01). Further, the random effect of age ([sigma] = 0.93, p < 0.01) suggests that there was significant variability in the initial "growth" of self-esteem within individuals. Hence individuals followed diversely changing patterns of self-esteem in early adolescence. Note also the large random effect for the intercept ([sigma] = 6.17, p < 0.01). This indicates that initial levels of self-esteem were highly diverse among the sample.

Model 2 estimated the effect of sex and the interaction of sex by age on self-esteem. It also introduced family income as a control variable. Sex as a main effect does not have a significant impact on changes in self-esteem. Moreover, the interaction between age and sex did not attain statistical significance, thus initially casting doubt on the hypothesis that the age trends in self-esteem differ for males and females. The random effect of age remained at 0.93, indicating that neither the sex nor the sex by age interaction explained any of intraindividual variability in the age effect. The coefficient associated with income indicates that those from higher income families tended to have higher self-esteem than others, net the effect of age and sex.

Stressful life events were entered into Model 3 as a time-varying covariate. Additionally, life events by sex was included as an interaction term. Life events as a main effect had a significant negative effect on self-esteem development ([beta] = - 0.13, p < 0.01). Even after controlling for the age-related curvature in self-esteem, those who experienced a greater number of life events experienced significantly decreasing self-esteem. The random effect for life events was 0.15 (p < 0.05), suggesting that there was substantial variability in the effect of life events on self-esteem across individuals. The life events by sex interaction was not significant. Age, [Age.sup.2], and [Age.sup.3] remained highly significant, but the random effect of age dropped slightly (0.91). Thus, including life events in the model explained a small amount (~2%) of the intraindividual variability in the age effect. In this model, the sex variable and age by sex interaction continued to have nonsignificant effects.

Finally, in Model 4 family cohesion and an interaction between cohesion and life events were included in the model. As a main effect, cohesion had a significant positive effect on self-esteem ([beta] = 0.21, p < 0.01). However, the interaction between family cohesion and life events did not attain significance. In this model, after controlling for the effects of income, sex, cohesion and their various interactions, Age was borderline significant ([beta] = 0.68, p = 0.06), but [Age.sup.2], and [Age.sup.3] continued to have significant effects, thus showing that the curvature identified was not due to these variant and invariant characteristics. The life-events main effect was signifi-

Table I.

Growth-Curve Models of Self-Esteem, Family Health Study, 1992-99

Predictor	Model 1			Model 2		
Fixed effects						
Intercept	-0.27		(0.69)	-3.24	(**)	(0.80)
Age	1.23	(*)	(0.38)	1.16	(*)	(0.39)
[Age.sup.2]	-0.28	(**)	(0.07)	-0.28	(**)	(0.07)
[Age.sup.3]	0.02	(**)	(0.01)	0.02	(**)	(0.003)
Income				0.37	(**)	(0.07)
Sex				0.90		(0.59)
Life events						
Family cohesion						
Interactions						
Age x Sex				0.16		(0.09)
Life Events x Sex						
Life Events x Cohesion						
Random effects						
Intercept	6.17	(**)		6.04	(**)	
Age	0.93	(**)		0.93	(**)	
Life events	—			—		
Level-1 error	4.52			4.52		

Predictor	Model 3			Model 4		
Fixed effects						
Intercept	-2.91	(**)	(0.80)	-2.19	(*)	(0.75)
Age	1.06	(*)	(0.38)	0.68		(0.37)
[Age.sup.2]	-0.27	(**)	(0.22)	-0.18	(*)	(0.06)
[Age.sup.3]	0.02	(**)	(0.003)	0.01	(*)	(0.003)
Income	0.33	(**)	(0.07)	0.22	(**)	(0.06)
Sex	0.89		(0.58)	0.92		(0.54)
Life events	-0.13	(**)	(0.03)	-0.09	(**)	(0.02)
Family cohesion				0.21	(**)	(0.01)
Interactions						
Age x Sex	0.15		(0.09)	0.19	(*)	(0.09)
Life Events x Sex	0.06		(0.04)	0.05		(0.03)
Life Events x Cohesion				-0.001		(0.001)
Random effects						
Intercept	5.93	(**)		5.28	(**)	
Age	0.91	(**)		0.86	(**)	
Life events	0.15	(*)		0.10		
Level-1 error	4.48			4.37		

Note. The results represent a set of nested multilevel growth-curve models. Coefficients are provided with standard error in parentheses.

(*) p < 0.05

(**) p < 0.01.

cant while the life events by sex interaction continued to be nonsignificant. Interestingly, the age by sex interaction term emerged as a significant coefficient ([beta] = 0.19, 0 < 0.05), demonstrating that, once one controlled for the effects of life events and family cohesion, males and females differed in their pattern of self-esteem "growth." The random effect of age decreased slightly in Model 4. This suggests that family cohesion accounted for some of the intraindividual variation in the age effects on self-esteem, but its impact was not dramatic.

There is substantial evidence that male and female adolescents cope with stress in diverse ways (Mirowsky and Ross, 1990; Vaux and Ruggiero, 1983), but the growth-curve models used in the above analysis did not support this evidence. However, some research has shown that male and female young adults do differ in the ways in which they cope with stress (Porter and Stone, 1995). Hence our results may be due to the different age groups in the analysis. To test whether sex and stressful life events may affect self-esteem only among adolescents, we stratified the sample into an older cohort (ages 14-16 in Year 1) and a younger cohort (ages 11-13 in Year 1). As suspected, the effect of the sex by life events interaction was significant only among the younger cohort ([beta] = 0.22, p < 0.05), a group that ranged in age from 11 to 19. The interaction effect indicated that female self-esteem was affected to a greater extent than male self-esteem by stressful life events. The interaction term was significant among the older cohort, however.

Sensitivity Analysis

An important consideration when using a growth-curve analysis involves the assumptions about the residuals (Litell et al., 1996; Singer, 1998). A standard growth-curve model assumes that the residuals are independent and identically distributed across time points in the longitudinal data (cf. Karney and Bradbury, 2000). However, longitudinal data often do not meet this assumption. For instance, residuals from longitudinal models are often autocorrelated (Goldstein, 1995; Singer, 1998). Unlike other software that is commonly used to estimate growth-curve models (e.g., HLM), SAS's Proc Mixed allows one to specify several different variance/covariance matrices for the residuals, thus allowing one to evaluate the effect that different assumptions about the residual terms have on the results of the model. To determine the impact of these assumptions on the results presented above, five models were compared to the final model in Table I.

Table II presents the results of this sensitivity exercise. The first model was the final model from Table I. The second and third models assumed that the residuals were correlated over time (autocorrelation), yet these correlations were assumed to decay at a constant, whereas in Model 3 (ARH(1)) the within-year variances of the residuals were allowed to differ over time. Coefficients and standard errors from these 2 models were not substantially different from the original model, although model comparisons using AICs suggested that these 2 models fit the data slightly better than the final model from Table I. However, the variance/covariance matrices implied by these models were not positive definite, so the reader should be cautious when interpreting their results.

Models 4 and 5 assumed that the correlations between the residuals at each time point were constant (compound symmetry). Model 4 (CS) restricted the within-year residual variance to the constant, while Model 5 (CSH) freely estimated the within-year

residual variances. The results of Model 4 and Model 5 were not substantially different than the results of the original analysis. Once again, however, the variance/covariance matrix implied by Model 5 was not positive definite, so little faith should be put in its results.

Model 6 allowed the correlations of the residuals across years to be estimated freely from the data (i.e., an unstructured covariance structure; see Singer, 1998). Much like the previous models, the coefficients were not substantially different from those of the original model. As with several of the other models, however, the variance/covariance matrix implied by the model was not positive definite.

The results of this sensitivity analysis suggested that the growth-curve findings were robust to a variety of assumptions about the relationships among the within- and between-year residuals. Hence one may be confident in the results that demonstrated the impact of the time-variant and time-invariant explanatory variables on self-esteem. It is highly unlikely that the results were due to specific assumptions about the model's residuals.

Discussion

The goal of this study was to build upon previous adolescent self-esteem research by using growth-curve models to examine if there were significant changes in self-esteem from early adolescence to young adulthood. In addition to examining age effects on self-esteem, we also examined whether life events, gender, and family cohesion influence changes in self-esteem during adolescence. The advantage of the hierarchical growth-curve model was that it allowed us to build upon previous research by examining not only mean-level changes (fixed-effects), but also intraindividual changes (random-effects) (cf. Block and Robins, 1993). Furthermore, the sample used in this study furnished an extensive view of changes in self-esteem from early adolescence (age 11) to early adulthood (age 21). Each of these attributes allowed a more precise test of developmental theory predictions about shifts in self-esteem.

The results of the growth-curve models provided mixed support for the hypotheses. As predicted, age had a significant effect on self-esteem. Specifically, controlling for the effects of the other variables, age had a significant nonlinear (cubic) effect on self-esteem, suggesting that self-esteem changes significantly during adolescence, thus supporting developmental perspectives on this intrapersonal construct (James, 1983; McCandless, 1970; Rosenberg, 1979; Santrock, 1986; Sprinthall and Collins, 1984). Previous research has reported mixed results concerning adolescent self-esteem changes, but most of this research has focused on mean-level changes and has failed to consider the potential nonlinear effects of age (Block and Robins, 1993; Kling et al., 1999). Thus, the intraindividual changes found in the above model provide important insight into the dynamics of adolescent self-esteem. The results indicated that not only did the developmental path of self-esteem fluctuate significantly, but that these respondents did not follow

Table II.

Sensitivity Analysis of Growth-Curve Models of Self-Esteem

Predictors	Final model	AR (1)
Fixed effects		
Intercepts	-2.19 (*) (0.75)	-1.76 (*) (0.75)
Age	0.68 (0.37)	0.52 (0.40)
[Age.sup. 2]	-0.18 (*) (0.06)	-0.15 (*) (0.07)
[Age.sup. 3]	0.01 (*) (0.003)	0.01 (*) (0.004)
Income	0.22 (**) (0.06)	0.22 (**) (0.06)
Sex	0.9 (0.54)	0.67 (0.51)
Life events	-0.09 (**) (0.02)	-0.09 (**) (0.02)
Family cohesion	0.21 (**) (0.01)	0.21 (**) (0.01)
Interactions		
Age x Sex	0.19 (*) (0.09)	0.22 (*) (0.08)
Life Events x Sex	0.05 (0.03)	0.05 (0.03)
Life Events x Cohesion	-0.001 (0.001)	-0.001 (0.002)
AIC	-16039.4	-15962.4
Predictors	**ARH (1)**	**CS**
Fixed effects		
Intercept	-1.93 (*) (0.73)	-2.19 (*) (0.75)
Age	0.62 (0.39)	0.68 (0.37)
[Age.sup. 2]	-0.17 (*) (0.07)	-0.18 (*) (0.07)
[Age.sup. 2]	0.01 (*) (0.004)	0.01 (*) (0.003)
Income	0.22 (**) (0.06)	0.23 (**) (0.06)
Sex	0.64 (0.51)	0.92 (0.54)
Life events	-0.09 (**) (0.02)	-0.09 (**) (0.02)
Family cohesion	j0.21 (**) (0.01)	0.21 (**) (0.01)
Ineractions		
Age x Sex	0.22 (*) (0.08)	0.19 (*) (0.09)
Life Evens x Sex	0.05 (0.03)	0.05 (0.03)
Life Events x Cohesion	-0.001 (0.001)	-0.001 (0.001)
AIC	-15958.1	-16040.4
Predictors	CSH	UN
Fixed effects		
Intercept	-2.16 (*) (0.71	-1.99 (*) (0.71)
Age	0.66 (0.36)	0.63 (0.38)
[Age . sup. 2]	0.18 (*) (0.06)	-0.16 (*) (0.07)
[Age . sup. 3]	0.01 (*) (0.003)	0.01 (*) (0.003)
Income	0.23 (**) (0.06)	0.21 (*) (0.06)
Sex	0.84 (0.53)	0.57 (0.52)
Life events	-0.10 (**) (0.02)	-0.10 (**) (0.02)
Family cohesion	0.21 (**) ().01)	0.20 (**) (0.01)
Interactions		
Age x Sex	0.19 (*) (0.09)	0.24 (*) (0.08)
Life Events x Sex	0.06 (0.03)	0.07 (*) (0.03)
Life Events x Cohesion	-0.001 (0.001)	-0.001 (0.001)
AIC	-16029.6	-15948.5

Note. The final model above is Model 4 from Table I. Coefficients are provided with standard errors in parentheses.

(*) p < 0.05.

(**) p < 0.01.

the same self-esteem developmental patterns; changes in self-esteem varied significantly among individuals.

Although there was no main effect of gender on self-esteem across adolescence, there were significant gender differences in the effects of age on self-esteem. This indicates that gender has an important influence on changes in self-esteem. As shown by the positive sex by age-interaction coefficient in the growth-curve model (see Table I, Model 4; cf. Zimmerman et al., 1997), fluctuations in self-esteem were significantly more dramatic among females than among males. Female self-esteem decreased substantially from age 12 to about age 17. In contrast, males' self-esteem increased until age 14, decreased until about age 16, but then increased in early adulthood. Females first experienced a decline in self-esteem between the ages of 12 and 13, a time when most females have entered puberty. This is a time when females often become more aware of their bodies and may feel that their body shape is not what they assume it should be (Simmons and Rosenberg, 1975). Males, however, experienced the first general decline in self-esteem between the ages of 14 and 15, approximately the time when most males move from middle to high school. It has been suggested that during this period of school change males often feel that they have regressed on the social "food chain" (Chubb et al., 1997; Wigfield et al., 1991). Females of this age are often interested in the older boys at their high school, class work becomes more difficult, and there is stiffer competition for a place on athletic teams or for positions in school clubs. The sex difference in the age effect may also be explained by the different effects puberty has on males and females. As mentioned above, females often become dissatisfied with their body image during the early stages of puberty. Perhaps this dissatisfaction involves primarily those females who perceive a movement from an "ideal" body shape (slim) to a bigger, more curvaceous body (Hill and Lynch, 1983). However, males tend to fill out from a less than "ideal" body shape (slim) to a more muscular, "masculine" figure. Interestingly, the random effect of age was not explained at all by sex differences or by the age by sex interaction. Therefore, variation across individuals in the age effect was independent of gender.

One potential explanation for the variation in the age effect, as observed in Model 2, involved the impact of stressful life events. Indeed, by introducing life events into the model, a modest portion of the random age effect was explained. Moreover, life events had a significant effect on changes in self-esteem, even after accounting for the effects of age and the other explanatory variables in the model. This effect is particularly important because experiencing a high level of difficult life events, which are often out of a youth's control, puts self-esteem at risk. Thus, those concerned with adolescent well-being, such as parents, teachers, and school counselors, should be aware of and provide support during the difficult times in an adolescent's life.

In the younger cohort, the effect of life events was not completely independent of sex, however. Rather, the life events by sex interaction was positive and significant, thus indicating that stress had a greater impact on changes in female self-esteem, although this finding may be limited to adolescence (see below).

This finding is consistent with previous work that has demonstrated that adolescent males and females react differently to stress (Aneshensel et al., 1991; Kliewer and Sandler, 1992; Mirowsky and Ross, 1990; Vaux and Raggiero, 1983). A common explanation is that adolescent females tend to internalize their reactions to life's difficulties, whereas males tend to externalize their reactions (Leadbeater et al., 1995; Siddique and D'Arcy, 1984). Thus, females are more likely to react to stress with attenuated self-esteem and perhaps more depressive symptoms, while males are more likely to react with aggressive behavior and delinquency. Although we had no feasible way of fully gauging this hypothesis, among the younger cohort, our models supported the portion about females and their reactions to life events. It has been proposed that this reaction to stress is attributable to socialization—females are socialized to value relationships; thus, they will not react to stress aggressively for fear of damaging those relationships, but instead turn to internalized reactions to cope with their difficulties (Leadbeater et al., 1995).

However, the results also indicate that by young adulthood the impact of life events on self-esteem no longer differs by sex. This is consistent with research that has found that young adult males and females do not differ significantly in the ways in which they deal with stressful life events (Porter and Stone, 1995). Porter and Stone (1995), for instance, suggested that sex differences among young adults are due to the types of stressors experienced, not the coping mechanisms per se. Thus, as adolescents move toward young adulthood, males and females often experience many of the same types of stressors—going to college, living on their own, marriage, and so forth—consequently, their reactions to these life events are quite similar and their self-esteem is affected adversely in the same way.

The results of the model also suggested that being an adolescent member of a cohesive family is associated with increased self-esteem over time. This finding agrees with previous work that has shown similar effects for various mental health and developmental outcomes (Barber and Olsen, 1997; Blaske et al., 1989; Yoshikawa, 1994). It has also been proposed that social support, such as family cohesion, buffers the effects of stressful life events (Cohen and Willis, 1985). Our results did not support this contention, suggesting that changes in self-esteem are not a result of the buffering effects of a cohesive family. Thus, it seems that during adolescence and early adulthood, those who come from a cohesive family simply have higher self-esteem than do those from a noncohesive family (Roberts and Bengtson, 1996; Yabiku et al., 1999). This is likely due to the love and general support these adolescents feel from their families.

Although this study has made an initial attempt to study the growth curves of self-esteem over a substantial period of the early life course, the results are limited somewhat by the fact that the sample was not collected randomly. Nevertheless, the ample did include a large group of adolescents who were potentially exposed to substantial stress in their lives. Future research with a random samples, however, would provide additional evidence about the nature of self-esteem development during this age period. Moreover, the number of time points limited the number of time-varying covariates that could be entered into the model. Bryk and Raudenbush (1992) have recommended no more than 3 time-varying covariates for a 7-point random-effects growth-curve model. Future research with more data points is desirable because it would allow additional random effects to be entered into the model.

In sum, this study has modeled a general developmental pattern of self-esteem from early adolescence to young adulthood. Specifically, it has patterned 2 levels of development—the development across individuals and the development within individuals. Consistent with theories of adolescent development, at both levels the models supported the notion that self-esteem is a dynamic, changing construct during adolescence and young adulthood. Specifically, the results are consistent with Santrock's notion that adolescents' self-concept and self-esteem change substantially during adolescence (Santrock, 1986). Furthermore, changes in self-esteem were related to a number of dynamic and static factors. Within individuals, we found that life events and family cohesion have significant effects on changes in adolescent self-esteem, with the former attenuating self-esteem and the latter associated with increasing self-esteem. Across individuals, we have found that females, on average, report lower self-esteem than males, even during young adulthood. This general pattern is conditioned by age and exposure to stressful life events, however. In particular, the self-esteem gap is largest during the middle adolescent years, and it appears to become more narrow as males and females enter young adulthood. Moreover, female adolescent self-esteem seems to be more sensitive to changes in stressful life events than is male adolescent self-esteem, suggesting that sex-specific socialization patterns may disadvantage female adolescents when they are faced with stressful life events.

ACKNOWLEDGMENTS

This research was funded by NIDA grant DA05617. We thank Felicia Cerbone and Dean Gerstein for sharing the Family Health Study data with us. We also thank two anonymous reviewers for helpful suggestions on an earlier draft of this paper.

References

Aneshensel, C. S., Rutter, C .M., and Lachenbruch, P. A. (1991). Social structure, stress, and mental health: Competing conceptual and analytic models. Am. Sociol. Rev. 56: 166-78.

Banex, G. A., and Compas, B. E. (1990). Children's and parents' daily stressful events and psychological symptoms. J. Abnorm. Child Psychol. 18: 591-605.

Barber, B. K., and Olsen, J. A. (1997). Socialization in context: Connection, regulation, and autonomy in the family, school, and neighborhood, and with peers. J. Adolesc. Res. 12: 287-315.

Bijlereld, C. J. H., and van der Kamp, Th. L. J. (1998). Longitudinal Data Analysis: Design, Models, and Methods. Sage, Thousand Oaks, CA.

Blaske, D. M., Borduin, C. M., Henggler, S. W., and Mann, B. J. (1989). Individual, family, and peer characteristics of adolescent sex offenders and assaultive offenders. Dev. Psychol. 25: 846-855.

Block, J., and Robins, R. W. (1993). A longitudinal study of consistency and change in self-esteem from early adolescence to early adulthood. Child Dev. 64: 909-923.

Bolognini, M., Plancherel, B., Bettschart, W., and Halfon, O. (1996). Self-esteem and mental health in early adolescence: Development and gender differences. J. Adolesc. 19: 233-245.

Brown, K. M., McMahon, R. P., Biro, F. M., Crawford, P., Sebreiber, G. B., Similo, S. L., Waclawiw, M., and Striegel-Moore, R. (1998). Changes in self-esteem in black and white girls between the ages of 9 and 14 years. J. Adolesc. Health 23: 7-19.

Bryk, A. S., and Raudenbush, S. W. (1992). Hierarchical Linear Models: Applications and Data Analysis Methods. Sage, Newbury Park, CA.

Cairns, E., McWhirter, L., Duffy, U., and Barry, R. (1990). The stability of self-concept in late adolescence: Gender and situational effects. Pers. Indiv. Differ. 11: 937-944.

Chassin, L., Rogosch, F., and Barrera, M. (1991). Substance use and symptomatology among adolescent children of alcoholics. J. Abnorm. Psychol. 100: 449-463.

Chiam, H. (1987). Change in self-concept during adolescence. Adolescence 22: 69-76.

Chubb, N. H., Fertman, C. I., and Ross, J. L. (1997). Adolescent self-esteem and locus of control: A longitudinal study of gender and age differences. Adolescence 32: 113-129.

Cohen, L. H., Burt, C. E., and Bjorck, J. P. (1987). Life stress and adjustment: Effects of life events experienced by young adolescents and their parents. Dev. Psychol 23: 583-592.

Cohen, S., and Willis, T. A. (1985). Stress, social support, and the buffering hypothesis. Psychol. Bull. 98: 310-357.

Compas, B. E. (1987). Coping with stress during childhood and adolescence. Psychol. Bull. 101: 393-403.

Compas, B. E., Davis, G. E., and Forsythe, C. J. (1985). Characteristics of life events during adolescence. Am. J. Community Psychol. 13: 677-691.

Compas, B. E., Malcarne, V. L., and Fondacaro, K. M. (1988). Coping with stress events in older children and young adolescents. J. Consult. Clin. Psychol. 56: 405-411.

Compas, B. E., Orosan, P. G., and Grant, K. E. (1993). Adolescent stress and coping: Implications for psychopathology during adolescence. J. Adolesc. 16: 331-349.

Deihl, L. M., Vicary, J. R., and Deike, R. C. (1997). Longitudinal trajectories of self-esteem from early to middle adolescence and related psychosocial variables among rural adolescents. J. Res. Adolesc. 7: 393-411.

Dumont, M., and Provost, M. A. (1999). Resilience in adolescents: Protective role of social support, coping strategies, self-esteem, and social activities on experience of stress and depression. J. Youth Adolesc. 28: 343-363.

Duncan, T. E., Duncan, S. C., Strycker, L. A., Li, F., and Alpert, A. (1999). An Introduction to Latent Variable Growth Curve Modeling. Eribaum, Mahwah, NJ.

Dweck, C. S., Davidson, W., Nelson, S., and Enna, B. (1978). Sex differences in learned helplessness: II. The contingencies of evaluative feedback in the classroom and III. An experimental analysis. Dev. Psychol. 14: 268-276.

Eccles, J. S., Midgley, C., Wigfield, A., and Rueman, D. (1993). Development during adolescence. Am. Psychol. 48: 90-101.

Goldstein, H. (1996). Multilevel Statistical Models. Edward Arnold, London.

Graber, J. A., Brooks-Gunn, J., and Petersen, A. C. (eds.) (1996). Transitions Through Adolescence: Interpersonal Domains and Context. Earlbaum, Mahwah, NJ.

Harper, J. F., and Marshall, E. (1991). Adolescents' problems and their relationship to self-esteem. Adolescence 26: 799-808.

Harter, S. (1993). Causes and consequences of low self-esteem in children and adolescents. In Baumeister, R. (ed.), Self-Esteem: The Puzzle of Low Self-Regard. Plenum Press, New York, pp. 87-111.

Hill, J. P., and Lynch, M. E. (1983). The intensification of gender-related role expectations during early adolescence. In Brooks-Gunn, J., and Peterson, A. (eds.), Girls at Puberty: Biological and Psychosocial Perspectives. Plenum, New York, pp. 201-228.

Hirsch, J. H., and DuBois, D. L. (1991). Self-esteem in early adolescence: The identification and prediction of contrasting longitudinal trajectories. J. Youth Adolesc. 20: 53-72.

Hoffman, M. A., Levy-Shiff, R., Sohlber, S. C., and Zarizki, J. (1992). The impact of stress and coping: Developmental changes in the transition to adolescence. J. Youth Adolesc. 21: 451-469.

Hoffmann, J. P., and Cerbone, F. G. (1999). Stressful life events and delinquency escalation in early adolescence. Criminology 37: 343-373.

Hoffmann, J. P., Cerbone, F. G., and Su, S. S. (2000). A growth curve analysis of stress and adolescent drug use. Subst. Use Misuse 35: 687-716.

Hoffmann, J. P., and Su, S. S. (1998). Parental substance use disorder, mediating variables, and adolescent drug use: A nonrecursive model. Addiction 93: 1351-1364.

Horney, J. D., Osgood, W., and Marshal, I. H. (1995). Criminal careers in the short-term: Intraindividual variability in crime and its relation to local life circumstances. Am. Sociol. Rev. 60: 655-673.

James, W. (1983). The principles of Psychology. Harvard University Press, Cambridge, MA. (Original work published 1890)

Johnson, J. H., and McCutcheon, S. M. (1980). Assessing life stress in older children and adolescents: Preliminary findings with the life events checklist. In Sarason, I. G., and Spielberger, C. D. (eds.), Stress and Anxiety (Vol. 7). Hemisphere, Washington, DC, pp. 111-125.

Karney, B. R., and Bradbury, T. N. (2000). Attributions in marriage: State or trait? A growth curve analysis. J. Pers. Soc. Psychol. 78: 295-309.

Kliewer, W., and Sandler, I. N. (1992). Locus of control and self-esteem as moderators of stressor-symptom relations in children and adolescents. J. Abnorm. Child Psychol. 20: 393-413.

Kling, K. C., Hyde, J. S., Showers, C. J., and Buswell, B. N. (1999). Gender differences in self-esteem: A meta-analysis. Psychol. Bull. 123: 470-500.

Kreft, I., and De Leeuw, J. (1998). Introducing Multilevel Models. Sage, Thousand Oaks, CA.

Kroger, J. E. (1980). Residential mobility and self concept in adolescence. Adolescence 15: 967-977.

Larson, R., and Asmussen, L. (1991). Anger, worry, and hurt in early adolescence: An enlarging world of negative emotions. In Colton, M. E., and Gore, S. (eds.), Adolescent Stress. Causes and consequences. Aldine de Gruyter, New York, pp. 21-41.

Leadbeater, B. J., Blatt, S. J., and Quinlan, D. M. (1995). Gender-linked vulnerabilities to depressive symptoms, stress, and problem behaviors in adolescents. J. Res. Adolesc. 5: 1-29.

Lempers, J. D., and Clark-Lempers, D. S. (1992). Young, middle, and late adolescents' comparisons of the functional importance of five significant relationships. J. Youth Adolesc. 21: 53-96.

Littell, R. C., Milliken, G. A., Stroup, W. W., and Wolfinger, R. D. (1996). SAS System for Mixed Models. SAS Institute, Cary, NC.

McCandless, B. R. (1970). Adolescents: Behavior and Development Dryden Press, Hinsdale, IL.

McCubbin, H. I., Patterson, J. M., and Wilson, L. R. (1981). Family Inventory of Life Events and Changes. Family Social Science Department, University of Minnesota, St. Paul.

Mirowsky, J., and Ross, C. E. (1989). Social Causes of Psychological Distress. Aldine de Gruyter, New York.

Newcomb, M. D., and Harolow, L. L. (1986). Life events and substance use among adolescents: Mediating effects of perceived loss of control and meaninglessness in life. J. Pers. Soc. Psychol. 51: 564-577.

Newcomb, M. D., Huba, G. J., and Bentler, P. (1981). A multidimensional assessment of stressful life events among adolescents: Derivation and correlates. J. Health Soc. Behav. 22: 400-415.

Nottelmann, E. D. (1987). Competence and self-esteem during the transition from childhood to adolescence. **Dev. Psychol. 23:** 441-450.

Olsen, D. H., Portner, J., and Lavee, Y. (1990). FACES-III. University of Minnesota, Family Social Science Department, St. Paul.

O'Malley, P. M., and Bachman, J. G. (1983). Self-esteem: Change and stability between ages 13 and 23. Dev. Psychol. 19: 257-268.

Petersen, A. C., Kennedy, R. E., and Sullivan, P. (1991). Coping with adolescence. In Colton, M. E., and Gore, S. (eds.), Adolescent Stress: Causes and Consequences. Aldine De Gruyter, New York, pp. 93-110.

Porter, L. S., and Stone, A. A. (1995). Are there really gender differences in coping? A Reconsideration of previous data and results from a daily study. J. Soc. Clin. Psychol. 14: 184-202.

Raudenbush, S. W., and Chan, W. (1993). Application of a hierarchical linear model to the study of adolescent deviance in an overlapping cohort design. J. Consult. Clin. Psychol. 61: 941-951.

Roberts, R. E. L., and Bengtson, V. L. (1996). Affective ties to parents in early adulthood and self-esteem across 20 years. Soc. Psychol. Q. 59: 96-106.

Rosenberg, M. (1979). Conceiving the Self Basic Books, New York.

Santrock, J. W. (1986). Life-Span Development, Brown Publishers, Dubuque, IA.

Savin-Williams, R. C., and Demo, D. H. (1984). Developmental change and stability in adolescent self-concept. Dev. Psychol. 20: 1100-1110.

Siddique, C. M., and D'Arcy, C. (1984). Adolescence, stress, and psychological well-being. J. Youth Adolesc. 13: 459-473.

Simmons, R. G., and Blyth, D. A. (1987). Moving into Adolescence. Aldine De Gruyter, New York.

Simmons, R. G., and Rosenberg, F. (1975). Sex, sex roles, and self-image. J. Youth Adolesc. 4: 229-258.

Singer, J. D. (1998). Using SAS PROC MIXED to fit multilevel models, hierarchical models, and individual growth models. J. Educ. Behav. Stat. 24: 321-355.

Snijders, T., and Bosker, R. (1999). Multilevel Models: An Introduction to Basic and Advanced Multilevel Modeling. Sage, Thousand Oaks, CA.

Sprinthall, N. A., and Collins, W. A. (1984). Adolescent Psychology: A Developmental View, Addison-Wesley, Reading, MA.

Su, S. S., Hoffmann, J. P., Gerstein, D. R., and Johnson, R. A. (1997). The effects of home environment on adolescent drug use and depression. J. Drug Issues 27: 851-877.

Swearingen, E. M., and Cohen, L. (1984). Measurement of adolescents' life events: The junior high life experiences survey. Am. J. Community Psychol. 13: 69-85.

Vaux, A., and Ruggiero, M. (1983). Stressful life change and delinquent behavior. Am. J. Community Psychol. 11: 169-183.

Wigfield, A., Eccles, J. S., Mac Iver, D., Rwuman, D. A., and Midgley, C. (1991). Transitions during early adolescence: Changes in children's domain-specific self-perceptions and general self-esteem across the transition to junior high school. Dev. Psychol. 27: 552-565.

Wylie, R. (1979). The Self-Concept: Vol. 2. Theory amid Research on Selected Topics. University of Nebraska Press, Lincoln, NE.

Yabiku, S. T., Axinn, W. G., and Thornton, A. (1999). Family integration and children's self-esteem. Am. J. Social. 104: 1494-1524.

Youngs, G. A., Jr., Rathge, R., Mullis, R., and Mullis, A. (1990). Adolescent stress and self-esteem. Adolescence 25: 333-341.

Yoshikawa, H. (1994). Prevention as cumulative protection: Effects of early family support and education on chronic delinquency and its risks. Psychol. Bull. 115: 28-54.

Zimmerman, M. A., Copeland, L. A., Shape, J. T., and Dielman, T. E. (1997). A longitudinal study of self-esteem: Implications of adolescent development. J. Youth Adolesc. 26: 117-141.

Fostering Social-Emotional Learning in the Classroom

Linda K. Elksnin; Nick Elksnin

Teachers face enormous challenges meeting both the academic and social-emotional needs of learners in their classrooms. In this article we discuss ways in which teachers can promote social-emotional learning. First, we discuss the construct of emotional intelligence and how it can be improved through social-emotional learning. We then review strategies teachers can use to improve learners' emotional, social, and interpersonal problem solving skills.

It is estimated that between 15 and 22 percent of U.S. youth have social-emotional difficulties warranting intervention (Cohen, 2001; Mogno & Rosenblitt, 2001). Students at risk for school failure are particularly vulnerable for social-emotional problems. For example, 75 percent of students with learning disabilities (LD) exhibit social skills deficits (Kavale & Forness, 1996), and the U.S. Department of Education (1996) reported that 29 percent of adolescents with disabilities require social skills instruction beyond high school.

Regular education classrooms include ever-increasing numbers of at-risk students. For example, special education students receive most, if not all, of their education in regular education classrooms (U.S. Department of Education, 2001). It is clear that teachers face enormous challenges meeting learners' academic and social-emotional needs. In this article we discuss ways in which teachers can promote social-emotional learning in their classrooms. First we discuss the construct of emotional intelligence and how it can be improved through social-emotional learning. We then review strategies teachers can use to improve learners' emotional, social, and interpersonal problem solving skills.

Emotional Intelligence and Social-Emotional Learning

The term emotional intelligence was first used in 1990 by Salovey and Mayer, who offer this definition:

Emotional intelligence involves the ability to perceive accurately, appraise, and express emotion; the ability to access and/or generate feelings when they facilitate thought; the ability to understand emotion and emotional knowledge; and the ability to regulate emotions to promote emotional and intellectual growth (Mayer & Salovey, 1997).

Goleman (1995) popularized the construct of emotional intelligence in his book, Emotional Intelligence: Why It Can Matter More Than IQ. The term EQ, or emotional quotient, was coined by Bar-On (1997) to differentiate emotional intelligence from cognitive intelligence, which is measured by intelligence tests. EQ is thought to be comprised of five domains (Goleman, 1995; Mayer & Salovey, 1997):

- knowing ones' emotions
- managing one's emotions
- motivating oneself
- recognizing emotions of others
- effectively using social skills when interacting with others

Less genetically determined than IQ, emotional intelligence can be taught by teachers and parents. Even more encouraging is that EQ skills overlap, creating a "spillover" effect: Teaching one skill improves other EQ skills. Social-emotional learning (or social-emotional education) involves using procedures and methods to promote EQ.

Within two years after publication of Goleman's book, more than 700 school districts implemented social emotional learning (SEL) programs designed to teach students social-emotional skills (Ratnesar, 1997). SEL programs focus on emotional awareness, social skills, and interpersonal problem solving (Cohen, 2001). In the sections that follow, we discuss ways in which teachers can foster social-emotional learning in their classrooms.

Emotional Awareness

The ability to perceive and understand emotions develops with age. Children as young as three can identify sadness, happiness, and fear using nonverbal cues such as facial expression, gestures, and voice tone (Nabuzoka & Smith, 1995). At this age they begin to understand causes of feelings. However, children who are at risk for school failure may only acquire these skills through direct instruction (Gumpel & Wilson,

1996; Most & Greenbank, 2000). In addition, many children (and some adults) may require help in understanding subtle shifts in emotion represented by family groupings as identified by Bodine and Crawford (1999):

> *Anger: Fury, outrage, resentment,*
> *wrath, exasperation, indignation,*
> *vexation, acrimony, animosity,*
> *annoyance, irritability, hostility*
> *Sadness: Grief, sorrow, cheerlessness,*
> *gloom, melancholy, self-pity,*
> *Loneliness, dejection, despair (p. 82)*

Understanding one's own emotions is prerequisite to self control and anger management (Bodine & Crawford, 1999). Understanding the emotions of others is essential if learners are to read social situations accurately and respond to them appropriately. Without emotional understanding, students will misread the behaviors of others. Teachers can help learners increase their emotional understanding by teaching nonverbal communication skills and by becoming emotion coaches.

Nonverbal Communication Skills

Most (i.e., 93%) of emotional meaning is conveyed without words: Fifty-five percent through facial expressions, body posture, and gestures, and thirty-eight percent through tone of voice (Mehrabian, 1968). In order to understand one's emotions and the emotions of others, learners must have adequate nonverbal communication skills. Nowicki and Duke (1992) and Duke, Nowicki, and Martin (1996) identified six areas of nonverbal communication: paralanguage, facial expressions, postures and gestures, interpersonal distance (space) and touch, rhythm and time, and objectics. Instructional goals are for learners to recognize nonverbal messages of others and to effectively express themselves nonverbally. Teachers can reach these goals by using activities described in Table 1.

Paralanguage. Paralanguage is comprised of nonword sounds that convey meaning. Examples include tone of voice, rate of speech, emphasis and variation in speech, and nonverbal sound patterns such as "mmmmmmmm." Learners need to understand how voice tone conveys emotion. In order to avoid cognitive conflict voice tone and words must match. Similarly, learners need to recognize that speech rate conveys emotion. They also should be aware of their own speech rate and be able to adjust it to meet listeners' needs. Emphasis and variation in speech conveys and changes meaning. The sentence "I didn't say you stole the car," takes on different meanings depending on which word is emphasized:

> **I** *didn't say you stole the car.*
> *I* **didn't** *say you stole the car.*
> *I didn't say* **you** *stole the car.*
> *I didn't say you* **stole** *the car.*
> *I didn't say you stole the* **car.**

Table 1
Activities for Teaching Nonverbal Communication Skills

Area of Nonverbal Communication	Activity
Paralanguage	
Tone of Voice	Identify emotions when teacher reads sentence using different voice tones.
	Read a script when given different situations surrounding different emotions.
Nonverbal Sound Patterns	Use different types of paralanguage to express feelings.
Rate of Speech	Match rate with emotions such as happy, angry, sad.
	Tape voice and count number of words spoken per minute; compare with others.
Facial Expressions	Demonstrate "resting face."
	Make facial expressions to convey different emotions.
	Identify emotions conveyed by people in public, on TV, and in magazines.
Postures and Gestures	Assemble a dictionary of gestures/postures conveying specific emotions.
	Demonstrate postures under formal/informal situations.
Interpersonal Distance and Touch	Identify types of conversations that should/should not occur in each spatial zone.
	Discuss feelings when personal space is invaded.
	Demonstrate a touch for an emotion when role playing.
Rhythm and Time	Estimate length of time to complete activities.
	Keep track of number of times late or on time.
	Describe examples of public and private time.
Objectics	Develop dress codes for specific situations and use magazine pictures to illustrate.
	Describe image conveyed by dress when observing people in public.
	Develop dictionary of "in" styles.

Facial Expressions. People are expected to look at other's faces during conversation, and learners may need to be taught to engage in eye contact. Ability to read facial expressions is related to understanding that the face includes three zones: forehead and eyes, nose and cheeks, and mouth. Awareness of facial zones and the resting face (a person's unconscious facial expression) can be taught directly.

Postures and Gestures. Learners must learn to interpret postures and gestures and to use them appropriately. For example, the teacher may regard a student as bored and disinterested by how that student sits in class.

Interpersonal Distance (Space) and Touch. Hall (1966) identified four spatial zones among Americans: intimate zone (i.e., nearly touching to 18 inches away), personal zone (i.e., 18 inches to 4 feet away), social zone (i.e., 4 to 12 feet away), and public zone (i.e., 12 feet and more). Learners need to be taught about these zones as violating a zone may result in a serious faux pas. Learners who respect classmates' personal space are more accepted by peers and are less apt to get into difficulty when working with others. Learners also need to know about mental space that holds private topics. Learning to read people to determine if they feel that their mental space has been invaded is a useful skill. Finally, students also must learn what constitutes appropriate and inappropriate touching.

Rhythm and Time. Some principles of rhythm and time students need to understand and practice include being in sync with others, managing time, arriving on time, and knowing the difference between private and public time. Students need to be able to read messages conveyed through others' use of time (e.g., being made to wait in the doctor's office) and have their use of time match the intended message (e.g., spending time with friends means you care about them). Many learners need direct instruction in how to estimate and manage time.

Objectics. Objectics includes style of dress and hair, use of jewelry and cosmetics, and personal hygiene that allow learners to fit in with a group. Learners need to understand the difference between image (self perception) and impression (other's perception of an individual). Objectics are particularly important for young adolescents, whose desire to fit in is overpowering. Teachers and parents should not pretend to understand preadolescent and adolescent fashion rules, but should rely instead on observing children in school and magazines, at the mall, and on TV. Students may need to be taught how to dress to convey their desired image and how to dress for different situations.

Emotion Coaching

Once learners acquire adequate nonverbal communication skills, emotional understanding can be further improved through use of emotion coaching, a technique developed by John Gottman (1997). Teachers and parents acting as emotion coaches can use a five-step process to provide guidance about emotions. Parents and teachers first need to be aware of the learner's emotion. Gottman recommends that adults put the child's situation into an adult context. For example, how we feel when our boss dresses us down during a staff meeting is similar to how a child feels when a teacher reprimands the child in front

of the class. Step Two involves recognizing uncomfortable emotions as teaching opportunities and discussing feelings rather than punishing or criticizing. Emotions are validated rather than evaluated during Step Three. Step Four involves helping the learner label his emotion. The skills learned during nonverbal communication lessons will help learners use words to label how they feel. The final step involves helping the learner solve the problem that led to the feeling. Problem solving is discussed in detail elsewhere in this article.

Social Skills

Adequate interpersonal skills are an important component of emotional intelligence. Types of social skills include interpersonal behaviors needed to make and keep friends, such as joining in and giving compliments; peer-related social skills valued by classmates, such as sharing and working cooperatively; teacher-pleasing social skills related to academic success, such as listening and following directions; self-related behaviors, such as following through and dealing with stress; communication skills such as attending to the speaker and conversational turn taking; and assertiveness skills (Elksnin & Elksnin, 1998). Learners demonstrate two types of social skills problems: acquisition problems and performance problems.

Acquisition Problems

An acquisition problem occurs when a learner lacks specific social skills. Each social skill must be taught directly. Teachers can prepare to teach a social skill by providing the learner with a definition of the skill, the steps required to perform the skill, a rationale for learning the skill, situations in which to use the skill, role play situations in which to practice the skill, and social rules that govern skill use (see Elksnin & Elksnin, 1995).

Social skills are taught during role playing. The teacher first performs each skill step while talking out loud to model cognitive decisions. The teacher then guides the learner through the skill while providing specific, informative feedback to improve performance. Finally, the teacher provides opportunities for the learner to independently practice the skill. Many social skills curricula are available. A well-developed social skills program provides a taxonomy of social skills, along with analyses of skills steps.

Performance Problems

Performance problems occur when the learner knows how to perform the skill yet fails to do so. Causes of performance problems include failure to determine when to use a skill or failure to receive adequate reinforcement for skill use. In the first case, coincidental teaching can be used to encourage students to practice skills. In the second case, classmates can be recruited to praise the learner for using the skill.

Coincidental teaching. Coincidental teaching involves teaching social skills as situations occur in the natural environment (Schulze, Rule, & Innocenti, 1989). Teachers can use coincidental teaching in their classrooms and teach parents to use it at home. The first step is to identify social skills to target during the day and situations that call for skill use. For example, the teacher may identify "sharing" as the target skill and cooperative groups and free play as situations likely to require sharing. After situations are identified, the teacher determines times during the day that are supportive of coincidental teaching. For example, while the teacher is actively monitoring cooperative learning groups may not be the best time to coincidentally teach social skills. Once appropriate situations and times are identified, the teacher looks for opportunities for learners to use the skill, prompts learners to use the skill, and praises learners following skill use. Teaching parents to coincidentally teach provides students with even more practice opportunities (Elksnin & Elksnin, 2000).

Peer reinforcement. Often learners who perform social skills fail to receive reinforcement from classmates. These learners may even be punished for past mistakes (Scott & Nelson, 1998). In these situations, teachers must recruit peer support. Two examples of peer-mediated interventions illustrate the power of the peer group to enhance social skills performance. The first example is positive peer reporting, which involves reinforcing peers with tokens when they publicly praise appropriate social behavior. Jones, Young, and Friman (2000) taught peers to give positive feedback to socially rejected, delinquent adolescents by looking at the learner, smiling, stating a positive thing the learner did or said, and verbally praising the learner. Steps were posted on class bulletin boards as reminders. Peer acceptance of rejected learners improved and the number of positive statements made by their peers increased. In a second study, elementary-aged learners were taught how to recognize socially appropriate behavior (Skinner, Cashwell, & Skinner, 2000). They then were asked to "tootle," or tell the teacher when peers behaved in a socially appropriate manner, rather than "tattle," or tell the teacher when peers did or said something inappropriate. Socially appropriate behavior of students in this fourth-grade classroom increased substantially.

Problem Solving

In addition to possessing adequate social skills, emotionally intelligent learners are effective social problem solvers (Salvin & Madden, 2001). Problem solving can and should be taught, and it is important for teachers to model problem solving by "thinking out loud." Learners can be taught to problem solve using this sequence (D'Zurilla & Goldfried, 1971):

1. Define the problem.
2. Generate possible solutions.
3. Select a solution.
4. Predict outcomes if solution is implemented.
5. Select an alternative solution if predicted outcome is not positive.
6. Evaluate outcome after solution is implemented.
7. Decide what to do in a similar situation.

The FIG TESPN Routine and Social Skill Autopsies are two approaches that incorporate these steps that are especially useful in the classroom.

FIG TESPN Routine. Elias, Tobias, and Friedlander (1999) developed the FIG TESPN Routine as a process parents and children can use to solve social problems. Teachers also can use this routine. The eight steps of FIG TESPN include

1. Feelings cue me to thoughtful action.
2. I have a problem.
3. Goal gives me a guide.
4. Think of things I can do.
5. Envision outcomes.
6. Select my best solution.
7. Plan the procedure, anticipate pitfalls, practice, and pursue it.
8. Notice what happened, and now what?

During Step One, learners are taught that bad feelings signal a problem that needs to be solved. Learners are taught that problems cannot be solved effectively without labeling the emotion or the bad feeling. The teacher can use many of the strategies discussed earlier to increase emotional understanding. Step Two emphasizes that the learner "owns" the problem. He may not have caused the problem, but it is his responsibility to solve it. During this step, learners also learn that actions, not feelings, solve problems. Step Three focuses on goal setting to direct actions and reduce stress. Learners generate possible solutions during Step Four. Learners are taught that every action has consequences during Step Five. Based on predicted outcomes learners select a solution to the problem during Step Six. The original problem is revisited at this point. Step Seven emphasizes that problems are likely to occur when implementing any plan. By anticipating problems before implementing a plan, learners are less likely to become discouraged. During the final step of FIG TESPN, learners self-evaluate and are taught that not all plans will be successful. Several curricula that focus on interpersonal problem solving also are available.

Social Skill Autopsies. Lavoie (1994) recommends using social skill autopsies after the learner experiences a negative (or positive) social outcome. Autopsies involve analyzing the events surrounding a social outcome by asking the learner what she did, what happened when she did it, and what she will do in a similar situation based upon the positive or negative direction of the outcome. Autopsies should only be conducted privately and only after the learner has dealt with her emotions. For this reason, they can be used as part of the emotion coaching process. The obvious advantage of social skill autopsies is that they can be used any time and any place. If school personnel and parents "autopsy" social behavior, learners will become more skillful interpersonal problem solvers.

Conclusion

Emotional intelligence may be as important as, or even more important than, cognitive intelligence. Many learners, particularly those at risk for school failure, do not possess the social-emotional skills needed to be emotionally intelligent. However, these skills can and should be taught. In this article we reviewed ways in which teachers can improve learners' emotional understanding, social skills, and interpersonal problem-solving ability. Social-emotional learning enables learners to effectively "understand, process, manage, and express the social and emotional aspects of [their] lives" (Cohen, 2001).

References

Bar-On, R. (1997). BarOn Emotional Quotient Inventory, user's manual. Toronto, ON: MultiHealth Systems, Inc.

Bodine, R. J., & Crawford, D. K. (1999). Developing emotional intelligence. Champaign, IL: Research Press.

Camp, B. W., & Bash, M. A. S. (1985a). Think aloud, grades 1-2. Champaign, IL: Research Press.

Camp, B. W., & Bash, M. A. S. (1985b). Think aloud, grades 3-4. Champaign, IL: Research Press.

Camp, B. W., & Bash, M. A. S. (1985c). Think aloud, grades 5-6. Champaign, IL: Research Press.

Cartledge, G., & Kleefeld, J. (1991). Taking part. Circle Pines, MN: American Guidance Service.

Cartledge, G., & Kleefeld, J. (1994). Working together. Circle Pines, MN: American Guidance Service.

Cohen, J. (Ed.). (2001). Caring classrooms/intelligent schools: The social emotional education of young children. NY: Teachers College Press.

Coombs-Richardson, R., Evans, E. T., & Meisgeier, C. H. (1996a). Connecting with others, K-2. Champaign, IL: Research Press.

Coombs-Richardson, R., Evans, E. T., & Meisgeier, C. H. (1996b). Connecting with others, 3-5. Champaign, IL: Research Press.

Coombs-Richardson, R., Evans, E. T., & Meisgeier, C. H. (1996c). Connecting with others, 6-8. Champaign, IL: Research Press.

Duke, M. P., Nowicki, S., Jr., & Martin, E. A. (1996). Teaching your child the language of social success. Atlanta, GA: Peachtree.

Dygdon, J. (1993). CLASSIC. Brandon, VT: Clinical Psychology Publishing Company.

D'Zurilla, T. J., & Goldfried, M. R. (1971). Problem solving and behavior modification. Journal of Abnormal Psychology, 78(1), 107-126.

Elias, M. J., Tobias, S. E., & Friedlander, B. S. (1999). Emotionally intelligent parenting. New York: Harmony Books.

Elksnin, L. K., & Elksnin, N. (1995). Assessment and instruction of social skills. San Diego: Singular.

Elksnin, L. K., & Elksnin, N. (1998). Teaching social skills to students with learning and behavior problems. Intervention in School and Clinic, 33, 131-140.

Elksnin, L. K., & Elksnin, N. (2000). Teaching parents to teach their children to be prosocial. Intervention in School and Clinic, 36, 27-35.

Goldstein, A. P. (1997). The PREPARE curriculum. Champaign, IL: Research Press.

Goldstein, A. P., & McGinnis, E. (1997). Skill-streaming the adolescent. Champaign, IL: Research Press.

Goleman, D. L. (1995). Emotional intelligence: Why it can matter more than IQ. New York: Bantam Books.

Gottman, J. (1997). Raising an emotionally intelligent child. New York: Simon & Schuster.

Gumpel, T., & Wilson, M. (1996). Application of a Rasch analysis to the examination of the perception of facial affect among persons with mental retardation. Research in Developmental Disabilities, 17(2), 161-171.

Hall, E. (1966). The hidden dimension. New York: Doubleday.

Hazel, J. S., Schumaker, J. B., Sherman, J. A., & Sheldon, J. (1996). ASSET. Champaign, IL: Research Press.

Jones, K. M., Young, M. M., & Friman, P. C. (2000). Increasing peer praise of socially rejected delinquent youth: Effects on cooperation and acceptance. School Psychology Review, 15, 30-39.

Lavoie, R. (Producer). (1994). Learning disabilities and social skills with Richard Lavoie: Last one picked ... first one picked on. Washington, DC: WETA.

Kavale, K. A., & Forness, S. R. (1996). Social skills deficits and learning disabilities: A meta-analysis. Journal of Learning Disabilities, 29, 226-237.

Mannix, D. (1993). Social skills activities for special children. West Nyack, NY: Center for Applied Research in Education.

Mayer, J. D., & Salovey, P. (1997). What is emotional intelligence? In P. Salovey & D. J. Sluyter (Eds.), Emotional development and emotional intelligence: Educational implications (pp. 3-31). New York: Basic Books.

McGinnis, E., & Goldstein, A. R. (1997). Skill-streaming the elementary school child. Champaign, IL: Research Press.

McGinnis, E., & Goldstein, A. P. (2003). Skill-streaming in early childhood. Champaign, IL: Research Press.

Mehrabian, A. (1968). Communication without words. Psychology Today, 24, 52-55.

Most, T., & Greenbank, A. (2000). Auditory, visual, and auditory-visual perception of emotions by adolescents with and without learning disabilities, and their relationship to social skills. Learning Disabilities Research & Practice, 15, 171-178.

Mugno, D., & Rosenblitt, D. (2001). Helping emotionally vulnerable children: Moving toward an empathic orientation in the classroom. In J. Cohen (Ed.), Caring classrooms/intelligent schools: The social emotional education of young children (pp. 59-76). NY: Teachers College Press.

Nabuzoka, D., & Smith, K. (1995). Identification of expressions of emotions by children with and without learning disabilities. Learning Disabilities Research & & Practice, 10, 91-101.

Nowicki, S., Jr., & Duke, M. P. (1992). helping the child who doesn't fit in. Atlanta, GA: Peachtree.

Ratnesar, R. (1997, September). Teaching feelings 101. Time, XXX, 62.

Salovey, P., & Mayer, J. D. (1990). Emotional intelligence. Imagination, Cognition, & Personality, 9, 185-211.

Salovey, P., & Sluyter, D. J. (Eds.). (1997). Emotional development and emotional intelligence: Educational implications. New York: Basic Books.

Schulze, K. A., Rule, S., & Innocenti, M. S. (1989). Coincidental teaching: Parents promoting social skills at home. Teaching Exceptional Children, 21, 24-27.

Scott, T. M., & Nelson, C. M. (1998). Confusion and failure in facilitating generalized social responding in the school setting: Sometimes 2 + 2 = 5. Behavioral Disorders, 23(4), 264-275.

Skinner, C. H., Cashwell, T. H., & Skinner, A. L. (2000). Increasing tottling: Effects of a peer-monitored group contingency program on students' reports of peers' prosocial behaviors. Psychology in the Schools, 37, 263-270.

Slavin, R. E., & Madden, N. A.(2001). One million children: Success for all. Thousand Oaks, CA: Corwin.

Shure, M. B. (2001a). I can problem solve, elementary. Champaign, IL: Research Press.

Shure, M. B. (2001b). I can problem solve, kindergarten. Champaign, IL: Research Press.

Shure, M. B. (2001c). I can problem solve, preschool. Champaign, IL: Research Press.

Stephens, T. M. (1992). Social skills in the classroom (2nd ed.). Odessa, FL: Psychological Assessment Resources.

U.S. Department of Education (1996). Eighteenth annual report to Congress on the implementation of The Individuals with Disabilities Education Act. Washington, DC: Author.

U.S. Department of Education (2001). Twenty-third annual report to Congress on the Implementation of the Individuals with Disabilities Education Act. Washington, DC: Author.

Waksman, S., & Waksman, D. D. (1998). Waksman social skills curriculum. Austin, TX: PRO-ED.

From *Education*, Vol. 124, No. 1, Fall 2003. © 2003 by Education Magazine. Reprinted with permission.

Gendered reminiscence practices and self-definition in late adolescence[1]

The purpose of this study was to examine gender differences in the emotional construction of life-threatening events (LTEs) that were chosen as self-defining by late adolescents. European American college students (41 women, 25 men) whose average age was 19 were selected from a larger sample (*n* = 139) because they reported at least 1 LTE among 3 self-defining memories. Memory narratives were elicited with a questionnaire (Singer & Moffitt, 1991–1992) and coded for emotional position. As expected, tough, action-packed positions were more prevalent in men's narratives, and compassionate positions were more prevalent in women's narratives. Unexpectedly, narratives that emphasized one's own vulnerability (fear or sadness) were equally prevalent for men and women, and women's emotional discourse was more conditional upon type of event, i.e., deaths vs. assaults. Findings provide the most explicit evidence to date that some gendered reminiscence practices found in prior studies of children are reflected in late adolescents' self-defining reminiscences. Implications are also discussed for a more situated understanding of gendered reminiscence pratices and for theories of identity development.

KEY WORDS: gender; autobiographical memory; identity; trauma.

Avril Thorne; Kate C. McLean

INTRODUCTION

In recent years, personal reminiscence increasingly has been viewed as a cultural practice that channels emotional development and the development of a sense of self (Fivush, Brotman, Buckner, & Goodman, 2000; Miller, 1994; Snow, 1990). Studies of children's reminiscences have identified robust differences in how boys and girls are taught to elaborate emotional events, differences that have been found to be incorporated in their own emotion talk in middle and late childhood. To date, however, most gendered reminiscence research has focused on emotional reminiscence without explicitly linking such reminiscence to self-definition. This trend is understandable in studies of children, for whom a concept of self is only beginning to emerge, but connections between gendered reminiscence and self-definition have also been neglected in studies of late adolescents, for whom a concept of self is much more developed. This study was designed to examine whether gendered findings with regard to emotional reminiscence that have been obtained in studies of children extend to the self-defining memories of late adolescents. This study may be the most explicit inquiry to date as to whether gendered reminiscence practices are integral to self-definition in late adolescence.

Gendered Reminiscence Practices in Childhood

The most robust gender differences in children's emotional expression have been found in the context of narratives about past experiences that involve negative emotions (Fivush et al., 2000). Mothers have been found to discuss happy experiences equally with pre-school-aged daughters and sons, but experiences of sadness are more often discussed with daughters than with sons (Fivush, 1989, 1991; Fivush et al., 2000; Kuebli & Fivush, 1992). When talking about frightening events, girls use more emotion words than boys do (Fivush et al., 2000), and boys are more likely than girls to deny ever having been scared (Hudson, Gebelt, & Haviland, 1992). By middle childhood, girls, compared to boys, report having felt sad more often and in more social contexts (Buckner & Fivush, 1998; Stapley & Haviland, 1989). Boys, more so than girls, expect negative consequences for expressing sadness (Fuchs & Thelen, 1988).

Girls' greater sensitivity to their own feelings of fear and sadness also extends to the feelings of others. Pre-school girls, more so than boys, have been found to display empathy for others' feelings (Eisenberg, Miller, Shell, McNalley, & Shea, 1991; Zahn-Waxler, Cole, & Barrett, 1991) and to engage in nurturant interactions (Leaper, 1991). In reminiscences about memorable events,

4–9-year-old girls, more so than boys, emphasized communal themes and referenced family members (Ely, Melzi, Hadge, & McCabe, 1998).

The robustness of such findings led Fivush et al. (2000) to conclude that gendered reminiscence practices extend to self-definition; that is, girls, more so than boys, may come to view experiences of fear and sadness as a more integral part of themselves and their relations with others. The possibility that gendered reminiscence practices can channel a child's sense of self has been pursued in necessarily indirect ways because a concept of "self" requires a cognitive sophistication that does not emerge until late childhood or adolescence (Damon & Hart, 1988). By mid- to late adolescence, however, the question, "Tell me a memory that is self-defining, that helps you to understand who you are as a person," becomes meaningful.

Gender and Self-Defining Memories in Adolescence

Although the period from adolescence to early adulthood has long been characterized as the era in which identity becomes a primary concern (Erikson, 1963), the role of personal reminiscence in this process has only recently been emphasized. Building on the work of Erikson, McAdams (1985) characterized identity as becoming a primary concern when adolescents begin to notice incongruities between themselves in the present and past and to imagine different possibilities for the future. Efforts to unify the past, present, and anticipated future presumably underlie the process by which adolescents ponder their life experience and select particular events as especially meaningful for understanding who they are and could be.

Because of the theoretical linkage between identity and reminiscence in adolescence, researchers who study adolescents' memory narratives tend to examine themes of identity achievement and intimacy rather than vulnerability (e.g., McAdams, Hoffman, Mansfield, & Day, 1996; McLean & Thorne, 2001; Orlofsky & Frank, 1986). This trend may reflect theoretical assumptions that learning to manage vulnerability is a childhood task and that adolescents move on to tackle the more age-relevant tasks of identity and intimacy (Erikson, 1963). Although feelings of fear and sadness, and vulnerability more generally, do not occupy a central spot in theories of adolescent development, events that threaten one's basic sense of safety tend to be highly memorable for both children and adolescents (Pillemer, 1998). Pre-school-aged children, for example, have been found to produce longer narratives to probes about car wrecks and hospitals than to probes about pets and vacations (Ely et al., 1998). In a college student study that used a variety of word prompts, Robinson (1976) found that physically traumatic events such as accidents and injuries were most frequently recalled, followed by romantic episodes.

Although life-threatening events (LTEs) such as accidents and injuries tend to be highly memorable, we do not know whether such events are regarded as self-defining by adolescents, nor have gender differences in emotional construal of such events been explicitly examined. The only study that seems to have examined such questions found that women college students rated their self-defining memories as sadder than did men, who rated their self-defining memories as happier; 10 other emotion words, including fear, did not show significant gender differences (Singer et al., 2001). Because Singer et al. (2001) did not report the kinds of events that were selected, such as injuries or romantic episodes, the finding that women more often rated their memories as "sad" is somewhat difficult to interpret: Was it because of differences in the selection of events, with men selecting happier events, or in the construal of events, or both? Similar ambiguities characterize other findings with regard to gender differences in adolescents' emotional construal of past events. For example, in a study of depressive rumination, Nolen-Hoeksema (1986; reported in Nolen-Hoeksema, 1987) found that young women were more prone to ruminate (i.e., ponder, talk to others, cry) when in a depressed mood than were young men, who tended to avoid rumination. However, the kinds of depressing events that were selected, and the degree to which the events were regarded as self-defining, were not assessed.

This Study

The purpose of this study was to examine gender differences in late adolescents' emotional construal of self-defining events that are likely to engage feelings of fear or sadness. Feelings of fear tend to be activated by a physical or psychological threat to the self, and feelings of sadness by loss and separation from those that one cares about (Izard, 1977). In pondering the kinds of life events that seem most likely to engage feelings of fear or sadness, we settled upon events that severely threaten the physical well-being of self or valued others. Such events include severe accidents and physical assaults, which are likely to elicit fear, and deaths of valued others, which are likely to elicit sadness.

The first phase of the study examined the prevalence of such LTEs in late adolescents' self-defining memories. Although prior studies of autobiographical memories in adolescence suggest that LTEs are highly memorable, theories of adolescence do not emphasize the self-salience of such events, and the degree to which such events are regarded as self-defining is unknown. This study thus pioneered exploration of the degree to which LTEs are regarded as self-defining by late adolescents.

The second phase of the study was designed to examine the prevalence of gender differences in emotional discourse about LTEs that are regarded as self-defining. Research on children's responses to adverse events suggests that there are three primary emotional positions, or stances, that are often taken vis-a-vis such events: Toughness, Vulnerability, and Compassion. The Tough position highlights action in response to adversity with minimal references to emotion. Such a position has been called "John Wayne" discourse (Talbot, Bibace, Bokhour, & Bamberg, 1996), because John Wayne, the Hollywood actor, emphasized action rather than emotion and portrayed fearlessness in the face of events that might make others cower and shake. A second emotional stance, the Vulnerable position, emphasizes one's own emotional vulnerability. Unlike Toughness, the Vulnerable position focuses on one's own feelings of pain, fear, sadness, or helplessness. A third position with regard to traumatic experiences is to show concern for others. The Compassionate position expresses care, concern, or sympathy for others who are also impacted by the event, rather than exclusively focusing on one's own feelings of vulnerability. On the basis of research reviewed earlier and primarily conducted with children, men were expected to emphasize Tough positions, and women were expected to emphasize Vulnerable and Compassionate positions in recounting LTEs.

STUDY 1

Participants

The initial sample consisted of 192 students (63% women) between the ages of 18 and 23, who were enrolled at a public university (M = 19.5 years, SD = 1.2 years). Participants engaged in the research to fulfill a requirement in various psychology courses. The majority (73%) of the sample self-identified as European American, 13% as Asian, 10% as Latino/a, and 4% as other ethnic backgrounds. Because sample sizes were small for other ethnic groups, and because gender and emotion findings primarily have been reported for European American samples, European Americans were selected for this study. The final sample consisted of 139 (63% women) European American college students who averaged 19.6 years of age (SD = 1.2).

Self-Defining Memory Questionnaire

Participants responded to a questionnaire that asked them to describe three self-defining memories. The first page of the questionnaire described features of a self-defining memory (Singer & Moffitt, 1991-1992, p. 242). A self-defining memory was defined as

1. At least 1-year-old. (2)

2. A memory of a specific event (3) in your life that you remember very clearly and that still feels important to you even as you think about it now.

3. It is a memory that helps you to understand who you are as an individual and might be the memory you would tell someone else if you wanted that person to understand you in a more profound way.

4. It may be a memory that is positive or negative, or both, in how it makes you feel. The only important aspect is that it leads to strong feelings.

5. It is a memory that you have thought about many times. It should be familiar to you like a picture you have studied or a song (happy or sad) you have learned by heart.

To understand best what a self-defining memory is, imagine you have just met someone you like very much and are going for a long walk together. Each of you is very committed to helping the other get to know the "Real You.… " In the course of conversation, you describe several memories that you feel convey powerfully how you have come to be the person you currently are. It is precisely these memories that constitute self-defining memories.

On the next three pages of the questionnaire, participants were asked to write a description of each of three self-defining memories, including a caption for the event, their age at the time of the event, where they were, whom they were with, what happened, and how they and any others present responded to the event. They were asked to include details that would help an imagined friend see and feel as they did. After providing an event narrative, they were then asked to estimate with how many different people they had shared the memory, and, if they had a specific memory of having told the event to someone else, to describe a memorable telling of the event. The analyses for this study focused on the description of the original event rather than on the telling event, for which data were sparse (for a discussion of findings with regard to telling the events, based on a portion of the present sample, see Thorne & McLean, in press).

Coding of Life Events

Each self-defining memory was sorted into one of four categories of life events. Event categories were developed inductively to arrive at a limited number of categories that were mutually exclusive, and that comprehensively covered the range of events that were chosen as self-defining. The four types of life events were LTEs, relationship events, achievement events, and leisure events (see Thorne & McLean, 2001). Independent coders reliably differentiated LTEs from other kinds of events (overall K = .94).

Life-threatening events were defined as events in which a severe threat to one's own or another's physical well-being structured the narrative. Mortality concerns were not necessarily emphasized in the narrative, but if the description of the event indicated the possibility of severe physical injury or death to oneself or others, the event qualified as life-threatening. LTEs included severe accidents, physical assaults, and deaths (K = 1.00). The following life-threatening memory is about a death:

> I was in the seventh grade when a good friend called me up after school crying. Her 24-year-old brother had been in a car accident and was dead. Immediately, I started crying and felt sick to my stomach. This was not only my first experience

Table I. Percentage of Self-Defining Memories for Each Type of Event

Event type	Overall		Mean		Women		t(135)	p
	M	SD	M	SD	M	SD		
Life-threatening	0.22	0.27	0.21	0.25	0.23	0.29	-0.48	ns
Relationship	0.40	0.34	0.36	0.32	0.43	0.36	-1.20	ns
Leisure	0.20	0.26	0.23	0.25	0.18	0.26	1.20	ns
Achievement	0.12	0.20	0.16	0.22	0.10	0.19	1.82	ns
Miscellaneous	0.06	0.16	0.05	0.13	0.07	0.18	-0.79	ns

Note. n = 52 men, 85 women; two-tailed t tests for gender differences.

with death, but it was someone that was too young to die. My mother and I attended the Scottish funeral that was held in town. Hearing bagpipes to this day makes me cry.

Relationship events were defined as events in which a particular interpersonal relationship was emphasized, usually with a parent or peer. Themes in such events usually emphasized moving toward, away from, or against another person, for example, intimacy, separation, or interpersonal conflict (K = .94). The following relationship memory is about a divorce:

We had just moved to San Diego and my father, away in Germany, had just been re-stationed after Vietnam. My father was due to return home soon, after years of being gone. When he returned he wasn't very close to any of us. My parents argued a lot. And so my mom tells me, I asked my mom, "Why doesn't dad love me anymore?" Shortly after, my parents were divorced.

Achievement events were defined as events that emphasized effortful attempts at mastery with regard to vocational, material, social, or spiritual goals, regardless of the outcome. Such events included winning a competition; learning to drive a car; passing, failing, or struggling with an important exam; getting into college; mastering the urge to eat; and establishing a new life upon immigration (K = .85). The following achievement memory is about a decision to quit professional dancing:

After 14 years of dance training I decided to quit. I was a professional dancer and I hated it. I went to my instructor's condo with my boyfriend because my family would not support me in my decision. I told my instructor that I was extremely unhappy and I could not go on in this business. I was crying, consumed with feelings of guilt and relief. She was surprisingly understanding and I felt like a free person for the first time without the trappings of the complex dynamics of a dance studio (e.g. eating, dressing, acting…).

Leisure Events

Leisure events centered on recreational activities such as hobbies, parties, travel, or sports. Emphasis was on recreation, play, or exploration. Spiritual moments that were framed as moments in themselves, rather than as a decision to redirect one's life, fell into this category rather than into the achievement category (κ = .94). The following leisure event involves encountering an owl during a hike:

I was on a trail below my parents' house taking an enjoyable walk alone. While passing a tree which my family and I always call "the big oak tree" I suddenly jerked my head upward—meeting eyes with this owl. My immediate reaction was one of amazement and then appreciation. Its eyes were locked with mine—an intense gaze that is hard to describe A raw, honest, soulful feeling emanated from the owl's eyes. There was nothing fake or misleading in its eyes and that was what was so refreshing but also alien. I felt lucky, and I wanted to tell someone about it.

Results

Most participants (87%) described three self-defining memories (range = 1–4). Women tended to offer more self-defining memories than did men, M = 2.94, SD = 0.39, versus M = 2.81, SD = 0.44; t(135) -1.85, p < .07, two-tailed, but conventional levels of significance were not reached. To control for slight gender differences in the overall number of memories described, data were analyzed in terms of percentage of memories per event type. For example, a person who provided three memories, one of which was about an LTE, received a score of .33 for the LTE category. Similarly, a person who provided two memories, one of which was about an LTE, received a score of .50 for the LTE category.

Table I shows the average percentage of self-defining memories per event type. In the overall sample, relationship events were the most prevalent (40%), followed by LTEs and leisure events (22 and 20%, respectively), and, lastly, achievement events (12%). Comparisons between men and women for each event yielded no significant findings. For both men and women, relationship events were the most prevalent kind of event, and LTEs and leisure events were each about half as prevalent as relationship events. Although less prevalent than relationship events, LTEs were sufficiently prevalent to render subsequent analyses useful. (4)

STUDY 2

Participants

The sample consisted of 41 women and 25 men from Study 1 who reported at least one LTE. Representation from the original sample was 48% for both men and women. Participants averaged 19.5 years of age (SD = 1.2), and age did not differ for men and women, $t(64) = -0.10$, ns.

Coding of Emotional Positions

Emotional positions in narratives of LTEs were first coded together by the authors. All the narratives were then independently coded by a reliability coder who was blind to the hypotheses and to the participants' gender. The categories were defined as mutually exclusive, and interrater agreement was acceptable; the overall kappa was .89. Disagreements between the authors and the reliability coder were settled by consensus. Four emotional positions were coded.

Toughness

Physical toughness and endurance in the face of adversity was the hallmark of this position. Such narratives were dense with descriptions of physical action, and the focus was on self-survival. Explicit references to feelings of fear, pain, or suffering on the part of self or others typically were not mentioned and, if mentioned, were not emphasized ($\kappa = .83$). Here is an example of a Tough narrative about a bicycle accident. Despite the severity of the injury, the narrative contains no explicit references to fear or suffering:

> About halfway down the 12-mile trail I was coming around a right turn going about 30 and there was a huge water bar across the trail, my front tire landed in it and stopped, and I kept going. My arm slapped the ground before I landed and that's when it broke. I knew it was broken the second it happened, before I even landed. I remember looking up at my arm and having it look like I had two elbows.... Because of that day I now have two steel rods and 13 screws in my arm.

Vulnerability

Vulnerable narratives emphasized one's own feelings of fear or sadness, without reference to caring or concern for others. The dominant feeling in the narrative was of being overwhelmed by the event ($\kappa = .93$). Here is an example of a Vulnerable narrative about an assault by a dog:

> I was outside playing in the back yard. It was a sunny day and I was trying to put flower seeds in the ground that my dad had gotten for me. I heard a noise from behind me, and I turned around and saw the neighbor's dog come crawling from underneath the fence. These two German shepherds came charging at me. They both jumped and knocked me over. They were biting at me while I lay there, screaming at the top of my lungs. My mom heard the commotion and charged out of the house and chased off the dogs. To this day I have a fear of large dogs.

Compassion

Care or concern for others was the hallmark of these narratives. Concern for oneself might also be expressed, but the narrative also expressed concern for others ($\kappa = .82$). In the following narrative, the participant expresses concern for a friend and indebtedness to the friend's deceased father, in addition to expressing self-vulnerabilty.

> I was at college when I found out that my best friend Susan's father had passed away.... I froze and all I could think about was how worried I was for Susan. I couldn't imagine what I would do if one of my parents died. He had changed my life only months before he passed.... I couldn't even stand up; I was in the fetal position on the floor bawling. I was so worried about her.

Existential Awe

This emotional position was not anticipated but was apparent in some of the narratives. The hallmark of this narrative was an emphasis on one's feelings of awe or fascination in the face of death or near-death, an intellectual fascination that took precedence over feelings of fear or sadness ($\kappa = 1.00$). The following narrative about a near-death experience on a rafting trip exemplifies the Existential Awe position:

> On a river rafting trip, I got tossed out of my kayak and got pulled under. I was stuck under water until I struggled to free myself just in time. I saw my life pass before my eyes as I was running out of air. It made me understand my own mortality better.

Results

Most of the participants (71%) reported one LTE, and some reported two (23%) or three (6%). Women (M = 1.44) reported slightly more LTEs than did men, M = 1.20, $t(64) = 1.80$, $p < .08$; however, conventional levels of significance were not reached. To control for slight gender differences in frequencies of self-defining LTEs, percentages were employed rather than frequencies, as in Study 1.

Table II. Features of Life-Threatening Event Memories: Means for Men and Women

Feature	Men		Women		t(64)	p
	M	SD	M	SD		
Age of reporter	19.48	1.12	19.51	1.27	-0.10	ns
No. of traumatic event narratives	1.20	0.41	1.44	0.67	-1.80	ns
Age at which memorable event occurred	12.56	4.88	13.08	3.77	-0.49	ns
Words in event narrative	105.34	50.30	170.45	82.97	-3.97	0.001
Event type (% total LTE)						
Deaths of loved ones	0.18	0.38	0.53	0.46	-3.37	0.001
Accidents	0.56	0.49	0.28	0.39	2.48	0.05
Physical assaults	0.26	0.44	0.19	0.33	0.68	ns
Emotional positions (% total LTE)						
Toughness	0.36	0.47	0.13	0.32	2.13	0.05
Compassion	0.10	0.29	0.35	0.45	-2.80	0.01
Vulnerability	0.40	0.48	0.49	0.46	-0.74	ns
Existential awe	0.14	0.34	0.00	0.00	2.06	0.05

Note. Levene's test for equality of variances was used for t tests; two-tailed t tests.

Preliminary Analyses

In preliminary analyses we examined basic features of the memories: narrative length, participants' reported age at the time of the original occurrence, and type of LTE. As can be seen in Table II, the LTEs occurred on average at age 13, for both men and women.

Women's memory narratives were significantly longer than were men's, M = 170 words versus 105 words, respectively, t(64) = -3.97, p < .001, which supports findings from prior reminiscence studies (e.g., Fivush & Reese, 1992; Singer et al., 2001).

Gender differences were also found for type of LTE. As is shown in Table II, the majority of women's LTEs centered on deaths (53% for women, 18% for men), t(64) = -3.37, p < .001. The deceased were mostly family members or friends, but also included beloved pets and strangers. The majority of men's LTEs, on the other hand, concerned accidents (56% for men vs. 28% for women), t(64) = 2.48, p < .05. Automobiles, rafts, and bicycles were usually the vehicles in such accidents, and the participant was the main person who was injured. The final category of LTE, physical assaults in which the participant was a victim, showed similar base rates for men and women (26% vs. 19%, respectively), although women more often reported physical assaults that involved rape or sexual abuse. Of 7 assaults reported by men, 1 (14%) involved sexual abuse; of 13 assaults reported by women, 5 (38%) involved sexual abuse.

Emotional Positions

As can be seen in Table II, two of the hypothesized three emotional positions showed anticipated gender differences. Tough narratives were more prevalent for men (36%) than for women (13%), t(64) = 2.13, p < .05, and Compassionate narratives were more prevalent for women (35%) than for men (10%), t(64) = -2.80, p < .01.

Unexpectedly, however, Vulnerable narratives showed a similar prevalence for men and women (40 and 49%, respectively), t(64) = -0.74, ns. Analyses within gender showed that Vulnerable positions were as prevalent as gendered positions: For men, the proportion of Vulnerable positions equaled the proportion of Tough positions (38%, respectively). For women, the proportion of Vulnerable positions, 49%, did not differ significantly from the proportion of Compassionate positions, 35%, paired t(40) = -1.02, ns. (5)

The fourth emotional position, Existential Awe, was significantly more prevalent for men than for women, t(64) = 2.06, p < .05. However, because this position showed such a low base rate (13% for men, 0% for women), it was not included in the final analysis.

Emotional Positions and Kinds of LTEs

In the final analysis we explored whether the three focal emotional positions (Toughness, Compassion, and Vulnerability) were associated with particular kinds of LTEs. Because distributions for these variables were positively skewed, Spearman correlations were employed. As can be seen in Table III, positions and event types showed no significant correlations for men. For women, however, four of the nine correlations were statistically significant, which indicated women's conditional use of two emotional positions: Compassionate positions characterized women's narratives about deaths (r = .55, p < .001), and Tough positions characterized women's narratives about physical assaults (r = .53, p < .001).

Table III. Spearman Correlations Between Emotional Positions and Kinds of Life-Threatening Events

Emotional position	Accident		Assault		Death	
	M	F	M	F	M	F
Toughness	0.32	-0.01	-0.10	0.53 ***	-0.28	-0.31 *
Compassion	-0.06	-0.29	0.26	-0.45 **	-0.18	0.55 ***
Vulnerability	-0.32	0.24	0.05	0.13	0.33	-0.28

Note. n = 25 men, 41 women.

* p < .05. ** p < 0.01. *** p < 0.001, two-tailed.

DISCUSSION

Results of this study confirmed that LTEs were regarded as self-defining by late adolescents, and that men more often took tough, nonemotional positions in recounting such events, whereas women more often took compassionate positions. Because LTEs (severe accidents, assaults, and deaths of loved ones) can be assumed to evoke feelings of fear or sadness at some level, and because these events were regarded as self-defining, the findings provide explicit empirical support that two gendered reminiscence practices found in prior studies of children are also reflected in self-definitions in late adolescence: denial of fear for men (toughness) and concern for others (compassion) for women.

Although the findings with regard to Toughness and Compassion suggest that gendered reminiscence practices extend to self-definitions in adolescence, this was not the case for positions of Vulnerability, which emphasized one's own feelings of fear or sadness. Counter to expectations, we found that Vulnerability positions were equally prevalent for men and women. In fact, for men, Vulnerability was as prevalent as Toughness, and for women, Vulnerability was as prevalent as Compassion.

The high base rate of Vulnerable positions for men and women might be explained in several ways. One possibility is that Vulnerability positions were more tied to depression than to gender. Although rumination on one's own sadness has been found to be more common for late adolescent females than for males in prior research (e.g., Nolen-Hoeksema, 1987), the present sample may have included as many depressed men as women. However, on the basis of post hoc analyses of participants who offered several LTEs as self-defining, the depression explanation does not seem very plausible. Of the 19 participants who reported more than one LTE, the majority (n = 15) took different emotional positions for each event, for example, one Vulnerable position and one Tough or Compassionate position. If depression is a chronic emotional state, participants who consistently took Vulnerable positions would seem the most likely to be depressed, but they constituted a small minority of the sample. However, in the absence of depression measures, the possibility that Vulnerability was symptomatic of depression remains viable.

A second possibility is that the cross-gender prominence of Vulnerability reflects an emotional maturation that occurs for many youth on the brink of adulthood. For example, Erikson (1968) viewed vulnerability as an outgrowth of the struggle with identity and as integral to the experience of the identity crisis. A third possibility is that the self-defining memory task tends to press for disclosure of Vulnerability. These possibilities could be explored by comparing findings across a broader array of adolescent and adult age groups and by comparing the base rate of Vulnerability positions obtained with self-defining memory probes versus more general autobiographical memory probes.

The lack of significant gender differences in Vulnerability was surprising, because a number of researchers have found that girls and women are more likely to express their own feelings of fear and sadness than are boys and men (e.g., Fivush et al., 2000). Our lack of significant gender differences in Vulnerability may have been a function of our mutually exclusive coding categories. The expression of one's own fear or sadness was defined as the sole emphasis of Vulnerability narratives, whereas self-vulnerability could also be mentioned in Compassionate narratives. We may have thereby underestimated the frequency of vulnerability in the sample, especially for women, who showed a higher frequency of Compassionate narratives than did men. We constructed the Compassionate category to allow mention of vulnerability because we found that expressions of compassion for others also tended to reference expressions of self vulnerability. The co-occurence of vulnerability and compassion within such narratives is an int eresting phenomenon for future research.

Women's More Conditional Use of Emotional Positions

Although men and women reported similar proportions of LTEs in their self-defining memories, different kinds of LTEs were chosen by men and women: men disproportionately reported accidents, and women disproportionately reported deaths of significant others. Men's focus on accidents was not surprising because men are more accident-prone than are women in late adolescence (Massie, Campbell, & Williams, 1995). However, women's focus on deaths was surprising, because there is no reason to expect that young women more often experience deaths of significant others than do young men.

Women's focus on death may reflect the communal orientation that has often been found in prior studies of girls' and women's reminiscences (e.g., Fivush et al., 2000; Woike, 1995). Death was the only kind of LTE that happened to others rather than to oneself, and women not only selected such events more often than did men, but also used the communal, Compassionate position to describe such events. The contribution of this study is that the communal orientation was found to be highly situated; it emerged in the selection of events that directly harmed others rather than oneself and in the specialized application of communal discourse to construe such events.

The present findings also suggest a neglected sphere (i.e., deaths) in which women are asked to rise to the communal occasion. Studies of gender and emotion in childhood have not focused on deaths per se, perhaps because deaths of loved ones may be shielded from children. However, deaths of pets are quite commonly experienced by children, and it would be useful to explore how parents talk about such events to daughters and sons. If our findings were to show parallels in studies of parent-child reminiscence, parents would more extensively elaborate past events involving death with daughters than with sons, and would particularly emphasize feelings of fondness for the dead and concern for the welfare of the survivors.

Overall, men's application of emotional positions was relatively less conditional than that of women, that is, less specialized for particular kinds of events. For men, none of the correlations between emotional positions and type of LTE reached probability levels of $p < .05$, whereas four of the nine correlations were statistically significant for women. Although this finding needs to be replicated with larger samples, the finding makes sense, given the fact that emotion talk, in middle-class White U.S. samples, is a predominantly feminine practice, and may have evolved some highly specialized rules and contexts of application. Beginning in early childhood, girls are exposed to more elaborated talk about emotions (Fivush et al., 2000). Part of that exposure may concern deaths of significant others. Women, for example, may more often be recruited to express condolences to grieving families, whereas men may more often be excluded from rituals related to grieving; this exclusion may restrict men's opportunities for talking about death and for expressing verbal concern for the well-being of the survivors.

The other conditional pattern shown in women's emotional positions concerned their specialized use of Tough narratives to describe experiences of being physically assaulted. Although men used Tough narratives proportionately more than did women, men's use of this position was not tied to a particular kind of event. Women's tendency to position themselves as tough and

agentic in responding to physical assaults might have reflected the feminist values of their college community, which encourages rejection of victimization. (6)

LTEs and Identity Development in Adolescence

The finding that LTEs were quite prevalent in the sample extends prior findings with autobiographical memories to the more specific domain of self-defining memories. Nearly half of the men and half of the women in the present sample included at least one LTE in their three self-defining memories. LTEs did not swamp the sample of memories—relationship memories were nearly twice as prevalent—but were more prevalent than theories of normal adolescent development would suggest (Erikson, 1963).

From the perspective of theories of autobiographical memory, the salience of LTEs centers on their disruption of everyday routines. Highly disruptive events produce cognitive dissonance, and efforts to resolve the dissonance can include self-rumination as well as social sharing with others (Rime, Mesquita, Philippot, & Boca, 1991; Tait & Silver, 1989). Furthermore, LTEs can produce enduring changes in one's relations with others, as when a loved one dies, and in one's own health status, as when one experiences a permanent injury in an accident.

From the perspective of theories of adolescent development, LTEs are perhaps the ultimate challenge to identity. Identity becomes a primary concern when adolescents begin to notice incongruities between themselves in the present and past and to imagine different possibilities for the future (Erikson, 1963; McAdams, 1985). Confronting LTEs is perhaps the ultimate incongruity. As adolescents come to understand who they are and their place in society, they must also face the possibility of their absence. Confronting the possibility of death is an important and neglected aspect of identity development in adolescence.

Very few of the participants in this study took a purely cognitive position with regard to the incongruity of life and death, as shown by the scarcity of the Existential Awe position. Such narratives intellectualized the prospect of death. Although fascination with the possibility of death may be a fleeting experience for many adolescents, the scarcity of this position in the overall sample of narratives, and its total absence in women's narratives, suggests that a purely cognitive position with regard to the incongruity of life and death is not an enduring feature of adolescent identity.

The more prevalent positions with regard to LTEs entailed presenting oneself as a tough survivor (Toughness), as having suffered tremendously (Vulnerability), or as caring for others despite one's own suffering (Compassion). These positions may not have told the whole story, but they conveyed how late adolescents wanted to be viewed as persons: "This is my memorable brush with death, this is what it meant to me, and this is how I coped with it." In locating these self-defining stances in the context of particular kinds of LTEs, the results of this study illuminate neglected contexts that are fertile ground for the construction of personal and gender identity.

ACKNOWLEDGMENTS

We thank Julia Haley for her thoughtful coding of the narratives and Campbell Leaper for comments on a prior draft of this paper.

NOTES

1. Portions of this study are discussed in Thorne and McLean (in press), which used a smaller sample and focused on telling narratives rather than on event narratives.
2. Events that are at least 1-year old are more likely to remain memorable than are very recent events (Thompson, Skowronski, Larsen, & Betz, 1996).
3. Instead of using the phrase "memory of a specific event in your life," Singer and Moffitt (1991–1992) used the term memory from your life. Otherwise, our description of a self-defining memory was the same as that of Singer and Moffitt.
4. When the two largest ethnic minority groups in the overall sample (Latino/a and Asian descent) were examined separately, each group tended to show patterns that were similar to the European American patterns reported in Table I, although sample sizes were comparatively small (Latino/a descent: 7 men, 11 women; Asian descent: 9 men, 15 women).
5. Latino/a descent participants (4 men, 7 women) and Asian descent participants (4 men, 6 women) tended to show gender patterns that were similar to those in Table II, with the exception that Asian descent men and women reported proportionately more deaths than did the other ethnic groups, and no assaults.
6. For a discussion of reminiscences with regard to sexual assaults, see Thorne and McLean (in press).

REFERENCES

Buckner, J., & Fivush, R. (1998). Gender and self in children's autobiographical narratives. Applied Cognitive Psychology, 12, 455–473.

Damon, W., & Hart, D. (1988). Self-understanding in childhood and adolescence. New York: Cambridge University Press.

Eisenberg, N., Miller, P. A., Shell, R., McNalley, S., & Shea, C. (1991). Prosocial development in adolescence: A longitudinal study. Developmental psychology, 27, 849–857.

Ely, R., Melzi, G., Hadge, L., & McCabe, A. (1998). Being brave, being nice: Themes of agency and communion in children's narratives. Journal of Personality, 66, 257–284.

Erikson, E. H. (1963). Childhood and society (2nd ed.). New York: W. W. Norton.

Erikson, E. H. (1968). Identity, youth, and crisis. New York: W. W Norton.

Fivush, R. (1989). Exploring sex differences in the emotional content of mother-child conversations about the past. Sex Roles, 20, 675–691.

Fivush, R. (1991). Gender and emotion in mother-child conversations about the past. Journal of Narrative and Life History, 1, 325–341.

Fivush, R., Brotman, M., Buckner, J. P., & Goodman, S. H. (2000). Gender differences in parent-child emotion narratives. Sex Roles, 42, 233–253.

Fivush, R., & Reese, E. (1992). The social construction of autobiographical memory. In M. A. Conway, D. C. Rubin, & W. Wagewnaar (Eds.), Theoretical perspectives on autobiographical memory (pp. 1–28). Dordrecht, Netherlands: Kluwer.

Fuchs, D., & Thelen, M. H. (1988). Children's expected interpersonal consequences of communicating their effective state and reported likelihood of expression. Child Development, 59, 1314–1322.

Hudson, J. A., Gebelt, J., & Haviland, J. (1992). Emotion and narrative structure in young children's personal accounts. Journal of Narrative and Life History, 2, 129–150.

Izard, C. E. (1977). Human emotions. New York: Plenum.

Kuebli, J., & Fivush, R. (1992). Gender differences in parent-child conversations about past emotions. Sex Roles, 12, 683–698.

Leaper, C. (1991). Influence and involvement in children's discourse: Age, gender and partner effects. Child Development, 62, 797–811.

Massie, D. L., Campbell, K. L., & Williams, A. E (1995). Traffic accident involvement rates by driver age and gender. Accident Analysis and Prevention, 27, 73–87.

McAdams, D. P. (1985). Power, intimacy, and the life story: Personological inquiries into identity. New York: Guilford.

McAdams, D. P., Hoffman, B. J., Mansfield, E. D., & Day, R. (1996). Themes of agency and communion in significant autobiographical scenes. Journal of Personality, 64, 339–378.

McLean, K. C., & Thorne, A. (2001). Adolescents' self-defining memories about relationships. Manuscript submitted for publication.

Miller, P. J. (1994). Narrative practices: Their role in socialization and self-construction, In U. Neisser & R. Fivush (Eds.), The remembering self: Accuracy and construction in the self-narrative (pp. 158–179). New York: Cambridge University Press.

Nolen-Hoeksema, S. (1987). Sex differences in unipolar depression: Evidence and theory. Psychological Bulletin, 101, 259–282.

Orlofsky, J., & Frank, M. (1986). Personality structure as viewed through early memories and identity status in college men and women. Journal of Personality and Social Psychology, SO, 580–586.

Pillemer, D. B. (1998). Momentous events, vivid memories. Cambridge, MA: Harvard University Press.

Rime B., Mesquita, B., Philippot, P., & Boca, S. (1991). Beyond the emotional event: Six studies on the social sharing of emotion. Cognition and Emotion, 5, 435–465.

Robinson, J. A. (1976). Sampling autobiographical memory. Cognitive Psychology, 8, 578–595.

Singer, J. A., Albert, D., Lally, R., Lizotte, M., Molina, C., & Scerzenie, S. (2001). Gender and self-disclosure in self-defining memories: Agentic and communal themes. Manuscript submitted for publication.

Singer, J. A., & Moffitt, K. H. (1991–1992). An experimental investigation of specificity and generality in memory narratives. Imagination, Cognition, and Personality, 11, 233–257.

Snow, C. E. (1990). Building memories: The ontogeny of autobiography. In D. Cicchetti & M. Beeghly (Eds.), The self in transition (pp. 213–242). Chicago: University of Chicago Press.

Stapley, J. C., & Haviland, J. M. (1989). Beyond depression: Gender differences in normal adolescents' emotional experience. Sex Roles, 20, 295–308.

Tait, R., & Silver, R. C. (1989). Coming to terms with major negative life events. In J. S. Uleman & J. A. Bargh (Eds.), Unintended thought (pp. 351–381). New York: Guilford.

Talbot, J., Bibace, R., Bokhour, B., & Bamberg, M. (1996). Affirmation and resistance of dominant discourses: The rhetorical construction of pregnancy. Journal of Narrative and Life History, 6, 225–251.

Thompson, C. P., Skowronski, J. J., Larsen, S. F., & Betz, A. L. (1996). Autobiographical memory: Remembering what and remembering when. Mahwah, NJ: Erlbaum.

Thorne, A., & McLean, K. C. (2001). Manual for coding events in self-defining memories. Unpublished manuscript, University of California, Santa Cruz.

Thorne, A., & McLean, K. C. (in press). Telling traumatic events in adolescence: A study of master narrative positioning. In R. Fivush & C. Haden (Eds.), Connecting culture and memory: The development of an autobiographical self. Mahwah, NJ: Erlbaum.

Wolke, B. A. (1995). Most memorable experiences: Evidence for a link between implicit and explicit motives and social cognitive processes in everyday life. Journal of Personality and Social Psychology, 68, 1081–1091.

Zahn-Waxler, C., Cole, P., & Barrett, K. C. (1991). Guilt and empathy: Sex differences and implications for the development of depression. In J. Gerber & K. A. Dodge (Eds.), The development of emotion regulation and dysregulation (pp. 243–272). Cambridge: Cambridge University Press.

Avril Thorne, Department of Psychology, University of California, Santa Cruz, California. To whom correspondence should be addressed at Department of Psychology, 277 Social Sciences 2, University of California, Santa Cruz, California 95064; e-mail: avril@cats.ucsc.edu.

Kate C. McLean, Department of Psychology, University of California, Santa Cruz, California.

UNIT 5
Family Relationships

Unit Selections

Key Points to Consider

- Can parents and teens be friends? Should they be friends?

- If a teen disobeys a parent or teacher, how should the adult manage the situation?

- When family conflict occurs, what resources are available to teens and parents?

- Are today's youth too busy? Are they trying too hard to be "super kids"? If yes, what can be done about it?

- Do parents or other adults play a crucial role in preventing teens from experimenting with drugs, tobacco, and alcohol?

 **Links: www.dushkin.com/online/**
These sites are annotated in the World Wide Web pages.

CYFERNET: Cooperative Extension System's Children, Youth, and Family Information Service
http://www.cyfernet.org/
Help for Parents of Teenagers
http://www.bygpub.com/parents/
Stepfamily Association of America
http://www.stepfam.org

When 17-year-old Marie was rejected by the college her choice, she sought her parents for comfort. But when her parents suggested going to a movie with them to cheer her, she was stunned. Why would she want to go with them when she could go with a friend instead? Clearly the family is important to the adolescent, but the relationship is not the same as it was in childhood. How should parents react? How involved should parents be with their adolescent?

In order to understand the influence of the family on its members, the family needs to be viewed as a *system*. This means that parents do not simply shape their child; rather, each part of the family influences the other parts. For example, just as parents influence their children's behavior, children influence not only their parents' behavior, but their parents' relationship with each other. A child who complies with parental rules may put less stress on the parents than a child who is consistently in trouble. The compliant child's parents may argue less with each other over issues like discipline. Similarly, the parents' marital relationship influences how each parent interacts with the children. Parents whose marriage is stressed may have less patience with children or may be less available to help their children. This means that factors affecting one part of the system have implications for the rest the system.

We can describe adolescents as changing in three major areas: biology, cognition, and social skills. Adolescents enter puberty, parents see their children become sexually mature individuals. How parents react to this may be influenced by a variety of factors, including the parents' view of their own development. Parents who see their own attractiveness or health or sexuality decline may react to their child's development very differently than do parents who have a more positive view of themselves.

Adolescents' cognitive development may also distress their relationship with their parents. As adolescents become more cognitively sophisticated, they frequently become more questioning of parental rules. Although the adolescent's demand for reasons underlying parental judgments may reflect newly developed cognitive skills—a positive development from an intellectual perspective—it may increase conflicts with parents. Parents who expect their rules to be obeyed without question may be more upset by their child's arguments than are parents who expect to discuss rules and rule violation.

Concurrent with these physical and cognitive changes, adolescents also undergo social changes. These include increased demands for autonomy and independence. Parents whose children were docile and compliant prior to adolescence may feel their authority threatened by these changes. Parents may find it more difficult to discipline children than before. This may be especially problematic for families who had difficulty controlling their children earlier in childhood.

Although families may be viewed as a system, there is no one form that this system takes. In the 1950s the ideal form of the family system was a breadwinner father, a homemaker mother, and "Leave it to Beaver" type children. Today families take many different forms. About 50 percent of American adolescents will live in single-parent families for some period. This rate is higher

Amos Morgan/Getty Images

for African Americans. About 75 percent of women with school-age children are employed outside the home. About 21 percent of American children live in *blended families*, with step-siblings and a step-parent. It is clear that there is no "typical" family. Does this mean that the family plays a less significant role in the life of the adolescent? The research indicates no. The family is still among the most important influences on an adolescent. How well adolescents resist peer pressure, how successful they are developing an identity, how capable they become in making independent decisions, and what they strive for in the future all seem to be predominantly influenced by the family. A remaining question is, what characteristics of the family predict success in these areas?

Diana Baumrind—a leading researcher on the effects of differing parenting styles on adolescent development—proposed that some styles of parenting result in more competent, independent children than do other styles. She classified parents as authoritative, authoritarian, or permissive. *Authoritative parents* encourage their children to discuss rules, rather than expecting children to obey without question. When the rules are broken, authoritative parents do not address this in a punitive manner. They neither ignore the offense nor do they use punitive discipline. They often use reasoning. Like authoritative parents, *authoritarian parents* also set clear rules and limits. However, authoritarian parents are more likely to expect their children to obey without question. These parents can sometimes be punitive as well. *Permissive parents* fall into two categories. Some permissive parents have a warm relationship with their children, but they do not impose many controls on them. Other permissive parents are basically uninvolved in the lives of their children.

Baumrind and others have investigated the relationship between parenting styles and social competence in adolescents. Issues such as how well adolescents resist peer pressure, how well adjusted they are, or how many problems they have with delinquency have been investigated. It was found that children from authoritative families, where parents are emotionally warm to their children but have clear rules, limits, and controls, generally scored best. This was found to be the case regardless of family structure.

The articles in this unit demonstrate some of these aspects of the family as a system. The first article speaks to precisely what is discussed above. In *Friends Forever*, Karen Fanning explains that more often than not adolescents and their parents are not usually in conflict. Instead, Fanning maintains, adolescents and their parents typically are friends. We must recognize, however, that there are a few stormy relationships between parents and their teens. The second article in this unit explicates why children disobey and are noncompliant with parental requests. The author casts both parents and teens as culpable in these conflicts. A companion piece follows; the article reveals that teens and parents who feel helpless about continuing family conflict can turn to support groups.

Besides teen noncompliance, there are other issues that throw a family system out of balance. One common issue is that today's adolescents are overwhelmed by being superteens. Today's teen may be overcommitted to academic clubs, athletic teams, community organizations, and so forth to obtain societal approval and admission to a competitive college. *In Learning to Chill*, families who have said "enough is enough" are showcased.

Because families are so influential on youth, parental communication is important. The way parents communicate to their teens about alcohol, tobacco, and other substance use is important and may help prevent the surrender to peer pressure and to experiment with and use these substances. Most parents timidly broach the subject of drug use and then bury it in a conversation with other subjects. Parents can do much more to guide their children on this subject.

Friends Forever

Believe It or Not, Many Teens Actually Get Along With Their Parents. Read on to Find Out the Secret of Their Success

Karen Fanning

Last summer, Kim Lerner saw one of her favorite bands, Matchbox Twenty, perform live. Sitting with her at the show at the Meadows Music Theater in Hartford, Connecticut, were her cousin and her father.

Her father? Since when do dads and their teenage children attend concerts together? In Kim's life, it happens quite often.

"My dad and I like the same music and like to go to concerts together," says the 16-year-old from Cheshire, Connecticut. "He laughs because I'm getting into all these older rock bands, like Led Zeppelin and Pink Floyd, that he's been listening to his whole life."

While not all teens are ready to dive into the mosh pit with Mom and Dad, contrary to popular belief, most aren't at war with their parents. In fact, in a recent Gallup Youth Survey, 97 percent of American teenagers, ages 13 to 17, reported that they get along with their parents very well or "fairly well."

Making It Work

Healthy relationships between teens and parents don't just happen. Making them work requires effort on both sides, because adolescence is a time of uncertainty for parents as well as for teenagers.

"Adolescents have to recognize that parents spend the first 12 years raising their kids and getting closer to them," says Stan J. Katz, a clinical psychologist in Beverly Hills, California. "Parents are ready when kids turn 13 and all of a sudden become rebellious and don't want to go on family vacations or sit at the dinner table. Parents are shocked at this kind of behavior."

As children make their way through adolescence, that shock turns into anxiety. When teens begin to pull away and assert their independence, parents feel shut out. Fear-

ful that their kids will get mixed up in drugs or the wrong crowd, they often respond by instituting a lot of rules to try and keep their kids in line.

Clue In Mom and Dad

But it doesn't have to be that way. While teens are entitled to their privacy, experts say the more they tell their parents about their lives—school, friendships, social life—the less parents will worry. If parents trust their children are being honest with them, they won't feel the need to snoop or nag.

"My dad knows my friends, so he trusts me when it comes to where I go and who I am hanging out with," says John Reynolds, a junior at Santa Susana High School in Simi Valley, California. "He gives me a lot of freedom to go out with my friends."

While most teens agree that healthy relationships require good communication, in many cases, actions speak louder than words. John says he shows his father and stepmother respect by doing chores.

"They always help me, so I always want to return the favor," he says. "I wash the cars. I vacuum. I clean the bathrooms. I watch my little brother and sister."

Staying Calm

Even teens and parents who do get along have their share of quarrels and disagreements over a range of issues—from clothes to curfews to grades. While arguments are a normal part of any relationship, what's most important is how parents and teens settle their disputes. In the heat of the moment, it's easy for tempers to flare, but experts agree keeping cool, calm and collected is critical.

"The best way to get parents to listen is to speak to them in a voice they can hear, "says Mary Lamia, a clinical psychologist in Mann County, California. "That means a voice that is rational and calm. That means a voice that is not angry. All they'll hear is the anger. They won't hear the message."

Louis Young, 16, of Baltimore, Maryland, says yelling and screaming turns his parents off. Instead, when he and his parents have a disagreement, he tries to remain composed.

"I have the type of relationship with my parents where I try not to lose my head," Louis says. "I try to talk to them calmly. I'll discuss what I want to do and why it should be done. It's kind of like arguing a court case."

Hear the Other Side

But like all successful lawyers, teens must also be willing to listen to the other side of the story—their parents' version.

"I try to listen to what my parents say," Kim says. "They usually have pretty good advice because they've been teens. They've had similar experiences."

And even when that advice isn't exactly what she wants to hear, Kim knows that her parents have her best interests in mind—and for that, she is thankful.

"I know kids whose parents don't want to be part of their lives," Kim says. "My parents have always been there for me. I can go to them whenever I need to."

Support Network Eases Problems for Parents of Out-of-Control Teens

BY STEPHANIE DUNNEWIND

Five of them were there when the businesswoman had to speak to the judge at her daughter's court sentencing for drug use. They were there when she called at 1 a.m. for help. And they were there, every two weeks, at a restaurant to support her in her struggles.

"This group saved my marriage, it saved me and it really saved my daughter," said the Seattle businesswoman, who asked not to be identified. "My daughter humbled me and brought me to my knees. Through this group, I was able to stand up again."

The Changes Parent Support Network in Seattle offers support groups for parents with out-of-control teenagers—kids who do drugs, cut school, run away, shoplift, steal or hit family members. Besides the weekly groups, members are encouraged to form smaller "teams" whose members provide more personalized counsel.

"Parents feel so hopeless," said Detective Jennifer Baldwin of the Redmond (Wash.) Police Department, who spoke to the group and serves on its board of directors. "They feel like there's nowhere to go."

Baldwin garnered lots of nods—and some tears—when she prefaced a speech to the group by quoting her pastor. "He said that when you have a baby, your heart leaves your body and becomes them, walking around out there."

These parents' hearts aren't just walking around. They're drugged out on crystal meth, arrested for choking their mother, threatening suicide, lying for money to buy drugs, hanging out with prostitutes, stealing checks.

It's easy for parents of young children, or those with grown children who made it through adolescence unscathed, to brush off these parents' pain by figuring the kids turned out that way because the parents messed up somehow.

Listen at a Changes support group for just a few minutes, however, and it's overwhelmingly obvious that while no parent will claim to be perfect, none are heartless. They're heartbroken.

"They helped me through the worst time in my life," said one mother.

The group acknowledges parents' anguish in wondering where a daughter is when she stays out all night. It acknowl-edges the difficulty of refusing to bail a son out of jail and the embarrassment of asking for a restraining order against one's own child.

But Changes doesn't focus on the past. Instead, it emphasizes learning how to live with the present and alter the future.

"They don't just sit and share stories back and forth," Baldwin said. "It's about developing new ideas of what to do when things go sideways."

The group's philosophy is this: "We can control only ourselves and our home," said Changes Executive Director Terri Suzuki. "We make small changes in our own behavior and the child responds to those changes. But we can't control our child."

The 20-year-old group incorporated as a nonprofit in 1996. The Seattle group and one in Redmond, which splintered off last spring, draw 30 or more people each week, while smaller groups operate in three other Washington locations—Des Moines, Kent and Bremerton.

Changes is the first place many parents feel safe to talk about how terrible home life is.

"At work, someone will talk about how their son was accepted to Harvard, and another will say, 'Mine's going to Yale,' " said Suzuki, who was awakened at 6 one morning by police after her then-teenage daughter stole a cab ride. "You can't just say, 'Mine's going to jail.' "

When parents attend their first meeting, they always think their story is the worst, said the Seattle businesswoman. "But you soon realize yours is nothing. This group gets you off the pity party."

Most parents have one or two children besides their "star" child, so named because that child's name carries an asterisk next to it on the parent's nametag at group meetings. That's the child who brought them—usually in desperation—to the group, but parents are quick to point out that they also have a son in law school, say, or a daughter who is a teacher.

Even after their children have moved out, many parents stay to counsel new members who are going through what they did.

"Parents can learn so much from other parents who are not professionals but who have been through the fire themselves," said Roland Tam Sing, a therapist with Family Reconciliation

Services, a Washington state program that helps troubled families. "For new parents, meeting veteran parents who have seen their kids through a crisis can help them realize there is a light at the end of the tunnel."

As part of the program, parents make a stand, or a long-term goal, and then set weekly steps to gradually achieve it.

At a recent meeting, parents went around the room sharing their goals (no "try" allowed): "I will not give in to my kid's demands." "I will not allow my children to take advantage of me." "I will not parent my adult children."

One mother said her week's aim was to find a way to connect with her son. After promising not to "ACE" (advise, criticize or explain to) her teenager, "it's just silence," she said. "It's kind of sad—if I'm not ACEing my kid, I'm not talking to him."

Another mom's stand—"I will let my child experience the consequences of his behavior"—translated into her weekly step of not nagging her son about his upcoming probation meeting. She would drive him there if he asked, but she wasn't going to set it up for him.

"We hold kids responsible for what they do, while society wants to hold parents responsible," said Suzuki.

In a crisis situation, most parents react and then consider better options, Suzuki said. Thus the group's motto: Think. Plan. Act.

Much of that planning happens not in the larger group meetings, but in five- to eight-member teams. Some teams stay in contact by e-mail, while others meet in person or talk by phone.

When one woman's son stole a car and drove to California, the police wanted her to come down and get him. She called her team members, who supported her decision to hold her son accountable for his actions.

For Suzuki, accountability meant setting a curfew for her daughter, who would stay out all night. If her daughter wasn't home when expected, Suzuki called the police to report her as a runaway.

While the teams offer support, they also hold members to their promises. "Your biggest work happens in your team," said Virginia Day, the group's representative.

Her team threatened to drop her if she and her husband didn't stop blaming each other for their son's problems. "That's what it took," Day said.

She asks team members to read letters before she sends them to her son, who is in a school for troubled teens in Mexico.

Members who attend court hearings help by taking notes to make sure the parent remembers all the key points. "The parent in that situation is so emotional it's easy to forget what goes on," Suzuki said.

When she met with her daughter's principal, eight members of her support team showed up. She would drive her daughter to school but her daughter sneaked out.

"I was doing everything I could to keep her in school, but I knew they wanted to blame me for it," she said.

She believes her team's presence helped demonstrate her commitment to the principal.

"There was a huge change in attitude," she said. "It was now, 'How do we work to solve this?'"

Learning To Chill: Overloaded at school and overscheduled at home, stressed-out kids— with their parents' blessing—are saying 'Enough!'

Susan Schindehette

Last year, not long after entering Peterson Middle School as an accelerated sixth grader, Wendy Gregg hit the wall. "If you were late or your homework was incomplete, you got a gold note, and three gold notes was detention," says the formerly perfectionist 11-year-old from Sunnyvale, Calif. "I had seen detention in movies, but I didn't know what it was. I thought only weirdos got it, or people who smoked."

Wendy never actually did time herself, but despite three hours a night of homework, she soon saw her usual A's replaced by B minuses. "I felt pretty stupid," she says, recalling how mortified she was at being assigned to write about why she had fallen off the honor roll. She began to break out in cold sweats and often had stomachaches. In her class photo, says principal Bob Runyon, "Wendy was the only one not looking at the camera. She was staring off to the side."

In January, when Wendy's "scary feelings" were diagnosed as anxiety attacks, her parents—Jenny, 37, a homemaker, and Bill, 41, an aerospace engineer—did a major rethink. "My husband and I decided to pull her out of the pressure cooker," says Jenny. The Greggs took Wendy out of Peterson and homeschooled her for a semester. They reprioritized, making more time for her piano lessons, basketball and I Love Lucy videos. Says her mother: "We reclaimed a lot of her time."

Last month a buoyant Wendy returned to Peterson as a seventh grader in a standard curriculum. Whenever she starts to tense up, she pulls out the "stress kit" that she made in her local Girl Scout troop—a white paper bag painted with a lake and stocked with Silly Putty (for squeezing out tension), notes from friends, an origami bird and her favorite blue nail polish. "Last year I would have been scared," she says of returning to school. "This time I was so excited I couldn't stop smiling."

Wendy's story is hardly unique. From Portland to Peoria, experts say, plenty of kids are nearing meltdown from stress. The evidence is obvious: third graders hauling 25-lb. book bags to class; 12-year-olds juggling their soccer schedules on PalmPilots; a growing number of teens teaming up with $200-an-hour business consultants to teach them CEO-style time-management skills.

According to studies by such groups as the Centers for Disease Control and the American Institute of Stress, nearly half of kids report stress symptoms from headaches to short tempers; children as young as 9 are now experiencing anxiety attacks; and from 1980 to 1997 the number of 10-to-14-year-olds who committed suicide increased 109 percent. In an era when 40 percent of school districts have eliminated recess and 21 percent of teens rate a lack of time with their parents as a top concern, children risk becoming what a paper by the Harvard University admissions office recently termed "dazed survivors of some bewildering lifelong boot camp."

The source of the trouble is easy to track: anxiety-ridden moms and dads. Determined to get their children into increasingly competitive colleges and a tight job market down the road, today's parents are demanding more academic rigor (and thus more homework), even in grade school. To further beef up future resumes—and, often, to keep the kids occupied while both parents hold down jobs—they're also cramming after-school hours with extracurricular activities. The upshot, says Dr. Alvin Rosenfeld, a New York City psychiatrist and author, is that "parenting has become the most competitive sport in America." Adds Georgia Witkin, assistant professor of clinical psychology at Mount Sinai School of Medicine: "It's as if an epidemic is spreading from us to them."

How To Help Your Kid Cope

If your child seems unduly worried or scared, is day-dreaming too much or having trouble sleeping because of academic pressure and overscheduling, says Georgia Witkin, director of the Stress Program at Mount Sinai School of Medicine in New York City, try the following:

- Establish regular mealtimes and bedtimes. Predictability helps reduce kids 'stress.
- Schedule unstructured play periods. If neither parent can be home, hire a responsible teen as an overseer.
- As a role model, make sure your kids see you relaxing with a book or listening to music—not just paying bills and cleaning house.
- Plan stress-reducing family time with your children, whether it's a picnic, outdoor games or just a round of Monopoly.
- If your kids are overwhelmed by homework, don't be afraid to let teachers and school administrators know.

The good news is that some families—and organizations—have begun to fight back. Last September, for instance, the Girl Scouts introduced a Stress Less badge, awarded so far to more than 60,000 8-to-11-year-old girls (including Wendy Gregg). The entire town of Ridgewood, N.J., encouraged its citizens to clear their calendars for a "Ready, Set, Relax!" family night last spring. In Austin 6-to-12-year-olds can enroll in a program that teaches them painting, dancing and acting—without the pressure to achieve that often accompanies such extracurriculars. "Once in a while we get a call from a parent saying they want their child to be in a 'real 'production, like Oliver! or Annie," says Jeanne Henry, the city's cultural arts education supervisor. "We explain that if the kids come here after school and feel like doing nothing, that's okay. They can do nothing."

Public schools are joining the stress-busting movement as well—and not only in affluent communities. When teachers in San Francisco noticed in 1997 that students were stressed out, they started teaching yoga. Today Cathy Klein, 30, offers it to her second graders at the inner-city Daniel Webster Elementary School. "Yoga calms me," says 6-year-old Filoi Sevatase, a regular at the twice-weekly, 20-minute sessions. "I like doing it when I'm mad or sad, like when my sister hits me or makes me cry." That relaxation technique is also on the curriculum in Atlanta preschools, where 4-year-olds learn to center themselves with the help of a Copee Bear hand puppet. Reports program director Gloria Elder: "Ninety-five percent of their teachers say it helps."

But the biggest push comes from parents like Bill Doherty, 57, a social sciences professor and father of two who lives in Roseville, Minn. In 1999, when he began noticing "6-year-olds with daily planners," Doherty helped launch Putting Family First, a local organization dedicated to reclaiming family time. One of the group's first seal-of-approval certificates went to the conference-winning Wayzata High School football team coached by Brad Anderson, 38. The team has long refused to bench players when they skip practice for family obligations. Josh Rounds, 18, a senior middle linebacker, says that when he missed the first week of practice because of a family vacation, "it was no problem. I got right back into football when I came home."

Anderson says his own family has experienced scheduling overload firsthand. "As a parent you want to provide opportunities for your kids—gymnastics, swimming, church choir, Brownies, piano lessons. But my wife and I had to sit down with our PalmPilots to figure out how we were going to get them from one thing to another." Instead the couple decided to pare back, limiting their two girls to no more than two after-school activities each. Now, he says, "the kids 'favorite thing is family night—playing a game of Battleship together or going to an outdoor concert."

In the nearby town of Plymouth, the Peterschmidt family came to a similar decision three years ago, when they almost lost themselves in a blur of frenetic activity. "I can't bear to look at the calendar from that year. It was crazy," says mother Margaret, 45, who goes by the nickname Bugs. "Every night we'd say, 'What's next? 'before running to get Max to his church group or Betsy to soccer." Max, 14, who is just starting ninth grade at Wayzata High, also shudders at the memory: "Trumpet, Scouts, violin, advanced math, church youth group, recreational soccer. And I was depressed because I felt like I had no time to do anything at all." Adds Betsy, now 11, who was equally overscheduled: "I needed a break."

The kids weren't alone in feeling stressed out. In the fall of 1999 a chronically tired Bugs went to the doctor, who found that she had walking pneumonia. During a week of mandatory bed rest, she recalls, "my kids gave me all kinds of stress-relieving gifts—an aromatherapy candle, a little fountain for the kitchen counter. It was a clear message."

137

One that she and her husband, Eric, 47, a marketing director for Honeywell, finally heeded. Today, after curtailing their schedules, the Peterschmidts are enjoying a newfound tranquility. "Life is so much better now," says Bugs. "But it's like finding religion or quitting smoking: You don't realize how good you feel until you've done it." These days dinner's on the table at 6:15—no phone calls allowed. Family members talk to one another. The kids roast marshmallows and play flashlight tag—"like tag but with light," Betsy explains. "And it's in the dark, so it's much funner."

Each week, Max has a violin lesson, while Betsy takes piano from a teacher who comes to the house. "We don't have huge blowups like we used to," says Bugs. As for Peterschmidt pere: "When I come home from work," marvels Eric, "the first thing my son says is, 'Dad, how was your day?' Isn't that neat?"

Parent-Adolescent Communication About Alcohol, Tobacco, and Other Drug Use

For this study, 67 adolescent African American and Caucasian adolescents were interviewed about their parent-adolescent conversations regarding alcohol, tobacco, and other drug (ATOD) use. Analyses indicated that fewer than half of the youth had engaged in a conversation with one or more parent about ATOD use and that significantly more adolescents felt closest to and preferred talking with their mothers about risky topics than to other family members. Moreover, the results suggested that parental antidrug messages were part of the ongoing discourse of family life rather than structured in an isolated "drug talk," as is advocated in contemporary media. This article argues for a clearer definition of the parent-adolescent conversation, discusses implications for targeting mothers as prevention agents, and introduces risk socialization theory.

Michelle A. Miller-Day
Pennsylvania State University

It is no secret that the United States government has an action plan to wage a war on drugs. One cannot open the newspaper or watch television without being exposed to antidrug media messages and advertisements calling for parents to talk with their children about alcohol and other drugs. Beginning in 1998, the U.S. Congress appropriated $195 million for the Partnership for a Drug-Free America antidrug media campaign (Partnership for a Drug-Free America, 1998). This campaign is ongoing and pervasive, striking for the continuous placement of public service messages in television during prime viewing hours and in other key media. Yet, it is not clear if parents are actually talking with their children about drug use.

Family Communication and Alcohol, Tobacco, and Other Drug Use (ATOD)

Social learning theory (Bandura, 1986; Patterson, 1982) focuses on the importance of family process variables in learning and subsequent performance. This theory guides much of the socialization research and considers parental behavior and attitudes as critical components of adolescent socialization. Indeed, one parenting variable consistently identified as important in affecting adolescent behavior is parent-adolescent communication (Patterson, Reid, & Dishion, 1992). Yet, little research has focused on how actual parental communication strategies influence drug attitudes (Beck & Lockhart, 1992; Klingle & Miller, 1998; M. A. Miller, Alberts, Hecht, Trost, & Krizek, 2000). Moreover, there is no real communication theory from which to make claims about parent-youth communication and risk.

Clearly, family interaction influences children's behavior, and because family is the social unit primarily responsible for modeling communication behavior and teaching social skills, family interaction might also provide models for competencies related to drug resistance and use (Baumrind, 1991; Noller, 1994; Patterson & Yoerger, 1997; Socha & Stamp, 1995). In fact—although peers play a crucial role in levels of current adolescent drug use—the attitudes and behaviors of parents, the overall quality of family life, and the relationship between parents and children are what play the most crucial role in adolescent behaviors such as initiation and experimentation with ATOD (Brown, Mounts, Lamborn, & Steinberg, 1993; Hoffman & Su, 1998; Kumpfer & Alvarado, 1995; M. A. Miller et al., 2000).

Before children develop relationships with peers, they have relationships with family members. The behavior of adolescents' family members and their relationships with those members influence and shape attitudes and values toward drugs and drug use (Newcomb, 1995). According to Kandel (1996), scholars who view family influences as less important than peer influences are ignorant of the central role family relationships play in influencing adolescents' values, norms, and behavior. Coombs, Paulson, and Richardson (1991) noted, for instance, that parental influence may be more important than peer influence in young people's reasons for nonuse. Quality of family life consistently emerges as a pronounced influence on adolescent substance use behavior (Gullota, Adams, & Montemayor, 1995; Hawkins, Catalano, & Miller, 1992).

The nature of family communication is influenced by the frequency of parent-child interactions but also may be influenced by whom the child interacts with in the family context. The nature of family talk may be different for mothers and fathers (Socha & Stamp, 1995). Stafford and Dainton (1995) suggested fathers talk about fewer topics and focus on rules, academic achievement, and instrumental tasks. Some studies reveal that fathers spend little to no time in one-on-one conversation with their children during middle childhood or adolescence (Buerkel-Rothfuss, Fink, & Buerkel, 1995; Secunda, 1992), and other studies demonstrate a link between fathers' attitudes about drug use and their children's attitudes and behavior regarding drug use (Brook, Whiteman, Gordon, & Brook, 1984).

Mothers, conversely, tend to talk with their children more often and talk about a wider variety of topics than do fathers (Hetherington & Stanley-Hagan, 1995; Youniss & Smollar, 1985). Pipp, Shaver, Jennings, Lamborn, and Fischer (1985) suggested that adolescents feel closer and more attached to their mothers than to their fathers. In addition, there is evidence in the risk literature that positive general communication with mothers is associated with less risky behavior (Hutchinson & Cooney, 1998; Miller, Kotchick, Dorsey, Forehand, & Ham, 1998).

Indeed, only a smattering of studies have examined family efforts to discuss ATOD use, and many of these studies conceptualize family communication as a static variable that is of either poor, inadequate, or good quality. We know little about whom children talk with in their families about drug risks and whether that communication is effective.

Furthermore, few studies have included ethnicity when looking at family factors and drug prevention (Catalano et al., 1992). Although drug use is a problem for many families, the implications appear to be worse for families of color (Fullilove & Fullilove, 1995). In particular, African Americans suffer greater health and judicial consequences from their use than do other groups (Bass,

1993). Moreover, Blackwell (1991) suggested minority research considering environmental factors such as family life has been "virtually nonexistent" and that closer examination of the family—the African American family in particular—is needed when looking at drug use etiology (Botvin, Schinke, & Orlandi, 1995).

Based on this review of previous research, the primary purpose of this study is to determine if and how African American and Caucasian youth are engaging in conversations about ATOD with parents. A secondary purpose of this study is to determine if there is a relationship between parent-adolescent conversations about ATOD and adolescents' drug-resistance behavior. The following questions and hypotheses were posed for this study:

Research Question 1: Do adolescents engage in conversations with their parent(s) about ATOD use?

Research Question 2: Are there differences between African American adolescents' communication and Caucasian adolescents' communication about ATOD use?

Hypothesis 1: Adolescents will prefer talking with mothers than with any other family member about important topics such as ATOD use.

Hypothesis 2: Fewer adolescents who talk with parents about ATOD use will accept offers of ATOD than will adolescents who do not talk with parents about ATOD.

METHOD

Participants

This research was part of a larger research project examining adolescents' drug offer-resistance episodes. In the larger study, adolescent self-reports of drug use and descriptions of offer-resistance episodes were elicited from participants to determine what drugs they had been offered, what strategies they had used to successfully resist offers, and which strategies had failed.

Two inner-city schools, two inner-city churches, and two inner-city community center sites within a 10-mile radius in the mid south were randomly chosen from all the schools, community centers, and churches within that radius. Then, a purposive, stratified sample (the same numbers of participants were randomly selected from each site) was selected from the adolescent volunteers who returned signed consent forms. A final sample of participants included 67 adolescents who ranged in age from 11 to 17, with a mean age of 12.97; 74.6% (n=50) were 13 years old or younger. Approximately 60% (n=40) of the sample were African American, 40.3% (n=27) were Caucasian, 56.7% (n=38) were male, and 43.3% (n=29) were female. Interviewees were paid $5 and offered coupons for free food at a local yogurt store and/or McDonald's restaurant.

Interviews

Interviews were conducted based on an interview schedule with open-ended questions similar to that used in Hecht, Trost, Bator, & MacKinnon (1997) and M. Miller (1998). This schedule was used to elicit students' experiences by asking them to describe any offer and refusal episode they experienced in the past 2 years. Questions pertaining to family communication were asked at the end of the interview schedule and included questions pertaining to family structure, general parent-adolescent communication, communication with friends about ATOD, and parent-adolescent communication regarding ATOD.[1] Adolescents who reported that they talked with someone about ATOD were subsequently encouraged to describe and elaborate on their stories, thus capturing adolescents' points of view.

Analysis

Analysis of the interview data was conducted through a series of procedures whereby the interview tapes were audiotaped and transcribed by the researcher. The transcriptions were then subjected to content-coding procedures used in previous drug prevention studies (Hecht et al., 1997; M. Miller, 1998). Three researchers were trained in coding the interviews using a dichotomous categorization system. This system consisted of identifying the presence or absence of dichotomous yes-no classifications for each question in the interview; for example, "The student indicates that his or her father lives in the household, yes or no?" or "Offered marijuana in the past 2 years, yes or no?" Three interview transcripts were than randomly selected and read by each researcher and a preliminary list of categories for each question was determined through open coding of the three transcripts. Saturation of each category was important to account for all responses to the interview question. These categories were than labeled and described, and they ultimately constituted the dichotomous coding system.

After the core categories were determined for the family communication items, the three interviews were coded into those categories, rotated among coders, and recoded. Absolute percentage agreements and kappa values (range = .71 to 1.00) were deemed adequate. Discrepancies were discussed, coders refined their understandings of categories, and then they agreed to proceed. Thus, an additional transcript was selected and coded by all three coders, and the minimum absolute percentage agreement increased from a kappa value of .71 to .90. The remaining 63 interviews were divided among the three coders, and each transcript was read a minimum of three times and then analyzed for the presence or absence of that response category.

RESULTS

Due to the time-restricted, conversational nature of the interview, not all respondents were asked all of the items. Thus, the total percentages for each category may not total 100%.

Parent-Youth Communication About ATOD Use

Out of 67 total respondents, 43.3% (n=29) of the adolescents indicated they had communicated about ATOD use with their parents. Hence, 56.7% (n=38) had not communicated about ATOD use with their parents. Moreover, 40.3% (n=29) reported they had communicated solely with friends about the risks of using ATOD. To assess differences across adolescents who did and did not communicate with their parents about ATOD with adolescents who did and did not communicate with their friends about ATOD a 2 x 2 chi-square analysis was employed. Results indicated the adolescents who talked with parents about ATOD were significantly more likely to extend that talk into their peer groups, $\chi^2 (1) = 18.504, p < .01$.

When drug talks with parents did occur, they tended to be perceived as assertive conversations in which parents clearly articulated that drugs are bad. Whereas 29 students reported engaging in an actual conversation with parents about ATOD use, 11 more reported parents were more likely to merely mention to their children not to indulge in ATOD use. Therefore, a total of 59.7% of the sample suggested that their parents at least mentioned prevention messages to their adolescent children.

Ethnicity and Adolescent Communication About ATOD

The second research question examined the issue of ethnic differences in communication about ATOD use. Results provided no evidence of ethnic differences between African Americans and Caucasians regarding communication about ATOD; both groups reported talking about ATOD with parents fairly equally. Of African American youth, 45% (n = 18) reported talking with their parents compared with 40.7% (n=11) of Caucasian youth.

Another 2 x 2 chi-square analysis was employed to assess if this ethnic difference was significant, omitting categories with fewer than five in any given cell (Kennedy, 1992). The chi-square analysis was computed for ethnicity (African American or Caucasian) and for whether adolescents talked with parents about ATOD (yes or no). Results indicated that ethnicity was not a significant factor in parent-adolescent communication about ATOD, $\chi^2 (1) = .453$, not significant.

Aside from who participated in ATOD discussion, this study investigated adolescents' perceptions of drug use prevalence among members of their own ethnic group. Another 2 x 2 chi-square analysis was computed crossing ethnicity (African American and Caucasian) with respondent perceptions of whether members of their own ethnic group used more ATOD than did other ethnic groups (yes or no). The results indicated 50% ($n = 20$) of the African Americans compared with 18.5% ($n = 5$) of Caucasians perceived members of their own ethnic group to use more ATOD than do other ethnic groups, and this difference was statistically significant, $\chi^2 (1) = 6.669, p < .02$.

Mother-Adolescent Communication

The composition of the households in this study included mostly mothers (94%, $n=63$), fathers (65.6%, $n=44$), siblings (77.6%, $n=52$), stepfathers (9%, $n=6$), and extended family members including aunts, uncles, cousins, and grandparents (16.4%, $n=11$), with no stepmothers in the households. Respondents noted that they were around their families a lot, with 49.2% ($n=33$) reporting frequent contact with their parents and 29.8% ($n=20$) reporting moderate contact with their parents. One male youth reported he did not spend any time with his parents; he lives with a grandparent. A total of 13 respondents did not provide a response to this issue.

Respondents were asked who they were closest to in their families and with whom they felt most comfortable talking about important topics such as ATOD use. Frequencies were first computed for closeness, and results indicated that 67.2% ($n=45$) of all respondents felt relationally closest with their mothers; this consisted of adolescents who lived with their fathers ($n=30$) and who do not live with their fathers ($n=15$). A chi-square analysis was employed to assess differences between those who reported they were closest to their fathers (yes or no) and those closest to their mothers (yes or no), with a significant margin of respondents indicating they felt closest to their mothers, $\chi^2 (1)=11.99, p .01$. Yet, when two additional analyses were employed to assess difference across gender and ethnicity, computing those closest to their mothers (yes or no) with gender (male or female) and ethnicity (African American or Caucasian), results indicated that neither gender , $\chi^2 (1)=.522$, not significant, nor ethnicity, $\chi^2 (1)=.007$, not significant, was significantly related to closeness with mothers.

Mother, as predicted in the first hypothesis, was also the preferred conversational partner for important topics. Frequencies were first computed for the item "Who in your family do you feel most comfortable talking with about important topics," and the results indicated that 70.1% ($n=47$) of all respondents preferred talking with their mothers about important topics. This is in contrast to 11.9% ($n=8$) of the respondents who preferred talking with their fathers, 7.4% ($n=5$) who preferred talking with

their grandparents, 7.4% ($n=5$) who preferred talking with their siblings, and 2.9% ($n=2$) who preferred talking with other extended family members. Two separate chi-square analyses were then conducted computing reported preference for mothers (yes or no) with gender (male or female) and ethnicity (African American or Caucasian). Results indicated that neither gender, $\chi^2 (1)=.001$, not significant, nor ethnicity, $\chi^2=1.137$, not significant related to selecting mothers to talk with about important topics.

Communication About ATOD and Adolescents' Acceptance or Rejection of ATOD Offers

Last, a 2 x 2 chi-square analysis was employed to assess whether parent-youth communication about ATOD (communicates with parents with ATOD or does not communicate with parents about ATOD) was significantly related to rejection of ATOD offers (accepted drug offer or rejected drug offer). The second hypothesis predicted that adolescents who reported talking with parents about ATOD would also report rejecting offers of ATOD. Although statistical significance was almost attained, this hypothesis was not supported, $\chi^2 (1) = 3.453, p < .06$. Yet, of the nine adolescents who reported accepting a drug offer, 77% ($n = 7$) indicated they had not communicated with one of their parents about the risks of ATOD. Thus, communication with parents about the risks of ATOD may possibly be a significant factor in determining who would accept or reject a drug offer.

DISCUSSION

The primary purpose of this study was to determine if and how African American and Caucasian youth engaged in conversations about ATOD with parents. Results suggested that parent-youth talks advocated by the media might not actually occur for many adolescents. Indeed, most of the adolescents in this study reported they did not engage in conversations about drugs with parents. Moreover, these findings suggest youth may receive antidrug messages in more subtle ways than in sit-down conversations with their parents. The content and form of these more subtle messages are often not readily apparent, and a review of the literature did not reveal substantive information about the informal, casual messages parents use to prevent their adolescents from engaging in ATOD use.

Parents are powerful socializing agents in the lives of children, and they are in the unique position to engage children in ongoing, rather than singular, dialogues about risky situations and decision making. Defining what conceptually constitutes a conversation about ATOD risk in the minds of parents and adolescents may be fundamental to the pursuit of this line of research. Actual sit-down, parent-adolescent conversations about

ATOD use may occur less frequently than communication of intermittent messages mentioned by parents to their children in the ongoing dialogue of daily life. This trickle of messages from parents to their adolescent children during day-to-day interaction may be more important than sit-down drug talks encouraged by the media. The implication is that in addition to the content of the messages included in parent-adolescent discussions of ATOD, family and adolescent scholars must examine the day-to-day family interaction that may reinforce, contradict, complement, or illustrate the antidrug use messages indicated by the media.

This investigation also examined African American and Caucasian communication about ATOD use. The results did not reveal evidence of systematic differences between African American and Caucasian parent-adolescent communication about ATOD. Although these results suggested that African American adolescents perceived African Americans as a whole as involved in more ATOD use than are other ethnic groups, this perception is contrary to prevalence data. Recent prevalence statistics indicate ATOD use is more prevalent among Caucasian than among African American adolescents (Bass, 1993; Johnston, O'Malley, & Bachman, 1989, 1997; Parker, 1995a, 1995b). Further investigation is necessary regarding ethnicity and perceptions of drug use prevalence. These findings imply that whereas African American youth may overestimate ATOD use among African Americans, Caucasian youth may underestimate use among Caucasians.

This study also supports and extends current knowledge regarding mother-adolescent relationships. Results suggest that adolescents not only report feeling most comfortable talking generally with their mothers but also were most likely to select mothers as the persons they would speak with about ATOD. The adolescents in this study felt emotionally closest with their mothers and they also felt most comfortable talking about risky topics with their mothers. The critically important nature of mother-adolescent communication about risky issues has vast implications for substance abuse prevention and family education efforts. Given that adolescents may choose to talk with mothers rather than anyone else about risky issues and that they feel closer to their mothers, mothers may be logical targets for drug education and intervention programs.

A secondary purpose of this study was to determine if there was a relationship between parent-adolescent conversations about ATOD and adolescents' drug-resistance behavior. The relationship was close to achieving statistical significance and with a larger sample would most likely do so. It is clearly implicit in the media and in other prevention efforts that parent-youth conversations about the risks of ATOD are expected to effectively prevent (or at least delay) adolescent drug use (Kumpfer & Alvarado, 1995; M. A. Miller et al., 2000; Newcomb, 1995), yet this assumption is not theory driven. The theoretical approach that implicitly guides this expectation in much of the literature is social learning theory (Bandura, 1986); however, this theory is focused primarily on modeling parental behavior rather than on the socialization of conservative norms through communicative practices. Perhaps rather than a focus on the single-shot drug talk advocated by the media, scholars should seek to build a risk socialization theory that explains how parents, as ongoing socializing agents, communicatively promote conservative norms for risky behavior (e.g., drug use) and empower their children to make individually responsible decisions regarding risky behavior.

There is much to be learned about parent-adolescent communication and effective messages to prevent adolescent drug use. There continues to be a gap in our knowledge about the kinds of dialogue that mediate risk, and there is no theoretical framework on which to base our ongoing inquiry. Despite these gaps, K. S. Miller and his colleagues (1998) offered a starting point for building a theoretical basis with their following prescription for parent-child dialogues:

> Dialogues should be continuous and sequential (building one upon the next as a child's cognitive, emotional, physical, and social development and experiences change) and time-sensitive (i.e., information is immediately responsive to the child's questions and anticipated needs, rather than programmed curriculum).

Limitations

There were several limitations to this study. First, conducting family communication research with the responses and perceptions of only one family member limits the generalizability of this research. To date, other studies provide evidence that parents often believe they have communicated antidrug messages to their children, whereas their children do not share that perception (Partnership for a Drug-Free America, 1999). This kind of research would be more powerful if interactional data were obtained to define and assess what constitutes parent-adolescent communication about ATOD. A direction for this line of research is toward gathering more interactional data from multiple family members and using multiple methods.

Second, because this study was imbedded within a larger study, detailed accounts of parent-adolescent conversations were not probed in more depth to gain detailed information regarding how the parent-adolescent conversations that did occur were conducted. Further research may focus on conversational analyses by documenting the parent-youth talks in laboratory settings. Moreover, the sample in the current investigation was limited to organization that would permit probing adolescents' family issues. Although the overall size of the sample hampers the statistical power of these findings, the findings still add to our knowledge of parent-adolescent communication about risky issues while challenging existing assumptions about drug talks and the process of this communication.

Regardless of methodology, family communication about ATOD use is an area of research that will continue to be important to parents and to our nation as we continue to wage our war on drugs. The victors in the end will invariably be the children.

NOTE

1. The interview schedule can be obtained by contacting the author.

REFERENCES

Bandura, A. (1986). *Social foundations of thought and action: A social cognitive theory.* Englewood Cliffs, NJ: Prentice Hall.

Bass, L. (1993). Stereotype or reality: Another look at alcohol and drug use among African-American children. *Public Health Reports Annual, 108,* 78–85.

Baumrind, D. (1991). The influence of parenting style on adolescent competence and substance use. *Journal of Early Adolescence, 11,* 56–95.

Beck, K. H., & Lockhart, S. J. (1992). A model of parental involvement in adolescent drinking and driving. *Journal of Youth and Adolescence, 21,* 35–51.

Blackwell, J. E. (1991). *The African-American community.* New York: HarperCollins.

Botvin, G. J., Schinke, S., & Orlandi, M. A. (Eds.). (1995). *Drug abuse prevention with multiethnic youth.* Thousand Oaks, CA: Sage.

Brook, J. S., Whiteman, M., Gordon, A. S., & Brook, D. W. (1984). Parental determinants of female adolescent's marijuana use. *Development Psychology, 20,* 1032–1043.

Brown, B. B., Mounts, N., Lamborn, S. D., & Steinberg, L. (1993). Parenting practices and peer group affiliation in adolescence. *Child Development, 64,* 467–482.

Buerkel-Rothfuss, N. L., Fink, D. S., & Buerkel, R. A. (1995). Communication in the father-child dyad: The intergenerational transmission process. In T. J. Socha & G. H. Stamp (Eds.), *Parents, children, & communication: Frontiers of theory and research* (pp. 63–85). Hillsdale, NJ: Lawrence Erlbaum.

Catalano, R. F., Morrison, D. M., Wells, E. A., Gillmore, M. R., Tritani, B., & Hawkins, J. D. (1992). Ethnic differences in family factors related to early drug initiation. *Journal of Studies on Alcohol, 53,* 208–217.

Coombs, R. H., Paulson, M. J., & Richardson, M. A. (1991). Peer vs. parental influence in substance use among Hispanic and Caucasian children and adolescents. *Journal of Youth and Adolescence, 20,* 73–88.

Fullilove, R. E., & Fullilove, M. T. (1995). Conducting research in ethnic minority communities: Considerations and challenges. In G. J. Botvin, S. Schinke, & M. A. Orlandi (Eds.), *Drug abuse prevention with multiethnic youth* (pp. 255–294). Thousand Oaks, CA: Sage.

Gullota, T., Adams, G., & Montemayor, R. (1995). (Eds.). *Substance abuse in adolescence.* Thousand Oaks, CA: Sage.

Hawkins, J. D., Catalano, R. F., & Miller, J. Y. (1992). Risk and protective factors for alcohol and other drug problems in adolescence and early adulthood: Implications for substance abuse prevention. *Psychological Bulletin, 12,* 64–105.

Hecht, M. L., Trost, M. R., Bator, R. J., & MacKinnon, D. (1997). Ethnicity and sex similarities and differences in drug resistance. *Journal of Applied Communication Research, 25,* 75–97.

Hetherington, E. M., & Stanley-Hagan, M. M. (1995). Parenting in divorced and remarried families. In M. Bornstein (Ed.), *Handbook of Parenting: Vol. 3. Status and social conditions of parenting* (pp. 233–254). Hillsdale, NJ: Lawrence Erlbaum.

Hoffman, J. P., & Su, S. (1998). Parental substance use disorder, mediating variables and adolescent drug use: A non-recursive model. *Addiction, 93,* 1351–1364.

Hutchinson, M. K., & Cooney, T. M. (1998). Patterns of parent-teen sexual risk communication: Implications for intervention. *Family Relations: Interdisciplinary Journal of Applied Family Studies, 47,* 185–194.

Johnston, L. D., O'Malley, P. M., & Bachman, J. G. (1989). *Drug use, drinking, and smoking: National survey results from high school, college, and young adult populations, 1975–1988.* Washington, DC: Government Printing Office.

Johnston, L. D., O'Malley, P. M., & Bachman, J. G. (1997). *National survey results on drug use from the Monitoring the Future Study, 1975–1995* (National Institutes of Health Publication No. 97-4139). Rockville, MD: National Institutes of Health, National Institute on Drug Abuse.

Kandel, D. B. (1996). The parental and peer contexts of adolescent deviance. An algebra of interpersonal influences. *Journal of Drug Issues, 26,* 289–315.

Kennedy, J. J. (1992). *Analyzing qualitative data: Log-linear analysis for behavioral research* (2nd ed.), New York: Praeger.

Klingle, R. S., & Miller, M. (1998). *Family education efforts and family members' substance use as predictors of adolescent substance abuse.* Paper presented at the Western States Communication Association convention in Denver, Colorado.

Kumpfer, K. L., & Alvarado, R. (1995). Strengthening families to prevent drug use in multiethnic youth. In G. J. Botvin, S. Schinke, & M. A. Orlandi (Eds.), *Drug abuse prevention with multiethnic youth* (pp. 255–294). Thousand Oaks, CA: Sage.

Miller, K. S., Kotchick, B. A., Dorsey, S., Forehand, R., & Ham, A. Y. (1998). Family communication about sex: What are parents saying and are their adolescents listening? *Family Planning Perspectives, 30,* 218–239.

Miller, M. (1998). The social processes of drug resistance in a relational context. *Communication Studies, 49,* 358–375.

Miller, M. A., Alberts, J. K., Hecht, M. L., Trost, M., & Krizek, R. L. (2000). *Adolescent relationships and drug use.* Hillsdale, NJ: Lawrence Erlbaum.

Newcomb, M. D. (1995). Drug use etiology among ethnic minority adolescents: Risk and protective factors. In G. J. Botvin, S. Schinke, & M. A. Orlandi (Eds.), *Drug abuse prevention with multiethnic youth* (pp. 105–129). Thousand Oaks, CA: Sage.

Noller, P. (1994). Relationships with parents in adolescence: process and outcome. In R. Montemayor, G. T. Adams, & T. Gullota (Eds.), *Personal relationships during adolescence* (Vol. 6). Thousand Oaks, CA: Sage.

Parker, K. D. (1995a). Predictors of alcohol and drug use: A multi-ethnic comparison. *Journal of Social Psychology, 135,* 581–591.

Parker, K. D. (1995b). Prevalence of cocaine use: A multi-ethnic comparison. *The Western Journal of African-American Studies, 19,* 30–47.

Partnership for a Drug-Free America. (1998). *The boomer-rang: Baby boomers seriously underestimating presence of drugs in their children's lives* (Report to the Office of National Drug Control Policy). New York: Author.

Partnership for a Drug-Free America (1999). *Partnership attitude tracking study* (Report to the Office of National Drug Control Policy). New York: Author.

Patterson, G. R. (1982). *A social learning approach: Coercive family process.* Eugene, OR: Castalia.

Patterson, G. R., Reid, J. B., & Dishion, T. J. (1992). *A social learning approach for antisocial boys.* Eugene, OR: Castalia.

Patterson, G. R., & Yoerger, K. (1997). A developmental model for late-onset delinquency. In W. D. Osgood (Ed.), *Motivation and delinquency: Vol. 44 of the Nebraska Symposium on motivation* (pp. 119–177). Lincoln: University of Nebraska Press.

Pipp, S., Shaver, P., Jennings, S., Lamborn, S., & Fischer, K. W. (1985). Adolescents' theories about the development of their relationships with parents. *Journal of Personality and Social Psychology, 48,* 991–1001.

Secunda, V. (1992). *Women and their fathers.* New York: Dell.

Socha, T. J., & Stamp, G. (1995). *Parents, children, & communication: Frontiers of theory and research.* Hillsdale, NJ: Lawrence Erlbaum.

Stafford, L., & Dainton, M. D. (1995). Parent-child communication within the family system. In T. J. Socha & G. H. Stamp (Eds.), *Parents, children, and communication* (pp. 3–22). Hillsdale, NJ: Lawrence Erlbaum.

Youniss, J., & Smollar, J. (1985). *Adolescent relations with mothers, fathers, and friends.* Chicago: University of Chicago Press.

Michelle A. Miller-Day is an assistant professor of communication arts and sciences at the Pennsylvania State University. Her most recent book is the coauthored text Adolescent Relationships and Drug Use *(2000). She is interested in interpersonal interactional processes that serve as risk and protective factors for problem behaviors.*

From *Journal of Adolescent Research,* Vol. 17, No. 6, November 2002, pp. 604-616. © 2002 by Sage Publications. Reprinted with permission.

UNIT 6
Peers and Youth Culture

Unit Selections

Key Points to Consider

- Do you think teens from around the world are becoming more and more alike due to globalization? Is this a trend with which you agree? Is it important to preserve cultural variations?

- Is popularity among peers more important to adolescents than to other children? Do you feel that at times popularity can be a "toxic" issue among teens? How so?

- In what negative ways do adolescent peers influence each other? In what positive ways do they influence one another?

- Are there aspects of adolescent popular culture that you find distasteful? Are there aspects that you like and appreciate? What dimensions of teen culture differentiate your likes and dislikes?

- Are there methods other than face-to-face communication that teens use to connect with each other? What are the advantages and disadvantages of these methods? Are some methods (e.g. the internet) more precarious than others?

Links: www.dushkin.com/online/
These sites are annotated in the World Wide Web pages.

Higher Education Center for Alcohol and Other Drug Prevention
http://www.edc.org/hec/

Justice Information Center (NCJRS): Drug Policy Information
http://www.ncjrs.org/drgswww.html

National Clearinghouse for Alcohol and Drug Information
http://www.health.org/

Hakim won't spend time with his family anymore; he prefers to "hang out" with his friends on the basketball court and all his sister cares about is what her friends think of her. Both of them are teenagers. Their parents bemoan the loss of influence over their children's behavior and the increasing insinuation of peers into their children's lives. The image of the powerless parent versus the persuasive peer is stereotypical but is inconsistent with current research and theory about relationships during adolescence. Parents who believe this stereotype run the risk of missing danger signals in their children's behavior and of abdicating too much responsibility at a time when their children still need parental guidance and structure.

Adolescents are without a doubt more peer-oriented than any other age group. But it is simplistic to assume that peer influence is always negative and that it outweighs parental influence. Research demonstrates that the nature of the parent-child relationship is consistently the best predictor of adolescent psychological health and well-being. Adolescents who have poor relationships with their parents are precisely the adolescents who are most susceptible to negative peer influences. Poor parent-adolescent relationships are *not* the norm during the pubertal years, but, rather, conflicted relationships more likely represent a continuation of poor family relationships from childhood.

Research also indicates that most adolescents feel close to and respect their parents. Most adolescents share their parents' values, especially when it comes to moral, religious, political, and educational values. The school the adolescent attends, the kind of neighborhood the parents live in, whether the parents attend religious services, and what parents do for a living all influence their children. Parental choices such as these have a definite impact on their children for the network of friends they select.

Several factors have contributed to the misconception that adolescents reject their parents in favor of peers. First, peers play a greater role in the adolescent's day-to-day activities, style of dress, and musical tastes than do parents. Second parents often confuse the adolescent's struggle for autonomy with rebellion. G. Stanley Hall's views of adolescence as a biologically necessary time of "storm and stress" contributed to this confusion as well. Similarly, Anna Freud, arguing from her father's psychoanalytic tradition and her own experience with troubled adolescents, maintained that the adolescent-parent relationship is highly laden with conflicts causing adolescents to turn to their peers. According to Anna Freud, such conflicts ensure a successful resolution of the Oedipus/Electra complex. This model of intense parent-adolescent conflict has not been empirically supported and can be detrimental if parents fail to seek help because they believe intense conflict is "normal" during adolescence.

Another myth about peer influence during adolescence is that it is primarily negative. As Thomas Berndt discusses in his research, peer influence is mutual and has both positive and negative effects. Peer pressure is rarely coercive, as is popularly envisaged. It is a more subtle process where adolescents influence their friends and the friends influence them. Just as adults

Ryan McVay/Getty Images

do, adolescents choose friends who already have similar interests, attitudes, and beliefs.

Until recently, researchers paid little attention to the positive effects of peers on adolescent development. Among other things, friends help adolescents develop role-taking and social skills, conquer the imaginary audience referred to in the last unit, and act as social supports in stressful situations. Although they decry peer pressure as an influence on their children, no thinking parents would want their son or daughter to be a social outcast without friends.

Another misconception about peer relations is that teen culture is a unified culture with a single way of thinking and acting. A visit to any secondary school today will reveal the variety of teen cultures that exist. The formation of peer groups and adolescent crowds is partly a function of school structure and school activities. As in past decades, one can find jocks, populars, brains, delinquents, and nerds. One would also encounter members of today's grunge and body-piercing crowds. Media attention is often drawn toward bizarre or antisocial groups further contributing to the myth that peer influence is primarily negative.

Music is very much a part of youth culture, although there is no universal type of music liked by all adolescents. One way adolescents have always tried to differentiate themselves from adults has been through music. On the other hand, adults today are concerned that music, movies, and television have gone too far in the quest for ever more shocking and explicit sexual and violent content. Widespread and easy access to the Internet has also compounded concerns about the types of material today's adolescents are exposed to.

In addition to school and leisure activities like sports, adolescents today spend considerable time in the part-time work force. Work has usually been seen as a positive influence on adolescent development. Society points to the positive outcomes of developing responsibility and punctuality, knowledge of the working world, and appreciating the value of money. Research does corroborate the existence of the positive effects of work, but adolescents have been spending an increasing number of hours in the work force. Recent studies find that adolescents who work over 20 hours per week are more involved in drug use and delinquent activity, have more psychological and physical complaints, and perform more poorly in school. Although there may be a tendency for adolescents who are predisposed toward such behaviors to be disengaged from school and, therefore, work more in the first place. Longitudinal data suggest that working exacerbates these tendencies.

In this unit on peers and youth culture, various aspects of the youth phenomenon are explored. The first introductory article addresses the question of whether there is a global teen culture despite the existence of all the other cultures in the world. The answer is "yes" and "no". American teens seem to have a unique, cutting edge style, but more and more youth around the world are trying to emulate it. Marketers promulgate a heterogeneous youth culture by essentially promoting a global youth culture. They do this by using the same appeals to various youth groups worldwide.

The next two articles focus on peer influences. Recent research on alpha girls (dominant girls) has captured America's attention. Researchers contend that some girls become bullies and isolate their less popular peers. In some situations, the ostracism can be brutal. The second article in this unit examines the phenomenon of alpha girls. A companion article also examines the role peers play in risky behaviors. Some studies demonstrate that friends can influence the initiation of risky behaviors; however, friends can also play a large role in preventing risky behaviors.

The final two essays in this unit discuss media influences on adolescents. The first article presents research on the effects of rap music. Interestingly, the author concludes that rap music has both positive and negative effects. Finally, close online relationships in a sample of American adolescents are examined in the last article. Many teens are contacting strangers online and attempting to meet with them face-to-face. Research on whether these relationships have beneficial or harmful elements is disclosed.

Global Teen Culture— Does It Exist?

* It's shock news. Teenagers—everybody's favorite stereotypes—aren't in fact a homogenous group of hormonal horrors, but a complex and sophisticated collection of consumers, according to a study from market research agency RoperASW Europe. The research seeks to explode popular myths about marketing to a global teen audience.

Many modern teens live very similar lives to older consumers in their own countries. Ten per cent of all teens are already working full-time, rising to 31% of 17-19 year-olds. In the UK, 11% of the 17-19 year old group are already parents to children of their own. These busy consumers hardly fit into the 'Kevin the teenager' bratty stereotype.

Teenagers are affected more by the values of the country and culture in which they live than a global 'youth culture', according to the research. In Japan, they viewed open-mindedness as very important, as did their older Japanese counterparts. Saudi and Egyptian teenagers rated faith as an important asset. And American teenagers were more interested in freedom.

Nick Chiarelli, associate director at RoperASW Europe, says: "We were surprised that teens tended to have the same fundamental values as their parents rather than other people of the same age around the world. 'Global teen culture' is a superficial expression where everyone drinks Coke and wears Nike trainers, but deep down, teens have very different values that depend more on their background than their age."

However, Michelle Cfas, consultant at youth agency Beatwax disagrees: "There is definitely a coherent global teen market—that's why kids in a slum in Sao Paulo aspire to wear Nike as much as kids in Los Angeles, Sydney, Delhi, Manchester or even Baghdad."

Teenagers in the developed world—North America, Western Europe and some parts of developed Asia—see individuality as a particularly important value. Forty-seven per cent of 13-14 year-olds describe individuality as very important to them. This figure drops as people age, with 40% of people in their twenties and 38% of people in their forties choosing individuality as a very important trait." I think teens in the UK are slightly more extreme versions of British people in general," says Chiarelli.

In other areas, the figures tell a different story. Only 26% of Chinese teenagers rate individuality as an important characteristic—no doubt a reflection of the country's communist past. However, even this figure is greater than the percentage of people in their thirties who find this important—only 11%.

There are some homogenous patterns within the global teen group. Most teenagers put a high value on qualities such as wisdom, knowledge and learning. Thirty-nine per cent of 13-14 year-olds describe the need for knowledge as extremely important. This dips to only 20% among the older 50-60 year-old age group. Teens are a group of people who are open and receptive to new ideas.

Teenagers also want to have fun with their friends. Thirty-seven per cent of 13-14 year-olds think that this is extremely important, as opposed to only 20% of older 50-60 year-old consumers. Even people in their twenties are not so concerned by friendships as the teenage audience.

But Beatwax's Cfas warns that the teen market is too complex for generalisations: "It is too simplistic to say that teens are influenced by one thing or another. Teens can be influenced by many things, such as age, peers, parents, the media as well as their location."

So how does this research benefit marketers? Teens are in fact more open to brands and marketing than many older consumers. Only 53% of those over the age of 40 feel that having more global brands is a good thing, whereas 67% of teenagers support this idea.

When asked to rate their favourite brands, it is interesting to note that teens choose many of the same brands as their parents. Sony, Microsoft, BMW, Discovery Channel, Mercedes, Disney and Coca-Cola are all listed by both those over the age of 40 and teenagers as the best global brands.

But while these brands are popular with all ages, they appeal much more strongly to younger consumers than their older counterparts. Sixty-five per cent of 13-16 year-olds profess to really like CocaCola, while only 37% of 50-65 year-olds feel the same way. A similar tale can be told for most global brands, such as Disney and Microsoft. These brands all appeal to young consumers but their allure has faded slightly for older customers.

The ways to reach teenagers through marketing are also quite obvious. The top ten hobbies for both boy and girl teenagers show that music and films are a very important way of reaching young audiences around the world. Sixty-two per cent of male teenagers and 76% of female teenagers enjoy music while 52% and 54% respectively are interested in films.

Both groups are also interested in pop culture, entertainment and sport. "It did strike us that there were fewer differences between male and female teenagers than might have been expected. There are a lot of stereotypes about boys liking sport, but the research showed that it was important to girls too. But the key things that really bring teenagers of both genders together are films and music," comments Chiarelli.

Fifty per cent of teenagers around the world actively seek information on the music they like. And there is good news for the record industry. In Western Europe and the US, over 90% of teens listen to pre-recorded music and even in the lowest penetration markets, India and Saudi Arabia, it is over 60%.

But Beatwax's Cfas warns that just because teens can be targeted through one consistent medium like music, it does not mean they will respond to the same brands: "Teen girls in Manchester might aspire to the same thing in music but different things in clothes; one might like Top Shop while another aspires to Burberry."

Teens also enjoy finding out about and using new technologies. Forty-three per cent of teenagers claim that they find technology exciting and use it as much as they can. This figure drops to 36% among the allegedly trend-setting twentysomethings and as low as 22% in the 30+ age group.

Thirty-seven per cent of teens also play electronic games every week—six times the adult figure. This rises to 60% among boys aged 13-14 years old. "Teens are much more likely to use technology for fun and leisure purposes, such as playing music or streaming videos. Adults are more likely to use technologies for more mundane purposes, such as e-banking or news," says Chiarelli.

It is a similar story in the mobile phone market. Penetration is high among young people—63% of teens own a mobile. This figure rises to 90% in Hong Kong, Germany, Sweden, Italy, Singapore and Taiwan. The percentage of 40+ year-olds owning mobiles is only around 59%. But both groups are looking for quite different things from their handsets. Teenagers again focus on the fun applications, such as text messaging, rather than the more practical and serious side of the technology.

But Chiarelli is hoping that RoperASW Europe will learn more about teens than their leisure activities through the study. Chiarelli thinks that there is still more to be learnt about the fundamental attitudes of teenagers around the globe.

He says: "We're interested in exploring some of the more surprising things that we found out. There are some very serious parts of this research, such as how teens feel about serious issues that might affect them, like AIDS or terrorism.

"But one of the most interesting things is the way that lots of non-Western and even Western countries are turning back to religion or more traditional ways of life. Teens are normally more keen on experiencing life and change than older people, but it would be interesting to see if teens are affected by this trend too. We want to look beyond the superficial to better understand the fundamental values held by teenagers."

New research explores effects of rap music on adolescents.

(Artist: Dr. Dref/Hitman, Kurupt, Nate Dogg & Six-Two, Album: The Chronic 2001, Song: Xxplosive)

Xxplosive, West coast shit My nigguh-ish ways attract, girls that used to turn they back Causin me to yank they arm and pose like I would do the harm Now I'm sayin thank you cause they tell me, my shit's the bomb Xxplosive ... for my niggaz drinkin Cognac, smokin weed, always pack mo' than one, firearm, chrome rims, ridin' on Chronic in yo' system, let me know, my shit's the bomb—Xxplosive ...

While lyrics like these sometimes titillate and inspire adolescents, some researchers and parents are shocked by the message these offensive words might be sending. If you turn to any of the music television channels, you're likely to find both male and female artists from a variety of ethnic backgrounds spewing songs filled with violent, raunchy language, misogynistic allusions, sexual innuendo—sometimes blatant references to lewd sexual acts—and suggestive dancing. To the dismay of adults, rap has become the musical choice of some teens.

According to Brad H. Reddick, M.D., a clinical fellow at Harvard Medical School, and Eugene V. Beresin, M.D. of Massachusetts General Hospital, music plays a vital role in a teen's life. In an article published in Academic Psychiatry, they write, "It forms the background of car rides and social gatherings, and it also informs the adolescent about the adult world through the lens of the artists' lives, language and role modeling." They further explain that through music, teens establish a communal environment that, in some cases, represents old fashioned family structure. The isolation created by the Interact, the prevalence of single-parent homes and dearth of youth community programs, particularly in the inner city, creates the need for an alternative "family."

Does this mean that rap music is primarily to blame for increased substance use and abuse, escalating violence, sexual promiscuity and lowered self-esteem in adolescents? In a prospective study, Gina M. Wingood, Sc.D., MPH, Ralph J. DiClemente, Ph.D. et al., evaluated the effect of exposure to rap music videos on African-American females. They established a baseline and assessed whether it might be a predictor of the occurrence of health risk behavior and sexually transmitted diseases. The screening process took place from December 1996 through April 1999. Recruiters focused on African-American girls living in non-urban,

lower-socioeconomic neighborhoods and who were enrolled in school health classes or were patients at county health department clinics to assess their eligibility for participation in an HIV prevention program. A total of 522 single African-American females between the ages of 14 and 18 who had been sexually active for the six months prior to the study qualified.

According to Wingood, the participants were given a survey with questions pertaining to their media viewing habits. "We asked them how many hours a day and how many days a week they might listen to rap music videos," she says. "The we computed the number of hours a week they would listen to rap music videos." In addition to frequency, Wingood et al. assessed the primary types of rap music videos, i.e., gangsta, bass or hip-hop, and with whom the videos were watched. The researchers also considered each subject's age and employment factors as well as level of involvement in extracurricular and religious activities. Of importance to the outcome, too, was the amount of parental monitoring, notes Wingood.

The researches used univariate analyses to describe music video viewing characteristics at baseline. Bivariate analyses appraised the correlation among the adolescents' level of exposure to rap music videos at baseline, potential covariates and the incidence of health risk behaviors during a 12-month follow-up. The authors note that the health risk behaviors and covariates that were strongly associated ($p < 0.05$) with exposure to rap music videos in bivariate analyses were included in logistic regression analyses. Links between level of exposure to rap music videos at baseline and the rate of each health risk behavior during the 12-month follow-up were identified through a separate logistic regression analysis.

Of the 522 study participants, 92.2 percent completed 12-month follow-up assessments. Analysis revealed that the median hours of weekly exposure to rap music videos at baseline, at six-months and at 12-months was 14 hours, 14 hours and 12 hours, respectively. According to the authors, these figures indicate relatively stable viewing habits. Those subjects who were unemployed and under less parental supervision demonstrated greater exposure to rap music videos.

Wingood et al. found that at the 12-month follow-up, 37.6 percent of the participants had contracted a new sexually transmitted disease; 4.8 percent had struck a teacher; 12.1 percent reported being arrested; 14.8 percent had engaged in sexual intercourse with someone other than their steady partner; 44.2 percent reported using drugs and 44.4 percent consumed alcohol. These results indicate that, after controlling for covariates, greater exposure to rap music videos is independently associated with a wide range of negative health outcomes.

Those subjects with greater exposure were three times more likely to have hit a teacher; more than 2.5 times as likely to have been arrested; twice as likely to have had multiple sexual partners and more than 1.5 times as likely to have contracted a new sexually transmitted disease or used drugs and/or alcohol during the course of the 12-month follow-up.

Although these findings might be somewhat startling, Wingood views them cautiously. "I don't want to say there's a causal effect between rap music videos and these adverse health events," says Wingood, "because there's obviously other issues that could help explain this relationship.

She cites peer pressure and adolescent developmental issues as important potential mediating factors.

"Rebellion, the need for autonomy and independence is often associated with risky behavior. So something in the whole adolescent developmental time period may also be associated with these results," she says. She adds that violence on television and in films often has a negative impact on adolescent health. Rap music is simply a newer media that may contribute to those adverse effects.

Cheryl L. Keyes, Ph.D., associate professor in the Department of Ethnomusicology at UCLA, finds the problem of aggression and violent behavior in teens much more complicated than simply listening to and viewing rap music videos.

"The [Wingood] study puts the blame on rap, but it's a much more complex issue than that," she says. "It boils down to a child is a child and needs leaders and role models." And those, she states, are found in the home. "Disturbingly, there is no mention of the importance of parenting in the study."

Keyes says, "It's become a deeper issue of running behind the money. Parents want their kids to have the best, so they work overtime. They can't be there to raise their kids so television raises them." Rather than placing the blame for teen problems strictly on rap music, she emphasizes the critical role of parental guidance and responsibility. During those times when adolescents are not under the watchful eye of family, Keyes advocates community involvement in the overall welfare of teens through workshops that create dialogue and educate adolescent girls. She feels the issues at hand are much broader than some studies would lead the public to believe.

Although not reported explicitly in this study, Wingood considers parental monitoring key in reducing potential negative effects of any media. She also asserts that producers and performers have a public responsibility "in terms of producing more socially healthy videos." She says, "They know, of course, that sex and violence sells and that images of drug use don't hurt either. But they should have some social responsibility as well."

Travis L. Dixon, Ph.D., assistant professor of communication studies and faculty associate at the Institute for Social Research at the University of Michigan, downplays the detrimental effects of rap music videos. He cites the tendency to automatically attach negative connotations to any new media innovation from television to computers. "But we need to differentiate how people respond."

He points out that any type of media, not only rap videos, may increase tendencies toward aggression. Admittedly, rap songs in particular normalize certain negative, immoral and often illegal practices. For example, Dixon notes the acceptance of the idea that you can acquire material wealth from non-traditional jobs, such as selling drugs. However, he sees a positive side to the issue. "Rap allows anyone to become culturally expressive," he says. "It can be an empowering force."

To date, not enough studies involving the effects of rap music on African-American women have been performed, according to Dixon. He predicts that in the next five years, additional, broader-based studies will be conducted to evaluate an individual's response to the message and influence of rap music.

Eric Gordy, Ph.D., assistant professor of sociology and communications at Clark University in Worcester, Mass. also finds it hard to blame rap alone for the violence in the world. He points out that violent crimes existed long before the dawn of rap music and aggressive songs. "There is a culture of glamour about violence that makes it something to be appreciated rather than feared," he says. "It's hard to say that rap music is different from police shows or the news about war in Iraq." Most of the concerns that people bring to the table—inequality, violence and sexuality—don't originate with entertainment, according to Gordy. "These issues are real social problems."

In fact, rap music represents cultural identity for African-Americans, Gordy explains. "It's probably a mistake to look at rap in isolation from the rest of the literary and musical tradition that African-Americans have built up. It's part of a long tradition of homegrown expression by people who have not had access to the mainstream," he says. "They use a humorous—and sometimes disrespectful—attitude to read a situation and turn it into art."

Wingood and her colleagues plan to conduct another study with a larger study sample and include white and Latina adolescents as well as males, in an effort to see whether exposure to rap music videos might produce any positive effects.

Reddick BH, Beresin EV: Rebellious rhapsody: metal, rap, community and individuation. *Academic Psychiatry* 2002; 26 (1):51-59.

Wingood GM, DiClemente RJ, Bernhardt JM, et al.: A prospective study of exposure to rap music videos and African American female adolescents' health. *American Journal of Public Health* 2003; 93(3):4370-439.

From *The Brown University Child and Adolescent Behavior Letter*, Vol. 19, No. 6, June 2003. © 2003 by Manisses Communications Group. Reprinted with permission.

CLOSE ONLINE RELATIONSHIPS IN A NATIONAL SAMPLE OF ADOLESCENTS

Janis Wolak; Kimberly J. Mitchell; David Finkelhor.

This paper uses data from a national survey of adolescent Internet users (N = 1,501) to describe online relationships. Fourteen percent of the youths interviewed reported close online friendships during the past year, 7% reported face-to-face meetings with online friends, and 2% reported online romances. Two hundred forty-six youths provided details about one close online relationship. Most of these relationships were with same-age peers (70%) and crossed gender lines (71%). Many intersected with face-to-face social networks because they were initiated by introductions from friends or family (32%), involved people who lived in the vicinity (26%), were known to parents (74%), included offline contact by mail or telephone (70%), or involved face-to-face meetings (41%). Few youths reported bad experiences with online friends.

Surveys indicate that large numbers of youths use the Internet to communicate with others (Roberts et al., 1999; Rosenbaum et al., 2000). As Internet use has expanded among young people, there has been much speculation and some anxiety about the impact of its increasing prevalence. One area of concern has been the ease with which online communications like e-mail, instant messages, and chat rooms permit young people to converse with and form relationships with people they have never met face-to-face. There is a small but growing body of research about online relationships, which focuses largely on how the anonymity of Internet communications affects the quality of social ties that are developed online (Lea & Spears, 1995; Turkle, 1995) and how online relationships may affect offline social ties (Kraut et al., 1998). Further, media stories about manipulative adults who use the Internet to lure teenagers into meetings for illicit sexual purposes have raised fears that the anonymity of online relationships makes them rife with deception and dangerous, especially for adolescents (Armagh, 1998). In the midst of the discussion, there is little empirical information about the extent to which populations of Internet users are forming online relationships with people they have never met

face-to-face and the extent to which these relationships spill over into face-to-face social networks. Some researchers have gathered data on this topic from small online samples (Katz & Aspden, 1997; Parks & Floyd, 1996), but these data are not generalizable to a larger population of Internet users.

This paper uses data from the Youth Internet Safety Survey, a national telephone survey of youths ages 10 through 17, to describe the incidence and kinds of online relationships formed by adolescents, and to provide details about close online friendships, romances, and face-to-face meetings with online friends.

METHOD

The Youth Internet Safety Survey used telephone interviews to gather information from a national sample of 1,501 young people, ages 10 through 17, who were regular Internet users. "Regular" Internet use was defined as using the Internet at least once a month for the past six months on a computer at home, a school, a library, someone else's home, or some other place. This definition was chosen so that the sample would include a range of both heavy and light Internet users. Telephone numbers of households with children in the target age group were identified through another large national survey with which these researchers were involved. (This was the Second National Incidence Study of Missing, Abducted, Runaway and Thrownaway Children, a survey of over 16,000 households with children, which was conducted between February and December 1999.)

The interviews for the Youth Internet Safety Survey were conducted between August 1999 and February 2000 by experienced interviewers. Upon reaching a household, an interviewer speaking with an adult screened for regular Internet use by a 10- to 17-year-old youth in the household. When an eligible youth was identified, the interviewer conducted a short interview with the parent or caretaker who knew the most about the youth's Internet use and then asked for permission to speak with the youth. When parental consent was given, the interviewer described the survey to the youth and obtained his or her consent. Youth interviews lasted from about fifteen to thirty minutes.

They were scheduled at the convenience of youth participants and arranged for times when they could talk freely and confidentially. Youth respondents received brochures about Internet safety and $10.

PARTICIPATION RATE

Sevently-five percent of the households approached completed the screening necessary to determine their eligibility for participation in the survey. The completion rate among households with eligible respondents was 82%. Five percent of parents in eligible households refused the adult interview. Another 11% of parents completed the adult interview but refused permission for their children to participate in the youth interview. In 2% of eligible households, parents consented to the youth interview, but youths refused to participate.

Sample

The final sample consisted of 1,501 youths (boys 790, girls = 708). The mean age was 14.14 years (SD = 1.96). Table 1 further describes the demographic characteristics of the sample.

Instrumentation

The primary purpose of the Youth Internet Safety Survey was to assess how often young people encounter unwanted sexual solicitations, pornography, and harassment online. The interview included questions about the existence of online relationships because some youth Internet users have been sexually solicited in the context of these relationships. Youths were asked a series of questions about those with whom they communicated online, distinguishing between communications with people the youth knew "in person" (or "face-to-face") and

people they first met online (i.e., "In the past year, have you been online with people you don't know in person, but you met online through friends or family? For example, a friend introduced you to someone through e-mail?").

All youths were asked, "In the past year, has there been anyone you met on the Internet who you have chatted with or exchanged e-mail with more than once?" Youths who answered yes were asked about casual friendships: "Sometimes when you chat or e-mail with someone several times, they start to feel like friends. I mean you get to know them some and to like them. In the past year, have you started to feel like you were friends with anyone you met on the Internet but didn't know in person?"

Also, all youths were asked three questions about close online relationships. First, "Have you had a close friendship with someone you met on the Internet who you didn't know in person? I mean someone you could talk online with about things that were real important to you." Second, "have you had a romantic online relationship with someone you met on the Internet? I mean someone who felt like a boyfriend or girlfriend." And third, "Has there been anyone you met on the Internet who you later met in person?" Youths who answered yes to one or more of these three questions about close online relationships were asked a series of follow-up questions about "the person you've known online who you've had the most contact with in the past year."

Analysis

Frequencies were run on variables describing characteristics of close online relationships. In some cases, Pearson chi-square tests and odds ratios were used to compare characteristics of groups.

RESULTS

Frequency and Types of Online Communications with Strangers

Most of the youths (55%) used chat rooms, instant messages, e-mail or other forms of online communications in the past year to converse online with people they did not know face-to-face. This 55% included youths who were introduced to online friends by face-to-face friends or family members (38% of youths), youths who met people online through chat rooms, instant messages, and similar forums (33%), and youths who met people online when they were using the Internet to get information for things like school projects (20%). (Some youths were in more than one category.) Thirty-nine percent of youths reported chatting or exchanging e-mail more than once with someone they met online, and 25% reported casual online friendships. Fourteen percent of youths reported a close online friendship, 7% a face-to-face meeting with someone they met online, and 2% an online romantic relationship. Overall, 17% of youths had formed at least one close online relationship in the past year (a close relationship, face-to-face meeting, or romance). Five percent reported more than one type of close online relationship (i.e., a close friendship and a romance or a meeting).

	Table 1 Youth and Household Characteristics	
Characteristic	All youths (N = 1, 501)	Youths with close online relationships (n = 258)
Age of youth		
10	4%	2%
11	8%	3%
12	11%	5%
13	15%	14%
14	16%	15%
15	18%	24%
16	17%	19%
17	13%	18%
Mean age	14.14	14.75
Sex of youth		
Male	53%	48%
Female	47%	51%
Race of youth		
Non-Hispanic White	73%	79%
African-American	10%	7%
American Indian or Alaska Native	3%	1%
Asian	3%	2%
Hispanic White	2%	3%
Other	7%	6%
Don't know/refused to answer	2%	1%
Marital status of parent/guardian		
Married	79%	76%
Divorced	10%	13%
Single/never married	5%	6%
Living with partner	1%	1%
Separated	2%	2%
Widowed	2%	2%
Youth lives with both biological parents	64%	61%
Highest level of completed education in household		
Not a high school graduate	2%	2%
High school graduate	21%	22%
Some college education	22%	24%
College graduate	31%	32%
Postcollege degree	22%	20%
Annual household income		
Less than $20,000	8%	8%
$20,000 to $50,000	38%	39%
$50,001 to $75,000	23%	25%
More than $75,000	23%	22%
Type of community		
Small town	28%	33%
Suburb of large city	21%	18%
Rural area	20%	16%
Large town (25,000 to 100,000)	15%	16%
Large city	14%	15%

Note. Primary caretakers provided demographic information, except for race which was provided by the youths. Some categories do not add to 100% because of rounding and/or missing data.

Gender and age of youths with close online friendships. Girls were more likely than boys (29% vs. 23%, p < .01, OR = 1.4, CI = 1.1 to 1.8) to report casual online friendships. Nineteen percent of girls and 16% of boys had formed at least one close online relationship in the past year (a close friendship, romance or face-to-face meeting). Girls were somewhat more likely to report a close friendship than were boys (16% vs. 12%, OR = 1.4, CI = 1.0 to 1.9), but girls (6%) and boys (7%) were equally likely to report meeting online friends in person and forming romantic relationships (2% for both). Seventy-six percent of the close online relationships occurred among youths who were age 14 and older.

Characteristics of Close Online Relationships

Type of relationship. The majority (95%, n = 246) of the youths who reported close online relationships provided details about one online relationship from the past year (see Table 2). Of these, 75% were identified as close friendships, 41% included face-to-face meetings, and 7% were described as romantic relationships. (Some relationships were in more than one category.) Twenty-three percent of the close friendships involved face-to-face meetings, as did 28% of the romances.

Initial encounters. Fifty-nine percent of close online relationships originated in chat rooms, 30% through instant messages or e-mail, 5% in gaming sites, and 6% some other way. Thirty-two percent of youths were introduced to their online friend by a face-to-face friend or family member. For example, an 11-year-old boy said his grandfather suggested he get in touch with an 11-year-old cousin. Also, several youths mentioned meetings through instant messages based on profiles posted online.

Gender of online friends. Two-thirds of the relationships reported by girls were with boys, and 79% of those reported by boys were with girls. Girls were less likely than boys to report cross-gender relationships (p < .05, OR = 0.5, CI = 0.3 to 0.9). Few of these cross-gender relationships were described as romantic or sexual. Teens who were age 14 through 17 were much more likely to report cross-gender relationships than were the younger youths (79% vs. 50%, p < .001, OR = 3.7, CI = 2.0 to 6.7).

The nature of the relationships. Sixty-four percent of youths stated that common interests drew them to their online friends. Mutual interests specified during interviews included ballet, skiing, skating, paganism, role-playing games, acting, musical theater, Star Trek, scary movies, and comic strips. Several youths mentioned books and reading. Some of the youths volunteered additional details. A 14-year-old girl said she became friends with a 14-year-old boy because they were both "against the porno stuff". An 11-year-old girl said of her friendship with a 16-year-old girl, "I taught her how to pitch a softball over the web." A 14-year-old girl said of her relationship with a 15-year-old boy, "He is a pretty good friend, a close friend, someone I can talk to about personal things."

Several of the youths had established online friendships with adults. A 15-year-old boy said he became close friends with a 24-year-old man when the 15-year-old made a web page for the man's music group. A 17-year-old girl reported a close friendship with a woman in her forties which sprang from encounters in a chat room run by a well-known self-help group. One youth described meeting his 40-year-old uncle online before they ever met face-to-face.

Vicinity of online friends. Eighty-four percent of youths knew where their online friend lived. Few youths reported relationships with people from other countries. Twenty-six percent of the relationships were with people who lived within a one-hour drive of the youths.

Offline contact. Seventy percent of close online relationships included offline contact by mail or telephone after the initial online encounter. Over one-third of youths received telephone calls. Further, 41% of the youths who answered follow-up questions about an online relationship reported face-to-face meetings with their online friends.

Parents' knowledge.

Seventy-four percent of youths said a parent knew about their close online relationship.

Romantic and sexual relationships. Seven percent of youths who answered follow-up questions about a close online relationship called their relationships romantic (n = 18). Most of these youths (61%) were age 14 through 17. Fifty-six percent of these relationships were reported by girls. None involved same-sex partners. Most (72%) were described as both romances and close friendships. About one-quarter (28%) involved face-to-face meetings. Almost all (83%) involved youths who were within one year in age of each other and only one involved an adult who was more than 5 years older. (That instance was a relationship between a 17-year-old boy and a 29-year-old woman. The boy told the interviewer he ended the relationship when he learned the woman was married.)

All youths were asked if their online relationship was "sexual in any way." Only four, all boys ages 14 to 16, said "yes" to this question. The girls with whom they were involved were ages 15 through 17. Three of the four relationships included face-to-face meetings, all three of which were known to the youths' parents. In two instances the girls lived near the boys. The third girl, who did not live nearby, had been introduced to the boy through a friend or family member. The fourth relationship involved two 15-year-olds who had exchanged mail, but there were no phone calls or face-to-face meetings.

Looking at the romantic and sexual relationships together, 22% were initiated by introductions from face-to-face friends or relatives. There was offline contact by mail or telephone in most cases (78%), and parents knew about two-thirds of the relationships.

Characteristics of Relationships Involving Face-to-Face Meetings

Connections with social networks. The close online relationships that resulted in face-to-face meetings were different from other close online friendships in several ways (see Table 2). Significantly higher numbers were initiated through introductions by friends or family, and higher numbers involved online

Characteristic	All (n - 246)	No face-to-face meeting (n - 145)
Table 2 Characteristics of Close Online Relationships with Face-to-Face Meetings Compared to Those with No Face-to-Face Meetings		
Gender of youth		
Male	47%	42%
Female	52%	58%
Age of youth		
10	2%	3%
11	4%	1%
12	5%	6%
13	14%	14%
14	15%	18%
15	24%	24%
16	18%	16%
17	18%	18%
Mean age	14.71	14.75
Age range of online friends		
10 through 13	16%	15%
14 through 17	67%	66%
18 through 24	13%	16%
25 through 44	2%	3%
Age difference of youth and online friend		
Friend 2 or 3 years younger	4%	4%
Same or within 1 year in age	70%	63%
Friend 2, 3 or 4 years older	18%	23%
Friend 5 or more years older	8%	10%
Boy-girl or girl-boy relationship	71%	73%
Type of relationships		
Close friendship	75%	98%
Romantic	7%	9%
Face-to-face meeting	41%	-
Parties met online		
In a chat room	59%	68%
Using instant messages	22%	17%
Through e-mail	8%	5%
In a gaming site	5%	5%
Other	6%	5%
What brought them together		
Same interest	64%	70%
Through family/friend	32%	21%
Getting information	4%	3%
Online friend lived within one-hour drive (n - 210)	31%	9%
Offline contact (multiple answers possible)		
Online friend sent mail	58%	57%
Online friend called on telephone	38%	18%
No offline contact by mail or telephone	30%	40%
Parent knew about relationship	74%	69%
Relationship was sexual in any way	2%	1%
Online friend did something to make youth feel uncomfortable	2%	1%

Table 2 continued	
Characteristic	Face-to-face Meetings (n - 101)
Gender of youth	
Male	55%
Female	48% *
Age of youth	
10	1%
11	7%
12	3%
13	14%
14	12%
15	25%
16	21%
17	18%
Mean age	14.68
Age range of online friends	
10 through 13	18%
14 through 17	70%
18 through 24	10%
25 through 44	2%
Age difference of youth and online friend	
Friend 2 or 3 years younger	3%
Same or within 1 year in age	81%**
Friend 2, 3 or 4 years older	11% *
Friend 5 or more years older	5%
Boy-girl or girl-boy relationship	71%
Types of relationships	
Close friendship	43%***
Romantic	5%
Face-to-face meeting	all
Parties met online	
In a chat room	47%
Using instant messages	30%
Through e-mail	12%
In a gaming site	3%
Other	7%
What brought them together	
Same interest	55%*
Through family/friend	49%***
Getting information	11%*
Online friend lived within one-hour drive (n - 210)	71%***
Offline contact (multiple answers possible)	
Online friend sent mail	58%
Online friend called on telephone	66%***
No offline contact by mail or telephone	16%***
Parent knew about relationship	81% *
Relationship was sexual in any way	3%
Online friend did something to make youth feel uncomfortable	3%

Note. 246 youths answered a series of questions about a close online relationship.
* p [less than or equal to] .05
** p [less than or equal to] .01
*** p [less than or equal to] .001.

friends who lived within an hour of the youths. There was more offline contact by telephone, and more of these relationships were known to parents.

More than half of the face-to-face meetings involved relationships that were not described as close friendships or romances. Virtually all of the youths in this category (89%) lived within an hour's drive of their online friend. (These face-to-face meetings may have been casual events where a youth encountered an online acquaintance at a group event like a high-school game or in the presence of a mutual friend.)

Safety concerns about meetings. Sixty percent of the youths who attended a face-to-face meeting told a parent prior to the meeting. Of those who did not tell a parent, most did tell a friend about the meeting. However, 10% told no one. Also, almost one-quarter of the youths (23%) were alone when they met their online friend. (See Table 3.)

Expectations about online friends. We asked youths who attended face-to-face meetings, "When you first met this person, did she (he look the way you expected she (he) would look?" About four-fifths of youths said yes. Of the 21% who said the individual looked different, personal appearance was the main source of discrepancy. In 4% of meetings, the person's age was different than the youths expected. (The online friends in these cases were all teenagers, with one exception, and that was the uncle, described above, who met his teenage nephew online before they ever met face-to-face.)

Bad Experiences with Online Friends

We asked youths whether their online friends did anything to make them "even a little uncomfortable," or whether anything frightening happened at face-to-face meetings, and we also asked them to rate any discomfort or fright on a scale of one to five and to describe what happened. Two percent of youths (n = 4 reported that their online friend did something to make them uncomfortable and one youth reported being frightened. A 10-year-old girl was a little uncomfortable (1 on a scale of 1 to 5) because a 12-year-old boy told her he loved her. A 15-year-old girl felt a little uncomfortable (1 on a scale of 1 to 5) because her online friend, a 16-year-old boy, "kept talking about death." These instances did not involve face-to-face meetings.

Two youths reported discomfort after face-to-face meetings. A 16-year old boy who described a meeting with an 18-year-old girl was very uncomfortable (4 on a scale of 1 to 5) because she smoked marijuana. Another instance was potentially exploitative. A 16-year-old girl reported a close online friendship with a man in his thirties followed by a face-to-face meeting in a public place. She was a little uncomfortable (1 on a scale of 1 to 5), because he asked her to spend the night in his hotel room. She declined his request. One 16-year-old girl was frightened after a face-to-face meeting with a 17-year-old at a public place. She became afraid (3 on a scale of 1 to 5) when the boy followed her and a friend who had accompanied her from the meeting place.

We also ask whether youths were harmed, saw others harmed, or were exposed to illegal activity at face-to-face meetings. No one reported being harmed or witnessing harm. Except for the marijuana incident described above, no one reported witnessing illegal activity.

Table 3 Characteristics of Face-To-Face Meetings

Characteristics	Face-to-face meetings (n - 101)
Youth told parent about first face-to-face meeting	60%
Youth told friend about first face-to-face meeting, but not parent	29%
Youth told no one about first face-to-face meeting	10%
Someone accompanied youth to first face-to-face meeting	77%
Youth was accompanied by (n - 78)	
Friend	71%
Parent	13%
Sibling or other relative	13%
Other	4%
Meeting was within one-hour drive of where youth lived	82%
Meeting occurred at	
Public place, like mall, pa sports event	71%
Youth's home	5%
Someone else's home	10%
Other	12%
Online friend did not look the way youth expected	21%
What was different than youth expected	
Age	4%
Height or weight	12%
How face looked	15%
The way they dressed	8%
Online friend did something to make youth afraid at meeting	
Youth was physically or sexually assaulted by online friend	0%

Limitations

This is exploratory data. Because online relationships were not the main focus of this survey, we did not attempt to determine the number of online relationships these youths developed or to measure the duration or quality of the relationships. Thus, the relationships that youths described may not typify the full range of close online relationships of youths in general. Moreover, research about youth Internet use is a new undertaking. Procedures for inquiring about this realm have not been standardized or validated, and this study did not use measures that had been evaluated or validated in other research. In terms of the sample, some youths declined or were barred by their parents from participating, and we do not know whether their inclusion would have changed the results. Also, we cannot be sure the youths who participated were fully candid.

DISCUSSION

This survey found that, in the past year, most youth Internet users between the ages of 10 and 17 used the Internet to converse with people they had never met face-to-face. However, most of these online conversations did not lead to close relationships or face-to-face meetings. Some were one-time encounters, and others were short-lived exchanges or casual friendships. Nonetheless, a significant number of youths developed close friendships online (14%), had face-to-face meetings with people they met online (7%), and developed romantic relationships via the Internet (2%). Given the extent of Internet use among young people in the age categories covered by this survey, and given adolescents' natural interest in forming close relationships, the number of youths involved in close online friendships, romantic relationships, and face-to-face meetings with online friends is quite large and likely to increase as Internet use grows.

Age-related characteristics. With a few exceptions, youths were using the Internet to pursue relationships with peers. Most of the close online relationships occurred between youths who were close enough in age that they might attend school together or be together in other environments where teenagers and young adults would commonly meet.

A few of the youths had close friendships with adults who were significantly older. Cases where adults have used online relationships to manipulate and exploit adolescents have been a focus of concern by law enforcement, and we did find one relationship that looked exploitative. However, most of the relationships between adolescents and adults seemed benign. This is probably one of the areas where the Internet reflects "real life." Young people who go online can meet helpful and interesting adults who can offer valuable companionship and advice, but they can also run into people who would cause them harm.

Gender differences. The stereotype that girls, but not boys, use the Internet to form relationships is not bolstered by the data. The boys were as likely as the girls to converse online with people they did not know face-to-face and to report face-to-face meetings and online romances. Girls were somewhat more likely to report both casual and close online friendships, but the differences were not large.

Cross-gender relationships. Interestingly, we found that most close online relationships crossed gender lines. This is in contrast to face-to-face relationships where same-sex relationships predominate (Hartup, 1993). Among youths, the Internet may be serving as an important vehicle for communication between the genders, especially for teenage boys, who reported higher rates of cross-gender relationships than did girls. The unique qualities of Internet communication may facilitate contact between teenage girls and boys in a number of ways. The Internet may provide adolescents with a means of getting acquainted that is free of the distraction and awkwardness generated by the physical presence of someone of the opposite sex. Youths may feel less self-conscious online and more likely to be judged on their "inner" self than on their physical characteristics. For some, communication may be easier because they can compose what they are going to say. Also, teens may feel freed

from adolescent social networks where face-to-face friends and acquaintances can gossip and judge their behavior. The Internet may provide an appreciated level of privacy.

Few of the cross-gender relationships reported on were described as romantic or sexual. Of course, there is considerable anecdotal evidence that youths use the Internet to explore sexual topics. It is possible that youths were not entirely frank about the sexual aspects of the online relationships they reported, or they may not have picked relationships with sexual aspects when they chose a relationship about which to answer follow-up questions. On the other hand, nervousness about adolescent sexual activity may cause adults to have an exaggerated sense of how often young people are using the Internet to pursue sexual interests. In fact, the Internet may be providing a venue for adolescent boys and girls to get to know each other outside of the teen dating context.

Social context of close online relationships. Most of the close online relationships formed by youths intersected with face-to-face social networks, especially in relationships where face-to-face meetings ensued.

These intersections came about in three ways. First, many relationships with online friends were initiated through social networks, when online contact was arranged or suggested by face-to-face friends or family members. Many of these online introductions may have been sparked when mutual friends brought together youths who shared interests, since most close online relationships sprang from mutual interests. The Internet makes communication easy and inexpensive for youths. Outgoing teens may enjoy extending their social networks and pursuing their interests via the Internet, and shy teens may be comfortable approaching other youths by e-mail or instant message or in a chat room, especially when they can claim a mutual acquaintance.

A second way close online relationships intersected with face-to-face social networks is that many involved online friends who lived in the vicinity. The teens in these relationships may have been congregating at local web sites that sometimes act as community Internet "hangouts." Visiting these web sites is the cyberspace equivalent of cruising the local hamburger stand or hanging out at the mall. Youths can also meet other local youths by putting their schools or towns in profiles that are posted online. Many teens who are conversing with online friends who live in their vicinity may be using the Internet to expand their local social circles by meeting youths from neighboring high schools or town.

Third, close online relationships intersected with social networks because most were known to parents. This means youths are probably talking about their online relationships, and their families and friends are probably commenting, questioning and helping teens to make judgments about these relationships. These sorts of conversations allow for some degree of scrutiny of online relationships within face-to-face social networks and some oversight about whether they fit into the larger social networks to which youths belong.

Offline contact. Close online relationships were not confined to cyberspace. Most of the youths had received mail from their online friends and many had talked on the telephone with them. Face-to-face meetings happened in 41% of the relationships which youths described. We did not ask questions about the sequence of different kinds of contact, but our data suggest that online friendships are pursued similarly to face-to-face friendships, with people desiring more contact and more forms of contact as they get to know and like one another. The Internet may be providing new meeting places for adolescents, but relationships that are initiated in cyberspace do not appear to be isolated from other kinds of contact and communication.

Expectations about online friends. The idea that online friends may disguise their true identities and motives is a recurring theme in discussions of online relationships. However, while the reports about face-to-face meetings of parties to online relationships in the data may not precisely represent online relationships as a whole, they do suggest that many online relationships are what they seem.

Safety. Initial face-to-face meetings between online friends are the first point where there is physical contact between them and where misconceptions and deceptions about identity become apparent. These meetings are considered the primary source of danger in online relationships. This survey suggests that while most young people follow basic safety rules about face-to-face meetings, informing parents and bringing friends or family members to meetings, some youths did not take these precautions. This finding is certainly a matter of concern.

In some of these cases, the intersections between close online relationships and face-to-face social networks discussed above probably help to minimize the possibility of deceit and, thus, danger. Mutual acquaintances can vouch for the identities of online friends. Local social networks can provide contacts to verify online identities. Discussions with friends and family members can be "reality checks" for online relationships. It may be that the more ways an online friendship intersects with face-to-face networks, the safer it is. Law enforcement reports indicate that online relationships can be dangerous, and the more dangerous ones may be those that are isolated from the family and friends that youths interact with in daily life. Offline contact by mail and telephone in these relationships may cut both ways. If mail and telephone calls are exchanged in relationships that intersect with networks of friends and family members, they may provide additional means of verifying identity and of determining the compatibility of the relationship. But if these types of contact occur in secret, they may allow for greater manipulation by an exploiter.

CONCLUSION

Given the interest adolescents naturally have in forming close relationships and the amount of time and emotional energy they put into their relationships, it is not surprising that the Internet has become another means by which young people expand their social networks and form close relationships with others. Moreover, in many respects, these online relationships appear to be similar to and to intersect with the face-to-face relationships created and maintained by adolescents.

This is not the first survey to note that Internet friendships are relatively common and that they tend to spill over into real life. Katz (1997) and Parks (1996) reported similar but less detailed results using online samples.

The Internet is a medium with unique qualities. Some of these qualities, like anonymity, may make cyberspace a particularly intriguing place for young people, who tend to be both socially awkward and eager to connect with others. But the Internet is just one of many technological advances to which adults are adjusting and youths are growing up with. It is important to understand the role of close online relationships in the context of adolescent relationships in general and to study their impact on adolescent development. We need to gauge what is safe and healthy about online relationships and what is hazardous, so that their dangerous aspects can be avoided. But it also seems that online relationships are best viewed as integral parts of adolescent life rather than isolated from other aspects of it.

REFERENCES

Armagh, D. (1998). A safety net for the Internet: Protecting our children. *Juvenile Justice*, 5(1), 9-15.

Hartup, W. W. (1993). Adolescents and their friends. *New Directions for Child Development*, 60, 3-22.

Katz, J. E., & Aspden, P. (1997). A nation of strangers? *Communications of the ACM*, 40(12), 81-86.

Kraut, R., Patterson, M., Lundmark, V., Kiesler, S., Mukopadhyay, T., & Scherlis, W. (1998). Internet paradox: A social technology that reduces social involvement and psychological well-being? *American Psychologist*, 53(9), 1017-1031.

Lea, M., & Spears, R. (1995). Love at first byte? Building personal relationships over computer networks. In S. Duck (Ed.), *Under-studied relationships: Off the beaten track* (pp. 197-233). Thousand Oaks: Sage Publications.

Parks, M. R., & Floyd, K. (1996). Making friends in cyberspace. *Journal of Communication*, 46(1), 80-97.

Roberts, D. F., Foehr, U. G., Rideout, V. J., & Brodie, M. (1999). Kids & media @ the new millennium: A comprehensive analysis of children's media use. The Henry J. Kaiser Family Foundation.

Rosenbaum, M., Altman, D., Brodie, M., Flournoy, R., Blendon, R. J., & Benson, J. (2000). NPR/Kaiser/Kennedy School Kids & Technology Survey. Retrieved March 1, 2000, from http:www.npr.org/programs/specials/pool/technology/technology.kids.html.

Turkle, S. (1995). Life on the screen: Identity in the age of the Internet. New York: Simon & Schuster.

The data for this paper came from the Youth Internet Safety Survey, funded by the U.S. Congress through the National Center for Missing and Exploited Children. The authors would like to thank the members of the Family Violence Seminar at the University of New Hampshire for their helpful comments.

Janis Wolak, Kimberly J. Mitchell, and David Finkelhor, Crimes against Children Research Center, University of New Hampshire.

UNIT 7

Teenage Sexuality

Unit Selections

Key Points to Consider

- Are the sex lives of teens any different from the sex lives of other people? How so?

- Do you think it is difficult in the United States to be a gay teen? What are your personal feelings about homosexuality?

- Why are American parents so uncomfortable teaching their children about sexuality? From where do most teens learn about sex?

- Should the schools offer sex education classes? What information should such programs contain?

- Do you think the abstinence or "just say no" programs for sexuality or drugs are working? What other messages do you think might be effective?

- Why and how do politicians play a role in sex education programs? In your opinion, should they be able to dictate what information teachers teach?

 **Links: www.dushkin.com/online/**
These sites are annotated in the World Wide Web pages.

American Sexual Behavior
   http://www.norc.uchicago.edu/online/sex.pdf
CDC National AIDS Clearinghouse
   http://www.cdcnpin.org/
Welcome to AboutHealth
   http://www.abouthealth.com/

Kirk Weddle/Getty Images

Based on the music they listen to, the television shows they watch, or the movies they attend, it is clear that sex is frequently on the minds of adolescents. In fact, one statistic indicates that teenage boys think of sex on the average of once every 5 minutes! Unfortunately for adolescents today, the sexual issues that concern them run the gamut from "When should I start dating?" to "Will I get AIDS?" How has society, whether in the form of the government, schools, or family, dealt with these concerns? The answer seems to be, not very consistently and—frequently—not very well.

The articles in this unit generally pertain to two topics. The first topic is sexual attitudes and behavior of adolescents. The first few articles address the concerns adolescents have about a variety of areas related to sexuality and about how adolescents behave sexually. Although prepubescent children are interested in sex and may engage in some sexual exploration of their own or other people's bodies, interest in dating and in interacting in a sexual manner with others seems to increase rapidly with the on-

set of puberty. The vast majority of adolescents indicate that they have a boyfriend or girlfriend. By age 13 about 20 percent of boys say that they have touched a girl's breasts; a similar proportion of girls concur. By the end of the teen years, the majority of adolescents have engaged in coitus. Ten percent of teenagers in the United States become pregnant each year—twice the rate of other industrialized nations. Twenty-five percent of new cases of HIV are in adolescents under age 18.

Adolescents are clearly engaging in sexual behaviors. This is not only normal, but it is an important part of development. Understanding oneself as a sexual being is a significant component of identity formation. It seems, therefore, that society would want to understand how adolescents view human sexuality. The reality is that research on what adolescents want more information about and how much adolescents already know is surprisingly limited. Part of the reason for this lack of information is the taboos our society has concerning talking about sex. For example, when was the last time a study asking adolescents how often they masturbate was revealed in a popular magazine? Probably not recently. This is a sensitive topic, and parents are reluctant to allow their adolescents to talk about it even though the majority of people have masturbated. How much less is known, then, about the concerns of adolescents who are homosexual—a far more controversial subject? How much is really known regarding how girls feel about sexual harassment and what they are willing to do about it?

Research on sexuality is limited not only by taboos but also by society's clinging to myths about romantic relationships. Ours is a society that worries about adolescent sexuality, yet it does not train adolescents in social skills for dating. Adolescents are presented with the myth that they should find love with no problems, yet, in reality, romance and relationships must be actively worked on. Adolescents are expected to date, but they are not taught how to act on a date, how to communicate with a partner, or how to avoid or remove themselves from uncomfortable situations while on a date. When adults discuss sex with adolescents, they generally focus on the dangers surrounding sexual behavior. They do little to prepare adolescents for the emotional aspects of relationships. Likewise, knowledge about many areas of adolescent sexuality is severely limited.

The articles selected for this first section demonstrate the wide variety of issues faced by adolescents. For example, the first article in this unit covers information about the sex lives of teenagers. The author, Lynn Ponton, suggests that all teens have sex lives, even if only imagined in daydreams. Ponton provides a list of topics for adults who want to discuss sexuality with adolescents. A companion article pertains to adjustment of gay and lesbian youth. They, too, have sex lives or at least sexual imagination which they may keep even more private than do heterosexual teens. What adults who work with these minority youth should know is reviewed in this second article.

The second general topic in this unit involves sex education issues. Research on where adolescents learn about sex has long been performed. The results are quite consistent—adolescents' primary sources of information on sex are other adolescents. Schools and mothers also seem to contribute some information. For example, adolescents are most likely to learn about sexually transmitted disease from teachers. On the other hand, many girls learn about menstruation from their mothers. Fathers are less frequently cited by adolescents as a source of information on sex.

Why aren't parents and schools assuming more responsibility for educating children about sex? Researchers have speculated that parents do not know what to discuss with their children or how to present information effectively. Parents may also be inhibited by their own embarrassment with the topic. This does not mean parents wish their children to be ignorant about sex. Some surveys concluded that 85 percent of American families want schools to include sex education. Part of the reason for this is because parents wish their children to be knowledgeable about transmission of HIV. However, when sex education is left up to the schools, other problems are incurred. For example, what topics should be covered in school? In how much detail should various topics be covered? It may be acceptable to teach adolescents about conception or pregnancy, but if the adolescents bears a child, should the school also teach child care? How much information on prevention and transmission of HIV should be included?

The articles on sex education at this end of this unit include the one entitled, *What to Tell Kids about Sex*. The article basically is about sex education and the controversies that surround it. The author, Kay Hymowitz, claims that sex education programs in schools are changing from abstinence only education to comprehensive sex education programs. Two sister articles offer an in-depth look at one particular controversy swirling around sex education—the role of Congress, both political and financial—in providing sex education in public schools. One essay takes the "yes" side, that Congress should fund more abstinence-only programs while the other essay supports the "no" view that funding only abstinence education puts sexually active teens at risk.

THE SEX LIVES OF TEENAGERS

Lynn Ponton

All teenagers have sexual lives, whether with others or through fantasies, and an important part of adolescence is thinking about and experimenting with aspects of sexuality.

But when are teens ready to become sexually active and when are their parents ready to accept their teens being sexually active? This article explores this question as well as the many taboos and stereotypes that surround our beliefs about teenage sexuality.

TEENS' ATTITUDES TOWARD SEX

I believe that before teens become sexually active they need to ask themselves several important questions including: whether they are engaging in sexual activity for themselves; whether they feel rushed by a partner or the situation; whether their bodies feel ready; whether they trust their partners; and whether they would be comfortable saying no, even at the last minute.

As part of my research for my book, *The Sex Lives of Teenagers*, I had the opportunity to speak with hundreds of teens about what their sexuality means to them. Some answered that it made them feel lovable, or more adult. Some described intense physical pleasure. Some told how it nurtured intimacy with another person or fulfilled a desire to become pregnant, or promoted status in their peer group, or allowed for a surrender to desire or to another person.

For some it brought relief from boredom or escape from life's pressures or an opportunity to test out biological equipment. For others it involved reenactments of a sexually traumatic event from the past, or was useful as a tool for barter in obtaining money or material goods. Some characterized it as an expected part of a current relationship, a representation of "true love," a useful weapon, or a personal expression of growth and spirituality.

CULTURE AND TEEN SEXUALITY

The imperatives about knowing more about adolescent sexuality extend to the culture at large. Our culture is plagued with conflict about how to handle sexuality. Parts of this country are extremely restrictive, discouraging masturbation, homosexuality, and even adolescent sex, and labeling them as crimes, sin, or sickness. Adults try to discourage young people from becoming sexually active by lecturing them about the virtues of virginity and by making it difficult for teens to obtain contraception, rather than by openly discussing sexual matters.

While the views of teenage sexuality presented in the media suggest that the United States is a sexually permissive culture, in fact in contrast to many of the Scandinavian and some European countries, the United States is a fairly restrictive sexual culture characterized by strong taboos, poor communication, and restrictive gender roles.

Teens struggle to discover their sexuality in a culture that is giving them highly conflicted, inconsistent messages. It is a tribute to their energy and power that many are able to develop healthy sexual lives. Many, sadly, are not.

Sexual education efforts in this country are paralyzed by these same conflicts. Many states insist on abstinence-only sex education efforts and do not allow access to contraception or discussion of sexual orientation. Teens' views of their sexuality, however, may differ from those of adults. For many teens, the ways of sex are fraught with struggle, but also filled with excitement and pleasure.

The sexual culture of the United States is not only confused, alternating its message between restrictive and permissive, but violent as well. Violent sexual images are often transmitted through the media, but teens experience this violence in other ways too. Teen's struggling with their sexual identity or orientation fear that violence will be directed at them if they deviate from the norm. this affects all teens at some point in their lives, because at some point almost every teen feels that he or she is sexually different and fears reprisal.

The narrow gender and sexual orientation norms affect all teens. Narrow gender roles force a macho identity on boys who are striving to become men in a patriarchal culture. Boys feel the pressure to rapidly acquire experience and become sexual experts. For girls, the message is more contradictory.

On the one hand, they, too, are encouraged to become powerful with their sexuality, told explicitly and implicitly to use it as their main source of control. On the other hand, girls who do this are often cast out as sluts.

The double standard continues. Teens of both sexes are fearful as they struggle to develop and understand their sexual orientation. Frightened of their own feelings and the culture's reaction, some scapegoat others. Many adults encourage this attitude. Tolerance and understanding of sexual diversity are too little discussed or understood.

IMPACT OF RISK-TAKING

Fifty percent of America's 16-year-olds are having sexual intercourse, a figure that is actually lower than those in many developed countries. The United States excels in one area, however, that of dangerous sexual risk-taking; i.e. unprotected sexual intercourse resulting in unwanted pregnancy and sexually transmitted diseases.

For generations, this country has struggled with adolescent risk-taking of all types. American culture is defined by risk-taking. The successful pursuit of the American Dream virtually requires it, but we are not a society particularly adept at risk assessment.

The general attitude about risk-taking is only one factor that contributes to higher rates of sexual risk-taking, however. Attitudes about sexuality also pay an important role. Into this restrictive, confusing and punitive picture came the Human Immunodeficiency Virus (HIV). The lethal risks associated with HIV have been frightening for parents and teens alike. More than one quarter of those infected with the virus acquire it as teenagers. The crisis has encouraged the United States to begin to examine its attitudes about sexuality.

In a recent interview with Jocelyn Elders, the former U.S. Surgeon General, she said that she believes HIV has done more to change attitudes toward sexuality and sex education than anything else in the past decade. It has forced the United States to look at an area of taboo and to begin talking about teen sexuality. However, Dr. Elders also said, "we need to know what our teens are doing in the backseats of cars, and we don't." She's right about that, and of course it's not just what's going on in cars. Teens are sexually active everywhere—most commonly in their homes. Before we find out where teens are doing what sexually, we need to be able to both listen and talk with them about sexuality.

HIV is one factor that is forcing our culture to reexamine teen sexuality, but there is another—the teens themselves. Gilbert Herdt, professor of sexuality at California State University at San Francisco, notes that young people questioning their sexuality aren't satisfied with the answers they have been given, and are struggling to define a better world, one that is more tolerant and understanding of sexual diversity. Many of these teens have joined support groups, have written about their struggles, and have spoken out on these subjects with peers.

WHAT CAN WE DO?

We need to inform ourselves, consult with others and advocate for children and teens. Many parents know that they should prepare themselves to guide their child through the teen years but when they think about sex, they shut down. Rather than letting embarrassment paralyze them, it should act as a clue, helping parents detect what they are afraid of. In talking with teens about sex, it is important to be direct, using simple language, and admit to your own embarrassment.

In general, teens don't like jokes about sex unless they are telling them, so begin slowly in this area. Enforcing rigid gender roles or sexual orientation can be extremely damaging. The wise parent recognizes that adolescence is about taking risks, sexually and in other ways, and will want his or her teen to have safe, healthy options, even if this means engaging in activity that runs counter to parental values.

Helping society understand this taboo and complex subject may seem overwhelming, but educating ourselves is an important place to begin, followed by having conversations with the teens that we work with and parents. It is a challenge that I believe we are ready for.

Questions for teenagers to ask themselves:

■ Are you doing this for yourself?

■ Do you feel rushed by your partner, the situation, or yourself?

■ Is your body ready? Do you feel physical arousal and desire?

■ Do you trust your partner? Can you talk freely with him/her?

■ Would you be comfortable saying no, even at the last minute?

■ Have you and your partner practiced with other sexual experiences prior to deciding to have intercourse (foreplay using hands, mouth, genital and hip pressing, etc.)?

■ Have you planned for protection from pregnancy and sexually transmitted disease?

■ Are you able to engage in sexual activity without getting drunk or high first?

■ Are you knowledgeable about sex? Do you know what oral, anal, manual and vaginal intercourse are?

■ Have you thought about the impact of this event on your life, considering whether it matches your values?

Lynn Ponton, M.D., is professor of psychiatry at the University of California at San Francisco. She can be contacted by e-mail at lynnponton@aol.com and on the Internet at www.askdrponton.com.

Source: Lynn Ponton: The Sex Lives of Teenagers: Revealing the Secret World of Adolescent Boys and Girls (2000, Dutton).

Know sexual identity, homosexual adjustment issues before counseling GLBT youth

Arthur Lipkin

Even the high-achieving young homosexual can feel like a fraud if his or her status is contingent on concealing a dark secret.

Gay, lesbian, bisexual and transgender (GLBT) students have special problems growing up and keeping safe in environments that tend to be homophobic. Troubled GLBT youngsters confide in teachers and counselors they presume unlikely to be condemning. Sometimes just a passing expression of tolerance can indicate that one is open-minded: a poster on a wall, a book on the shelf, a word spoken against heterosexism.

Clarly, if the adult confidante is uncomfortable in such a role, he or she should refer the student elsewhere for gay-positive counseling, taking care to thank the young person for the trust. But when adults are open to the prospect, they should:

- Have a list of community resources available to GLBT young people.

- Be prepared to listen carefully.

- Be familiar with the issues.

- Know what questions to ask and when to do so.

Trained therapists are usually good listeners. But a student's distress can prompt a well-meaning counselor or teacher to jump in too soon with a "Hooray, you're gay." And as much relief as that sentiment often brings, mere affirmation is rarely enough. Sometimes it may even be distressing.

It takes time to understand each youngperson's world. Every individual brings a different constellation off family history and culture, religion, race/ethnicity, class, age, gender, relational history, degrees of "being out (of the closet)," and amount of contact with the homosexual community.

Not every problem a GLBT student ahs is related to sexuality. Still, these youth face unique challenges to healthy adjustment in the universal adolescent realms of safety, belonging, self-worth, independence, closeness and good relationships, competence and self-awareness.

Harassment begins early

Homophobic name-calling starts in the early grades, where it is both the most common form of name-calling and the kind most feared by all schoolchildren. Harassment intensifies at pre-adolescence and often becomes physical. But schools are not the only dangerous places; intimidation and violence also occur on the playing field, on the streets and even in the home.

Many GLBT youth have no sense of belonging. Alienation from peers, family and church often leads to devastating isolation, the primary cause of suicidality. Though there is ample disagreement over gay teen suicide statistics, no one has challenged the frequency of depression and loneliness that are its precursors. After all, what is more important to an adolescent than fitting in somewhere? We cannot overlook the consequences of exclusion in Littleton, Colorado, where the "goth" misfits, reportedly tormented as "faggots," took others down with them in their suicidal rage.

Establishing self-worth is difficult for all stigmatized minorities. Unlike other minority youth, who most often share identities with their families and can usually depend on a safe and prideful haven from bigotry, gay youth rarely have gay families to come home to. Moreover, they often lack gay-friendly families. Even the high-achieving young homosexual can feel like a fraud if his or her status is contingent on concealing a dark secret.

Conservative attacks on the "self-esteem movement" claim that self-worth should not be encouraged in the "unworthy." What they ignore are the victims of prejudice whose self-esteem is diminished by wanton bombardment. These children deserve a compensatory boost to reach parity with their schoolmates. Once they have learned not to degrade themselves on the irrelevant bases of race, gender, or sexuality, they can move on to better criteria for judging people.

Arthur Lipkin, Ed.D., is the author of Understanding Homosexuality, recently published by Westview Press. This text provides a foundation in gay/lesbian studies and offers models for equity, inclusion and school reform by bringing together topics related to homosexuality and education to make the gay, lesbian, bisexual and transgender experience part of a democratic multicultural vision.

Understanding Homosexuality will help teachers, administrators, counselors and policy-makers understand the significance of gay and lesbian issues in education; aid communication between gay/lesbian students and their families in the school community; promote the inclusion of gay and lesbian curricula in a range of disciplines; and further the healthy development of all students through reducing bigotry, self-hatred and violence.

Understanding Homosexuality is available in hardcover for $69. The book can be ordered from Westview Press at (800) 386-5656.

Achieving independence

Adolescents strive for independence, both practical and moral. But GLBT youth often have difficulty affirming that gay is good in a culture that tells them it is wrong, if not evil. Achieving day-to-day independence also is problematical. They undertake a journey that can jeopardize the material support of family and friends.

Some youth are actually thrown out of the home, fired from work, excommunicated from churches and dismissed from social organizations. Racial, ethnic and religious minority youth who come out as homosexual have a particular fear of cultural disinheritance as a consequence of asserting their sexuality independence.

Closeness and good relationships demand honesty. One cannot bond with family members or peers from whom one hides. Some GLBT youth immerse themselves in academics or hobbies to avoid intimacy. Some become jesters as a shield from personal disclosure; some minister fervently to others' needs to divert attention from their own. Those who cannot be open may seek surreptitious impersonal sex. When self-hatred and secrecy dictate these erotic practices, there is less capacity for deeper connections.

Gays and lesbians may have a hard time developing confidence in their own agency and abilities. Regardless of whether they blame their own sexuality or fault others for being homophobic, the expectation of failure can be self-fulfilling. Psychological assault from family and others contributes to their giving up on themselves. Some gay and lesbian youth doubt their own efficacy because they have struggled in vain against their sexual desires. As adolescent girls, lesbians may feel doubly powerless and lose purposefulness. Schoolwork and attendance may suffer from their lack of confidence as well as fears of ridicule and attack. Then academic failure just reaffirms their sense of incompetence.

At their core, feelings of homosexual ineptitude relate to gender and sex-role stereotyping. Gay has become synonymous with male incompetence and immaturity. Lesbians who embrace "male competencies" are seen to be failures as women. Many gays and lesbians are disconcerted, particularly when they are young, by challenges to their gender identity. Some internalize the idea that their sexuality precludes them from claiming the stereotypical attributes and perfecting the conventional skills of their gender.

Denial inhibits self-awareness

Homosexual youth are deterred from self-awareness by the twin ogres of denial and admonishment. Beset with fear and abetted by a culture that warns against and denies homosexuality, they sometimes are deluded into thinking that they can choose to be someone else. GLBT adolescents have feelings that, once acknowledged, can explode their private and public identities. Inner conflict builds as they grapple with a new self and its certain social stigmatization.

Teachers, counselors and therapists therefore must be well informed about sexual identity development and about homosexual adjustment and counseling issues. We must be able to help troubled GLBT youth rid themselves of any internalized homophobia that interferes with their growth and cripples their resilience. As a precondition we should examine the heterosexist (or internalized homophobic) biases in our own professional practice and interpersonal relationships.

Arthur Lipkin is an instructor at the Harvard Graduate School of Education and founder of the Gay and Lesbian School Issues Project. He is currently directing the Safe Colleges Program of the Governor's Commission on Gay and Lesbian Youth. He can be reached at arthur_lipkin@gse.harvard.edu.

From *The Brown University Child and Adolescent Behavior Letter*, Vol. 15, No. 12, December 1999. © 1999 by Manisses Communications Group. Reprinted with permission.

What to Tell the Kids about Sex

KAY S. HYMOWITZ

SEX education has been the Middle East of the culture wars and one of the longest-running, most rancorous battlegrounds of American social policy. For nearly 40 years, conservatives—many of them, though by no means all, observant Catholics and fundamentalist Christians—have been battling the increasing presence in the public schools of a permissive strain of sex education that came to be known as "comprehensive sexuality education." Unlike sex-ed programs from the first half of the twentieth century that had frowned on teen sex, comprehensive sexuality education affected a morally neutral or even positive stance toward adolescent sexual activity, supporting what was usually described as teenagers' "autonomous decision making," and promoting their use of contraception.

The spread of comprehensive sexuality education in the schools coincided with a steep rise in teen sexual activity. The number of teen girls who had had sex went from 29 percent in 1970 to 55 percent in 1990. Fourteen percent of sexually active teens had had four or more partners in 1971; by 1988, that number had increased to 34 percent. But though sex educators had sought to encourage teens to practice what they called "responsible decision making," their efforts did not seem to be paying off. Throughout the 1970s and 1980s American teenagers were not just having more sex; they were getting pregnant—and at rates that far surpassed those in other industrialized countries. Between 1972 and 1990, there was a 23 percent increase in the rate of teen pregnancy, and there was a similar increase between 1975 and 1990 in births to teen mothers.

The culture war

Thus it is hardly surprising that the new sex ed became a rallying point for the populist uprising that eventually gave rise to Reagan Democrats, the school-choice movement, and other grassroots groups chafing at the social upheavals of the sixties. Traditionalist parents opposed to sex education were often the working- and middle-class mothers of school-aged children. Sex educators, on the other hand, had influential friends in Washington and New York, including Planned Parenthood, the Sexuality Information and Education Council of the United States (SIECUS), and leading professional groups like the American Medical Association. While the federal government never directly funded comprehensive sexuality-education programs, over the years it did provide numerous funding streams, such as that from the Centers for Disease Control's (CDC) Division of Adolescent and School Health (DASH), that were often used to support them.

True, in the early years of the Reagan administration, traditionalists had one notable success in Washington when Congress passed the Adolescent Family Life Act (AFLA), earmarking $11 million for programs to "promote chastity and self-discipline." But "the chastity bill," as it came to be called, became bogged down in the courts when opponents charged that it violated the separation of church and state, and it remained a marginal cause and the subject of much eye-rolling among health professionals. At any rate, by the time AFLA was passed, 94 percent of school districts saw "informed decision making" as the major goal of sex education according to a 1981 study by the Alan Guttmacher Institute, and for years after that, comprehensive sex education, though often sanitized for middle-class communities, was the national norm.

Today, the reign of comprehensive sex ed appears to be faltering. This is largely due to Title V, a junior provision of the Personal Responsibility and Work Opportunity Reconciliation Act (PRWORA), the landmark 1996 welfare-reform bill. Title V put substantial money behind what is now known as "abstinence education"—that is, teaching children to abstain from sexual intercourse. States could receive $50 million a year for five years in the form of a block grant as long as they matched three dollars for every four from the federal government. In 2000, Congress added another abstinence initiative called Special Projects of Regional and National Significance (SPRANS). Today, the federal government earmarks over $100 million annually for abstinence education. But despite close analysis by researchers and journalists on the legislation and its impact on welfare mothers and their children, in the seven years since Congress passed welfare reform, Title V's rationale and legacy remain somewhat clouded.

A broad coalition

Critics and supporters of Title V can agree on one thing: At the time it was passed, it was a profoundly radical initiative. The architects of Title V believed that they were challenging not just the sex-ed establishment but American society overall. In a paper written for the American Enterprise Institute, Ron Haskins and Carol Statuto Bevan, congressional aides closely involved in writing Title V, conceded that "both the practices and standards in many communities across the country clash with the standard required by the law." And this, they wrote, "is precisely the point.... [T]he explicit goal of abstinence education programs is to change both behavior and community standards for the good of the country." Determined to avoid the fate of AFLA, whose language had been broad enough to sneak through some programs that were all but indistinguishable from those run by sexuality educators, the authors of Title V introduced a strict eight-point definition of abstinence education. These were "education or motivational programs" that had as their "exclusive purpose teaching the social, psychological and health gains from abstaining from sexual activity." Abstinence from sexual activity outside marriage, the definition also required, is "the expected standard for all school-age children." The bill allowed some flexibility—funded projects could not be inconsistent with any part of the definition but they didn't have to emphasize each part equally—but Title V was unusually specific, as well as unusually radical.

Yet much as abstinence education was promoted by social and religious conservatives determined to overthrow the liberal, nonjudgmental approach to sex ed, it also benefited from the reluctant backing of moderates frustrated with the status quo and the policies supporting it. Many Title V supporters saw a direct connection between welfare reform and sex-education reform; both could contribute to the battle against out-of-wedlock births tied to government dependency. PRWORA allows states to use a number of strategies intended to discourage out-of-wedlock births, such as a family cap and an end of direct payments to teen mothers; abstinence education was partly intended to be another weapon in that arsenal. Title V's eight-point definition of abstinence education includes several points whose purpose is to plant the ideal of childrearing inside marriage in young minds and to promote the idea that "bearing children out of wedlock is likely to have harmful consequences for the child, the child's parents, and society."

Moderates who eventually got behind abstinence education were also troubled by continuing high rates of teen pregnancy. True, by the early nineties, a decline in teen sexual activity, pregnancy, and abortion began, trends that continue to this day. According to the CDC's Youth Risk Behavior Survey, in 1991, 54.1 percent of high school students reported having sex; by 2001 that number was 45 percent. Those reporting multiple (more than four) partners declined from 18.7 percent to 14.2 percent. Pregnancy rates declined too—the CDC just announced that teen-birth rates decreased by another 5 percent in 2002, for a cumulative 28 percent decline since 1990. However, according to a 2001 study by the Alan Guttmacher Institute, even after the declines of the last decade, teen-birth, pregnancy,

and abortion rates in the United States remain considerably higher than those in France, Sweden, Canada, and Great Britain. Moreover, American girls are more likely to start having sex before age 15 and to have multiple partners than their counterparts in those countries. In the United States, a full 25 percent of high school seniors have already had four or more partners, a much rarer phenomenon in the contrasting countries.

What also made the 1990s decline in teen pregnancy and sexual activity look less impressive was the growing incidence of sexually transmitted diseases. When most parents of today's teenagers were their age, the only widely reported sexually transmitted diseases in the United States were syphilis and gonorrhea. By the last decade of the century, common STDs grew to encompass over 20 kinds of infections. They include not just the one everyone knows, HIV-AIDS, but other viral diseases that can be asymptomatic and that while not fatal, are difficult, and in some cases impossible, to cure. While condom use among teenagers increased—in 2001, 57.9 percent of teens who had had sex reported using a condom in the three months prior to the survey, up from 46.2 percent in 1991—teenagers were still contracting three million STDs every year, far exceeding rates in other industrialized countries.

Everyone for abstinence?

Within a short time after Title V was passed into law, it began to seem that the idea of abstinence for teenagers wasn't so radical anymore. Just about everyone connected to the business of sex education had taken to embracing the word abstinence—to the point of meaninglessness and much terminological confusion. A mere decade ago, abstinence was something of a laughingstock at places like the CDC and state departments of health. These days it is hard to find a state authority, sex-ed program, or organization, including Planned Parenthood, that doesn't promote "teaching abstinence." In using the term, educators sometimes mean they tell teens that abstaining from sex is one option to consider, much as comprehensive sex educators do. By "teaching abstinence," others mean they strongly encourage teens not to have sex, but still offer them information about how to use contraception. Both of these approaches fall under the now commonplace rubric "abstinence plus."

"Abstinence only" educators, on the other hand, teach abstinence as the only acceptable choice and discuss contraception almost entirely in terms of its failure to protect kids from pregnancy and STDs. To make matters more complicated, some abstinence supporters reject the "abstinence only" label as an overly narrow description of their goals and prefer "authentic abstinence." Meanwhile, the National Campaign Against Teen Pregnancy, the most prominent, middle-of-the-road organization in the business, has begun to promote an "abstinence first" message, apparently in order to clarify the ambiguity of "abstinence plus." Significantly, "abstinence only" programs are the only ones eligible for Title V money.

These skirmishes over terminology highlight the fact that even as American opinion leaders have grown more comfortable with the abstinence message, the handshake agreement about "teaching abstinence" only papers over a bitter, ongoing culture war. Not surprisingly, money and jobs, as well as ideology, are at stake.

For all the recent success of the abstinence forces, comprehensive sexuality education remains deeply embedded in the public-health infrastructure. While the number of schools teaching "abstinence only" has clearly grown, they are still in the minority: According to a recent article in Family Planning Perspectives, in 1988, 2 percent of school districts reported teaching abstinence as the sole way to prevent pregnancy whereas by 1999, 23 percent reported doing so. The liberal SIECUS receives money from the CDC to train teachers of curricula on HIV and AIDS that are indistinguishable from comprehensive sex-ed programs. A host of organizations including SIECUS, Planned Parenthood, the National Abortion Rights Action League, various AIDS and gay-rights organizations, as well as the National Association of County and City Health Officials, have begun a campaign entitled NoNewMoney.org to stop the federal government from putting any more funds behind abstinence education.

Meanwhile, teacher unions often balk at abstinence curricula. The New Jersey Education Association has opposed a legislative proposal to "stress abstinence." The National Education Association (NEA) suggests that members in "abstinence only" districts "lobby for those funds to be used in after-school community programs so schools can be free to teach a more comprehensive program." In 2001, the NEA and 34 national organizations including Planned Parenthood, Advocates for Youth, and the ACLU, put out a joint statement declaring abstinence education "ineffective, unnecessary, and dangerous" as well as a form of "censorship" and an "affront [to the] principles of church state separation." A number of states, including California, Oregon, Missouri, and Alabama have introduced "medically accurate" laws on the books that abstinence supporters claim are backhanded attempts to sabotage their programs.

An emotional appeal

What is it these programs actually teach? The most common accusation against them is that they are crude, didactic efforts to get kids to "just say no." Whatever truth this generalization may have held years ago, it does not hold up to careful scrutiny today. For one thing, today's abstinence programs are extremely varied. Title V funds over 700 programs. The Abstinence Education Clearinghouse, a resource organization founded 8 years ago, has 1,300 paid affiliates and includes 74 curricula in their directory, up from 49 just 2 years ago. The early curricula funded by AFLA tended to be created with conservative middle-American communities in mind. Today, many programs—like Title V itself—are targeting lower-income kids. Some programs are aimed at preteens, some late teens, others even in their twenties. Some are community-based, others are school-based. Of those that are school-based, some are one or two sessions, others much longer. Some involve peer mentoring, some adult mentoring, some parental education. Community-based programs might use ad campaigns or cul-

tural events or both. Some programs heavily emphasize delaying sex until marriage; others seem to be aiming to get kids to delay sex at least until they leave high school. Some programs get specific about what sexual behavior is permissible—one talks about avoiding the "underwear zone," another about going no further than holding hands and kissing—and some avoid these details altogether.

Still, today's abstinence programs share a few standard features. The first and most obvious is that they teach, as the Title V definition puts it, that "sexual activity outside the context of marriage is likely to have harmful psychological and physical effects." They aim to impress youngsters with the costs of ignoring the message, much the way drug or alcohol programs do, emphasizing the risk of pregnancy and sexually transmitted diseases. One widely used activity is a graphic slide show of the effects of STDs produced by the Medical Institute for Sexual Health in Austin, Texas. The gruesome slides of genital warts and herpes sores are reminiscent of pictures of diseased lungs shown in antismoking classes. Abstinence educators strongly emphasize—critics accuse them of actually lying about—the failure rate of condoms in protecting against pregnancy and STDs. Where comprehensive sex-ed programs promote safe sex and risk reduction—"Reducing the Risk" is the name of one well-known comprehensive program—abstinence programs are intent on risk elimination.

When critics charge abstinence education with being "fear based," they are overstating things; the newer abstinence curricula spend a relatively short amount of time on this sort of material. But there is no question that some of the warnings against sex tend toward the melodramatic. Abstinence educators are partial to stories of young people who have suffered heartbreak and misery after having sex with an unfaithful or diseased partner. In one of the more extreme examples of cautionary advice, "No Second Chance," a video sometimes shown in abstinence classes that has raised a lot of eyebrows in the media, a student asks a nurse, "What if I want to have sex before I get married?" "Well, I guess you have to be prepared to die. And you'll probably take with you your spouse and one or more of your children."

Most abstinence proponents believe premarital sex is genuinely destructive of young people's emotional and physical well-being, but some of them also cite several tactical reasons for their sensationalism. For one thing, they argue that kids should be scared. Early pregnancy does ruin lives; STDs can as well. It's not enough for kids to know how AIDS is transmitted, they argue; they need to dread the disease. For another, it makes sense to appeal to an age group partial to horror movies and gross-out reality shows—according to Health and Human Services, most programs are addressed to 9 to 14 year olds—through their emotions as well as their reason.

In fact, abstinence proponents believe that emphasizing the emotions surrounding sex sets them apart from the comprehensive sex-ed camp. They argue that comprehensive sex education gives the impression that sexual intercourse is a relatively straightforward physical transaction that simply requires the proper hygienic accessories. Abstinence proponents start with the assumption that sex elicits powerful crosscurrents of feeling that teenagers are unable to manage. Some cite new brain research showing that in adolescents the frontal lobes, the seat of judgment and self-control, are still undeveloped. They also believe that teens are not only incapable of mature, fully committed relationships but that teens have yet even to learn what such relationships are made of.

Character counts

There is much more to these programs than an appeal to the emotions. In the later-model abstinence programs, delaying sex is treated as part of a broader effort to adopt a mindful, take-charge attitude toward life. Curricula usually incorporate goal-setting exercises; some of the more intensive also include character education. The tag line on the cover of the "Game Plan" workbook, part of a curriculum for middle schoolers sponsored by the basketball star A.C. Green from one of the oldest abstinence organizations, the Illinois-based Project Reality, says, "Everybody has one lifetime to develop your Game Plan." The booklet asks students to write down answers to questions like "What are some of your goals for the future?" "What will it take for you to reach these goals?" The workbook also tries to anticipate some of the temptations that lure kids away from their "game plan." "Describe some activities that could make it difficult for you to accomplish your goals," it asks. One section tells students to "think about how much time you spend each day on … TV, radio/CD's, the Internet," and asks them to analyze media messages and consider "whether those messages will help them achieve their goals."

Character education reinforces these sorts of activities. As Operation Keepsake, a Cleveland area program, puts it, the point is "to develop strong character qualities for healthy relationships to endure." Character education is also supposed to promote the autonomy that would help kids resist the unhealthy influence of a powerful peer group and glamorous media. "It's OK to stand against the crowd," Operation Keepsake urges its students. Some programs also add community-service requirements to their character component, such as reading to the elderly at nursing homes.

A Washington D.C.-based program called Best Friends, a highly regarded intervention project created by Elayne Bennett, also emphasizes character development. Bennett developed her program after working with at-risk girls and being struck by how depression and the sense of helplessness often led to sexual activity as well as drug and alcohol use. Bennett was determined to instill in drifting young women a sense of their own efficacy, or what is called in more therapeutic circles "empowerment." Best Friends' Washington D.C. program is used in schools with a large number of high-risk girls, the vast majority of them African-American. Looking at pregnancy rates of the 14 and 15 year olds in her targeted population, Bennett concluded that she had to begin her program at age 11 when "[girls'] attitudes are still forming."

What is unique about Bennett's approach is that instead of softening children's allegiance to the peer group, she tries to turn it into a force for individual improvement. "The best kind of friend is one who encourages you to be a better person," is one of the program's core messages. The girls in a selected class are designated "Best Friends" who meet at least once a month with a teacher, and once a week in a special fitness class, as well as at events like fashion shows, cultural activities, and recognition ceremonies. Once or twice a year there is a motivational speaker, a married woman with a successful career from the surrounding community who tells her life story, including how she met and married her husband, a narrative that Bennett says the girls particularly relish. The program also relies a good deal on mentoring. Each girl has a teacher-mentor from her school with whom she meets 30 to 40 minutes per week when she can complain about trouble with another teacher or talk about problems at home or with friends. Best Friends Foundation now licenses programs in 25 cities, reaching a total of 6,000 girls, and has recently started a Best Men program for boys.

Changing hearts and minds

The most common objection to abstinence education has always been that it turns its back on reality. Kids are going to have sex no matter what you tell them, and the best thing to do is to teach them how to be mature and responsible about it, the argument runs. What evidence do we have that it is possible to teach kids to abstain from sex?

One thing we can say with some certainty is that it is possible to change kids' attitudes on the subject. Mathematica Research, which was awarded a federal grant to examine the problem, is conducting the most rigorous study to date of abstinence education, examining 11 diverse programs each involving 400 to 700 subjects. Mathematica began following its subjects several years ago when the children's average age was 12 and one-half and will continue to do so until they are 16 or 17, so the organization will not have its final results until 2005. But its 2002 interim report confirms that teenagers are open to the abstinence message when teachers are clear about their message and appear committed to kids' well-being. "Youth tend to respond especially positively to programs where the staff are unambiguously committed to abstinence until marriage," the researchers write, "and when the program incorporates the broader goal of youth development." This change in attitude is not likely with less thorough curricula, which kids often view as "just another class."

Indeed, though it's not clear how much abstinence programs can claim credit for the decline in teen sexual activity since the early 1990s, this trend does appear to signal a growing conservatism among young people on sexual matters. In its annual survey of college freshman, the Higher Education Research Institute has shown a decline from 52 percent to 42 percent between 1987 to 2001 of the number of respondents who agree with the statement, "If two people really like each other, it's all right for them to have sex if they've known each other for a very short time." The National Campaign Against Teen Pregnancy conducted a survey in which it asked, "When it comes to teens having sex over the past several years would you say that you have become more opposed, less opposed, or remained unchanged?" Twenty-eight percent of teens said they were more opposed, as compared with 9 percent who said they were less opposed.

Surveys consistently show that somewhere around two-thirds of teenagers who have had sex say they wish they had not. In the most recent example, the National Campaign asked, "If you have had sexual intercourse, do you wish you had waited longer?" Eighty-one percent of 12 to 14 year olds and 55 percent of 15 to 17 year olds answered yes. Some of these responses are undoubtedly influenced by the bedeviling "social desirability" factor, but the very fact that kids believe they should give a positive answer suggests that the abstinence message is not out of line with social attitudes. Interestingly, there are indications that adults are more likely to be skeptical of abstinence than teens. The National Campaign asked in a 2002 survey, "Do you think it is embarrassing for teens to admit they are virgins?" Thirty-nine percent of adults said yes, while only 19 percent of teens agreed, though this finding may conflict with a Kaiser Family Foundation survey showing 59 percent of kids agreeing with the statement, "There is pressure to have sex by a certain age."

What the data show

Regardless, wishes are not horses, and we are still left with the question of whether abstinence education actually makes kids abstain. The answer to that question is less clear. Just about everyone agrees that the decline in teen pregnancy that began in 1991 is partly attributable to a growing number of teenagers delaying sex, though there is vigorous disagreement about just how much can be chalked up to abstinence and how much to improved condom use. At any rate, a national decline in teen sexual activity cannot prove the impact of abstinence education per se, something that has been difficult to measure.

The key problem is finding well-designed research. The few early abstinence programs that did seem to show an impact on attitudes or behavior didn't use the sort of randomized control groups that more exacting researchers tend to trust. There are many studies of kids before and after attending a program, but either there is no control group, the control group comes from a different school, the sample size is too small, there was a follow-up only three months after the invention, but nothing longer term, or some combination of all of these.

"Emerging Answers," a 2001 review of the research on sex education sponsored by the National Campaign Against Teen Pregnancy, included only those programs that had been subjected to research with a rigorous experimental or quasi-experimental design. Douglas Kirby, the report's author and a senior researcher at ETR, an education research organization that also produces comprehensive sex curricula, was able to find only three abstinence programs that satisfied the study's requirements. (By contrast, there were 19 comprehensive programs that did so, of which 5 were considered successful.) And while none of the three abstinence programs could be shown to affect either sexual initiation, pregnancy rates, or condom use, the results do not lead to generalizable conclusions about abstinence

education. All three studies were of older-model programs, and as both Kirby's writings and Mathematica's research seem to confirm, straight didactic programs don't work with any message, abstinence or safe sex.

Another problem is that programs take time to test and refine. Up until two years ago there was little convincing evidence that comprehensive sex education was working. Four years before "Emerging Answers," Kirby wrote other less optimistic review of the research literature on sex education entitled "No Easy Answers," which concluded that "only a few programs have produced credible evidence that they reduced sexual risk-taking behavior," and even those results were limited to the short term.

Still, there are a few studies that provide what even the most scrupulous researchers might be willing to call "some evidence" that several abstinence programs are successful in getting kids to delay sexual initiation. One of the most intriguing, published in the Journal of Health Communication in 2001, looked at a community-based program called "Not Me, Not Now" in Monroe County, New York. In an effort to turn around high rates of teen pregnancy in and around the city of Rochester in the mid 1990s, the architects of "Not Me, Not Now" took a multifaceted approach to the problem: They spread the abstinence message through Internet sites, billboards, and community-sponsored events. Organizers also set up a youth-advisory panel, distributed 50,000 information packets for parents, and pushed abstinence curricula for middle schoolers. The results of the study show a decrease in the number of students who said they could "handle the consequences of intercourse" and a notable decline in sexual activity. Those who reported intercourse by the age of 15 dropped from 46.6 percent to 31.6 percent, and the rate of decline in teen pregnancy in Monroe surpassed that in comparison counties. But questions remain: Are students lying in their survey answers? Were there other interventions in the county that could explain the decline in teen pregnancy? These questions may yet yield firmer answers since "Not Me, Not Now" is one of the programs now being studied by Mathematica.

There are several reasons to anticipate that other abstinence programs will also have good results. The most suggestive finding in "Emerging Answers" is that service-learning programs that include time for contemplation and discussion are the most uniformly effective in getting adolescents to delay sexual initiation—even though they don't teach anything at all about sex. Kirby speculates that kids who are being supervised and mentored as they work in soup kitchens or hospitals develop close relationships with their teachers, increase their sense of competency, and gain a sense of self-respect from "the knowledge that they can make a difference in the lives of others." In general, Kirby finds that effective programs instill feelings of connectedness in kids. A number of earlier studies had shown that children who are more rooted in their peer group have earlier intercourse, while those more attached to their families and schools tend to begin having sex later. Connectedness, competency, and self-respect are precisely the goals of abstinence programs like Best Friends.

It's not just about sex

But the truth is, even if evidence emerges that one particular abstinence-education program drastically reduces teen pregnancy and STDs—or conversely, of a comprehensive program that makes teenagers use condoms 100 percent of the time—sex education will remain a flashpoint in the culture wars. What a society teaches its young about sex will always be a decision founded in cultural beliefs rather than science. In the case of sex education, those beliefs are not about efficacy; they are not even only about sex. They are in part about clashing notions of adolescence. Sexuality educators emphasize teens' capacity for responsible and rational choices and their right to opportunities for self-exploration. They see their role as empowering the young to make their own decisions. Abstinence educators imagine a more impressionable and erratic adolescent. They see their role as guiding the young.

The two camps also presume different notions of identity. Comprehensive sex educators place a great deal of emphasis on gender identity and sexual orientation. Abstinence-only educators, who for the most part don't mention homosexuality, locate identity in character as reflected through qualities like respect, self-control, and perseverance. And finally, there are conflicting notions of freedom at stake. Sexuality educators see freedom as meaning individual self-expression while abstinence proponents tend to understand freedom in a more republican sense—the capacity for personal responsibility that allows individuals to become self-governing family members and citizens.

But it is likely that for most Americans outside the culture-war zone these are not absolute distinctions. One of the most striking flaws of the entire sex-ed dispute is that both sides talk about 13 year olds in the same breath as they do 18 or for that matter 23 year olds. It's unlikely that most Americans see age differences as insignificant. According to Mathematica's interim report, a good deal of Title V money is being directed toward middle schools because there is a general consensus that younger teens need a strong message that they are not ready for sex. Perhaps because they believe that as kids age they develop a firmer sense of identity and have even achieved some measure of character, Americans are not as likely to think the same about older teenagers and young adults in their twenties. Certainly, abstinence until marriage seems an improbable outcome in a society where people marry on average at the age of 26, and where acceptance of premarital cohabitation is widespread. Still, in their appeal to kids' higher aspirations and need for meaningful connections, abstinence proponents are on to something that has been missing in the lives of many children of baby boomers. "My father wasn't a very responsible man. I want to be a better father when the time is right," the 18 year old son of divorced parents told the Indianapolis Star about his decision to remain abstinent. Comprehensive sexual education promises pleasure, but abstinence education pushes honor—and a surprising number of kids seem interested in buying.

KAY S. HYMOWITZ is a contributing editor to City Journal and author of Liberation's children (Ivan r. Dee, 2003).

Should Congress be giving more financial support to abstinence-only sex education? Yes

Abstinence is working to decrease teen pregnancy and is building character among our nation's youth.

Kathleen Tsubata

The current tug-of-war between "abstinence-only" and "comprehensive" sexual-education advocates is distracting us from the real issue. We are in a war against forces far more unforgiving than we ever have encountered. We must look at what works to save lives. My work brings me to deal with teens every day, in public schools, churches and community organizations, teaching HIV/AIDS prevention. I train teens to teach others about this genocidal plague that is sweeping nations around the world and depleting continents of their most-productive population. I can tell you that most teens have a very superficial understanding of HIV and that many are putting themselves at risk in a wide variety of ways.

While teen pregnancy is serious, it is still, in one sense, the lesser evil. It's a difficult thing to bear a child out of wedlock, with the accompanying loss of education, financial stability and freedom. However, compared to HIV, it's a walk in the park. Make no mistake about it: The choice of sexual activity is a life-and-death matter, as Third World nations are finding out in stark terms.

Having multiple sexual partners is the No. 1 risk factor for contracting HIV and 19 percent of teens have had four or more sexual partners.

"So teach them to use condoms!" we are told. Studies indicate that condoms, if used correctly and consistently, may lower the transmission rate to 15 to 25 percent. That's not a fail-safe guarantee, as any condom manufacturer under litigation quickly would point out.

But there are two additional problems with condoms being the central pillar of HIV prevention. First, correct usage of condoms is hard to achieve in the dimly lit, cramped back seat of a car. Second, and more importantly, kids simply make decisions differently than adults. Janet St. Lawrence, of the Centers for Disease Control and Prevention (CDC), related the results of one behavioral study to me in a phone conversation last year. In that study, teens reported using a condom for their first sexual contact with someone, and subsequent contacts, "until they felt the relationship was permanent," St. Lawrence said. Then they stopped using condoms. These teens were asked what defines a "permanent" relationship. "Lasting 21 days or longer," was their response. In other words, such a teen could start a relationship, initiate sex using a condom, decide after three weeks that it is "safe" to stop using a condom, break up and replay the whole cycle, convinced that this was responsible sexual behavior.

Teens are not realistic because they are young and not fully developed in key mental and emotional areas. They tend to imbue love with magical properties, as if the emotion is a sanitizing force, and that their trust can be shown by the willingness to take risks. Kids process information differently than adults. Parents know this. Saying "It's best not to have sex, but if you do, use a condom" is translated in their minds to "It's okay to have sex if you use a condom." Then, if they feel "this is true love," they convince themselves that even that is unnecessary. That's why during four decades of sex education we witnessed steep increases in sexual activity and the consequential increases in teen pregnancy, sexually transmitted diseases and poverty.

Only when abstinence education began in recent years did the numbers of sexually active teens go down - a full 8 percentage points from 54 percent of teens to 46 percent, according to the 2001 Youth Risk Behavior

Surveillance, published by the CDC. Simultaneously, teen pregnancies went down, abortions went down and condom use went up among those who were sexually active. Raising the bar to establish abstinence as the best method indirectly resulted in more-responsible behavior in general.

You would think such good news would have people dancing in the aisles. Instead, the safe-sex gurus grimly predict that increased abstinence education will result in teens giving in to natural urges without the benefit of latex. Or, the critics of abstinence-until-marriage education insisted that their programs (which pay lip service to abstinence) somehow reached teens more effectively than the programs that focused on abstinence. A third interpretation is that contraception, not abstinence, has lowered the numbers.

However, a study of lowered teen-pregnancy rates between 1991 and 1995 (published in Adolescent and Family Health by Mohn, Tingle et al., April 2003) showed that abstinence, not contraceptives, was the major cause of the lowered pregnancy rate. Another 1996 study, by John Vessey, of Northwestern University Medical School, followed up on 2,541 teens, ages 13 to 16, who completed an abstinence-education program. He reported that one year after completing the program, 54 percent of formerly sexually active teens no longer were sexually active. This puts to rest the idea that "once a teen has sex, they will continue to be sexually active."

It often is claimed that most parents want pro-contraceptive education for their kids. In fact, a nationwide Zogby International poll of 1,245 parents in February (see poll results at www.whatparentsthink.com) commissioned by the pro-abstinence Coalition for Adolescent Sexual Health found that when shown the actual content of both comprehensive and abstinence-only sex-education programs, 73 percent of parents supported abstinence education and 75 percent opposed the condom-based education, with 61 percent opposing the comprehensive sex-ed programs.

But what do teens themselves think? In a 2000 study by the National Campaign to Prevent Teen Pregnancy, 93 percent of the teens surveyed said there should be a strong message from society not to engage in sex at least until graduation from high school. Will abstinence education cause sexually active teens to be unable to find out about contraception? The small amount in abstinence-education funding requested by Congress ($135 million among three programs) is miniscule compared with the $379 million funding of only six of the 25 federal programs teaching contraceptive-based education. This is Goliath complaining that David is using up all the rocks.

But, in all good conscience, can we teach something that would put kids in danger of contracting HIV, even if at a somewhat-reduced risk? Can we glibly decide, "Oh, only 15 percent of users will die?" That's acceptable? The stakes simply are too high. Even one life is too important to lose. When we're talking about life and death, we can't settle for the soggy argument of "Kids are going to do it anyway." That's what used to be said about racial discrimination, drunk driving and cigarette smoking, but when people became serious about countering these behaviors, they receded. If we realize the necessity of saving every teen's life, we can't help but teach them that because sex is wonderful, powerful and life-changing, it must be treated with great care.

Sex is most pleasurable and joyful when there is no fear of disease, when both partners feel absolute trust in the other, when the possibility of a pregnancy is not a destructive one and when each person truly wants the best for the other. This takes self-development, investment, emotional growth, responsibility and a whole host of other elements a typical teen doesn't possess, unless they are guided. In reality, every person already is aware of the need to limit sexuality to certain times and places, like many activities. Sexuality is far more complex than the physical mechanics of orgasm. That stuff is pretty much automatic. It's far more important to know that orgasm is the perfectly engineered system for creating life, and for experiencing the fulfillment of love.

Abstinence isn't a vague ideal but a practical, feasible life skill. Studies show that kids who are able to say no to sex also can say no to drugs, alcohol and tobacco. The skills in one area automatically transfer to other areas of health. Learning to delay gratification can have positive impacts on academic goals and athletic accomplishments.

Without the soap-opera distractions of sex, kids feel more confident and free to enjoy the process of making friends, developing their own individuality and working on their dreams. That's why virtually no one looks back on the decision to be sexually abstinent and says "I wish I had never done that." But 63 percent of teen respondents who have had sex regretted it and said they wish they had waited, according to an International Communications Research of Media survey in June 2000 commissioned by the National Campaign to Prevent Teen Pregnancy. Further, 78 percent of the 12- to 17-year-old respondents said teens should not be sexually active, and only 21 percent thought sex for teens was okay if they used birth control.

Teens are telling us that they need support to resist the pressure to have sex. Even just making an abstinence pledge was found to delay sexual debut by 18 months on average, according to the National Longitudinal Study on Adolescent Health in 1997. And teens who know their parents have a strong belief and expectation of abstinence are far more likely to abstain, as shown in two 2002 studies released by the University of Minnesota Center for Adolescent Health and Development in which more than 80 percent of teens stayed abstinent when they knew their mothers strongly disapproved of premarital sex.

Even if it were only to end the spread of HIV/AIDS, that would be a valid reason to support abstinence education.

But teaching abstinence goes beyond preventing disease and unwanted pregnancy. It helps kids improve in the areas of self-esteem, academic attainments and future careers. It increases refusal skills toward drugs, alcohol and smoking. It equips teens with tools that they will use successfully throughout life, especially in their eventual marriage and family life. In other words, it has a positive ripple effect both in terms of their current and future life courses. In my estimation, that definitely is worth funding.

Tsubata is a regular contributor to the Washington Times as well as co-director of the Washington AIDS International Foundation. She teaches HIV/AIDS prevention in public schools and community venues and trains teens as peer educators. E-mail Kathleen Tsubata at kate@waifaction.org.

Should Congress be giving more financial support to abstinence-only sex education? No

Withholding information about contraception and teaching only abstinence puts sexually active teens at risk.

Cory Richards

Helping young people to understand the benefits of delaying sexual activity and to resist peer pressure is, and clearly should be, a cornerstone of sex education in the United States. Virtually no one disputes the importance of abstinence education. But support for abstinence-only education-which ignores or actually denigrates the effectiveness of contraceptives and condoms-is not based on scientific evidence; rather it is driven by a subjective moral and, for many, religious agenda. The nation's leading medical, public-health and educational organizations endorse sex education that includes positive messages about the value of delaying sexual activity along with information about condoms and contraceptive use to avoid sexually transmitted diseases (STDs) and unintended pregnancy. Public-opinion polls show that this also is the position of parents, teachers and young people themselves in the United States.

What does the evidence show?

- Teen-agers and young adults are at risk of unintended pregnancies and STDs for almost a decade between the time they initiate sexual activity and when they get married. By their 18th birthday, six in 10 teen-age women and nearly seven in 10 teen-age men have had sexual intercourse.
- Teen-age pregnancy happens. Nearly 900,000 American teen-agers (ages 15-19) become pregnant each year, and almost four in five (78 percent) of these pregnancies are unintended.
- Other countries do better. Despite recent declines, the United States has one of the highest teen-age pregnancy rates in the developed world. U.S. teen-agers are twice as likely to be- come pregnant as teen-agers in England, Wales or Canada and nine times as likely as those in the Netherlands and Japan.
- Teen-agers and young adults are at risk of STDs and HIV/AIDS. Four million teen-agers acquire an STD annually. Half of the 40,000 new cases of HIV infection in the United States each year occur to individuals younger than age 25. This means that every hour of every day an average of two young people become infected with HIV.
- Contraceptives and condoms are effective. While it is true that successfully abstaining from sexual activity is the only 100 percent guaranteed way of preventing pregnancy and disease, abstinence can and does fail. Extensive research demonstrates that correct and consistent use of contraceptives, including condoms, radically reduces one's risk of pregnancy and disease among those who are sexually active.

Despite the clear need to help young people make safe decisions regarding sexual activity so that they can delay the initiation of sexual intercourse and protect themselves from unintended pregnancy and STDs when they become sexually active, U.S. policymakers continue to promote school-based, abstinence-until-marriage education that fails to provide accurate and complete information about condoms or other contraceptives.

Overall, federal and matching funding from states for abstinence education that excludes information about contraception has totaled more than $700 million since 1996. There is, on the other hand, no federal program dedicated to supporting comprehensive sex education. Federal law contains an extremely narrow eight-point definition of abstinence-only education that sets forth specific messages to be taught, including that sex outside of marriage for people of any age is likely to have harmful physical and psychological effects. Because funded programs must promote abstinence exclusively, they are prohibited from advocating contraceptive use. They thus have a choice: They either must refrain from discussing contraceptive methods altogether or limit their discussion to contraceptive failure rates. Further, in many cases federal law prevents these programs from using their private funds to provide young people with information about contraception or safer-sex practices. Yet even today, many policymakers remain unfamiliar with this extremely restrictive brand of abstinence-only education required by federal law.

Considerable scientific evidence shows that certain programs that include information about both abstinence and contraception help teen-agers delay the onset of sexual activity, reduce their number of sexual partners and increase contraceptive use when they do become sexually active. Indeed, leading medical, public-health and educational organizations, including the American Medical Association, the American Academy of Pediatrics, the American College of Obstetricians and Gynecologists and the National Institutes of Health, support sex-education programs that both stress abstinence and teach young people about the importance of protecting themselves against unintended pregnancy and disease when they become sexually active.

In contrast, there have been few rigorous evaluations of programs focusing exclusively on abstinence. None of these has found evidence that these programs either delay sexual activity or reduce teen pregnancy. Finally, research on virginity-pledge programs and HIV-prevention efforts suggests that education and strategies that promote abstinence but withhold information about contraceptives (and condoms, in particular) may have harmful health consequences by deterring the use of contraceptives when teens become sexually active.

Despite similar levels of sexual activity among American teen-agers and their counterparts in other developed countries, teen-agers in this country fare worse in terms of pregnancy and STDs. U.S. teenagers are less likely to use contraceptives, particularly the pill or other highly effective hormonal methods. U.S. teen-agers also have shorter relationships and thus more sexual partners over time, increasing their risk for STDs. Evidence from other developed countries, moreover, suggests that when teen-agers are provided with comprehensive education about pregnancy and STD prevention in schools and community settings, levels of teen-age pregnancy, childbearing and STDs are low. Adults in these other countries give clear and unambiguous messages that sex should occur within committed relationships and that sexually active teen-agers are expected to take steps to protect themselves and their partners from pregnancy and STDs.

On certain topics, there is a large gap between what sex-education teachers believe they should cover and what they actually are teaching. The great majority of sex-education teachers think that instruction should cover factual information about birth control and abortion, the correct way to use a condom and sexual orientation. However, far fewer actually teach these topics, either because they are prohibited from doing so or because they fear such teaching would create controversy. As a result, a startling one in four teachers believes they are not meeting their students' needs for information.

The gap between what sex-education teachers think should be covered and what they actually teach particularly is acute when it comes to contraception. Sex-education teachers almost universally believe that students should be provided with basic factual information about birth control, but one in four teachers are prohibited by school policies from doing so. Overall, four in 10 teachers either do not teach about contraceptive methods (including condoms) or teach that they are ineffective in preventing pregnancy and STDs.

What many students are being taught in sex-education classes does not reflect public opinion about what they should be learning. Americans overwhelmingly support sex education that includes information about both abstinence and contraception. Moreover, public-opinion polls consistently show that parents of middle-school and high-school students support this kind of sex education over classes that teach only abstinence.

Parents also want sex-education classes to cover topics that are perceived as controversial by many school administrators and teachers. At least three-quarters of parents say that sex-education classes should cover how to use condoms and other forms of birth control, as well as provide information on abortion and sexual orientation. Yet these topics are the very ones that teachers often do not cover. Finally, two out of three parents say that significantly more classroom time should be devoted to sex education.

Similarly, students report that they want more information about sexual-and reproductive-health issues than they are receiving in school. Nearly one-half of junior-high and high-school students report wanting more factual information about birth control and HIV/AIDS and other STDs, as well as what to do in the event of rape or sexual assault, how to talk with a partner about birth control and how to handle pressure to have sex. Young people also need to receive information sooner: More than one-quarter of students become sexually active before they receive even a rudimentary level of sex education such as "how to say no to sex."

Abstinence-only programs also can undermine students' confidence in contraception by providing unbalanced evidence of its ineffectiveness. These programs miss the opportunity to provide students with the skills they need to use contraceptives more, and more effectively. Instead students may leave the program thinking that pregnancy and STDs are inevitable once they begin having sex.

To be sure, promoting abstinence to young, unmarried people as a valid and realistic lifestyle choice should remain a key component of sex education. But those who argue that this is the only message that should be provided to young people are misguided. The evidence strongly suggests that sex in the teen-age years-and certainly prior to marriage, which now typically occurs in the mid-20s is and will continue to be common, both in this country and around the world. Undermining people's confidence in the effectiveness of condoms and other contraceptive methods as a means of scaring them out of having sex is just plain wrong. Protecting our young people requires a balanced approach that emphasizes all the key means of prevention including effective contraceptive and condom use, as well as delaying sex. Ultimately, only such a comprehensive approach will provide young people with the tools they need to protect themselves and to become sexually healthy adults.

Richards is senior vice president and vice president for public policy at the Alan Guttmacher Institute and editor of The Guttmacher Report on Public Policy. He writes and lectures widely on sexual- and reproductive-health-related public-policy concerns. Contact Cory Richards at policyworks@guttmacher.org.

UNIT 8

Problem Behaviors and Interventions

Unit Selections

Key Points to Consider

- Why are teen suicide rates so high? Can we do anything to prevent teen suicide?

- Do you think adolescents are moody? How could you tell whether an adolescent friend is grumpy versus clinically depressed?

- Are American youth becoming more antisocial or uncaring about others? If yes, what do you think accounts for the trend?

- What drugs are popular with teens? What are the dangers of experimentation or consistent use of illicit drugs to teens?

- What is an eating disorder? Who is prone to such disorders? How are the various eating disorders treated?

- How has terrorism changed the way teens view the world? Or, are American teens fairly unaffected by terrorist events? For example, is pop culture more important to them? If so, why?

 **Links: www.dushkin.com/online/**
These sites are annotated in the World Wide Web pages.

Mental Health Net: Eating Disorder Resources
http://eatingdisorders.mentalhelp.net/

Mental Health Risk Factors for Adolescents
http://education.indiana.edu/cas/adol/mental.html

Questions & Answers about Child & Adolescent Psychiatry
http://www.aacap.org/about/q&a.htm

Suicide Awareness: Voices of Education
http://www.save.org/

Youth Suicide League
http://www.unicef.org/pon96/insuicid.htm

Natasha refused to go to school. Her parents could not understand why their daughter would not go. Finally, Natasha explained to her parents that school violence and bullying, substance abuse, and other issues made her school unsafe. She worried so much about safety that she was unable to learn. Are these issues what come to mind when adults think of adolescents? Do most teens feel as Natasha does? Are teens more vulnerable than either children or adults? Most importantly, how can the problems associated with adolescence risk-taking be prevented?

That adolescents can and do engage in high risk behaviors is not subject to much debate. The statistics on adolescent fatalities demonstrate their risk-taking behavior. The leading causes of death in adolescents are tragic: accidents, suicide, and homicide. Alcohol use is frequently involved, particularly in motor vehicle accidents. About half of the fatal motor vehicle accidents involving an adolescent also involves a drunk peer driver.

Why adolescents engage in high-risk behaviors is much debated. Some researchers believe that adolescent risk taking is related to cognitive development. They propose that adolescents possess a sense of invulnerability. Adolescents believe they are special and unique; things that could happen to others could not possibly happen to them. Other researchers believe at best this may apply only to young adolescents. By their midteens a majority of adolescents are too sophisticated to consider themselves invulnerable. Despite this, however, adolescents still take more risks than do adults.

If older adolescents do not perceive themselves as invulnerable, then why do they take risks? There are several possible explanations. One proposal is that adolescents may not perceive the risk. For example, adults may have a better sense of how fast they can safely drive given differing road conditions. Adolescents, simply because they are inexperienced drivers, may not recognize when road conditions are dangerous and so may not adjust their speed. Adolescents may engage in riskier behaviors than adults simply because they have the time and energy. Many adolescents have free time, money, and a car. Access to these may allow adolescents to put themselves in dangerous situations. Adults may work, do more household chores, and take care of their children. These adults may not have the time to drink, or take drugs, or joy ride.

Adolescents may also be less adept than adults at extricating themselves from high-risk behavior. For example, adults who attend a party where drugs are consumed may be more comfortable declining offered drugs than adolescents or they may be able to leave the party without depending on transportation from others. Some researchers indicate that society may be somewhat to blame for adolescents' risk taking. If impoverished adolescents have no chance of obtaining meaningful work, have limited access to recreational activities, and have little encouragement to go to school, then participation in drug-related or violent behavior may be the only options open to them. It may be up to society to provide these adolescents with an increased number of safe choices.

Adolescent risk taking activities can take many forms. The U.S. Public Health Service identifies several categories of behavior related to health risks for adolescents. Included are behaviors that may cause injuries, such as suicide and violence, use of tobacco or illicit drugs (including alcohol), and risky behaviors related to sexuality or eating disorders. All these can clearly threaten adolescents. Moreover, alcohol use seems to exacerbate many of the other risks, as indicated by the statistics on alcohol use and violent death. And drug use can be related to accidents, health problems, and violence. Violent behaviors are an increasing concern to society. Murder is the second leading cause of death in adolescence; it is the leading cause of death for African American male teenagers. Suicide rates in young people have tripled since the 1950s. Eating disorders are another threat to adolescents. Millions of adolescents suffer from anorexia nervosa or bulimia in the United States.

The articles in this unit investigate many of these issues. The first article concerns adolescent suicide. One reason suicide may occur is the failure to construct a healthy identity. Using Erikson's theory, the authors probe this issue in depth. The second article also relates to teen suicide. Perhaps depression is the precursor to adolescent suicide. In the next article by Harold Koplewicz, the author explains that depression may account for suicide and many other negative adolescent behaviors, including violence and wanton callousness toward others.

Barbara Penoyar/Getty Images

Along these same lines, the third article is about aggression and antisocial behavior in adolescents. The article raises the issue of undetected psychopathology as an explanation for violence and aggression in adolescence. Another explanation for risky behaviors in adolescence may be drug use. Ecstasy seems to be the rave for teens. How high school staff and parents can detect ecstasy use is at the center of the next article.

Two other issues that put adolescents at risk are the established issue of eating disorders and the newer issue of terrorism.

Teens are subject to eating disorders in our thin-obsessed world. It is easier to prevent such disorders than it is to "cure" them. Prevention usually falls on the shoulders of the parents, so this article explicates what parents can do to spot potential eating problems and prevent them. Finally, the newly reared head of terrorism can affect adolescents. Because fear of terrorism has made the world appear riskier, today's teens may well perceive a heightened fear of death and of anxiety in general.

Understanding Adolescent Suicide: A Psychosocial Interpretation of Developmental and Contextual factors

By Pedro R. Portes; Daya S. Sandhu; Robert Longwell-Grice

Adolescent suicide remains an international tragedy, yet a common denominator continues to elude researchers. Some adolescents internalize rejection and respond with suicide; other troubled adolescents engage in homicide before ending their own lives. One factor underlying suicide concerns the failure to construct a healthy identity. Using Erikson's theories on identity development as a framework, this paper examines the motives for and contexts of suicide among preadolescents, adolescents, and young adults, identifies specific school-age populations that are vulnerable to suicide, and discusses implications.

Suicide is a complex problem with ideology or beliefs as a common element that interacts idiosyncratically with any number of emergent identities pressing on the individual. One factor underlying suicide concerns the failure to construct a healthy identity. Much of the research on this issue focuses on adolescence, the period of time when individuals are most engaged in developing a healthy identity (Erikson, 1968; Coleman & Remafedi, 1989; Bar-Joseph & Tzuriel, 1990; Newton, 1995). Erikson (1968) noted that in extreme instances of delayed and prolonged adolescence, complaints of "I give up" and "I quit" are more than signs of mild depression—they are expressions of despair. Erikson acknowledged that suicide itself is an identity choice for some adolescents. Furthermore, suicide is increasingly occurring among people who are not adolescents, which may have to do with the inability to master Erikson's stages of development throughout the lifespan, beginning early in life.

Accomplishing developmental tasks in a given cultural context requires a sense of connectedness. As the institution of the family, which is the primary engine for healthy socialization, has weakened in modern society, individuals' risk for disturbances in identity formation mounts. For suicidal individuals, the family and society may have failed to provide the necessary conditions for sound development.

New trends in suicide are emerging for practically all ages and walks of life. Children, adolescents, and young adults appear to share in this "mis-solution," yet for quite different reasons. The purpose of this paper is to examine, within an Eriksonian framework, the different motives for and contexts of suicide among these three groups, to identify specific school-age populations that are vulnerable to suicide, and to discuss implications for school counselors and others. In so doing we will also look at how firearms and gender differences relate to suicide in the United States.

SUICIDE WITHIN AN ERIKSONIAN FRAMEWORK

The reasons for suicide vary, but seem to cluster around disruption of specific developmental tasks, vulnerability of the individual, and risk conditions in the immediate situation of the individual, such as lack of emotional support. From a sociocultural perspective, new norms may emerge (e.g., legalization of assisted suicide). Both the characteristics of the individual and the culture appear to interact in suicide ideation and attempts. This interaction becomes particularly life threatening when identity formation is obstructed in ways that the individual considers impossible to resolve.

Individuals who take their own lives vary in age. What prompts a 16-year-old to commit suicide as opposed to a 60-year-old? We need to recognize the different motives and life situations among children, adolescents, adults, and the elderly. According to Erikson (1963, 1968), there are eight stages in the lifespan, each of which poses conflicts or crises that need to be resolved positively and in a prosocial manner. Failure to do so may impact a person's personality development in a negative and cumulative way. Such failure may be understood as an important risk factor in the etiology of suicide and violent behavior.

Erikson was among the first theorists to indicate the importance of social context in understanding individual development. He witnessed the violence that took place during much of the twentieth century, and conflict resolution figured prominently in his work as he sought to establish a nexus between the individual and society. Some extensions of his work and other cultural-context models are presented here, with a focus on suicide. It is hoped that this will provide a means for understanding the socioemotional disturbances influencing life-threatening behavior.

Preadolescents

Research by Greene (1994) dispels many myths surrounding the suicide of children. Greene showed that children under the age of six experience true depression and that they are cognitively and physically able to implement a suicide plan. As Pfeffer (1993, 1994) shows, children are not too young to consider death. However, the exact mediating circumstances remain unclear from a theoretical perspective.

According to Erikson, how each developmental task is resolved (e.g., infancy: trust versus mistrust; early childhood: autonomy versus doubt and shame; preschool age: initiative versus guilt; school age: industry versus inferiority) defines to a considerable extent how healthy or unhealthy the person becomes and how well he/she is able to deal with future tasks or crises. The developmental history of the person varies depending on the extent to which trust was established in early attachments, a view that is currently well established (Bowlby, 1988). Failure to establish trust contributes to insecurity and poor adjustment in later life. Similarly, failure to establish autonomy leaves the individual subject to shame and doubt, which again can be carried over to the next stage. These may be seen as part of the maladjustment problems of children who internalize or externalize their anger. Anger emerges when socioemotional needs are not met in the contexts where development takes place, and this anger precedes violence. The antecedents of life-threatening behavior thus appear related to what may be regarded as a developmental sequence or syndrome rather than to any one specific experience.

If during this period prior to adolescence children are able to develop confidence by doing something well (i.e., learn to be competent and productive), they will be more likely to carry that confidence into the future. If during this time they fail at their endeavors and do not have a nurturing environment to give them support, they will more than likely carry feelings of inferiority and low self-esteem into their future developmental tasks. Parental separation and family dysfunction are generally associated with violent behavior at this age, particularly where conflict and anger have been present in the child's experience.

In our view, failure to resolve preadolescent crises successfully does appear to present a cumulative risk for suicide. This failure generally signals interference in the bonding process.

Adolescents

According to Erikson, individuals attempt to resolve the issue of identity versus role confusion during the teenage years. Adoles-

cents try to answer the question "Who am I?" so as to establish an identity in the sexual, social, ideological, and career domains. They often experience considerable stress in a variety of contexts as they attempt to forge an identity (Lock & Steiner, 1999). For example, the changing sex roles of men and women may exacerbate identity confusion. In addition, environmental stressors such as parental pressure for academic achievement, family mobility, the availability of drugs, and peer pressure can lead to depression (Capuzzi, 1994). Suicide seems to occur when stress, cognitive immaturity, and lack of emotional bonding interact and overwhelm an individual's ability to cope and to reason clearly. In one study, adolescents who had attempted suicide reported significantly more stress related to parents, lack of adult support outside the home, and sexual identity than did control groups (Wagner, Cole, & Schwartzman, 1995). Mood disorders are generally found in this population (Archer & Slesinger, 1999).

Some teenagers come from families with high expectations which, when coupled with identity confusion, feelings of inferiority, biological changes, and low self-esteem, are often too much to handle. In one study, school professionals were asked to identify individual, familial, and sociocultural factors which might make adolescents more vulnerable to suicide. Of 450 responses, half focused on the impact of the family; lack of parental support and alienation from and within the family were considered key risk factors (Grob, 1983). In the literature, parental absence or unavailability, poor communication between family members, conflict within the family, high parental expectations for achievement, and overt family pathology are generally considered the main risk factors.

Suicidal ideation is related to psychosocial distress, drug involvement, family stress, and unmet school goals (Thompson, 1994). Many adolescents become involved with drugs or alcohol in an attempt to reduce tension. Further, many adolescents who commit suicide are heavy users of alcohol or drugs (Laws & Turner, 1993). This suggests a two-factor process. First, drugs may provide some initial relief from distress. However, in masking distress chemically, the individual's cognitive development is undermined just as he or she may be beginning the difficult transition to formal operations. Drugs also tend to alienate the individual from his or her sources of social support. This leads to exacerbation of the crisis, overwhelming the individual's resources and making suicide seem the only option.

In discussing motives for suicide, Adler (1964) considered adolescents to be irrational, unrealistic, and illogical: "In dismissing interest in life and committing suicide, adolescents are able to accomplish something no one else is able to do. A person who considers himself or herself too weak to overcome life's difficulties acts 'intelligently' according to his or her goal of coping with the difficulties of life". Adolescents' intellectual functioning is in a state of transition and instability, and their ability to project themselves and others into the future is often limited. Elkind (1978) has referred to this unevenness in thought as "pseudostupity." It can be observed in people who fail to take into account the consequences of a successful suicide, particularly the effects on their families. Typically, the stressful situation that precipitates suicidal action is of a transitory nature and will abate over time (for example, the loss of a girlfriend or boyfriend); however, the adolescent's egocen tric, rigid here-and-now perspective reflects an inability to utilize his or her growing cognitive competencies.

Young Adults

During the early adult years, according to Erikson, the conflict of intimacy versus isolation is the predominant developmental issue. Individuals at this time seek companionship and love, which puts them at risk for rejection. Once rejected, they may become fearful of attempting closeness again. Not wanting to be hurt again, they may isolate themselves, which can lead to depression. Efforts by others to help is often met with anger or avoidance (McNeely, 1977). This decreases the social feedback available, compounding cognitive and emotional dissonance. In general, these persons have not achieved a positive identity in adolescence. The clinical literature supports the view that the less successful adolescents and young adults are in establishing healthy identities and intimacy, the more at risk they are for self-destructive behavior.

Suicide has been extensively studied among college students. Although research has shown that the overall suicide rate for this population is lower than it is for the population as a whole (Silverman, Meyer, Sloane, Raffel, & Pratt, 1997), there has been a dramatic increase in suicide among college students since 1950 (Lipschitz, 1995) and for those aged 15-24 in general (Hirsch & Ellis, 1993). Strang and Orlofsky (1990) reported that nearly 61% of college students experience some suicidal ideation during their college years—a frightening statistic.

It has been found that suicidal students have poorer parent relationships than do nonsuicidal students (Strang & Orlofsky, 1990) and come from families that are more rigid in their values, attitudes, and beliefs (Carris, Sheeber, & Howe, 1998). Associated with this rigidity, college students who feel that others have unrealistically high expectations of them are more likely to commit suicide (Dean, 1996). Adolescents from rigid families with unrealistic expectations often have problem-solving deficits and are unable to see a way out of perceived crises. Jones (1991) found that depression, hopelessness, helplessness, and loneliness were usually present in college students who attempted suicide, with hopelessness the best predictor of more lethal behavior. Certain personality types are more likely to be suicidal among college students, with introverts at higher risk than. extraverts (Street & Komrey, 1994).

Issues surrounding the intimacy versus isolation conflict are key determinants of whether young adults will attempt suicide. Crucial to the resolution of this conflict are the problem-solving skills that young adults learn (or fail to learn) in earlier stages of life.

GENDER DIFFERENCES

Not only do the dynamics of each developmental period affect adolescents' response to suicide ideations, there are also gender-based issues that need to be considered. What differentiates males from females who commit suicide?

In general, males learn to suppress their feelings (i.e., to keep their emotions inside), while females are encouraged to express them (i.e., that it is acceptable to cry, vent, and reach out to others). Suicide attempts are often a cry for help.

Suicide rates increase sharply at adolescence, starting significantly earlier for boys than girls (Aro, 1993). The adolescent male often acts quickly, using more violent means. Females, for the most part, use passive means of self-destruction: poison, gas, or pills (they have greater access to prescribed drugs through more frequent use of medical services). As Grollman (1971) noted, they prefer not to shed their blood or disfigure their bodies. Changes in gender roles may reduce the gap between males and females in suicide rates, as women are increasingly encouraged to take on more male-oriented characteristics.

RISK FACTORS AND FIREARM AVAILABILITY

Social learning theory (Bandura, 1977) is informative regarding adolescent suicide. Research has found that individuals whose parents had attempted suicide were more likely to attempt suicide than those without a family history of suicide. This is supported by social learning and cultural historical theory (Vygotsky, 1978). Grollman (1971) also reported that adolescents with a family history of suicide are more likely to take their own lives. However, how such patterns become established in the first place requires further research.

Some experts feel that suicide should not be discussed lest there be a "chain reaction." Often, when there is a suicide in a particular geographical area, others follow. This "solution" to an adolescent's problems seems driven by identification with the model or the model's situation. Males and females alike may also have a desire to "get back" at someone through suicide. The permanency of death may not be comprehended.

Each suicide attempt has an underlying message, and suicide completion indicates that the message was not received. Most people who attempt suicide threaten to do so beforehand, with over 80% of those contemplating suicide verbalizing their thoughts. Seventy-seven percent of adolescents state that if they were contemplating suicide they would first turn to a friend for help (King. 1999).

Whether a suicide attempt is successful often depends upon the method chosen. When someone uses a firearm, death is almost certain. Suicide by firearm is currently the third leading cause of death for adolescents and young adults in the United States (Duker, 1994), and 80% of suicides by older males are committed with firearms (Kaplan, 1994). Men tend to use firearms to kill themselves more often than do women, and this is attributed to the socialization of males in American society. For example, most males raised in the South have shot a gun before their thirteenth birthday. Females are less likely to be socialized to guns, and suicide by firearms is much less prevalent among them, except in the South, where female firearm suicide rates are highest. Recent studies, however, have shown an increase in the acceptance of firearms as a method of committing suicide for women (Adamek, 1996).

CONCLUSIONS

In attempting to understand suicide, it is difficult to specify a single pattern because those who commit suicide come from all walks of life and vary in background and motives. However, rates of suicide generally increase with age (Bingham, 1994) and males are more likely than females to commit suicide.

Suicide among the adolescent population is of major concern. The failure to resolve developmental crises, as described by Erikson, can lead to the belief that suicide is an acceptable solution to seemingly insurmountable problems.

Taking into account increasing economic difficulties for some, exposure to drugs and alcohol, and greater social alienation, suicide rates may continue to rise. Intervention needs to be multidimensional as well as developmentally differentiated. Research on suicide prevention (among adolescents in particular) indicates that there is a continuum of self-destructive behavior (Wolfle & Siehl, 1992). Pfeffer (1994) argues that a multifactorial approach that considers developmental concerns in all phases of life must be utilized to limit suicidal behavior.

Intervention, including screening, should begin early. Jackson, Hess, and van Dalen (1995) suggest that suicide intervention should begin at preadolescence. School counselors should be alert to the types of personal difficulties that could lead students to attempt suicide, and take appropriate and timely action. Awareness of the signs and symptoms of suicidal ideation should be a priority in the schools and in the community. Teachers and family members can work in partnership with school counselors to intervene when needed.

A family approach to intervention is especially important in light of recent evidence suggesting that parents may actually precipitate a child's suicide (Jacobson, Rabinowitz, Popper, & Solomon, 1995). A cost-effective strategy would involve educating parents in such areas as communication, problem-solving skills, and knowledge of child development, in an effort to avoid problems rather than merely react to them.

Interventions that help connect people and that improve an individual's self-worth can reduce potential suicides. These interventions can be conducted in a supportive social setting, such as the school. To the extent that families can be educated with regard to developmental issues, we may succeed in reducing individual vulnerability to maladjustment and neutralize external stressors. Further, families can be strengthened by macro-level economic policies.

A psychosocial model, focusing on the resolution of crises that constitute serious risk for suicide over the lifespan, offers direction to school counselors, psychologists, and teachers. This area is fertile for additional theory-driven research. Cross-cultural contrasts may also provide insights for suicide prevention and social promotion of psychological health. It is clear that there is a social learning component to self-destructive behavior and that the availability of guns interacts with unhealthy identity development. Thus, prevention is linked to the development of healthier conditions for positive identity development.

REFERENCES

Adamek, M. (1996). The growing use of firearms by suicidal older women, 1979-1992: A research note. Suicide and Life-Threatening Behavior, 26(1), 71-78.

Adler, A. (1964). Brief comments on reason, intelligence, and feeble-mindedness. In H. L. Ansbacher & R. R. Ansbacher (Eds.), Superiority and social unrest: A collection of later writings (pp. 41-49). Evanston, IL: Northwestern University Press.

Amato, P. R., & Keith, B. (1991). Parental divorce and the well-being of children: A meta-analysis. Psychological Bulletin, 110, 26-46.

Archer, R. P., & Slesinger, D. (1999). MMPI-A patterns related to the endorsement of suicidal ideation. Assessment, 6, 51-59.

Aro, H. (1993). Adolescent development and youth suicide. Suicide and Life Threatening Behavior, 23, 359-365.

Bandura, A. (1977). Social learning theory. Englewood Cliffs, NJ: Prentice Hall.

Bar-Joseph, H., & Tzuriel, D. (1990). Suicidal tendencies and ego identity in adolescence. Adolescence, 25, 215-223.

Bingham, C. R. (1994). An analysis of age, gender and racial differences in recent national trends of youth suicide. Journal of Adolescence, 17(1), 53-71.

Bowlby, J. (1988). A secure base: Parent-child attachment and healthy human development. New York: Basic Books.

Capuzzi, D. (1994). Preventing adolescent suicide (ERIC Document Reproduction Service No. 383 964).

Carris, M., Sheeber, L., & Howe, S. (1998). Family rigidity, adolescent problem-solving deficits, and suicidal ideation: A mediational model. Journal of Adolescence, 21, 459-472.

Coleman, E., & Remafedi, G. (1989). Gay, lesbian and bisexual adolescents: A critical challenge to counselors. Journal of Counseling and Development, 68, 36-40.

Cotton, R. C., & Range, L. M. (1993). Suicidality, hopelessness, and attitudes toward life and death in children. Death Studies, 17, 185-191.

Dean, P. (1996). The escape theory of suicide in college students: Testing a model that includes perfectionism. Suicide and Life-Threatening Behavior, 26, 181-186.

Duker, L. (1994). Youth suicide and guns (ERIC Document Reproduction Service No. 378 459).

Elkind, D. (1978). The child's reality: Three developmental themes. Hillsdale, NJ: Erlbaum.

Erikson, E. (1963). Childhood and society (2nd ed.). New York: W. W. Norton.

Erikson, E. (1968). Identity: Youth, and crisis. New York: W. W. Norton.

Evans, R. I. (1973). Jean Piaget: The man and his ideas (Eleanor Duckworth, Trans.). New York: E.P. Dutton.

Feenstra, J. S., Banyard, V. L., Rines, E. N., & Hopkins, K. R. (2001). First-year students' adaptation to college: The role of family variables and individual coping. Journal of College Student Development, 42, 106-114.

Garber, R. J. (1991). Long-term effects of divorce on self-esteem of young adults. Journal of Divorce and Remarriage, 17, 131-137.

Gilligan, C. (1982). In a different voice: Psychological theory and women's development. Cambridge, MA: Harvard University Press.

Greene, D. B. (1994). Childhood suicide and myths surrounding it. Social Work, 39, 230-232.

Grob, M. C. (1983). The role of the high school professional in identifying and managing adolescent suicidal behavior. Journal of Youth and Adolescence, 12, 163-173.

Groilman, E. (1971). Suicide: Prevention, intervention, postvention. Boston: Beacon Press.

Hirsch, J., & Ellis, J. (1993). Family support and other social factors precipitating suicidal ideation. (ERIC Document Reproduction Service No. 373 276).

Jackson, H., Hess, P., & van Delen, A. (1995). Preadolescent suicide: How to ask and how to respond. Families in Society, 76(5), 267-279.

Jacobsen, L., Rabinowitz, I., Popper, M., & Solomon, R. (1995). "Interviewing prepubertal children about suicidal ideation and behavior": Reply. Journal of the American Academy of Child and Adolescent Psychiatry, 34, 701.

Jones, J. W. (1991). Suicidality among college and university students: Contributing factors and preventive response (ERIC Document Reproduction Service No. 333 249).

Kaplan, M. S. (1994). Trends in firearm suicide among older American males. Gerontologist, 34, 59-65.

King, K. A. (1999). Fifteen prevalent myths concerning adolescent suicide. Journal of School Health, 69, 159-161.

Laws, K., & Turner, A. (1993). Alcohol and other drug use: The connection to youth suicide. Abstracts of selected research (ERIC Document Reproduction Service No. 362 818).

Lipschitz, A. (1995). Suicide prevention in young adults (age 18-30). Suicide and Life-Threatening Behavior, 25, 155-170.

Lock, J., & Steiner, H. (1999). Gay, lesbian and bisexual youths' risks for emotional, physical, and social problems: Results from a community-based survey. Journal of Child and Adolescent Psychiatry, 1, 297-304.

McNeely, J. (1977). The student suicide epidemic. Today's Education, 66(3), 71-73.

Newton, M. (1995). Adolescence: Guiding youth through the perilous ordeal. Scranton, PA: W. W. Norton.

Pfeffer, C. (1993). Too young to consider death? Think again. PTA Today, 19(2), 14-16.

Pfeffer, C. (1994). Developmental issues in child and adolescent suicide: A discussion. New Directions for Child Development, 64, 109-114.

Silverman, M., Meyer, P., Sloane, F., Raffel, M., & Pratt, D. (1997). The Big Ten Student Suicide Study: A 10-year study on suicides on Midwestern university campuses. Suicide and Life-Threatening Behavior, 27, 285-303.

Strang, S., & Orlofsky, J. (1990). Factors underlying suicidal ideation among college students: A test of Teicher and Jacob's model. Journal of Adolescence, 13, 39-52.

Street, S., & Komrey, J. D. (1994). Relationships between suicidal behavior and personality types. Suicide and Life-Threatening Behavior, 24, 282-292.

Thompson, E. (1994). Discriminating suicide ideation among high-risk youth. Journal of School Health, 64, 361-367.

Vygotsky, L. S. (1978). Mind in society. Cambridge, MA: Harvard University Press.

Wagner, B., Cole, R., & Schwartzman, P. (1995). Psychosocial correlates of suicide attempts among junior and senior high school youth. Suicide and Life-Threatening Behavior, 25, 358-372.

Wolfle, J., & Siehi, P. (1992). Case study of early personality traits of 10 adolescent suicides (ERIC Document Reproduction Service No. 377 423).

Pedro R. Portes, Daya S. Sandhu, and Robert Longwell-Grice, Department of Educational and Counseling Psychology, University of Louisville.

Reprint requests to Pedro R. Portes, Department of Educational and Counseling Psychology, University of Louisville, Louisville, Kentucky 40292.

From *Adolescence*, Winter 2002. © 2002 by Libra Publishers. Reprinted with permission.

More than Moody: Recognizing and Treating Adolescent Depression

Harold S. Koplewicz

Until recently, it was widely believed that young people had neither sufficiently formed egos, nor the brain development to cause the kind of chemical imbalance that is at the root of clinical depression. Indeed, twenty years ago depression in adults was often misdiagnosed, mistreated, and stigmatized. If the public, and even the medical world, couldn't entirely accept depression as a disease in adults, certainly innocent children had to be immune. Unhappily, we now know that this isn't the case. Not only does major depressive disorder exist in adolescents and, more rarely, in children, but the syndrome is in many ways clinically equivalent to the spiral of depression in adulthood.

The media is quick to wonder whether depression is an explanation for adolescents on murder sprees, for teenage mothers callously killing their newborns, for all the "children without a conscience" who made up the collage on a recent cover of People magazine. Parents wondered if the surliness, listlessness, hopelessness and despair their children were experiencing could be caused by something medical, something more than simply the natural—and not unhealthy—volatility of adolescence. Pediatricians, teachers, social workers, seemingly everyone whose lives brought them in contact with young people suddenly had in mind some child or teenager they felt was at risk. No doubt, many are at risk.

Prevalence

Upwards of 40 million Americans suffer from depression, and approximately 3.5 million of them are children and teenagers, according to a 1999 report by the United States Surgeon General. The studies indicate that as you read this, between 10 and 15 percent of the child and adolescent population show some signs of depression. It is still relatively rare among preteens and young children, so the vast majority of those affected are teenagers.

Significantly, studies estimate that in a given year as many as 8.3 percent of the adolescent population will begin exhibiting signs of major depression—compared with only 5.3 percent for adults. And while adults are much more apt to recognize their

depression and be treated, most teenagers will not receive the help they need.

As a group, perhaps the most affected are college students. Studies suggest that significant percentages of them have bouts of depression in which they feel hopeless and even suicidal. On the other hand, the widespread use of antidepressants means that some young people who might have been too debilitated to go to college in earlier years can now attend and succeed. In either case, parents today need to be especially alert to what depression in adolescents looks and feels like, and to be capable of helping their children perhaps long-distance.

Young people with depression don't suffer every day, or all their lives, or with the same intensity with each episode, but they do suffer. Whether they are entering middle school or finishing college, the pain of depression can seriously erode their capacity for joy and curiosity and for facing the developmental hurdles they must overcome to take their places as happy, productive adults. And at its worst, depression can lead to severe isolation and even suicide or violence toward others.

In 2002, five thousand young people in the United States will kill themselves. That's more adolescents than will die from all other illnesses—from cancer to AIDS—combined. Only traffic accidents and homicides take more adolescents than suicide. What is perhaps even more frightening are studies suggesting that every single day, in every single high school in America, teenagers are thinking about suicide or making actual attempts.

The most recent survey on youth risk behavior from the Centers for Disease Control reports that annually teenagers (19 percent or 3 million of all U.S. high-schoolers) had thought of suicide, and over 2 million of them made plans to carry it out. And some 400,000 made actual suicide attempts requiring medical attention. That comes to an average of more than 1,000 attempts a day nationwide, every day of the year. With a reasonable degree of confidence, we know that depression plays at least some role in most of them.

The problem is that adolescent depression is terribly underdiagnosed in this country. That statement applies to every socioeconomic group, though members of minority groups are the most neglected, as is the case in health care in general. It is in large part because major depression can be insidious that it is often unrecognized and untreated. Depression starts silently and slowly in most cases, and it is usually only when the symptoms become severe that others begin to take note. The costs are enormous. An adolescent with depression not only suffers at this crucial state in their development, but is at much higher risk of having depression as an adult.

Consider that some 20 percent of teenagers—one in five—report that they have had a major depressive episode that went untreated during their adolescence, according to a study by Dr. Peter Lewinsohn from the University of Washington. That's a striking number, and it may help explain why there are so many depressed adults.

"Depressed" is perhaps the most overused word in the English language—especially by teenagers. I'm so depressed, they say—even when they mean they're just upset about something. They don't say "I'm so demoralized," which would be a more accurate word. But despite this semantic abuse, there are many more teenagers who truly are depressed but who don't say they are—because they don't know that's what's wrong with them. Their parents, meanwhile, will be just as much in the dark.

Mallory is a 15 year old teenager and is absolutely crushed when her boyfriend breaks up with her, but it lasts only a few days or a couple of weeks. She bounces back. But if the sadness persists—if Mallory has become a different person, if she's lost her sense of humor, if her sleeping and eating habits are disturbed, and if she's become socially isolated and is suddenly having trouble keeping up with schoolwork—it may be that the breakup was the triggering event of an underlying depression that needs to be treated.

Treatment

Treatment itself is a delicate and controversial matter. Much has been written and said about kids and pills, and a good deal of the consternation ahs to do with a simple misconception: many people don't believe children can become psychiatrically ill. At the same time, hard questions need to be addressed: Are we changing our children's personalities with these medications? Is it right to set them on a course where they might have to take medicine, at least intermittently, for the rest of their lives? Is there a better way? Are HMOs, to say nothing of psychotherapy, for the sake of expedience or profit?

The truth is that while we know what works best for adults, we're still addressing that question for adolescents. There is abundant clinical evidence that antidepressants work for teenagers. But do they work better than cognitive behavioral therapy? Or is a combination of medicine and therapy best? What we do know is that most teenagers who respond to antidepressants for a first episode of depression will only need to take

the medication for six months to one year. Only those teens who have recurrent episodes of depression should take medication for the long-term.

Very important, too, is the understanding, support and cooperation of the child's parents, who will need to recognize that they can't use a "pull-yourself-together" or "kindness first" approach to a disorder that will not respond to either discipline or sympathy—any more than cancer or diabetes can be cured by a willed change of attitude.

Not only are many parents guilt-ridden over the diagnosis ("If my child is so unhappy, I must be doing something very wrong"), they are also loath to submit to the news that their child might have to be on medication for many months, or even years, even if the medication will treat the illness effectively.

More often than might be expected, coming to grips with a child's disease serves as a different kind of catalyst for parents: many come to understand that they, too, have suffered depression at some point or even throughout their lives and they, too, may need treatment. Thus, understanding and helping families to work more effectively is always a part of the treatment. MDD is rarely a disease that pops up once, is treated and then goes away for good.

Across the country there are excellent centers that specialize in treating depressed young people, and the field is fortunate to have so many dedicated and truly gifted researchers working to unlock the mysteries that remain. These people are saving teenagers' lives and advancing knowledge. But it's also true that over the last quarter century, one of the most widely acknowledged shortages in medicine has been in the field of child and adolescent mental health.

While ten million children and adolescents have a diagnosable psychiatric disorder right now, there are only 7,000 board-certified child and adolescent psychiatrists in the United States and fewer than 6,000 child psychologists. The overwhelming majority recognize that treatment is driven by diagnosis, but the fact that so many young people are brought in for help after having debilitating symptoms for many years means that we are failing at early identification and intervention. We wouldn't think of letting children with physical symptoms go without seeking treatment, dismissing the complaints with the timeworn words, "It's just a phase."

Sometimes it is a phase. Sometimes a teenager is just moody. But it is essential for parents, teachers, and pediatricians to be better equipped to recognize when it is more than that—when it is an illness crying out to be treated.

Harold S. Koplewicz, M.D. is the Arnold and Debbie Simon Professor of Child and Adolescent Psychiatry and the director of the NYU Child Study Center at New York University School of Medicine. He is the author of More Than Moody: Recognizing and Treating Adolescent Depression)Putnam: October, 2002).

From *The Brown University Child and Adolescent Behavior Letter*, Vol. 18, No. 12, December 2002. © 2002 by Manisses Communications Group. Reprinted with permission.

Aggression and antisocial behavior in youth

Daniel F. Connor, M.D.

Aggression and antisocial behavior in children and adolescents are central issues in our time. In the media everyday are stories of public school shootings, young children killing other young children, rising rates of youth crime and delinquency in the community and the growing trend of adjudicating youth charged with violent crimes as adults. This raises questions about the relationship between unrecognized and untreated mental illness and violence in youth.

Because school personnel and mental health clinicians may be faced with the task of evaluating and intervening with a potentially aggressive child, the purpose of this article is to highlight some important points about aggression and antisocial behaviors in children and adolescents.

Aggression and antisocial behaviors in youngsters are complex, heterogeneous conditions with multiple diverse psychosocial and neurobiological etiologies and consequences extending across the individual, family, and community environments. Because of this complexity, established antisocial behavior is not easily altered. However, recent research has documented some important findings that may help to guide efforts to diminish serious antisocial behavior in youths.

At-risk children

While most aggressive children do not grow up to be aggressive adults, it is now clear that a small percentage of aggressive children are at high risk to continue their aggressive behaviors into adolescence and adulthood. These children are called early starters. They demonstrate an onset of diverse aggressive behaviors (stealing, threats, physical fighting, lying, cheating, vandalism, fire setting, rule defiance) across multiple settings (home, school, community) beginning before age 10 years.

In early starter children, these behaviors are persistent across time and development and do not appear to be transient problems. These children are at risk to follow a trajectory of ever increasing severity and diversity of antisocial behaviors as they develop into adolescents and adults.

It is important to recognize that interpersonal conflicts and aggressive behavior are normative for infants, preschoolers, and children. Healthy aspects of aggression facilitate competence in social assertiveness, competition in games, and success in meeting daily life challenges. Observational studies indicate that approximately 50 percent of the social interchanges between children 12 to 18 months of age in a nursery school setting could be viewed as disruptive or conflictual, but by age 2 and 1/2 years the proportion of conflicted social interchanges drops to 20 percent. As children enter school physical aggression decreases and verbal forms of aggression increase. So, if internize the at-risk infant, preschooler, or child?

- The preschool child who largely directs aggression towards adults in out-of-home environments such as nursery school does not fit what is presently known about the normative aspects of aggression.
- The school-age child, who frequently and repetitively initiates physical attacks on others, rather than beginning to modulate overt aggression with words, may also be deviating from a normative developmental trajectory.
- The school-aged child who consistently uses physical aggression to obtain possessions from others may also be at-risk.
- The persistently hyperactive/impulsive child is at risk for antisocial behaviors since there is a significant overlap between hyperactivity/ impulsivity and aggression/conduct problems in children, especially in unstructured, unsupervised environments.

At-risk parenting

Over the past 50 years research in behavioral science has documented qualities of parenting and parent-child interactions that contribute to risk for continued aggression and antisocial behaviors in offspring. Early recognition and intervention to establish more effective parenting practices is important in interrupting the aggressive trajectory of the at-risk child. These include recognizing:

- Coercive parent-child interaction patterns: These occur when a parent sets a limit or asks the child to do something and the child resists or is oppositional and defiant. As the parent persists the child escalates eventually causing the parent to back down. The child then learns that escalating behavior allows them to escape aversive requests or demands (negative reinforcement). At the next parent-child encounter the child will once again use this strategy, and if successful, will be further reinforced. Eventually the child may generalize this oppositional strategy outside of the home into school and the community.

- Harsh and inconsistent parental discipline practices: Closely coupled with the above parent-child interaction pattern is the parental use of harsh and inconsistent discipline practices. Occasionally the parent will retaliate on the oppositional child. The child then becomes transiently compliant in the face of harsh punishment. The parent is negatively reinforced for aggressive behavior. The parent-child dyad becomes locked in a spiral of ever-escalating conflicted behavior. The harshness and inconsistency of the parental response further serves to reinforce maladaptive parent-child interactions that contribute to child aggressive behavior by modeling aggression as a means of solving interpersonal conflict.
- Failure to monitor and supervise children after school: Children whose parents do not know where they are after school and children whose parents are unaware of their friends and peer group, are at risk for engaging in more antisocial behaviors than closely monitored children.

Early intervention

It is becoming clear that effect sizes for interventions diminish as the at-risk child grows older. Family, educational and community treatments appear to be stronger for younger aggressive children and their families, rather than older aggressive children and teenagers.

To the extent that an early starter antisocial trajectory can be modified, the earlier the intervention, the better.

Transition points

Critical periods of development for diminishing aggressive behavior may be concentrated in the transitions from preschool to elementary school and during the transitions from late adolescence to the young adult years. At each of these points in development, research shows a proportion of antisocial and aggressive individuals desisting from further maladaptive behaviors.

Although the effect sizes of interventions diminishes as the antisocial child grows older, these "windows of opportunity" may represent times when concentrated treatment efforts might further interrupt a lifetime anti-social trajectory.

Verbal competency

Groups of persistently aggressive and antisocial children and adolescents consistently demonstrate diminished verbal competency relative to non-aggressive control samples. This dimin-

ished competency is reflected in overall poorer reading skills, increased incidence of learning disabilities, and poor expressive and receptive language skills in aggressive youngsters.

If a child is unable to articulate their moods, feelings, and frustrations verbally, they may be more at-risk to act them out behaviorally. Efforts to decrease antisocial and aggressive behaviors in youngsters need to emphasize early verbal and language skill acquisition as an anti-aggression primary prevention strategy.

Community interventions

Although the importance of safe neighborhoods, antipoverty efforts and educational access in the prevention of youth violence and antisocial behaviors cannot be under stressed, two other community interventions need emphasis.

- The role of violent media: American children are awash in violent images from television, magazines, movies, music and the Internet. While exposure to violent media does not cause violence or aggression de novo, it contributes through three mechanisms. Constant exposure to media violence may engender desensitization and a numbing of emotional response to real violence. Being submerged in a sea of media violence may contribute to a feeling that all people are more violent than they actually are and that the world is a very threatening place. Finally, violent media glamorize conflict resolution strategies emphasizing aggression - strategies that are easily adopted by impressionable youngsters. Communities might facilitate regulation of highly violent media as a primary youth violence prevention strategy.
- The role of handguns: At last estimate 60 million American homes contained at least one handgun. Having easy access to a gun at the point of interpersonal conflict increases risk for violent outcomes. Communities might facilitate handgun regulation as a primary youth violence prevention strategy.

Effectively intervening in the epidemic of youth antisocial behavior and aggression will require public health strategies coordinating evaluation and interventions across multiple educational, mental health, community, public policy, public safety and juvenile justice institutions.

The individual professional can help by supporting early recognition of at-risk children and families and supporting effective psychoeducational and parenting interventions delivered early in the at-risk child's development.

Dr. Connor is Associate Professor of Psychiatry, Director of Ambulatory Child and Adolescent Psychiatry, and Co-Director of Research in the Division of Child and Adolescent Psychiatry, University of Massachusetts Medical School, Worcester, MA.

Connor DF: Aggression & Antisocial Behavior in Children and Adolescents: Research and Treatment. New York, NY: The Guilford Press, 2002, 480 pages. To order, call 1-800-365-7006; or e-mail: info@guilford.com

Ecstasy: it's the rave.

Dixie Dennis; Michael Ballard.

National statistics reveal an alarming trend concerning the use of 3,4-methylenedioxymethamphetamine, which is better known as ecstasy. Results from the Monitoring the Future survey of 50,000 secondary youth reveal that use among 8th graders rose to 3.1%, 5.4% among 10th graders, and 8.2% among 12th graders. High school faculty and staff must be cognizant of this growing trend, understand the physiological effects of use, and recognize protective and risk factors among youth. It is imperative that school personnel and community-based organizations work together to implement primary, secondary, and tertiary prevention strategies as part of a comprehensive drug abuse prevention program.

Introduction

In 1874 the Women's Christian Temperance Union, an organization which grew out of the movement advocating prohibition, warned the nation about the negative effects of alcohol. Since then, educators have had the charge to warn against similar evils of the day (Rubinson & Alles, 1982). Today, there is a relatively new evil escalating in popularity and usage among adolescents which is chemically known as 3,4-methylene-dioxymethamphetamine or MDMA. The most common street name for this drug is ecstasy. Other names for the drug include Adam~ clarity, lover's speed, X, E, EX, and XTC (Lynskey, White, Hill, Letcher, & Hall, 1999; Johnston, O'Malley, & Bachman, 2000).

In pure form, MDMA is a white crystalline powder that is primarily ingested in pill or capsule form. It can be, however, snorted, smoked, or injected. The average cost ranges from $10.00 to $25.00 a hit (Inaba, Cohen, & Holstein, 1997).

In 1985, the Drug Enforcement Agency classified ecstasy as a Schedule I drug. This classification is reserved for any drug that is considered unsafe, has a high potential for abuse and is illegal to possess (Hanson & Venturelli, 1998). Despite the current classification, historically, users perceived the drug as one with few adverse effects (Jansen, 1997). Yet, numerous studies have documented the myriad of damaging effects of the drug on the human body.

Therefore, a heightened concern currently exists among public health officials concerning the escalating use and abuse of ecstasy. Former U.S. Secretary of Health and Human Services, Donna Shalala stated, "We are very concerned about the rise in the use of Ecstasy... . It is not a fun drug; it is not harmless. It is a dangerous drug" (Rayam, 2000). Educators, consequently, need to teach the effects and risks of ecstasy use as well as implement primary, secondary, and tertiary drug prevention strategies.

Physiological Effects/Side Effects

Ecstasy is known to have both stimulant and hallucinogenic properties (Hanson & Venturelli, 1998; Johnston, O'Malley, & Bachman, 2000). Yet, as a relatively new drug on the scene, ecstasy's adverse effects are not widely recognized. For example, many users believe ecstasy is relatively safe with no long-lasting effects (Schwartz, 1997). Conversely, current research is indicating ecstasy, even in small amounts, may cause severe reactions (Julien, 1998; Schwartz & Miller, 1997). State authorities in Maryland are so concerned about the epidemic proportion of students trying ecstasy, efforts are underway to educate doctors, parents, and teens about the "real problems" associated with its use (Gray, 2000).

Goldberg (2000) explained that effects of ecstasy last from 1-12 hours and may include feelings of love and calmness among users. Elk (1996) reported that the drug may "facilitate interpersonal relations, increase esteem, elevate mood, increase self-insight, and enhance communication and empathy." There are, however, a myriad of negative side effects, which may or may not be reversible. For example, Elk reported that ecstasy use decreases the amount of serotonin in the brain. Serotonin is associated with depression and sleep irregularities.

In addition to depression and sleep problems, Johnston, O'Malley, and Bachman (2000) and Weir (2000) report users experience a host of other side effects following ingestion which include confusion, anxiety, and paranoia, all of which may last several weeks after use. Physical effects include muscle tension, involuntary teeth clinching, nausea, blurred vision, chills, and sweating. When combined with physical exertion such as dancing, use of ecstasy may lead to hyperthermia and severe dehydration. Hyperthermia is an extremely serious condition characterized by a dramatic increase in body temperature and should be considered life threatening. Body temperatures of 110 [degrees] F have been reported following use of ecstasy. Hyperthermia is also a contributing factor in the development of renal failure (McEvoy, Kitchen, & Thomas, 1998).

Prior to human studies, research on monkeys, who were exposed to ecstasy for four days, showed brain damage present six to seven years later. Another alarming fact is that complications of ecstasy use are unpredictable and do not appear dose-dependent (Milroy, 1999). In other words, the degree of effect does not depend on the amount of ecstasy taken. Lacing and/or substituting are two factors that play a pivotal role in inconsistent complications. For example, drug dealers often substitute other dangerous compounds for ecstasy, or lace with a combination of other drugs or household cleaning products, which could prove fatal (Johnston, O'Malley, and Bachman, 2000).

Scope of the Problem

Even though the drug is considered new, it was patented in 1914 as an appetite suppressant. The drug resurfaced in the late 1970s as an adjunct to psychotherapy (Schwartz & Miller, 1997). Currently, the number of teenagers in America using ecstasy as a recreational drug has increased significantly. Statistics from the 1999 Substance Abuse and Mental Health Services Administration Survey (SAMHSA) reveal that Boston and St. Louis are U.S. cities with the highest increases in ecstasy use (Yourish, 2001).

Johnston, O'Malley, and Bachman (2000), authors of Monitoring the Future study, reveal that ecstasy is used by more teenagers today than cocaine. Monitoring the Future is an ongoing, 25-year study of approximately 50,000 secondary school youth in grades 8, 10, and 12 in over 400 schools across the U.S. regarding behaviors, attitudes, and values. The percentage of 8th graders who reported using ecstasy in the previous 12 months has risen from 1.7% in 1999 to 3.1% in 2000. Among 10th graders, ecstasy use rose from 4.4% in 1999 to 5.4% in 2000. Twelfth graders' use of ecstasy rose from 5.6% in 1999 to 8.2% in 2000. Ecstasy use among a 19- to 22-year-old follow-up group of college students rose from 0.5% in 1994 to 5.5% in 1999. In addition, the percentage of students who have "ever used" ecstasy is on the rise. Eleven percent of 12th graders report having ever used ecstasy. Clearly, the rise in use of ecstasy so far has been concentrated among teens and individuals in their early 20's. These young people, consequently, are those most likely to attend raves, the place where ecstasy is most often used.

Raves

Raves are all night dance parties, which first appeared in the U.S. in the mid 1980s and currently are attended by as many as 20,000 youth in some cities. Typically, rave participants ingest ecstasy and dance to repetitive electronic music. The "techno" computerized hypnotic, rhythmic rave music has been described as repetitive, loud, fast, and mindnumbing. Raves normally are held in farmers' fields due to the large number of attendees, but may be held at dance clubs or other locations where teenagers congregate. Exact locations of the parties are announced only a few hours in advance in an attempt to deter police surveillance (Weir, 2000). Use of other illicit drugs has also been reported at the raves in combination with ecstasy.

Not all participants who attend raves (identified as "ravers") use drugs, and only a minority of attendees consume alcohol. Most ravers agree that alcohol does not belong at raves (Salt, 1993). The cost of attending raves ranges from $10.00 to $50.00. Typically, ravers are between 15 and 25 years of age and are from middle-class backgrounds (Weir, 2000). Clothing apparel of rave participants includes baseball caps, tee shirts with logos, baggy pants, knapsacks, and plastic chains. Ravers often clutch infant toys and suck on pacifiers. Such appearances exemplify ravers' lack of pretension as well as a desire to mask differences based on physical attractiveness and sexual orientation (Weber, 1999).

Johnston, O'Malley, and Bachman (2000) warn that until young people see ecstasy as a dangerous drug, it is unlikely that the rave scene, or use of ecstasy in general, will turn around. Educators, therefore, need to teach adolescents—those who currently use, those who previously have used, and those who have not yet begun to use the drug—about the drug's adverse effects. Obviously, the personal decision to use illicit substances is influenced by many factors. These factors include experimentation, rebellion, peer approval, or simply boredom (Wilson & Kolander, 2000). Regardless of the reason, the drug has a significant impact on a young person's health and, therefore, primary, secondary, and tertiary preventive efforts are necessary, especially in schools where students spend one-third of their time.

Prevention Strategies

Primary prevention (harm-reduction) strategies are aimed at individuals who have not yet used ecstasy (usually early childhood) or have minimal experience (Levinthal, 1999). Primary prevention includes disseminating information on the effects and risks of taking ecstasy, as well as advising students not to attend raves alone despite the curiosity that surrounds the events (Weir, 2000). Primary prevention efforts must be initiated early in secondary schools and should address knowledge, attitudes, and behaviors through a comprehensive drug abuse prevention curriculum. In addition, skills training (e.g., refusal, decision-making, or problem-solving) is an essential component in this, as well as any, drug education program (Lohrmann & Wooley, 1998).

Once adolescents have used ecstasy and/or experienced hyperthermia, secondary prevention measures are warranted. Secondary prevention strategies target individuals who have had experience with the drug (Levinthal, 1999). Wilson and Kolander (2000) explain that secondary drug prevention strategies are for individuals who are believed capable of stopping. These adolescents must be made aware of signs and symptoms of use and abuse such as fluid and sodium loss after taking ecstasy while dancing. Taking frequent breaks from dancing and ingesting copious amounts of water is a secondary prevention practice to offset these loses (Weir, 2000). Secondary prevention also includes teaching adolescents about early signs of abuse, how to assist peers with problems, and where help is available for individuals with drug problems (Archambault, 1992). Other strategies to deal with this growing problem can be gleaned from the National Institute on Drug Abuse (NIDA). This organization launched a campaign two years ago to spend $54 million on educational initiatives to inform the public about rave drugs (National Institute of Drug Abuse [NIDA], 1999).

Tertiary prevention efforts are necessary when use of a drug is "fixed." The purpose of tertiary prevention programs is to reduce consumption and purchase of the drug. Again, adolescents are targeted because early drug use is one indication of later drug abuse patterns (Hawkins, Lishner, & Catalona, 1985). In other words, educators do not have to wait until students are "hooked" to receive tertiary prevention techniques about how to stop established abusive patterns.

Clearly, adolescents know where to purchase, and how to use, ecstasy. It appears, however, many do not know the effects and risks of use or the techniques to offset those effects and risks. Obviously, primary, secondary, and tertiary prevention programs are ideal to implement in schools where youth spend most of their time. Yet, we must extend beyond the school to collaborate with community members, law enforcement, civic groups, and public health officials. Dr. Alan Leshner, Director of NIDA, stated that ecstasy use by adolescents is not yet a national crisis but that we are trying to prevent one by getting in its path (NIDA, 1999). It will take many people working together to get in the path of a drug that many teens consider "the rave."

Role of High School Faculty and Staff

Annual statistics, which reveal a rising trend in use/abuse of ecstasy (Robert Wood Johnson [RWJF, 2001], illustrate a growing need for awareness among school personnel. In today's schools, "teachers usually are the first to notice a child's troubled behavior, but sometimes guidance counselors, coaches, other personnel, or peers notice it first" (Wilson & Kolander, 2000). Awareness alone, however, is not sufficient. These school personnel need to provide prevention strategies. Few schools, though, offer such strategies, and, of the ones that do, the approach is frequently disjointed.

An existing problem with current curricular offerings relates to the lack of comprehensiveness of subject content. For example, certain drugs such as ecstasy may be omitted from assigned readings or classroom activities within the curriculum while focusing on other illicit drugs. Specifically, even though ecstasy use is higher among adolescents than cocaine use (RWJF, 2001), many

drug curricula focus exclusively on cocaine. According to Elk (1996), "lack of information being taught to students in drug education programs where other frequently encountered drugs are discussed may encourage students not to question initial or subsequent use of ecstasy. By excluding discussions of ecstasy within such programs, awareness of its potential dangers may be minimized if students perceive this drug not worthy of discussion or that it is of minimal risk or danger compared to other drugs that are included in the curriculum."

The selection of, and proper use of, a comprehensive drug abuse prevention curriculum is vital. When deciding on a curriculum, the selection committee should adopt a curriculum that addresses the needs of the local high school. In order to be successful, Dusenbury and Falco (1995) suggest that the curriculum should be theoretically and research based, developmentally appropriate, culturally sensitive, provide normative education, include social resistance skills, incorporate interactive teaching techniques, provide adequate teacher training, and appropriate evaluation. A drug prevention program guide for secondary school faculty and staff to consider is listed in Table 1.

In-service training can make the difference in a program that works and one that does not. Training programs should include current scientific information as well as strategies specific to recognizing signs & symptoms of drug use/abuse. Wilson and Kolander (2000) have identified procedures faculty and staff can take following what they believe to be ecstasy-using behavior in a student. The procedures include:

1. Document the observed behavior in personal notes.
2. Talk to the student about the observation.
3. Talk to the parents about the concerns.
4. Seek counsel from personnel with expertise for resolving such problems.
5. Work with administrators in involving community agencies.
6. Follow-up with the student to determine what is being done.

TABLE 1: A HIGH SCHOOL DRUG PREVENTION PROGRAM GUIDE *

1. Set school standards (high expectations for students, positive learning environment).

2. Assess drug-use problem in school (surveys, establish/maintain records).

3. Set school drug policies (well defined and applied fairly/consistently).

4. Provide comprehensive drug-prevention curricula.

5. Offer positive peer programs.

6. Present resistance training (i.e., Teach students "how" to say no.).

7. Provide drug free activities.

8. Establish student assistance programs (in-school support, and outside referral).

9. Work with high-risk students.

10. Provide in-service training for teachers.

*Meeks, Heit, & Page (1995)

TABLE 2: PROTECTIVE AND RISK FACTORS *

Protective Factors:

1. Being reared in a loving, functional family
2. Being involved in school activities
3. Having positive self-esteem
4. Having clearly defined goals and plans to reach them
5. Having close friends who do not abuse drugs
6. Regularly practicing one's faith
7. Feeling a sense of accomplishment at school
8. Having adult role models including parents who do not abuse drugs
9. Having a healthful attitude about competition and athletic performance
10. Being committed to following the rules of the community
11. Having a plan to cope with life stressors

Risk Factors:

1. Being reared in a dysfunctional family
2. Having negative self-esteem
3. Being unable to resist peer pressure
4. Having difficulty mastering developmental tasks
5. Being economically disadvantaged
6. Lacking faith experiences and fellowship
7. Having a genetic background with a predisposition to chemical dependency
8. Experiencing family disruption
9. Experiencing depression
10. Experiencing pressure to succeed in athletics
11. Having difficulty achieving success in school
12. Having attention deficit hyperactivity disorder
13. Having immature character disorder
14. Having borderline personality disorders

*Meeks. Heit, & Page (1995)

Follow-up appears crucial for lasting results. To explain, Romano (1997) reported, "too often the training of school personnel ... lacks follow-up to assess the outcome of the training on school practices." This over site is true, especially as it relates to paraprofessionals within schools. Although the number of paraprofessionals (i.e., educational support staff) has increased, "their professional development experiences have not kept pace with their changing roles and responsibilities" (Romano, 1999). Yet, these support staff members play a vital role regarding school drug prevention success. In many cases, they interact with students in a very close manner as mentors, tutors, or by facilitating other classroom educational activities.

Finally, school personnel must become adept in recognizing risk factors existing among students. Faculty and staff also can help students build their individual protective factors. Protective factors are those factors, which, if present, significantly re-duce the likelihood of problems with drug use/abuse. Conversely, risk factors are those that increase the likelihood of problems with drug use/abuse. A detailed list of these factors is provided (see Table 2).

Conclusion

It appears imperative that secondary school faculty and staff understand, and take action against, the risk factors associated with increased use of ecstasy among youth. Also, faculty and staff can provide protective factors to students within comprehensive drug abuse prevention programs. According to Bernard (1991) a nurturing school climate is powerful in helping children both overcome incredible risk factors as well as increase their protective factors. Romano (1999) reported, "[drug] prevention must be an integral component of a school's basic structure and environment." Such a basic school structure utilizes the positive efforts of teachers, coaches, counselors, administrators, family resource/youth services centers, paraprofessionals, law enforcement, and parents in rendering children better able to resist the newest drug "rave" ecstasy.

References

Archambault, D. (1992). Adolescence: A physiological, cultural and psychological no man's land. In G. Lawson & A. Lawson (Eds.), Adolescent substance abuse, etiology, treatment & prevention (pp. 11-28). Gaithersburg, MD: Aspen.

Bernard, B. (1991). Fostering resiliency in kids: Protective factors in the family, school, and community. Western Regional Center for Drug-Free Schools and Communities. Portland, Oregon: Northwest Regional Educational Laboratory.

Dusenbury, L. & Falco, M. (1995). Eleven components of effective drug abuse prevention curricula. *Journal of School Health*, 65, 420-425.

Elk, C. (1996). MDMA (ecstasy): Useful information for health professionals involved in drug education programs. *Journal of Drug Education*, 26, 349-356.

Goldberg, R. (2000). Drugs across the spectrum (3rd ed.). Australia: Wadsworth Thomson Learning.

Gray, S. (2000, August 26). Md. mobilizes against use of ecstasy: Drug's rampant growth has officials rushing to warn teens, parents and police. *The Washington Post*, p. B2.

Hanson, G., & Venturelli, P.J. (1998). Drugs and society (5th ed.). Sudbury, MA: Jones and Bartlett Publishers.

Hawkins, J.D., Lishner, D., & Catalona, R.F. (1985). Childhood predictors and the prevention of adolescent substance abuse. In C.L. Jones & R.J. Battjes (Eds.), Etiology of drug abuse: Implications for prevention (pp. 54-125). Rockville, MD: NIDA.

Inaba, D.S., Cohen, W.E., & Holstein, M.E. (1997). Uppers, downers, all arounders (3rd ed.). Ashland, OR: CNS Publications, Inc.

Jansen, K. (1997). Adverse psychological effects of ecstasy use and their treatment [Online]. Available: http://ecstasy.org/info/karl.html

Johnston, L.D., O'Malley, P.M., & Bachman, J.G. (2000). "Ecstasy" use rises sharply among teens in 2000 [Online]. Available: www.monitoringthefuture.org

Julien, R.M. (1998). A primer of drug action. New York, NY: W.H. Freeman and Co.

Levinthal. C.F. (1999). Drugs, behavior, and modern society (2nd ed.). Boston, MA: Allyn and Bacon.

Lohrmann, D.K., Wooley, S.F. (1998). Comprehensive school health education. In E. Marx, S.F. Wooley, & D. Northrop (Eds.), Health is academic. Pp. 43-66. New York, NY: Teachers College Press.

Lynskey, M., White, V., Hill, D., Letcher, T., & Hall, W. (1999). Prevalence of illicit drug use among youth: Results from the Australian school students' alcohol and drugs survey. *Australian and New Zealand Journal of Public Health*, 23(5), 519-524.

Meeks, L., Heit, P. & Page, R. (1995). Drugs, alcohol and tobacco: Totally awesome teaching strategies. Blacklick, OH: Meeks Heit Publishing Company.

McEvoy, A.W., Kitchen, N.D., Thomas, D.G.T. (1998). Intracerebral hemorrhage caused by drug abuse. Lancet, 351, 1029.

Milroy, C.M. (1999). Ten years of ecstasy. *Social Medicine*, 92, 68-72.

Moon, D.G., Jackson, K.M. & Hecht, M.L. (2000). Family risk and resiliency factors, substance use, and the drug resistance process in adolescence. *Journal of Drug Education*, 30, 373-398.

National Institute of Drug Abuse will spearhead club drug prevention effort. (1999, December 13). Alcoholism & Drug Abuse, 11,3.

Rayam, S. (2000, December 13). More teens using ecstasy: 'Club drug' hits all age groups. *USA Today*, p. A1.

Robert Johnson Wood Foundation (2001, February). Substance abuse chartbook. Princeton, NY: Schneider Institute for Health Policy.

Romano, J.L. (1999). Prevention training of paraprofessionals in the schools: an examination of relevancy and effectiveness. *Journal of Drug Education*, 29, 373-386.

Romano, J.L. (1997). School personnel training for the prevention of tobacco, alcohol, and other drug use: issues and outcomes. *Journal of Drug Education*, 27, 245-258.

Rubinson, L., & Alles, W. (1982). Foundation of health education. Prospects Heights, IL: Waveland Press.

Salt, P. (1993). Rave review. *Nuts Times*, 89(50). 36-38.

Schwartz, R., & Miller, N. (1997). MDMA and the rave: A review. *Pediatrics*, 100(4), 705-708.

Webber, T. (1999). Raving in Toronto: Peace, love, unity and respect in transition. *Journal of Youth Studies*, 2(3), 317-336.

Weir, E. (2000). Raves: A review of the culture, the drugs and the prevention of harm. *Canadian Medical Association Journal*, 162(13), 1843-1848.

Wilson, R., & Kolander, C. (2000). Drug abuse prevention (2nd ed.). Sudbury, MA: Jones and Bartlett Publishers.

Yourish, K. (2001, February 12). Mapping addiction. *Newsweek*, 43.

Dixie, Dennis, Ph.D. Western Kentucky University Michael Ballard, Ed.D. Western Kentucky University

Prevention of Eating Disorders: Tips for Parents

No one denies that in the U.S. we live in a thin-obsessed society. The cultural ideals held up for us to emulate are either stick thin with surgically enhanced breasts (female) or powerful with clear muscle definition (male). As many vulnerable people, especially young people, try to achieve these unrealistic shapes and sizes, they diet, exercise, and drug themselves into dangerous eating disorders and medical jeopardy.

Eating disorders are much easier to prevent than to cure, and usually it is the job of parents to do the work of prevention. Most of your efforts will be carried out in the context of the family, not in organized programs. Keep in mind at all times that what you do is a much more powerful message than what you say.

Reject guilt. Most parents of eating disordered children are good people who have done the best they knew how to do as they raised their kids. In spite of their efforts, their children fell into anorexia, bulimia, or another disorder. Science is telling us that genetic factors that determine personality have more influence than previously suspected in the development of eating disorders. Those factors seem to be activated when a vulnerable person buys into the belief that losing weight will somehow make life happier and then begins to diet.

At that point parents tend to fall into guilt and denial. Neither is helpful. Instead of bemoaning what you did or didn't do (which may or may not have contributed to the current problem), take action and arrange an evaluation with your child's physician and a mental health specialist. The sooner treatment is begun, the easier it will be to turn matters around. The longer the symptoms are ignored, and the longer parents hope the behaviors are "just a phase", the harder the road to recovery will be.

We hope you read the following guidelines before the situation becomes critical. Use the suggestions to create a healthy environment for the growth of your child's self-esteem and to counter some of the destructive media messages about body image flooding today's young people.

- Give your family and friends the gift of a healthy role model. If you are a woman, get comfortable with your own body and enjoy it, no matter what its size and shape. Never criticize your appearance. If you do, you teach others to be overly concerned about externals and critical of their own bodies.

- Never criticize anyone's appearance, especially a woman or child's. Phrases like "thunder thighs" and "bubble butt," even if they are meant in jest, can wound deeply and puncture self-esteem. Remember that people are more than just bodies. They all have talents, abilities, hopes, dreams, values, and goals—just like you do. Treat them as you would like to be treated.

- Likewise, don't allow anyone in the family to tease others about appearance. Even playful teasing can produce negative consequences.

- Emphasize the importance of fit and healthy bodies, not thin bodies. The goals should be health and fitness, not thinness.

- Praise your children for who they are, their personal qualities, and what they do—not how they look. A child who feels unattractive but is told that he or she is good looking will feel only anxiety, not improved self-esteem, and you will lose credibility in her/his eyes.

- Especially important: Don't you diet. Ever. In the first place, diets don't work. They also send a dangerous and unrealistic message to kids about quick-fix solutions. Rather than diet, stick to a healthy routine of nutritious eating and fitness-promoting exercise. [Important fact: three risk factors for the development of an eating disorder are 1] a mother who diets; 2] a sister who diets; and 3] friends who diet. In addition, girls who diet severely are 18 times more likely to be develop an eating disorder than nondieters.]

- Encourage healthy eating, not dieting. There is a difference. Also, make eating tasty food OK. Demonizing french fries and ice cream only makes them forbidden fruit (to mangle the metaphor).

- Don't forbid certain foods. Don't define some food as "bad". Healthy eating has room for just about all foods in moderation. In addition, learn what normal development and weight gain look like. It's not what you see in magazines or on TV! Encourage normal, healthy development in your children.

- Make mealtime pleasant. Enjoy eating with family and good friends. Treat your family to a special meal once a week, at home or in a restaurant. Watching what you eat in the service of health is fine, but obsessive attention to calories, fat grams, and weight can set up a vulnerable person to fear food and the consequences of eating. For too many folks, these preoccupations and expectations lead to anorexia and bulimia.

- If a child is bound and determined to diet, get a physician or registered dietitian involved to supervise the effort. Doctors and dietitians can provide information about healthy eating and weight levels that can counteract myths about "good" and "bad" foods and realistic weight goals. In addition, if the diet gets out of control, the resource person will already be available to intervene.

- Help your children build and commit to an active lifestyle. You don't have to spend major money on athletic club memberships or promote organized sports, but encourage activities such as biking, walking, and swimming that are pleasurable and can be done every day. Physical fitness promotes healthy self-image.

- Talk to your children about normal body changes expected at puberty. Sometimes kids interpret developing female curve as "getting fat." Girls need to know that normal development is necessary for health in general and healthy childbearing in particular. Boys need to hear the message too so they can rise above the "no fat chicks" mentality so prevalent in adolescent male culture.

- Also talk to your children about the unrealistic images they see in magazines, on TV, and in the movies. Tell them that some models and actresses achieve their "look" by resorting to plastic surgery and eating disorders. It's the truth. Point out how advertisers prey on body image insecurities by sending vulnerable people messages about the benefits of being thin—and spending their money on the advertisers' products. Being thin doesn't make one popular and self-confident any more than smoking does, but the advertising techniques for cigarettes and diet products are almost identical.

- Most important of all, show people—don't waste your time telling them—how you take care of yourself in healthy, responsible ways. Demonstrate how a competent person takes charge, solves problems, negotiates relationships, and builds satisfying life without resorting to self-destructive behaviors.

From *The Brown University Child and Adolescent Behavior Letter*, Vol. 18, No. 3, March 2002. © 2002 by Manisses Communications Group. Reprinted with permission.

The effects of terrorism on teens' perceptions of dying: the new world is riskier than ever

Bonnie L. Halpern-Felsher Ph.D. and Susan Millstein Ph.D.

Adolescents assessed after the September 11, 2001 terrorist attacks perceived the risk of dying from general causes, a tornado, and an earthquake as dramatically higher than did adolescents assessed years before the attacks. Adolescents' heightened perceptions of vulnerability to death extended beyond the terrorist acts, and generalized to unrelated risks.

On September 11, 2001, terrorist attacks on the United States killed over 3000 people. These attacks were followed by reports of people being exposed to, infected by, and dying from, anthrax. Experiencing such disastrous events is known to increase people's perceptions of risk and vulnerability [1, 2, 3, 4 and 5]. Studies have been limited, however, to examining risk perceptions after one-time natural disasters (e.g., a tornado or hurricane) or disasters resulting from human error (e.g., Chernobyl, Three Mile Island, Challenger), and have focused on people's perceptions of risk concerning similar events. With few exceptions [4], studies have not examined perceptions after a disaster in which additional threats continue even weeks after the initial disaster, nor have they examined whether perceptions of greater risk generalize to unrelated events. We have data that allow us to examine whether ninth-grade adolescents surveyed after the September 11, 2001 terrorist attacks and their aftermath perceive a greater likelihood of dying from events that are unrelated to the actual terrorist attacks than do similar adolescents assessed before September 11, 2001.

Methods

Participants

Data were collected from three independent samples of ninth-grade students, aged 12.02–16.11 years, all of whom were attending public schools in middle to upper-middle class suburban communities in the Bay Area, Northern California. Although the adolescents in this study were approximately 3000 miles away from the actual attacks, recent data suggest that exposure to, and effects from, the attacks occurred throughout the country [6].

Data from Sample A1 ($n = 160$) were collected in the Fall and Spring of 1997–1998, 4 years before the attacks. Data from Sample A2 ($n = 119$) were collected in the Fall and Spring of 1999–2000, 2 years before the attacks. A third sample of 227 adolescents (Sample B) was assessed 4 weeks after the attacks, on October 8–9, 2001. Samples A1 and A2 represented different cohorts in the same longitudinal study; Sample B was part of a different longitudinal study. A1 and B participants began the study as ninth graders, whereas Sample A2 began as seventh graders. Data for this study come from the baseline surveys for Samples A1 and B, and from the fifth measure for Sample A2, during which time all participants were in the ninth grade. The Institutional Review Board at the University of California, San Francisco approved the study.

Procedures

Participants in Samples A1 and B were recruited from the classrooms. Students received study information and consent forms from the teachers, and were asked to bring the materials home to share with their parents. Interested participants signed the adolescent assent form and parents signed the parental consent forms; these were returned directly to the teachers. Participation rates for Samples A1 and B were 95% and 79%, respectively.

Participants in Sample A2 were recruited by mail. Letters explaining the study were mailed to the parents of all students enrolled in the participating schools. Interested participants returned the signed parent consent and adolescent assent forms. The participation rate using this methodology was 15%. This relatively low participation rate, coupled with possible effects of repeated measurements, make Sample A2 less comparable to Sample B than is Sample A1. However, Sample A2 (and Sample B) provides data on a critical item ("chance that you will die in the next year") that were not collected from Sample A1. Further, Sample A2 allows for a replication of the results found in comparing Sample A1 with Sample B.

Participants completed a self-administered questionnaire in groups of between 5 and 40 participants, either during class time or after school at the school district offices. They were given the same set of verbal and written instructions for completing the questionnaires. Research assistants were available to answer any questions. Refreshments were provided and participants were compensated for their time ($10 for Sample A1, $20 for Sample 2A, and an $11 movie gift certificate for Sample B).

Measures

Participants judged the probability that they would die in the next year and from two natural hazards. Risk judgments were assessed using quantitative response scales in which participants used any percentage estimate from 0% to 100%. Adolescents are able to use such scales [7], although there is evidence that individuals sometimes use the response of "50%" to reflect uncertainty (e.g., "a fifty-fifty" chance) rather than as an expression of numerical probability [8]. We analyzed the data both with and without participants who gave "50%" responses and these revealed no differences in the pattern of results; therefore, results for the full samples are reported. We also conducted separate analyses for males and females, and for white and non-white participants (the small number of non-white participants did not allow for further disaggregation). With one exception (noted in the text), the pattern of results did not change; therefore, results from the combined samples are presented.

Results

Differences in risk judgments across the three samples were tested using Analysis of Variance with Tukey-B follow-ups. Adolescents surveyed before September 11, 2001 perceived significantly lower chances of dying than did adolescents surveyed 4 weeks after the attacks. Chance of death in the tornado scenario was perceived, on average, as 34.62% before September 11, and as 64.33% after. Perceived risk for dying in an earthquake more than doubled, going from an average of 24.64% to 41.94%. Adolescents' perceived risk of dying from any cause increased significantly from 15.25% to 20.87%.

The only differences detected between Samples A1 and A2 were on the item concerning earthquakes; however, both samples showed significantly lower estimates of risk compared with Sample B. A marginally significant race-ethnicity by risk judgment interaction was detected for the item concerning the perceived risk of dying from any cause ($F = 2.48$, $p = .085$). On this item, increased perceptions of risk after the terrorist acts were only seen among non-white participants. No other race-ethnicity interactions emerged.

Discussion

Adolescents surveyed after the September 11, 2001 terrorist attacks perceived their risk of dying as dramatically higher than did adolescents assessed before the attacks. These heightened perceptions of vulnerability extended beyond the specifics of the initial terrorist attacks and generalized to unrelated risks. Perceptions of the world as a more risky place could have far-reaching implications, ranging from changes in adolescents' engagement in risk and/or health-promoting or prosocial behavior, differences in how youth view their own future and the value of preparing for that future [9], to consequences for their overall physical and mental health [10].

There are a few study limitations that warrant mention. First, because only ninth graders were included, this study does not represent the full developmental range of adolescents. Second, the racial and socioeconomic distribution of the sample limits our ability to generalize the findings to more heterogeneous populations. Finally, our method of recruiting Sample A2 yielded a low response rate. This rate does not necessarily mean that 85% of the students refused to participate. Instead, given the method of mailing information directly to the parents, we believe a significant number of families never received the information or never read it. In fact, 61% of parents did not return our initial postcard, which we specifically requested be returned regardless of interest in the study.

Despite these limitations, this is the first study to demonstrate that adolescents' heightened perceptions of vulnerability to death can extend beyond the initial disastrous event. Health care professionals should play an important role in assessing and responding to adolescents' needs, inquiring about the immediate and direct effects of the terrorist attacks as well as about adolescents' general attitudes and beliefs concerning their safety.

Acknowledgements

The authors gratefully acknowledge comments and assistance from Dean W. Felsher, Baruch Fischhoff, Julie H. Goldberg, Charles E. Irwin, Jr., and Holly Sigler on the manuscript. We are also grateful to all the study participants and their parents, as well as the schoolteachers and administrators who contributed to this study.

This research was supported in part by grants from the Tobacco-Related Disease Research Program, Office of the President, University of California (#9K-0072) and from the National Institute for Child Health and Human Development (#HD34412). Additional support for the authors was provided by a grant from the Maternal and Child Health Bureau (MCHB) of the Department of Health and Human Services (2 T71 MC 0003), the UCSF Academic Senate Committee on Research and the Raschen-Tiedenann Fund from the Research Evaluation and Allocation Committee, School of Medicine, UCSF.

References

1. B.M. Drottz-Sjoberg and L. Sjoberg, Risk perception and worries after the Chernobyl accident. *J Environ Psychol* **10** (1990), pp. 135–149.

2. R. Goldsteen, J.K. Schorr and K.S. Goldsteen, Longitudinal study of appraisals at Three Mile Island: Implications for life event research. *Soc Sci Med* **28** (1989), pp. 389–398. Abstract Absract + References PDF (1100 K)

3. B. Pfefferbaum, S.J. Nixon, P.M. Tucker *et al.,* Posttraumatic stress responses in bereaved children after the Oklahoma City bombing. *J Am Acad Child Adolesc Psychiatry* **38** (1999), pp. 1372–1379. Abstract-PsycINFO Abstract-EMBASE Abstract-MEDLINE **Full Text** via CrossRef

4. M. Schwebel and B. Schwebel, Children's reactions to the threat of nuclear plant accidents. *Am J Orthopsychiat* **51** (1981), pp. 260–270. Abstract-MEDLINE Abstract-PsycINFO

5. L.C. Terr, D.A. Bloch, B.A. Michel *et al.,* Children's symptoms in the wake of Challenger: A field study of distant-traumatic effects and an outline of related conditions. *Am J Psychiatry* **156** (1999), pp. 1536–1544. Abstract-EMBASE Abstract-PsycINFO Abstract-MEDLINE

6. M.A. Schuster, B.D. Stein, L.H. Jaycos *et al.,* A national survey of stress reactions after the September 11, 2001 terrorist attacks. *N Engl J Med* **345stop (2001), pp. 1507-1512. Abstract-Elsevier BIOBASE Abstract-EMBASE Abstract-PsycINFO Abstract-MEDLINE Full Text** via CrossRef

7. B. Fischoff, A.M. Parker, W. Bruine de Bruin *et al.,* Teen expectations for significant life events. *Public Opin Q* **64** (2000), pp. 189–205. Abstract-PsycINFO **Full Text** via CrossRef

8. W. Bruine de Bruin, B. Fischoff, S.G. Millstein and B.L. Halpern-Felsher, Verbal and numerical expressions of probability: "It's a fifty-fifty chance". *Organ Behav Hum Dec* **81** (2000), pp. 115–131.

9. B. Fischoff, E. Nightingale and J.G. Iannotta, Editors, *Adolescent Risk and Vulnerability: Concepts and Measurement,* Institute of Medicine, National Research Council, Washington, DC (2001).

10. R.J. Ursano, C.S. Fullerton and A.E. Norwood *Psychiatric Dimensions of Disaster: Patient Care, Community Consultation, and Preventive Medicine, American Psychiatry Association* (November, 2002) (http://222.psych.org/pract_of_psych/disaster.cfm).

Index

A

abstinence-only sex education, controversy over, versus comprehensive sex education, 170–175, 176–177, 178–180

academic achievement, effect of television viewing on, 80–84

accommodation, identity development and, 94

Adolescent Family Life Act (AFLA), sex education and, 170, 171, 172

Africa, 3–4

African Americans: effect of television viewing on academic achievement and, 80–81; effects of rap music and, 153–154; parent-adolescent communication about alcohol, tobacco and drug use and, 142, 143–144, 145; sense of belonging to school and, 57; violence and social injustice and, 6–13

aggression, 190–191

AIDS. *See* HIV

alcohol use, parent-adolescent communication about, 141–147

anorexia nervosa, 41, 197

antisocial behavior, 190–191

architecture, technology in classroom and, 74

arranged marriage, impact of globalization on ethnic identity formation and, in India, 99–100

B

balance, identity development and, 94

belonging, sense of, to school, 56–64

Bennett, Elayne, 173

Best Friends, 173

bicultural identity, impact of globalization on ethnic identity formation and, 100

Bill & Melinda Gates Foundation, 86

binge eating disorder, 41

bisexual students, counseling issues with, 168–169. *See also* homosexuality

body dysmorphia, 41

body image, 40–43; eating disorders and, 197, 198; media and, 40, 198

body mass index (BMI): body image and, 43; puberty and, 26

Bolivia, moral leadership training program in, 4–5

boredom, 8; class cutting and, 49–51

brain, neurodevelopment and psychopathology and, 31–34

breast cancer, early puberty and, 21, 29

bulimia nervosa, 41, 197

C

Cambodia, 4

Changes Parent Support Network, 136–137

character education, controversy over abstinence-only versus comprehensive sex education and, 173

chat rooms, online relationships and, 155–163

cheating epidemic, 76–79

class cutting, 47–55; boredom and, 49–51; conflict and, 51–52, 53, 54; intervention, 48; moral exclusion and, 52–53; prevalence of, 48; structural violence and, 53

class differences. *See* socioeconomic status

coercion, by parents, and antisocial behavior, 190–191

cognitive function, healthful eating and, 36, 37, 38

coincidental teaching, social-emotional learning and, 118

compassion, gender differences in reminiscence practices and self-definition and, 125, 126, 127, 128

comprehensive sex education, controversy over, versus abstinence-only sex education and, 170–175, 176–177, 178–179

computers, education and, 74–75

condoms, controversy over Congress giving financial support to abstinence-only sex education and, 176, 177, 178, 179

Condon, Richard, 98–99, 101–102

conflict, class cutting and, 51–52, 53, 54

conflict resolution programs, school violence prevention and, 68

Congress, controversy over, giving financial support to abstinence-only sex education and, 170, 171, 172, 176–177, 178–180

continuity, transition to independence process and, 71

contraceptives, controversy over Congress giving financial support to abstinence-only sex education and, 176, 177, 178, 179

cortisol, 32–33

cultural identity, rap music and, 154. *See also* ethnic identity

cultural identity formation, globalization and, 96–104

culture: global teen, 151–152; sex lives of adolescents and, 166–167

cutting. *See* class cutting

D

dehydroepiandrosterone (DHEA), 23, 25

dehydroepiandrosterone sulfate (DHEAS), 24, 25

depression, 188–189; neurodevelopment and, 31–32

dieting industry, body image and, 42

discipline, by parents, and antisocial behavior, 191

Dixon, Travis L., 154

dopamine, 33

double standard, sex lives of adolescents and, 166–167

drug abuse prevention, ecstasy and, 194

drug use: Ecstasy and, 192–196; parent-adolescent communication about, 141–147

dying, effects of terrorism of teen perceptions of, 199–201

E

early puberty, 21, 29–30

eating disorders: body image and, 40, 41, 197, 198; prevention of, and parents, 197–198

Ecstasy, 192–196

ectomorphic body shape, 41–42

education, 4; cheating and, 76–79; class cutting and, 47–55; demands of adulthood and, 14, 15; effect of television viewing on academic achievement and, 80–84; low-income and minority students and, 85–86; performance of girls in, 87–89; sense of belonging and, 56–64; social-emotional learning and, 115–120; stress and, 139; technology and, 74–75; transition to independence process and, 70, 72; violence and, 56, 65–69

Elders, Jocelyn, 167

electronic games, global teen culture and, 152

e-mail, online relationships and, 155–163

"Emerging Answers" (Kirby), 174

emotional awareness, social-emotional learning and, 116

emotional coaching, social-emotional learning and, 116–117

Index

Test Your Knowledge Form

We encourage you to photocopy and use this page as a tool to assess how the articles in *Annual Editions* expand on the information in your textbook. By reflecting on the articles you will gain enhanced text information. You can also access this useful form on a product's book support Web site at *http://www.dushkin.com/online/*.

NAME:

DATE:

_____

TITLE AND NUMBER OF ARTICLE:

_____

BRIEFLY STATE THE MAIN IDEA OF THIS ARTICLE:

_____

LIST THREE IMPORTANT FACTS THAT THE AUTHOR USES TO SUPPORT THE MAIN IDEA:

_____

WHAT INFORMATION OR IDEAS DISCUSSED IN THIS ARTICLE ARE ALSO DISCUSSED IN YOUR TEXTBOOK OR OTHER READINGS THAT YOU HAVE DONE? LIST THE TEXTBOOK CHAPTERS AND PAGE NUMBERS:

_____

LIST ANY EXAMPLES OF BIAS OR FAULTY REASONING THAT YOU FOUND IN THE ARTICLE:

_____

LIST ANY NEW TERMS/CONCEPTS THAT WERE DISCUSSED IN THE ARTICLE, AND WRITE A SHORT DEFINITION:

We Want Your Advice

ANNUAL EDITIONS revisions depend on two major opinion sources: one is our Advisory Board, listed in the front of this volume, which works with us in scanning the thousands of articles published in the public press each year; the other is you—the person actually using the book. Please help us and the users of the next edition by completing the prepaid article rating form on this page and returning it to us. Thank you for your help!

ANNUAL EDITIONS: Adolescent Psychology 04/05

ARTICLE RATING FORM

Here is an opportunity for you to have direct input into the next revision of this volume.
We would like you to rate each of the articles listed below, using the following scale:

1. **Excellent: should definitely be retained**
2. **Above average: should probably be retained**
3. **Below average: should probably be deleted**
4. **Poor: should definitely be deleted**

Your ratings will play a vital part in the next revision.
Please mail this prepaid form to us as soon as possible.
Thanks for your help!

RATING	ARTICLE
	1. Harnessing the Energies of Youth
	2. On (not) "Coloring in the Outline" (Transformations from Youth Through Relationships)
	3. The Future of Adolescence: Lengthening Ladders to Adulthood
	4. Developmental Markers in Adolescence: Implications for Studies of Pubertal Processes
	5. Early Puberty
	6. Adolescent Neurodevelopment and Psychopathology
	7. Why do Kids Eat Healthful Food? Perceived Benefits of and Barriers to Healthful Eating and Physical Activity Among Children and Adolescents
	8. Body Image: How Do You See Yourself?
	9. Are Students Failing School or Are Schools Failing Students? Class Cutting in High School
	10. Sense of Belonging to School: Can Schools Make a Difference?
	11. Challenges and Suggestions for Safe Schools
	12. Best Practices in Transition Programs
	13. Technology in the Classroom: How it is Changing (and Not Changing) Learning.
	14. The New Cheating Epidemic
	15. Television Viewing and Academic Achievement Revisited
	16. Studies Reveal Strengths, Weaknesses in Improving Rates of High School Graduation and College Completion for Low-Income and Minority Students
	17. Girls Rule
	18. Introduction: Identity Development Through Adulthood
	19. Coming of Age in a Multicultural World: Globalization and Adolescent Cultural Identity Formation
	20. The Dynamics of Self-Esteem: A Growth-Curve Analysis
	21. Fostering Social-Emotional Learning in the Classroom
	22. Gendered Reminiscence Practices and Self-Definition in Late Adolescence

RATING	ARTICLE
	23. Friends Forever
	24. Support Network Eases Problems for Parents and Out-of-Control Teens
	25. Learning to Chill: Overloaded at School and Overscheduled at Home, Stressed-Out Kids—with Their Parents' Blessing—Are Saying "Enough!"
	26. Parent-Adolescent Communication About Alcohol, Tobacco, and Other Drug Use
	27. Global Teen Culture—Does It Exist?
	28. New Research Explores Effects of Rap Music on Adolescents
	29. Close Online Relationships in a National Sample of Adolescents
	30. The Sex Lives of Teenagers
	31. Know Sexual Identity, Homosexual Adjustment Issues Before Counseling GLBT Youth
	32. What to Tell Kids About Sex
	33. Q. Should Congress be Giving More Financial Support to Abstinence-Only Sex Education? YES: Abstinence Is Working To Decrease Teen Pregnancy and Is Building Character Among Our Nation's Youth
	34. Q. Should Congress Be Giving More Financial Support to Abstinence-Only Sex Education? NO: Withholding Information About Contraception and Teaching Only Abstinence puts Sexually Active Teens at Risk
	35. Understanding Adolescent Suicide: A Psychosocial Interpretation of Developmental and Contextual Factors
	36. More than Moody: Recognizing and Treating Adolescent Depression
	37. Aggression and Antisocial Behavior in Youth
	38. Ecstasy: It's the Rave
	39. Prevention of Eating Disorders: Tips for Parents: From Anorexia Nervosa and Related Eating Disorders, Inc.
	40. The Effects of Terrorism on Teens, Perceptions of Dying: The New World is Riskier Than Ever

(Continued on next page)

NO POSTAGE
NECESSARY
IF MAILED
IN THE
UNITED STATES

BUSINESS REPLY MAIL
FIRST CLASS MAIL PERMIT NO. 551 DUBUQUE IA

POSTAGE WILL BE PAID BY ADDRESEE

McGraw-Hill/Dushkin
2460 KERPER BLVD
DUBUQUE, IA 52001-9902

Ilıluılllllıuıllıuıılllılılıllılııııhlılıll

ABOUT YOU

Name   Date

_____

Are you a teacher? ❐   A student? ❐
Your school's name

_____

Department

_____

Address   City   State   Zip

_____

School telephone #

YOUR COMMENTS ARE IMPORTANT TO US!

Please fill in the following information:
For which course did you use this book?

_____

Did you use a text with this ANNUAL EDITION?   ❐   yes ❐   no
What was the title of the text?

_____

What are your general reactions to the *Annual Editions* concept?

_____

Have you read any pertinent articles recently that you think should be included in the next edition? Explain.

_____

Are there any articles that you feel should be replaced in the next edition? Why?

_____

Are there any World Wide Web sites that you feel should be included in the next edition? Please annotate.

_____

May we contact you for editorial input?   ❐   yes ❐   no
May we quote your comments?   ❐   yes ❐   no